Day Care in Context

DAY CARE
IN CONTEXT

Greta G. Fein and Alison Clarke-Stewart

WITH THE SUPPORT OF THE
FOUNDATION FOR CHILD DEVELOPMENT

(FORMERLY THE ASSOCIATION FOR THE
AID OF CRIPPLED CHILDREN)

A WILEY-INTERSCIENCE PUBLICATION

JOHN WILEY & SONS
New York • London • Sydney • Toronto

843022

DJCC

Library of Congress Cataloging in Publication Data

Fein, Greta G.   1929-
    Day care in context.

    "A Wiley-Interscience publication."
    Bibliography: p.
    1. Day nurseries.   2. Child study.   I. Clarke-
Stewart, Alison, 1943-   joint author.   II. Foundation for Child Development.   III. Title.

HV851.F4   362.7'1   72-8588
ISBN 0-471-25695-1

Printed in the United States of America

10 9 8 7 6 5 4 3 2 1

Foreword

IN READING *DAY CARE IN CONTEXT,* ONE REFLECTS ON ITS
relevance for the current scene and the renewed interest in programs for children
and tries to place it in the context of one's personal experience.

As a physician my experience leads me to recall the educational process of
physicians. An initial period of learning in the basic sciences is required before
the student can embark on clinical experiences with patients. For those who have
been interested in day-care programs—and particularly in preparing staff for these
programs—we have not had a clear definition of the "basic science" knowledge
that should be available in a convenient source.

It is in this perspective that I see the significance of this book. It seems to
me that the authors have been remarkably resourceful in bringing together the
accumulated knowledge in the field of child development that has direct or even
potential relevance for day-care programs. Thus research reports from the fields
of education, psychology, and other social sciences have been assembled for practitioners and agencies in the fields of health, social work, early-childhood education,
day care, and the schools.

It is clear that a book designed to define the knowledge base on which
programs for young children can be developed could not serve as a cookbook
for the establishment of new programs. The authors properly have refrained from
suggesting "how to do it," with confidence that well-informed persons will be
led to a variety of constructive approaches in their work with young children
and their families.

Again, as a physician, I note that the authors have not attempted to review
the literature on developmental biology of the fetus and young child. This
comment is not intended as criticism, for such a review would have added greatly

to the length of the volume; another effort will be necessary to do justice to this field. It is appropriate to observe that much interesting research concerning the development of the nervous system, which may ultimately shed light on the relationships of the environment, early learning, and social and psychological development, is in progress. Many studies concerning nutrition and early development should provide us with more information for improvement in the care of young children.

The dynamic interpretation of child-development research presented makes it evident that day care cannot be viewed in a doctrinaire context. Various disciplines will need to be involved, some with greater emphasis earlier (as with health services) and relatively less later and vice versa. Clearly, all the child-care professions will need to contribute on a continuing basis. The flexible tone of the authors should also serve to encourage the exploration of new approaches for the care of young children and families, always in the search to foster greater growth and effectiveness.

Finally, the basic nature of this book suggests that the material should be useful to people in all cultures, for the development of children has a universality. Although day-care programs are at uneven stages of development in various countries, workers in all of them should find *Day Care in Context* useful in thinking and planning for their programs. Thus the authors have provided a service that should reach far beyond their own country.

JULIUS B. RICHMOND, M.D.

*Professor of Child Psychiatry and Human Development
and Professor and Chairman, Department of Preventive and Social Medicine,
Harvard Medical School
Psychiatrist-in-Chief, Children's Hospital Medical Center
Director, Judge Baker Guidance Center, Boston, Massachusetts*

Preface

AS A FOUNDATION WHOSE CENTRAL CONCERN FOR MORE THAN 70 years has been the prevention of handicapping conditions and the improvement of care for afflicted children, our program has evolved from service to research and recently has moved to encompass more broadly the experiences that influence, for good or ill, the growth and development of the young child. To reflect this broader objective, we are, as of September 1972, changing our name to the *Foundation for Child Development.*

We are pleased that *Day Care in Context* is the first book to be published under our new name, for the volume provides a tangible reflection of one approach by which the Foundation seeks to respond to current needs of children. I am delighted to have had the opportunity of working with and supporting the book's authors, Dr. Fein and Dr. Clarke-Stewart. Special attention is also due the 11 men and women listed below who were drawn together by the Foundation as an informal advisory committee for the authors. This group's collective wisdom and experience were of enormous assistance in the development of the focus and structure of the book.

Mr. Stanley Brezenoff
Dr. Urie Bronfenbrenner
Dr. Bettye M. Caldwell
Mrs. Barbara Finberg
Dr. Jerome Kagan

Dr. William Kessen
Dr. Jane Knitzer
Dr. Richard Nelson
Dr. Ronald Parker
Dr. Julius B. Richmond

Dr. Evangeline Ward

ROBERT J. SLATER, M.D.
President
1972

Credits

Context II

The Free Press for permission to quote from *Psycholinguistics* by Roger Brown, published in 1970; to Basic Books, Inc., for permission to quote from *Attachment and Loss*, Vol. 1, "Attachment" by John Bowlby, published in 1969; to The Columbia University Press for permission to quote from *Understanding Children's Play* by R. E. Hartley, L. K. Frank, and R. M. Goldenson, published in 1952; to John Wiley and Sons, Inc., for permission to quote from "A Syntax for Play and Games" by B. Sutton Smith in R. E. Herron and B. Sutton Smith (Eds.), *Child's Play*, published in 1971; to John Wiley and Sons, Inc., for permission to quote from *Studies in Cognitive Growth* by J. S. Bruner, R. R. Olver, P. M. Greenfield, published in 1966.

Context IV

The University of Chicago Press for permission to quote from "How Shall the Disadvantaged Child Be Taught?" by Blank and Solomon, published in *Child Development*, Vol. 40, 1969; to Prentice Hall, Inc., for permission to quote from *Teaching Disadvantaged Children in the Preschool* by Bereiter and Engelmann, published in 1966; to Brunner/Mazel, Inc., for permission to quote from "The National Impact Study of Head Start" by S. H. White in J. Hellmuth (Ed.), *Disadvantaged Child*, Vol. 3, "Compensatory Education: A National Debate," and for permission to quote from an article by Evans and Schiller in the same volume, "How Preoccupation with Possible Regression Artifacts Can Lead to a Faulty Strategy for the Evaluation of Social Action Programs," published in 1970.

Acknowledgments

WE WISH TO EXTEND OUR DEEPEST APPRECIATION TO THE Foundation for Child Development for its generous support of this book. In particular, we wish to thank Dr. Robert Slater for his steady and warm encouragement and for his choice of the perfect advisory committee for the task of writing about day care. Many thanks, too, go to Jane Dustan, Dr. Norman Sissman, Joseph MacCabe, and other people at the Foundation who came to our aid at critical moments during the long haul from conceptualization to writing to publication.

We greatly appreciate the suggestions made by our advisory committee— Urie Bronfenbrenner, Bettye Caldwell, Barbara Finberg, Jerry Kagan, William Kessen, Richard Nelson, Ronald Parker, Julius Richmond and Evangeline Ward —who, by their perceptive comments and clear perspectives helped us to focus on critical issues in day care and added to our appreciation of their complexity. Again, we owe special thanks to Jerry Kagan for his careful reading and stimulating comments on early drafts; to William Kessen for his transatlantic journeys and critical commentaries; to Mark Lepper without whose editorial help a second draft might never have been completed; to Mary Hellen who was a superb typist; and to Sara Batter who kept our accounts.

Last, we wish to thank those who read, approved, and commented on *Day Care in Context,* particularly Joseph Glick, Brian Sutton-Smith, and Richard Hackman.

GRETA G. FEIN
ALISON CLARKE-STEWART

New Haven, Connecticut
June 1972

Contents

CONTEXT III   THE FAMILY

CONTEXT IV EDUCATION

About the Book

WHENEVER A SERIOUS CHANGE IN SOCIALIZATION PRACTICES is about to be introduced into a society, a debate commences between the advocates of reform and those who fear the change because it challenges their ideology. Such a debate occurred when public schools were introduced and when women were given the vote. Contemporary American society is discussing several social changes at once: abortion on maternal request, legislation of psychotropic drugs, community control of public health and educational resources, and, of course, day care. Sharp polarities of opinion cloak each of these socially significant issues.

The past acts as a remarkably effective moderator of both unbridled enthusiasm and gnawing apprehension, for the history of social reform has an unequivocal message for contemporary Americans—no reform makes a new species of man. Day care will not breed a class of anxiety-free, creative, autonomous children nor will it destroy the child's trust in adults and build a valueless preadolescent. It would be equally foolish, however, to assume that this variant on child care will have no consequences for child or parent.

The need for child-care services outside the family is now in the forefront of consciousness in the United States. We used to ask whether preschool educational services were good or necessary, but now we ask how these services should be implemented and who should pay for them. In 1969 more than 30 million working women had more than 11 million children under 16 years of age, a figure that is eight times the comparable totals in 1940. Close to five million of these children were under 6 years of age. Since only 12% of this group can be cared for in licensed day-care centers, the vast majority of preschool children who have no grandmothers, aunts, or older sisters to care for them while their mothers are working either have baby-sitters at home or are taken to another woman's home for most of the day. This service is viewed by both the mother and the substitute caretaker as custodial, not as growth enhancing. There are several issues surrounding acceptance of federal aid in the crisis over the need for day-care centers. Who should get priority of enrollment in the centers? Who should determine the content of the programs? What should the content of these programs be? Each of these issues is complex and not easily answered.

Over the course of human history a rearing context in which the biological mother was the only caretaker during the opening years of the child's life has been the exception rather than the rule. In most cultures over the world mothers get help from aunts, grandmothers, cousins, and older children in the family. It is not easy, however, to transfer responsibility to other family members in today's modern American community. There are too many young parents who live too far from their families. Older children in the family go to school when they are 6 years old and are not around to help the mother with the infant. Thus the procedures that man has relied on for centuries are not appropriate to this generation of Americans. New child-rearing strategies are being invented and the concept of day care is becoming an increasingly popular choice.

Day care is a broad term that can include the paying of a next-door neighbor, the participation of parents in a block, or a spacious brick building where strangers take care of a child from early infancy until kindergarten. The differences among types of day care should not emphasize the physical facility but rather the psychological atmosphere. How is the child handled, what values is he taught, what kind of educational program is he exposed to, what kind of attitudes does he acquire—especially toward people? The child can be happy or sad, frightened or secure, trusting or angry in a neighbor's apartment, a commune, or a newly built day-care center.

Although there is no ideal set of goals or perfect set of experiences that every young child should be exposed to, independent of the community in which he lives, we must come to some decision about the kind of care that should be promoted. Since we in the United States applaud the ethnic pluralism in our country, it is not reasonable to assume that one kind of program is best for all children. Since parents must have a stake in the values and skills taught to their children, they should be involved in the implementation and strategies of care in day-care centers. Since there is no perfect set of traits for a child to possess, the task of deciding what his ideal psychological goals will be is an ethical rather than a scientific issue. There is some information, however, that psychologists can provide. *Day Care in Context* by Greta G. Fein and Alison Clarke-Stewart is a scholarly and extensive analysis of the knowledge base relevant to day-care procedures and should be extremely useful to those who make day-care decisions. Hopefully it will be read by parents, students, educators, and day-care personnel.

There are three positions from which one can evaluate the potential effects of day care: from the point of view of the society who will receive the children, the parents who want the service, and the child for whom the center was created. *Day Care in Context* emphasizes the perspective of the child and a brief word on the other views may be helpful.

Although it is precarious to predict possible consequences of day care, tentative guesses at least pose bases for discussion. One issue involves the community's assignment of the primary responsibility for the child's moral, intellective, and motivational development. We have passed through a long period during which members of the society agreed that the responsibility belonged to the family—nuclear or extended. If a third of the preschool children in the United States spend several years in group care with adults and children who are not kin, it is likely that we will gradually generate tacit agreement that the responsibility for the young child rests only partly with the family. This attitude will, in turn, lead to alterations in our theories of personality development, in which the role of peers and nonfamilial adults is given more power than it now enjoys. Our descriptions of children will contain fewer terms that attempt to capture individualistic traits, whereas more stereotyped categorizations may increase. Use of diagnostic phrases like "overprotected" or "rejected," which refer to parent-child relationships, will wane, and phrases like "socially cooperative," "withdrawn," "dominant," "autonomous," and "passive," which refer to behavior in groups, will become increasingly popular. We may begin to classify children by the characteristics of the center. Expectations of child behavior will be based on stereotyped classifications like "inner city" rather than the equally inexact phrase "deprived black family" or "middle-class suburban day-care center" rather than "upwardly mobile accelerating mother." These new terms will alter our perspective of the causes of personality deviation and necessarily our preferred therapeutic recommendations. There will probably be less individual psychological therapy with children and parents and more frequent manipulation of the peer group and the social context in order to remedy major or minor signs of psychopathology.

There are many social dividends to be derived from group day care. The center may promote more egalitarianism and may be the place where the battle against prejudice and racism will be won. Day care could lead to a cooperative organization between the public schools and the centers, for we need the nurturant labor of the junior high and high school student, and new intergenerational contacts can be established which should be beneficial to both. The day-care center may become one of the primary institutions of the next decade to promote the community as a central force and focus in American life.

From the perspective of the parent day care will allow many women who need or want to work to do so. Since these women want this freedom of choice, they are likely to feel more gratified. On the other hand, day care may attenuate the potential joys of parenthood. Affective involvement with the child may be less intense, and a basic rule of psychological dynamics states that the amount of pleasure extracted from a creative enterprise is proportional to the emotional investment in its creation.

The view from the child's perspective is more complicated. There should be increased autonomy, for a 4-year-old in a group of 15 preschoolers will have to be able to play alone and handle more crises without help. Unlike the family structure, adults will be less available to run to at the slightest provocation. The child will learn social skills a little earlier than he would under normal family arrangements. He will have to learn to control aggression against peers, to tolerate delay of gratification, to share possessions, and be realistic in the demands he makes on adults. All of these traits are potentially positive. On the other hand, he will become sensitized to the danger of being too different from the peer group, and he may not develop the indifference or callousness to peer rejection or disapproval that is more easily acquired by many family-reared children. As a result, there may be less push to risk peer rejection and less motivation to dominate or lead others if there is a substantial possibility of group disapproval or humiliation. The group will become a source of strength through the mechanism of identification and members of the group will become salient role models. Particular teachers may, for some children, become models as desirable as the parents. This dynamic will aid those with inadequate parents but not those with powerful, nurturant parents who could be used as resources for ego strength. The cohesiveness of the group may innoculate the child against the identity crisis seen in contemporary adolescents raised in nuclear families. The preschool child will extract strength from his identification with the group and will base his ideologies on those of the group. Alienation may be less likely and value crises less severe than those witnessed during the last half decade.

The Fein–Clarke-Stewart book takes reasonable positions on many of these issues. *Day Care in Context* argues strongly for parental involvement in the day-care center and minimal attenuation of the sense of responsibility the family should have for the child. It also argues that group care is not the only caregiving arrangement possible and may not be desired by all parents. Fein and Clarke-Stewart advance a new definition of a day-care center which emphasizes the "center" as an educational and social service for parents and children rather than as a place where children receive care in the absence of their parents. They urge the center to promote an arrangement in which the family will feel primary loyalty toward the child. The authors want the family's values to be respected and socialization practices—methods as well as content—to adhere to the family's preferences. This posture should maximize a sense of consistency in the child's mind and keep the balance of power with the family.

Preservation of the child's individuality is a recurrent theme in the book. The child is not to be forced to conform to the catechism of the center. Nurturant, warm, flexible interactions between adults and children are celebrated, with the child's individual growth, rather than his taming or control, the central aims. The child's dialect is to be respected and one-to-one interaction between adult and child prescribed as an effective way to promote language development. Creative play is encouraged as a means to promote divergent thinking and the facilitation of fantasy roles. Freedom, flexibility, openness, and respect for the child's individual identity summarize the basic message in the Fein–Clarke-Stewart manuscript.

Day Care in Context emphasizes the center's role in promoting the competence of children. It believes that language, communication, arithmetic, or other formal educational skills may be taught in the center, but the whole child is never to be forgotten. Fein and Clarke-Stewart argue that pluralism, respect for individuality, and parental responsibility should dominate the philosophy and curriculum of the day-care center. We concur with that conclusion. It should be noted that many eastern European countries initially chose a different bias. They decided to take control from the family and foster a group mind. Recent reports from these centers suggest that they are disappointed with that decision. Thus the recommendations in *Day Care in Context* have intuitive as well as empirical wisdom. The authors have done us all a high service.

JEROME KAGAN

Cambridge, Massachusetts
July 1972

Day Care in Context

Introduction

WHEN WE WERE INVITED IN THE SPRING OF 1970 TO PREPARE A
report on day care for the Association for Aid of Crippled Children, we did not
expect to find ourselves examining an enormously complex set of propositions
about children, families, and social programs. If foresight had permitted us a
glimpse of the magnitude of the problem, we might never have undertaken the
task. With hindsight we are not sorry that we did.

At the time we agreed to prepare this report our own work was becoming
increasingly concerned with two questions. What general principles can guide
the translation of research findings into effective designs for optimizing environments for children, and, conversely, how can significant elements of child-
development programming and child-rearing environments be systematically and
profitably studied? Our interest in these issues should have warned us that the
preparation of a report on day care would demand considerations well beyond
its institutional or service aspects. Indeed, we began to view day care as *what
happens* when conditions of caregiving and the capacities of children vary. As a
result we found outselves attempting to construct a multidimensional map that
would display events at the intersection of significant and complex variations. We
came to see "conditions of caregiving" as both determinants and consequences,
in part influencing the development of children from different initial levels while
being influenced by institutions (familial, educational, and political), by history,
and by national predispositions.

Inevitably our analysis grew into an examination of the contexts of day care—
a study of how historical and social factors, the changing needs of children and
families, and innovative educational programs might enter into a long-term

1

perspective for child-development programming. To anticipate our conclusions, we would promote day care as a viable and unique opportunity to learn how to repair those discontinuities that doggedly impede the efforts of researchers, planners, parents, and teachers and force each to operate as if the other did not exist, even though the enterprise must come to a standstill when it cannot draw fully on the resources of all those participating. Clearly, the contexts of day care are interconnected, even though interactions among them have yet to receive sustained attention.

In the preparation of this report it became evident that day care is inevitably viewed through a set of a priori assumptions about the nature of human development and human culture. In the belief that reasoned discussion cannot occur when biases are not clarified, we shall reveal our biases and how they have influenced our analyses of issues in day care.

ON BIASES

Ways of comprehending the child and ways of rearing him necessarily rest on assumptions about what the child brings to the task of growing up. At the extremes, theories concerning the child find the essentials of development either in the child himself or in the world around him (Kessen, 1965; Kohlberg, 1968).

Theories of development that locate the origins of the sense-making capacities in a sensible, ordered world often assume a child who is empty of content—a *tabula rasa* child—who comes into the world open to whatever impressions or structures the world might impose. This child is born infinitely malleable, responsive to human engineering as well as happenstance. The metaphor of the *tabula rasa* child has never ceased to attract those impatient for social reform. To some extent all education must attribute plasticity to the child and must assume that some important ingredient of development comes from outside the child. However, as more malleability is attributed to the child and as more of the essential ingredients for growth are attributed to a sensible, rich world, those who care for and teach him grow in importance. By the same token failure is likely to be attributed to those who carry out this task.

A belief in the openness and the plasticity of the child is often accompanied by a principle of primacy—the first things put in are those that determine development. Whether by accretions or by combination, by frequency of repetition, or by the absence of interfering habits, a primacy principle draws attention to the infant and to the earliest years of life. In the seventeenth century such speculations about the child's plasticity led to the first serious attempt to build a theory of infant instruction. The names of Comenius and, later, Seguin, Pestalozzi, and Itard are associated with these first great instructional prescriptions. In the eighteenth and nineteenth centuries infant schools sprang up all over Europe— in Manchester, London, New Lanaak, Leipzig, and Cremona. The fires of the infant education movement were fed by the faith that the shortest, most direct route to a better world was through the education of the child (Forest, 1927).

At the other extreme are those positions that assign the child a preformed or predetermined set of capacities for comprehending the world and an intuitive knowledge of what is best for his own growth (Hunt, 1963, 1964a, b). One can attribute to the child a smaller or larger store of inherent knowledge or sense-making capacity; but, as the child is given more of the essential know-how, child-rearing agents decline in importance and their role becomes one of ensuring the child's physical survival. Failures of development are attributed to defects in the child's natural equipment (Hunt, 1964a, b).

Practice, as opposed to theory, never follows such neat dichotomous categories: those who prescribe an intrusive, engineering environment can still assign failures to a defective perceptual apparatus; those who prescribe a nonintrusive educational environment can still blame failures on excessive interference.

As each position must call on the other at some point, it becomes clear that neither is sufficient in itself, for, when we demand too much of the child or the child-rearing environment as independent units, when we attribute to one or the other an exclusive control over change, we are expecting far more than either one can accomplish alone. As we interpret the current mood in child psychology, we find greater emphasis on the ongoing interaction between the child and his environment. The child is seen both as a shaper and as the one who is being shaped. Throughout this book we stress the continuing interaction between the child as an organizing agent and the environment as a coherent system which both changes the child and is changed by him.

Traditionally, adults have been thought of as initiating the child's contacts with people and things. They provide the child with playmates and with toys and tools for him to manipulate. It is becoming increasingly evident that the child, at the same time, plays an important role in stimulating the activities of adults. The national Head Start survey (Kirschner, 1970a) has well documented the power of children to energize communities, and other authors have spoken of the willingness of adults in democratic families to learn about a changing society under the tutelage of their children (Bennis & Slater, 1968). Parents will initiate contacts with strangers—teachers and neighbors—when these strangers have a bearing on the welfare of their children. The tradition in research and education of examining the ways in which adults activate and manage children is being balanced by attention to the ways in which children activate and manage adults (Bell, 1971).

Still another important trend has appeared within the last few years. Increasing numbers of those who would understand or change the child are willing to start where he is. Investigators are writing grammars to describe the language system of 2-year-olds. Others are observing with fine and precise detail the balance between the child's search for new sources of stimulation and maintaining contact with the mother. Still others are attempting to formulate principles that would govern the child's changing capacity to negotiate transactions with things. These studies reflect a fascination with the child's competence. The prevailing mood is one of "behold!" In order to adopt the role of beholder, one must make a distinction between the world perceived by adults and the world perceived by the child and be prepared to suspend adult modes of organization.

The development of competence is the goal of many educational ventures, but it is defined in different ways. As we, in this book, attempt to assign a meaning to the term competence, we find that the meaning most consistent with the view of an interacting, experimenting, constructing, and changing child is one that emphasizes the development of the ability to modulate transactions with people and things, to seek complexity and challenge, and to generate new procedures for dealing with novel and unexpected situations. To some extent such a definition is based on an understanding not only of the child's capacities but of his pleasures. The child's competence is represented in part by the nature of his attachments to people, his ability to create a "make-believe" world, his ability to receive and give information to others, and his ability to manipulate systematically the relationships between actions and outcomes. We do not conceptualize competence as a narrow set of intellectual skills but rather as a complex network of knowledge and talents that permits the child to deal in diverse ways with an increasingly differentiated world.

Some educational programs emphasize achievements and skills that are by-products of competence as we have defined it; for instance, the determined national effort to achieve universal literacy has led many early childhood programs to stress preparation for reading and arithmetic. Still other programs reflect the theme of the apocryphal professor who began his first lecture by saying, "Half of what I am about to tell you will not be true ten years from now, and I don't know which half that will be." These programs point up the *processes* of competence rather than its contents—the processes developed by the child to define problems, select relevant information, and coordinate that information into a coherent body of knowledge. Among these programs, too, there are differences. Some present the child with a sequence of ordered skills in a tightly packaged instructional program based on the notion that higher-order skills are combinations of lower-order skills. Other process-oriented programs see the same kinds of general skills growing out of child-initiated encounters with a rich and varied world of objects and people. A concern with competence also ties together the disarray of educational and child-welfare programs that are expected to ameliorate poverty and restore social justice. In today's world we find optimism in the growing respect of increasing numbers of people for the advantages of a pluralistic society—one that acknowledges and protects cultural and ethnic diversity—and for the need for institutional processes for formulating well-stated questions, multiple hypotheses, test procedures, and the alternative solutions that such a society would entail. Our particular biases lead us to believe that these are the conditions most likely to generate a viable set of national programs and strategies to deal with an unpredictable future. We wish to place in parallel the competence of the child and the competence of society. In a limited way we are proposing to tie goals for the child to a sense of what he is and we are not made uncomfortable by the implication that that is what society ought to be.

We wish to identify ourselves clearly as child psychologists. If, in the course of this report, we wander into sociology, economics, and political or administrative science, we do so only because of our growing realization that the child cannot be dealt with in isolation from his immediate environment or from the broader social context. The foundations of the child's confidence and trust in himself, his self-affection and self-respect, will reflect the feelings of those who care for him. These feelings, in turn, must reflect the corrosive influence of societal racism, inequality, and injustice. We hope that others with the specialized competencies we lack will do justice to issues that we must inevitably deal with superficially. If this book accomplishes no other end than to energize those in other areas to consider child-related issues, it will have accomplished its central purpose.

Our biases, which have led us to emphasize the child in context, have led us to a similar presentation of day-care issues. This book is about day care in context—beyond its traditional connotation of a "center." To some extent "center" thinking has drastically limited and narrowed day-care efforts. Several authors have speculated about why day care has so persistently retained a character of emergency and crisis. Some have placed the responsibility on narrow sights in social work that emphasize pathology and treatment (Kahn, 1962; Mayer & Kahn, 1965; Ruderman, 1968). Others have attacked cultural biases that the young child must be reared by its mother (Wolins, 1965). The poor quality of care typically offered in day-care centers (Ruderman, 1968) and the failure of programs to respond to consumer preferences and needs (Emlen, 1970) have also been cited.

It seems as though all these speculations tacitly recognize that day care, when it is set equivalent to centers, places emphasis on the walls and doors, the bricks and brass that separate the child from his family and neighborhood. Even more, day care has often been advanced as a solution to family or societal problems. Its adult orientation has often resulted in little but global attention to the variables and processes that influence the development of the child.

As we deal with day-care issues we go beyond day care as a "center" to day care as the environment in which children are reared. By proposing a broad view of day care we must deal with issues frequently excluded from day-care discussions. The context of day care is exceedingly complex and so are the issues.

ON ISSUES

What are the major issues in day care? At least two substantially different approaches to this question are possible. We could begin with a survey of prevailing debates and establish priorities according to the amount of attention or vehemence that a particular debate has attracted. Here the surveyor would adopt the position of a neutral recorder, commentator, and clarifier of dominant preoccupations. We have considered this mode and rejected it on several grounds. As a matter of principle we believe that issues are not necessarily what people argue about but are propositions with alternatives, implications, and assumptions. Moreover, a list of popular arguments may do a disservice by locking debate into the superficial features of problems. The real question of interest may not be the particular matter under debate but rather the problems from which a particular controversy evolved; for example, if measured by historical persistence, consensus, and vehemence, a major day-care issue is the ratio of adults to children in group care. We suggest that the adult-child ratio is primarily an administrative issue in the arena of legislative guidelines which require indices that can be unambiguously determined. In fact, not only are group environments more complex but governmental responsibilities for child-development programming are far broader. Behind these guidelines are the more fundamental issues of indexing and monitoring program quality and behind these issues are others that pertain to the conceptualization of an optimizing environment. As a practical matter we suspect that even when an apparently neutral approach to the designation of issues is taken personal biases and viewpoints *do* intrude and that dealing with issues is more difficult when such intrusions are not clearly identified.

Another approach assumes that issues originate in basic assumptions about day care and develop from positions taken at various choice points. The issue proposer need not explore all the alternatives at every choice point but rather should indicate his biases and what the options might be. This approach may enrich the arena of discussion by inviting alternatives but at the same time permit the consequences and implications of one argument to be projected. We believe that such a style fittingly expresses the notion that there are alternative ways of solving problems and that each set of alternatives brings with it a set of new problems and possible solutions.

ISSUE 1: THE SUBJECT MATTER OF DAY CARE

This we consider to be the superordinate issue in day care. The priorities assigned to day-care issues will differ if the day care is discussed from the point of view of economics, sociology, medicine, or child development. One can imagine a book on day care that took as its central concern the issue of working mothers in relation to costs, benefits, or national productivity. Another might deal with social institutions, their change and development. Such books would be of enormous value and quite different from one another. They would reflect the application of varying conceptual frameworks to a problem that is amorphous in the absence of such frameworks. We have chosen to define the child—his development and mode of functioning—as the overarching issue of day care. Having made this choice, other issues follow.

ISSUE 2: VIEW OF THE CHILD

Earlier in this discussion we indicated our preference for a representation of the child as actively engaged in making sense out of his world. We view the child as an extraordinary problem definer-problem solver whose development hinges both on the nature of the information available to him and on the kind of sense-making competence he has already acquired. Thus the child and his human and material environment interact to constrain and direct future development.

Two categories of environment—family and school—stand out as distinctive in the life of the child. Each has its own structures and regulating mechanisms; each is in itself a coherent system. Yet each environment also generates psychological variables that influence the child's development. The family is the environment of long-term continuity that provides the relatively small group of "others" of heterogeneous ages with whom the child will have life-long contact. The school represents planned systematic goal-directed interventions, homogeneous ages, and relatively large groups of people. These are but a few of the possibly relevant dimensions of environmental variation, and when their combinations and those of others are generated we come to the third issue in day care.

ISSUE 3: DIVERSITY OF ALTERNATIVES—BREADTH OF DAY CARE

A major question in day care concerns the variety and breadth of day-care alternatives. Day-care programming can reflect the ecology of current child-rearing environments by adapting them to the needs of various groups and individuals, or it can concentrate on a limited set of options that reflects the historical preoccupation with group programs. The broader perspective is likely to be nurtured by an emphasis on the development of children in contrast to an emphasis on welfare reform, women's liberation, or multiproblem families. This means conceptions of "day care" in the absence and in the presence of parents, in the home and out of the home, with relatives and with strangers, next door and 10 miles away. Emphasis on the development of the child creates new issues or rather brings forward those often obscured when day care is equated to particular social-political problems and to particular types of programming. These issues deal with the aims of day care with respect to the child.

ISSUE 4: AIMS OF DAY-CARE PROGRAMS

Discussion of diverse environments and alternatives cannot long proceed without attention to the diverse aims and purposes toward which these alternatives are directed. Superordinate goals may reflect conceptions of the ideal state of human society, assumptions about the nature of man, and the direction of human development. They may reflect assumptions about the specific skills needed to survive in the world of today. In discussing the inherent potential of human beings, one can stress their capacity to live by a rational, ethical system based on a commitment to the ideals of justice and human life or, conversely, one can stress man's inherent bent for destruction, conflict, and power. These themes span concerns that range from survival to actualization, from control to fulfillment; each emerges in current controversies about day care.

We have chosen a third theme, perhaps midway between the other two, and we have called that theme "competence." Competence stresses those capacities or processes that determine effective functioning in a range of situations. The notion of competence stresses the conceptual, affective, and motivational systems that apply equally well to school learning, job performance, political action, and social regulation. Competence systems are marked by their focus on active participation and on the reciprocity between the child's initiation of change and his accommodation to change. A concern with competence draws attention to the conditions under which mastery is acquired and includes the general assertion that these situations are characterized by moderate levels of stress and conflict.

ISSUE 5: THE DEPTH AND DIRECTION OF CHANGE

Protest is more effective than advocacy; failure is more salient than success; the critic is less vulnerable than the proposer. Briefly, it is safer to predict trends than to try to change them.

Current trend analysts suggest that increasing numbers of mothers will work, that the total number of parental working hours will increase, and that the overriding factor in the child's development will hinge on the quality of care in the absence of parents. Quite another trend is possible, however—one that moves toward a decrease in the total number of parental working hours. In the face of such a countertrend, the child's development would hinge on the quality of care provided by the parents. Although day care has been traditionally defined as child care in the absence of parents, there is no reason to ignore the rather large number of alternatives that can be generated.

It may be the case that drastic revisions of national values will be necessary for these alternatives to become viable. We might (somewhat fancifully, perhaps) point to the elaborate credit system that permits people to borrow for today against earnings in the future (buy now, pay later) and thus achieve monetary flexibility in relation to material goods and services. There is no analogous device for achieving role flexibility that permits people to borrow time for parenting when children are young against time for working when children are older (nurture now, work later) or for earning credits for parenting by working before the children are born (work now, nuture later)—but there could be.

How can we plan now for possibilities such as these? Urgently needed is some mechanism that would permit planning for the future but would be protected from immediate short-term enthusiasms or crises. Clearly called for is something like a "sheltered workshop" in which day-care–child-development programs that would anticipate what is needed could be formulated and tested.

Change, stability, and continuity are essentially developmental problems that appear in issues that are relevant to the child, the family, intervention programs, and society. In articulating a model of the child in which each level of child-environment interaction builds on a preceding level, we are proposing that the child is neither fixed and predetermined at birth nor does he become fixed and predetermined at any level of development. At each developmental level the past is conserved as the conditions necessary for future change are created.

We are suggesting that day care should concern itself with the processes underlying children's achievements, with the ways in which children solve problems and negotiate exchanges with people, and their expectations of success or failure, affection or abuse. These issues, which concern the depth of change in the child, have been perceptively analyzed by Glick (1969). If day care is to appreciate fully the issue of competence, it cannot rest with criterion performances such as the size of a child's vocabulary, his ability to count to 10, to avoid conflict, or to follow the rules. In each case it behooves us to inquire what the performance means: what is the child communicating, what is he counting, what conflicts is he avoiding, and what significance do the rules have for him?

In large measure our discussion of day care has been shaped by the selection and definition of issues suggested by our particular frame of reference and set of assumptions. These issues are not tendered as universal or exhaustive. So deep is our belief in the committed advocacy of alternative views that we submit ours in the hope that contrasting approaches to day care will emerge.

We raise these issues because the central theme of *Day Care in Context* is that day care can be considered as a major opportunity for advancing our knowledge of children and optimal growth schemes; that to confine issues in day care to the employment of women or the alleviation of welfare dependency, or to fail to promote open inquiry regarding the social, material, and psychological resources of American families, is to abdicate responsibility for social planning while continuing to promote schemes that may alter the texture of American society.

Day Care in Context is addressed to those who study the development of young children and to those who wish to apply child-development principles to the design of day-care programs. It argues that our understanding of the child will be incomplete and our programs for children will be only partly effective as long as there is a gap between theories of development and programming strategies.

We have considered five areas of major significance for the context of day care. Context I is a brief examination of the history of day care and current policy issues. Context II examines four developmental systems that have particular significance during the early years for day-care planning. In Context III we explore features of the family in relation to the development of the child and child-care programs, and Context IV deals with aspects of early childhood programs that have built on what is known about the child. Finally we discuss the context of day care in the light of national needs and current programs that bear on these needs, national policy in the light of the experiences of other nations, and possibilities for day-care policy in the future.

CONTEXT I

DAY CARE PAST AND PRESENT

DAY CARE HAS BEEN IN AMERICA FOR A LONG TIME. FOR MANY years it has been a sensitive barometer of national crisis. Day care is best known by the booms that came on the heels of the Civil War, the Depression, and World War II. These boom periods cannot be described simply as attempts to protect children whose mothers were drawn into the labor market. For example, the expansion of day care during the Depression occurred more in order to make jobs for unemployed teachers, nurses, and social workers than to care for the abandoned children of working mothers or to provide a service for troubled or disadvantaged families.

Today the nation is on the edge of another major day-care expansion. In 1938 approximately 300,000 children were in licensed programs; in 1945 there were almost a million. At the present time approximately 640,000 children are using licensed day-care facilities, but estimates of the number currently needing care have ranged from 2 to 4.5 million (Bernstein, 1969; Feldman, undated; Keyserling, 1965; Reed, 1968; Rosenberg & Spindler, 1970).

Before too many options are closed by the rapid expansion of day-care facilities the question whether the day-care programs of tomorrow will speak to issues that are central to the development of children must be posed. Many of these issues deal with the ability of people to function effectively in a technological and changing society. In large measure today's national crisis reflects a loss of confidence in the capacity of existing institutions to promote the competence of large numbers of children—intellectual or academic competence for some, emotional, creative, or social competence for others.

Day care has another history. From its beginnings in the early nineteenth century until the rise of the nursery school in the 1920's the day nursery was the only formal program for the care of young children. A conceptual history of day care over the last 150 years recapitulates the changing views of the child in America. Assumptions about him—what he starts with, what he ought to end with, and how he changes—have always been embedded in child-care practices and child development theories. To accuse the past of providing merely "custodial" care is to ignore those who attempted to do much more, who sought definitions and justifications for practice.

1

Historical Perspectives

THE HISTORY OF DAY CARE BETWEEN RECURRING CRISES IS A
history of reformers and kindly people. The first day nurseries in America
opened with a spirit of unbounded optimism inherited from the social reformers of Europe. Infant Schools of New England at the turn of the nineteenth century accommodated the children of the poor, but the central themes
behind these schools dwelt on the mind of the child and the education of all
children. Bronson Alcott, writing in a Boston magazine in 1828, enthusiastically
heralded the great opportunity provided by infant schools for ". . . observations
on the principles and methods of infant instruction. . . ." Readers were assured
that investigations would lead to ". . . improvements which will be introduced
to our systems of education . . . these experiments on the infant mind will operate
with a power that must cause a great and rapid change." A later article called
on its readers to have compassion for the

> . . . poor little ones who have no nursery and no mother deserving the name, and
> not to rest until every section of the city has its infant school . . . women know
> more than men do how much may be done towards forming the mental health
> and especially the moral character during the first four years of a child's life
> (Kuhn, 1947, p. 27).

In a widely circulated manifesto of 1823 the spirit of optimism and wonder
encircling the young child was summarized by Lord Henry Brougham:

> The truth is that he can and does learn a great deal more before that age [six
> years] than all he ever learns or can learn in all his after life. His attention is more
> easily aroused, his memory is more retentive, bad habits are not yet formed, nor is
> his judgment warped by unfair bias (Forest, 1927, p. 49).

The theme of social reform through pansophism—the teaching of all knowledge to all children—was adopted from Comenius, who, writing in the seventeenth century, gave infant education some of its most enduring principles. Comenius espoused the "School of the Mother's Knee," which would train the child's senses and bring about moral, religious, and physical development through play, games, fairy tales, rhymes, music, and manual activities. Instruction would be graded to match the child's development: from simple to complex, from the known to the unknown, and using direct contact with objects or at least pictures of objects. Comenius also argued that each infant should have only one teacher so that differences in teaching styles would not compound the difficulties inherent in learning different material (Eller, 1956; Forest, 1927).

The infant schools borrowed from Rousseau a confidence in the child to do things for himself, without compulsion from external authority, and from Pestalozzi the principle that teachers should select from among the objects available to the child those specially suited to illustrate abstract dimensions of shape, size, and color.

Kuhn (1947) has argued that the infant-education movement elevated the status of mothering. Mothers were discovered as the "molders of childhood" and the "effective teachers of the human race." Domestic tasks and child rearing took on a divine glow, but it was not long before "divinity" was divided . . . "the mother sways the dominion of the heart, the father that of the intellect." Although new experts were advising mothers to take infants "abroad . . . to cultivate the faculties of attention, comparison, of sight, sound, taste, smell and touch," mothers were also encouraged to engage in "sweet exchange of sentiments . . . and overt expression of love" . . . , a charge that was generalized to the role of women in "ruling by the affections" rather than "ruling by the intellect." To rule by anything is more emancipated than not to rule at all, and enthusiasm for mothering spread throughout the land, eventually reaching even rural areas. This period saw the growth of maternal associations—conservative, religious, and rural organizations for mothers.

Gradually this early spirit of enthusiasm for infant education waned. The sense of wonder and discovery dissipated. In its place formalism and punitiveness entered the infant school (Brubacher, 1947; Forest, 1927).

FROM WONDER TO REFORM

By 1840 a new emphasis had appeared. New medical discoveries oriented those concerned with the welfare of children to the importance of sanitation and health. Actuarial data disclosed a relationship between maternal employment and infant mortality. The first infant crèche for the children of working mothers opened in Paris in 1844, and in 1854 the first American crèche was established in collaboration with the Child's Hospital of New York City (Forest, 1927). The children, whose ages ranged from 15 weeks to 3 years, received regular medical examinations and were under the supervision of experienced nursemaids.

This concern for the child's physical well-being was soon expanded to concern for proper habits, orderliness, and manners. In some nurseries older children were trained to use a napkin, were expected to eat their meals in silence, and were marched about in line whenever it was necessary to leave the nursery room [National Association of Day Nurseries, Inc. (NADN), 1940]. One nursery anticipated today's fascination with operant conditioning and token economies:

> Tickets were given for punctuality, good behavior, and the proper performance of duties which were redeemable by articles of clothing (NADN, 1940, p. 3).

Some nurseries developed a curriculum:

> All the children of suitable age are employed by turns in performing different portions of the housework under the eye of the matron, thus affording them an excellent opportunity of becoming fitted for servants or future housekeepers (NADN, 1940, p. 3).

Sewing was taught to the girls as a suitable occupation for poor females. One group made the vocational aspect of the curriculum explicit when it organized the Rochester Industrial School Association in 1856 for the purpose of gathering

> into the school, vagrant and destitute children who from poverty or vice of their parents, are unable to attend the Public School, and who gather a precarious livelihood by begging and pilfering, to give them ideas of moral and religious duty, to instruct them in the elements of learning, and in different branches of learning, and thus enable them to obtain an honest and honorable support and become useful members of society (Shoemaker, 1965, p. 54).

The day nurseries of the mid-nineteenth century were certainly concerned with ameliorating the plight of abandoned and neglected children. Health, habits, and skills were not ignored. To say that these nurseries offered merely custodial care is to do them a great injustice. Yet their tone was sober and grim.

In the 1880's and 1890's immigrants from all over Europe came to America and settled in large cities. Irish, Italians, Jews, Germans, Russians, and Armenians became America's poor, the residents of tenement houses and ghettos. The settlement-house movement arose in response to the needs of the sweatshop toilers, the unwed mothers, the hungry, and the helpless. Robert A. Woods (1898) preached settlement-house functionalism. He argued that the resources of civilization needed to be available to the people they were intended to serve. An infant health station, for example, is useless to the mother who lives two miles away. Woods envisioned a comprehensive grouping of social services "capable of releasing the energies of all ages within an area of easy accessibility" (Kennedy, 1953, p. 27). Woods ranks among social work's early analysts. Social institutions, in his analysis, could carry out one of three functions: (a) relief, (b) rehabilitation, and (c) reconstruction. Relief and rehabilitation involve help that comes from outside the community. Reconstruction comes from within the community when the people involved take up a common cause to improve social conditions (Woods, 1898). By this classification the day nurseries of the late nineteenth century were relief institutions.

The first settlement-house nursery opened at Hull House in 1898. It came about quite simply because the children were there:

> During our first summer, an increasing number of these poor little waifs would wander into the cool hallway of Hull House. We kept them there and fed them at noon . . . our little guests noisily enjoyed the hospitality of our bedrooms under the so-called care of any resident who volunteered to keep an eye on them (Addams, 1910, p. 127).

The tradition of Jane Addams embodies compassion and respect for the poor. The immigrant working mother is "bent under the double burden of earning the money which supports her children and giving the tender care which alone keeps them alive" (Addams, 1910, p. 128). The early settlement houses were clearing houses of social service, broadly conceived as militant activism on behalf of juvenile courts, trade unionism, child labor, housing, sanitation laws, law enforcement, and woman's suffrage. The day nursery was seen as a provision made necessary by the exploitation of women, the "sweaty" shops, and the difficulties inherent in living in a strange and foreign land. Acculturation was a minor purpose compared with the view of the settlement as an "information and interpretation bureau," as a "big brother whose mere presence on the playground protects the little ones from bullies" (Addams, 1910, p. 127).

Evidence of acculturation began making its appearance in settlement-house activities and soon seeped into the nursery. By the turn of the century a few nurseries had added kindergartens (Fleiss, 1962; Hosley, 1963) and had adopted the model developed by Friedrich Froebel, which was based on the notion of a preformed child, born with latent, symbolic mental contents. These latent contents expressed universal laws of development and were represented by the symbols of the circle, the cube, and the triangle. The purpose of education was to provide the child with symbolic "gifts" and "opportunities" so that the order and laws of the mind could be expressed. Although Froebel recognized the active nature of the child and the importance of play, carefully prescribed objects ("gifts") and lessons ("opportunities") came to dominate practice. Once again the formal and regimented aspect of education prevailed.

It was during this period that day nurseries were first sponsored by boards of education. Nurseries were opened in the public schools of Gary, Indiana (Dewey & Dewey, 1919), and Los Angeles, California. The Los Angeles nurseries were explicitly concerned with parent education and the Americanization of the family (Whipple, 1929). Similar emphasis on parent education was made in the settlement houses and other voluntary day nurseries.

Parent education in these institutions began in an atmosphere of criticism of the ways and values of the poor, combined with the notion that education could change adults as well as children. Perhaps at an earlier time the prevailing belief was that the "poverty and vice" of the poor could be relieved only by the education of their children. The early settlement house activists placed the onus of child neglect on the machine, long working hours, and inhuman conditions rather than on the parent. The working mother who locked her children in the house, whose children were dirty and unfed, did not emerge as a bad mother but rather as a victim of a brutal system that permitted no alternatives. The early nurseries opened their doors uncritically to all. Mothers were not expected to participate or to contribute—obviously they could not.

Then the obvious was questioned. As views about the poor changed, reformers turned from institutions to individuals. Charity became helping people to help themselves: "The only charity which amounts to much is that which takes the form of education in some way" (NADN, 1940, p. 4). Attention turned to the parent deficient in knowledge and skills:

> She has no idea of how to economize money, time or strength; she is largely ignorant of the needs of her little ones, and though she may wish them to be moral and decent, she has no idea how to train them to these ends (NADN, 1940, p. 5).

Parent education was rendered in the form of teaching homemaking skills and the proper physical care of children.

At the same time the organized and articulate segment of the day-nursery movement began to worry that the unrestricted availability of the day nursery would diminish the parents' sense of responsibility for caring and providing for their children. The first admissions criteria were evolved to discourage mothers from going to work if they could possibly stay at home. Clergymen and board members began to visit the homes of applicants to determine whether the mother was either a "destitute widow" or a "woman with a sick husband."

NEGLECT AND DECLINE

Disillusionment and apprehension began to assail both practitioner and consumer. The National Federation of Day Nurseries, founded in 1898, forcefully drew attention to the poor quality of care offered by day nurseries. Social reformers campaigned for pension allowances for mothers. Grace Abbot argued that day nurseries were not a necessary part of child-welfare services and that the nation could well afford to support all mothers at home (Knight, 1966). Moreover, a 1912 survey indicated that day nurseries were used only to 71% of capacity. An interview study to determine why working mothers were keeping their children out of nurseries reported that mothers felt that (a) nurseries were not located in sections inhabited by them and (b) nurseries did not care for and educate their children in the proper way (Forest, 1927). The first Mothers' Pension Act was legislated in 1911 and by 1919 public assistance was available to mothers in 39 states.

As the virtues of staying home with her children received increasing stress, the competency of the poor mother—indeed, mothers in general—was increasingly disparaged. In discussions of public support for nursery education leaders were suggesting simultaneously that

> more lasting social good will results from conserving family life and relationships than from creating an increasing number of child-caring agencies (Gesell, 1922, p. 1033),

and that

> the modern family is in many instances presently inadequate to the task of educating young children according to the standards required by the best thought on the subject (Forest, 1927, p. 264).

The day nursery had begun its history in an atmosphere of glowing optimism. The mind of the child was seen as the key to a better society. In the ensuing years the emphasis shifted from mind to body, to practical habits and skills, to protection rather than change. Then doubts were expressed that day nurseries were giving adequate protection. Reformers argued that if protection were the central issue it would be better to keep mothers at home. However, suspicions that mothers were incapable of providing more than protection for their children were never advanced to defend the day nursery but rather became the central theme of the burgeoning nursery school movement.

THE RISE AND FALL OF NURSERY SCHOOLS

The decline of enthusiasm for day nurseries was accompanied by a rising enthusiasm for nursery schools. Whatever status the mother had acquired by 1820 was thoroughly undermined by 1920. The handbook of the National Society for the Study of Education proposed that the "prevailing criticism" of the "family's use of its opportunity to educate and shape the young child" called for a program of reform

> . . . either by eliminating much of the family's opportunity to mould the child or by demanding that the family be made more efficient by bringing its methods into harmony with scientific principles (Whipple, 1929, p. 78).

Mothers were faulted for not knowing how to keep the child profitably busy, and for encouraging excessive dependency. Freud and Flugel were cited in regard to the dangers of "too complete fixation" of the child on his parents. In exploring the relation between functions of nursery school and family, Forest suggested that

> the nursery school touches very closely upon the educational function of the home, and indeed undertakes certain aspects of child care which have until now been considered to be altogether the concern of the home. . . . It thus represents a new social attitude toward the respective rights and duties of the child, the parent, and the community (1927, p. 399).

In contrast to the day nursery, the nursery school had its sights on the middle and upper classes. The nursery school

> extends the values of the day nursery as a strategic point from which to gain strategic control of the often neglected preschool child, upward or outward, to include economic strata which could never be reached by the nursery (Forest, 1927, p. 398).

Despite profound philosophical differences, however, these early nursery schools were more like current day-care centers than like current nursery schools. A 1928 survey of nursery schools indicated that 60% had all-day programs, 8:30 to 4:30—not long enough to service working mothers but presumably long enough to overcome insufficiencies of the middle-class home. In the nursery school of this period children as young as 18 months of age were fed, napped, toileted, and given early social training.

The nursery school placed strong emphasis on parent education, but the kind it developed differed markedly from that attempted by the day nursery. In the day nursery parent education was a matter of teaching physical care of the child, sewing and cooking, and household skills and management (Addams, 1910; Woods, 1898). For the most part the day nursery ignored the cultural values of the mother in food, dress, and mothering styles. Attempts to assess the effectiveness of these efforts reported that mothers felt that the programs accomplished little, and it was difficult to attract participants. In the nursery school parent education emphasized the development of the child in courses of study and intensive observation of him at home and in school (Dewey & Dewey, 1919; Taylor, 1931; Whipple, 1929). Parent participation was often an admission requirement (Davis, 1932). A survey of 203 nursery schools in 1931 indicated that 79%

considered parent education to be a major activity, whereas only 20% listed relief for the mother as a primary goal (Davis, 1932).

Above all, nursery schools were for and about children. Advocates asserted that the developmental needs of the child for group association, a suitable play environment, expert guidance, and "wholesome detachment from the mother" could best be met by the nursery school (Forest, 1927).

Thus after a 100-year hiatus America rediscovered the child. If the first discovery had been marked by wonder, the second was marked by awe and perhaps even dismay. The first wave dwelt on the mind, the second on the emotions. The strong presence of Freud, Jung, and McDougall was reflected in the theme of the child dominated by inborn drives, instincts, and appetites.

Specialists were divided in their prescriptions for dealing with these powerful inner forces. Some argued for inhibition, whereas others warned of the dangers of repression; for example, one writer counseled:

> The perversion of interest-drives in many adults emphasized the importance of developing normal, healthy, and spontaneous drives in young children . . . they are pursued in the face of obstacles unless the individual is strongly conditioned against the drives (Davis, 1932, p. 17).

Another specialist warned of the harm that would come from the

> repression of the instincts and the appetites. . . . What the nursery school teacher can do is to prevent the unnatural suppression of primitive impulses . . . the morality of a civilized community must not be imposed on the child by the wholesale repression of his natural instincts (Owens, 1920, p. 6, cited in Forest, 1927).

This division in strategies for dealing with the child's emotions paralleled the division that frequently appears in strategies for dealing with the child's mind. One emphasis urged increased environmental intervention, the other would reduce intervention. The strategy chosen reflected assumptions about the equipment available to the child and how this equipment operates in the course of social or intellectual development.

Those who adopted the language of conditioning reflected the influence of Pavlov and Watson (Kessen, 1965). Presumably the child is born with a limited number of emotional reactions to specific stimuli and a limited number of inborn reflexes. In this analysis emotional control develops by conditioning and chaining. Habits, that is, conditioned responses, become superimposed by learning on the child's biological reflex endowment.

Those who adopted the language of psychoanalysis stressed the disruptive consequences of neurotic anxiety—the child's excessive fear of expressing antisocial, sexual, and aggressive urges. According to this position, the foundations of neurotic anxiety are established during the early years of life by the harsh repression of natural drives. Neurotic anxiety prevents the child from acquiring or utilizing those control mechanisms that would normally appear if the anxiety were not present. Mechanisms for controlling inborn drives were assumed to be part of the child's naturally developing equipment which can be interfered with but not provided by child-rearing agents.

In 1929 the National Society for the Study of Education, in a survey of nursery schools (Whipple, 1929) reported programs that employed the language of each of these points of view. More interesting, however, was the central pre-occupation of all programs with the management of routine functions such as sleeping, eating, and eliminating. It was in these functions that the emotions of concern were manifested and that mismanagement was thought to produce the most serious consequences for emotional and social development.

Another area of consensus appeared in the value assigned to play. All pro-grams were based on the natural interests of the child. The research of G. S. Hall and the score of those who followed (Hurlock, 1934) produced a list of activities children preferred, and it was from these lists that the now-standard nursery-school array of blocks, sand, clay, paints, and so on was derived. The child was seen as an active investigator and observer of the environment. The objective of the nursery school was to provide the time and equipment for "unhurried and undictated looking, listening and manipulation" (Davis, 1932, p. 17).

Play occupied the largest single part of the nursery school day. Benefits to the child were assumed to accrue simply from the opportunity to exercise his interests and to practice sensory-motor skills. As the work of Dewey began to capture the imagination of nursery school educators, the role of play became more refined. The benefits of play were elaborated. According to Dewey,

> the activities of the child . . . are the means by which he becomes acquainted with his world and by which he also learns the use and limits of his own powers (Dewey & Dewey, 1919, p. 10).

He also emphasized the

> need of intimate and extensive personal acquaintance with a small number of typical situations with a view to mastering the way of dealing with the problems of experience (p. 10).

He argued for learning related to "the motives that are furnished by their own powers and the needs that are dictated by their own conditions." (p. 2).

The key to learning, according to Dewey, lies in materials and situations that satisfy the purposes of the child, not the adult. As these ideas were applied, the adult was assigned the task of providing suitable materials and enjoined to interfere minimally in the child's activities. Intervention could be defended only in the case of aggressive or destructive behavior. Again, much of the discussion of teacher roles focused on the powerful and disturbing emotions. Although a heavy burden was placed on play to promote intellectual development, the recommended role for the adult was that of a watchful, retiring supervisor. The child could and would extract the benefits of play on his own. If the adult simply guarded the child properly against emotional stress, natural growth forces would ensure the unfolding of the child's inherent capacities.

THE NURSERY SCHOOL INFLUENCE

The nursery school movement dramatically elevated the status of those who would study or teach the young. In 1931 34% of the 203 nursery schools surveyed listed research as a major function and 43% listed teacher preparation (Davis, 1932). Yet it was not until the Depression that trained early childhood specialists appeared in the day nurseries. Consultants in early childhood education were made available to the WPA nurseries (Fleiss, 1962) and teachers were placed in day nurseries by training institutions (Beer, 1938). The nursery school teacher, however, functioned quite apart from the ongoing day-nursery program. Beer (1938), for example, speaks of the nursery school *in* the day nursery, and supervision of the nursery school teacher rested with a training institution.

This arrangement apparently satisfied no one. As reported by Beer (1938), the nursery school teacher attempted to develop the child's independence by letting him serve his own food, ignoring his slowness, while the day-nursery staff grumbled at the cold food on the child's plate. Those concerned with the physical care of the child worried about eating, tooth brushing, and elementary social skills; the nursery school teacher worried about expanding the child's expressive capacities and limiting the extent to which adult values would be imposed on him. Nonetheless, nursery school thinking and methods were gradually assimilated by the articulate segment of the day-nursery establishment (Cauman, 1956). By 1942 the educational and developmental philosophies of the day nursery and the nursery school were indistinguishable (Fleiss, 1962, Appendix A), and by 1950 one widely respected book in the field of early childhood education treated the day-care center as one kind of nursery school, identical to all other early childhood programs in its assumptions about the child, recommended curriculum, teacher behaviors, and so on (Read, 1950). Cauman (1956) argued that the only difference between the two lay in the status of the day nursery as a child-welfare service. More recently Murphy (1968b) advocated a comprehensive educational program for day care modeled after prominent nursery school centers.

The dominant theme in early childhood education gradually became a commitment to the unfolding, maturational characteristics of development propelled by a growth drive variously expressed as a "thrust" (Law, 1964), an "impulse" (University of the State of New York, *Child Development Guides,* 1968), or a "life force" (Gilbert, 1970).

Psychosocial development, as formulated by Erik Erikson (1950), softened the weight previously given to the negative, repressive characteristics of the child's human environment. Under the influence of psychosocial concepts, more attention was given to the adaptation of caregiving behaviors to tasks facing the child at each developmental level. Habit training and conditioning notions were abandoned. The child was seen as moving through sequential stages during which the major developmental tasks concerned his sense of trust, autonomy, and initiative. The outcome at each stage could be positively as well as negatively influenced by those who provided care. The development of trust or mistrust in infancy, for example, could be influenced by the mother's giving or witholding attention and care. The stress on negative and undesirable behaviors—aggression, jealousy, and dependence—and their expression and control, however, was retained. Substantial portions of the literature in the field, guides for teachers, and expositions of exemplary practice were devoted to the explanation and management of negative social behavior and strong emotional feelings (Read, 1950; University of the City of New York, *Child Development Guides,* 1968). The approach was often clinical in the tone of interpretation and prescription. Case workers in day care were urged to stress diagnosis and treatment within the nursery group setting (Hansan & Pemberton, 1965).

Play was recommended as the core of the day-care curriculum. Importance was attached to materials that children could adapt to their own purposes (Law, 1964) and to time for organizing thoughts and impressions (Hymes, 1968b). Play was seen as expressing the child's inner fantasy in which he could control outcomes. In play children "reveal themselves and their concepts of the world" (Read, 1950, p. 281). Hence observation of the child's play was seen as one way of understanding him. Play was also thought to provide a cathartic drain of negative feelings.

Specialists continued to stress the value of a protean teacher style that was discrete, "elusive and personal" (Law, 1964). The child-centered, permissive tradition of the nursery school in which the teacher watched and waited for the child's needs to emerge (Sears & Dowley, 1963) was adopted by the day-care educator. Language and intellectual development were relatively low priority aims, well behind meeting physical needs, attention to organic functions, controlling and expressing feelings, and developing motor and manipulatory skills (Sears & Dowley, 1963).

It is perhaps not surprising that little attention was given to the specific characteristics of day-care children. Beer (1938) wondered why "destructiveness is so hard to combat in the Day Nursery child." Holmes (1935) noted that children in the day nurseries were less fearful than children in nursery schools. Smith (1935) found substantial language differences between these groups that favored nursery-school children. More recently Upton (1969) reported intellectual and language deficits in day-care children on standardized tests. Still others (Hansan & Pemberton, 1965) commented on the lack of strong emotional ties to other people and the disciplinary and language problems that frequently appeared in day-care children. Glass (1949), on the other hand, failed to find differences in sleeping, eating, and elimination habits between children attending day nurseries and children cared for at home.

To the extent that children attending day nurseries were selected on the basis of family problems, one would expect to find considerable differences between day-care and nursery-school populations. Most certainly social-work prescriptions for admissions were strongly oriented toward such selection. Yet there are serious questions whether such admissions criteria were actually implemented. The available data (Beer, 1938; Mayer & Kahn, 1965) suggest that there were substantial socioeconomic differences between nursery-school and day-nursery groups which suggest differences in the abilities and behaviors of the children. Yet there is no indication until relatively recently (Hosley, 1963), that these differences were taken into account in day-care programming as it developed after the 1930's.

The extent to which the child-centered, permissive model advocated by the childhood specialist adequately reflects the typical day-care program is difficult to determine and has had only one serious examination (Prescott, Jones, & Kritchevsky, 1967). The informational literature distributed by day-care programs typically emphasizes the care and protection of the child, his physical activities, and his adjustment to the group. Intellectual development is usually seen in the context of play, although a few programs mention particular kinds of learning activity. Prescott et al. (1967) reported wide diversity in the teaching styles, program formats, and equipment among organized day-care centers in the Los Angeles area. One suspects from visits to local neighborhood-based centers in poverty areas that programming tends to be more structured, more academic, and also more concerned with acceptable social behaviors than that usually recommended by child-development specialists and usually found in nursery schools. One such strongly academic program was organized recently by a group of mothers in an inner-city neighborhood. The program emphasized the teaching of basic language skills and used procedures developed by O. K. Moore and equipment such as typewriters, tape recorders and line-a-times (Dixwell Pre-School Day Care Center, 1970).

The design of programs in response to the needs of particular groups of children has yet to become a part of deliberate day-care planning. Such designs might distinguish a total program oriented toward a particular population group (e.g., Spanish-speaking children, infants, or school-age youngsters). Even more, programs might consider ways of working with different children within the program (e.g., children from nuclear and extended families or outgoing and withdrawn children).

The history of day care in America can be seen as a succession of alternatives which, taken together, state themes that have a contemporary ring. We are still faced with contrasts in relief, rehabilitation, and reconstruction. We still shift from the mind of the child to his socialization and his physical well-being. The history of day care is a complex interlacing of assumptions about the child, the origin and repair of social inequity, and the function of social institutions. The aims of protection and health care, acculturation and education, the impact of social stress, and institutional change have influenced the shape of day care in the past and continue to do so today.

2

Policy Issues

THE MAJOR POLICY ISSUES OF TODAY HAVE THEIR ROOTS IN THE past. From the early optimism that the day nursery would usher in a new era in child rearing to the fear that mothers would abdicate responsibility for their children and from the desire to protect the lives of children to the belief that mothers should care for their children at home, day care has kaleidoscopically reflected the American *Zeitgeist*. Day care has been seen both as a hope for social rehabilitation and as a threat to family and church (Mayer & Kahn, 1965). It has persistently refused either to satisfy these hopes or justify the fears. The three major orientations toward day care which have grown out of the past provide a useful contrast of perspectives today: day care as a child-welfare service, as a public utility, and as an instrument of social change.

CHILD-WELFARE SERVICES

The purpose of day care has been most frequently described as a child-welfare service for the care and protection of children. At first all children who were neglected, abandoned, or without supervision were welcome. Gradually, however, admissions became formalized and qualified—first by the phrase, "destitute widows and those with sick husbands" and then by the phrase, "to support and strengthen the child's own family." The attempt to define the service created a focus on eligibility criteria and a constant discussion of the need for their expansion or reduction (Cauman, 1961; Dumpson, 1964; Goldsmith, 1965; McDermott, 1967; Ruderman, 1968; Yeomans, 1960).

Initially, eligibility criteria were expected to support the family by discouraging people from casual use of all day care for their children. At the same time

26

a collateral stress on day care as an alternative to foster or institutional care made its public appearance during the first White House Conference on Children in 1909 (Carstens, 1929).

Recent attempts have been made to elaborate the role of the caseworker in day-care settings beyond conducting application interviews and deciding whether day care would be a "constructive solution" to a particular problem (Hosley, 1964), a change in emphasis dictated perhaps by the relative infrequency with which agencies use day care as part of a treatment strategy (Pisapia & Haniwell, 1969). Many social workers consider a diagnostic intake study the "core" of day-care service when it is used as a casefinding device for the early detection of incipient or unexpressed social problems (Hansan & Pemberton, 1963; Mayer & Kahn, 1965; Stewart, 1968).

Yet day care as a service primarily for working mothers continues to be criticized by some social workers for offering "enriched custodial care that has little resemblance to a social work program" (Hansan & Pemberton, 1965, p. 150). Even broader concepts of the role of the caseworker include crisis intervention in the early stages of a parent-child problem, supportive services to the family, helping parents to seek treatment, direct casework with the day-care staff, and therapeutic services for the child (Bikle, 1965; Eckstein, 1962; Gilfillan, 1962; Hansan & Pemberton, 1965; Hosley, 1964; Rapoport & Cornsweet, 1969). This conceptual orientation of social workers to day care remains clearly rehabilitative and reflects the clinical and individualistic treatment orientation of the field.

Such an orientation has been subjected to critical scrutiny both in general (Mayer & Kahn, 1965; Schneiderman, 1964) and with regard to day care in particular (Ruderman, 1965). Schneiderman (1964), for example, has argued that demands for verbal communication, office visits, and confidence in professional competence make traditional casework services unsuitable for poor clients. In fact with these demands social-work services become effectively unavailable to the poor. Schneiderman proposed that the individualized, rehabilitative strategy be replaced by what amounts to a reconstructive strategy that would develop the competence of the poor at collective social action. This proposal constitutes a return to the settlement-house militantism of an earlier era and is expressed in day-care programs today by the approach of Etzkowitz and Schaflander (1969). Yet activist programs tend to place primary emphasis on adults. The day-care program is seen in relation to organizational, political, and social issues in the community, with somewhat less emphasis on the child.

Influential day-care publications still stress the problem-service view of day care [Child Welfare League of America Standards (CWLA), 1969; Ruderman, 1965]. Recommended eligibility requirements have been liberalized to include all the people who desire such services. Nevertheless, the intake study still receives top priority in descriptions of the role of the social worker in day-care settings. The Child Welfare League of America publication on day-care standards asserts that not all children of working mothers need day care as a child-welfare service without clarifying the criteria by which such "need" would be determined. In a study of mothers who use unsupervised family day care Willner (1966) reported that only 25 percent had the kind of personal family problems that customarily define the need for child-welfare services.

Day care, as a service, has retained several purposes (CWLA Standards, 1969). Day care is defined both as a *preventive service* to preclude the occurrence or aggravation of social, emotional, and health problems and as a *remedial or compensatory service* to reverse psychological damage. In addition, *supplementary* is a common qualifier of day care. It has its clearest meaning when day care is seen as an alternative to foster or institutional care. In other respects the term obscures most of the issues that are met when children are cared for by people other than their parents. One can argue, for example, that the child who is away from his parents 8 to 10 hours a day needs a mother surrogate, someone who will assume a mothering role in all respects. By the same token one might also argue that the child whose mother is not able to assume a mothering role also needs a mother surrogate so that his life experience will contain some regular and predictable warmth, responsiveness, and flexibility from another human being. For some children the expectations of nonparental caretakers may differ radically from those to which they are accustomed. Especially today, when the relevance of cultural and family values is receiving recognition, the term "supplementary" leaves the relationships between the child, the family, and the caregiving setting uncomfortably vague.

Despite frequent attempts to clarify the relation of social work to day care, social work has not played an active role in day-care programs. Only about 7% of the centers sampled by Ruderman (1968), for example, employed a social worker on a regular basis. Day care has been plagued chronically by a dearth of trained and experienced people in all areas (Costin & Gruener, 1964; Ruderman, 1965; Speer, 1966), so that even if day-care operators were to accept a casework emphasis adequately trained personnel would be difficult to locate.

SOCIAL NEEDS AND ACTUARIAL ALLOCATION

The emphasis on day care as an emergency treatment service has been challenged by those who view it as a normal need in a modern technological society (Kahn, 1962), as a "developmental" provision responsive to changing social needs rather than a service for underprivileged or inadequate people (Ruderman, 1965; 1968). The term "developmental," as it is used by those who raise this issue, does not refer to the changing needs of children but rather to the changing needs of society. Kahn (1962) suggested that in such a scheme the extent of the need would be predicted on an actuarial basis; that is, given information about the number of women in the labor market, the need for day-care services can be ascertained and "an allocation of resources in the light of social priorities and objectives democratically determined" (Kahn, 1962, p. 142) can be achieved. It is not clear, however, how statistical allocation bears on policy decisions that require analysis, debate, consensus, and a "community presence" (Kahn, 1963). Actuarial information can be a basis for choice only once the community has determined priorities among competing and often qualitatively different propositions. Actuarial data can be used to support alternative positions, but it is not helpful to confuse debates with decisions. How actuarial data are to be treated in the allocation of resources is very much an open question. If families are moving from urban to suburban areas, for example, should social action be undertaken to reverse the trend and, if so, how much of an urban population is desirable? Without an analysis of the problem, alternative solutions, and possible outcomes, actuarial distribution rules are either arbitrary or have their origins in unstated assumptions about the needs of children and their parents.

Several consequential issues grow out of the representation of day care as a "developmental provision." First, the suggestion seems to place day care more than ever in the position of an institution geared to relief. Day care has typically occupied this role in response to societal developments—war, economic distress, and industrial expansion. Advancing day care as a "normal" need in a modern society may be perilous if the existing social norm reflects chronic war, economic instability, and poverty rather than changing values with respect to working mothers or the needs of children. Second, the attempt to link relief to actuarial fluctuations comes alarmingly close to an escalator clause for social service which ties community services to deviations from some baseline level of distress. Surely the wisdom of formally relating day-care expansions or contractions to a state of relative emergency can be questioned. Of course, under these circumstances the emergency would not be defined as individual or family pathology but rather as social change that might endanger the well-being of children if the community failed to intervene. Yet within such a framework it is difficult to consider social reorganizations that speak to those chronic and perhaps unnecessary conditions of which inadequate child care may be but a symptom.

As an alternative, the notion that work must come in 20- or 40-hour bits, might be challenged. It might make sense to consider the total working hours of an individual's lifetime and distribute them according to family needs at a given time; the parents of small children, for example, might be expected to work no more than a total of 20 hours a week, whereas childless adults might be expected to put in a longer working week.

Finally, actuarial arguments have tended to tie solutions to established forms of service, namely day-care centers. Typically, the actuarial argument on behalf of day care contrasts the number of working mothers and the number of day-care centers (Bernstein, 1969; Kahn, 1962; Keyserling, 1965; Pines, 1968; Reid, 1970; Rosenberg & Spindler, 1970). The discrepancy between presumed need and existing facilities then becomes the measure of the emergency. Using this criterion, estimates of needed day-care placements have ranged from 2 million to 4.5 million, depending on whether the estimates included all the children under 6 years of age of full-time and part-time working mothers or all children, regardless of age, whose mothers work.

Alternative and more helpful estimation criteria are possible. An estimation formula might be based on those arrangements most likely to place the child in jeopardy. The formula adopted by the State of Illinois reflects this strategy by covering the

> percentage of children at each age level whose mothers are employed, and the percentage who are cared for by nonrelatives whether in the child's home, someone else's home or in group facilities, or who had no supervised care at all (Illinois Department of Children and Family Services, 1969, p. 4a).

Inherent in the Illinois formula is the notion that caregiving arrangements likely to be most damaging are those in which strangers care for children without familial or community safeguards.

If the Illinois formula were applied to national full-time maternal employment figures, 916,000 children under 6 years of age would need licensed day-care placement. Since approximately 640,000 places are currently available, the need for new ones comes to 276,000. Obviously not all mothers whose children are cared for by nonrelatives in unlicensed facilities would want to change and not all mothers whose children are cared for by relatives are satisfied with the arrangement. Other estimates of need might be based on an index of dissatisfaction that could yield from 10 to 32% overt criticism, depending on whether figures from Low and Spindler (1968) or Ruderman (1968) were used, and might go as high as 50% with a more liberal index of "would use if available" (Ruderman, 1968).

The Illinois formula turns out to be a relatively moderate estimate, yet its implications are nonetheless staggering. At an average teacher-child ratio of 10 to 1, 27,000 new teachers would be needed. At an average center size of 50 children roughly 3000 new buildings would be needed at a total cost of 500 million dollars. High-quality programming costs roughly 2000 to 2500 dollars per year for each child—another 300 million dollars. The gap between even a modest estimate of need (which does *not* include children who would need care if mothers now receiving welfare assistance were to obtain employment) and current fiscal plans is so staggering that an exaggerated statement of need is likely to discourage those concerned with the development of quality programs. Indeed, there is already ample precedence for low-cost programs and minimal standards. Since equipment and building costs are more or less fixed, there are two major ways in which day-care costs can be reduced: (a) a decrease in the adult:child ratio; (b) the employment of untrained people at low salaries.

In spite of Federal Interagency Day Care Requirements (Sugarman, 1968) of adult:child ratios of 1:5 for 3-year-olds and 1:7 for 5-year-olds, the State of California, for example, which has supported public day care since 1946, requires an adult:child ratio of only 1:8 for 2-year-olds and 1:15 for 5-year-olds. If the recent attempt to develop state guidelines in Connecticut anticipates a national trend, the pressure on state legislatures for minimal ratios will be acute. The theme will echo that of a churchman of 40 years ago, who, when criticized for the filth and impoverishment of the day nursery sponsored by the church, said, ". . . we cannot afford to do more and what would these working mothers do without us. They are grateful for this" (Whipple, 1929, p. 96).

The other source of economy in day care comes from low wages, which in turn depend on the employment of untrained workers. If career-development plans for day care are to become more than paper prospectives, day-care salaries and working conditions will have to improve. If they do not, the turnover of day-care employees will surely rise as workers find their way into better paid jobs in public schools. Unfortunately, there are no national figures for turnover rates in various child-care and -development programs. The scant data available suggest that present employment stability in day care is higher than in nursery schools—the median employment is three years for the former and two years for the latter (Ruderman, 1968)—which might reflect the relatively restricted job opportunities available to women with limited training and educational qualifications.

Most techniques for reducing day-care costs, then, operate on personnel: small adult:child ratios, low salaries, and the use of volunteers. Each of these cost-limiting techniques presents a rather special problem. As adult:child ratios decrease even competent caregivers are likely to find it increasingly difficult to find the time for more than routine physical care. Low salaries may discourage competent people from entering or remaining in the field. Volunteer workers can rarely offer more than a few hours a week, so that the large number of volunteers necessary to fill a staff position may reduce the child's opportunities to develop relationships with specific adults. On the other hand, there may be ways of deploying staff and using inexperienced workers or volunteers that will reduce costs without reducing the benefits received by the child. Detailed and tested models that deal with staffing patterns, staff roles, and training in child-care programs are urgently needed.

In the absence of such models the actuarial argument can rapidly deteriorate

to custodial care, possibly of the worst kind: attractive buildings and elegant equipment, the visible material indices of quality, coupled with unstable and shallow
human relationships, less visible but perhaps more powerful factors in suppressing
the optimal development of the child. An actuarial basis for the allocation of
national resources may be the most direct and practical way of ensuring that
they will be allotted. It is not, however, a panacea, and it is not free of intricate
problems and potential dangers.

SOCIAL CHANGE: EDUCATION AND COMPETENCE

In addition to its conception as a child-welfare service and a public utility, day
care has also been promoted as an instrument of social change. At the beginning
of the twentieth century the Americanization of the foreign born was a central
issue. Parent-education programs featured training in home-management skills
and public school nurseries sponsored programs that dealt with American history
and political values (Woods, 1898). The Los Angeles day nursery was started
because school-age children were staying home to care for younger siblings and
because it was thought that the day nursery would encourage parental participation in school activities.

Day care as an instrument for change has far different implications today.
Perhaps the broadest area of consensus can be found in the need to assure universal literacy. Preschool programs which express a concern for the child's mastery of academic skills are challenged by a steadily dwindling group of preschool
educators. It is highly unlikely that the acquisition of such skills will become
less important in the formulation of future programs.

There is a great need, however, to expand educational expectations beyond
mere skills. Such an expansion is already evident in the notion of "competence"
and the importance given to knowledge and skill-acquiring processes. Questions
of information organizing, decision making, and inquiry-sustaining motivational
mechanisms are receiving increasing stress (Hunt, 1964a, b; Sprigle, 1968). Relevant education is interpreted as developing the capacity of people to educate
themselves. Self-education hinges on wanting to know more, on identifying areas
in which knowledge is desired, on being able to call on strategies for seeking
and organizing knowledge, and on finding ways to determine the appropriateness of solutions and to revise solutions that do not work. Similarly, there is
heavier emphasis on the network of feelings and relations that connect the child
to the world about him, on the child's sense of worth, and on his feelings of
being able to function effectively in that world (Clark & Clark, 1950; Coopersmith, 1967; Zigler & Child, 1969).

By the same token, Americanization has in the past implied the denial of the cultural heritage of the family and the child by those who would change others as well as by those who wanted to be changed. Today more attention is given to the preservation and positive evaluation of minority cultures and the desirability of a pluralistic society (Baratz & Baratz, 1969; Gordon, 1969b; Hess, 1969; Labov, 1970). Practical implications of a pluralistic point of view are far-reaching and will influence program auspices, organization, staffing, training, and curriculum as much as the philosophical and theoretical perspectives that are adopted.

It is unfortunate, perhaps, that the educational potentials of day care are so often seen as the appropriate domain of boards of education and public schools (Mayer & Kahn, 1965). In the light of contemporary criticism of public education (Hart, 1969; Kohl, 1967; Kozol, 1967; Postman & Weingartener, 1969) and especially of the dimensions of criticism (i.e., unresponsiveness to both parents and children, oppressiveness, bureaucratic centralization, and dehumanization), the educational establishment would seem to be among the more questionable sponsors of early childhood programs. Indeed, available evidence challenges the notion that board of education sponsorship leads to quality programming. Ratings of public day-care centers in Oakland found them little better than proprietary centers and worse than voluntary centers (Ruderman, 1968). These findings are indirectly supported by a better controlled and more intensive study of centers in the Los Angeles area which failed to find differences in quality between public and proprietary auspices (Prescott et al., 1967). Although too few voluntary centers appeared in either study to support the statement that voluntary centers are of higher quality, more children were rated "exceptionally interested and involved" in voluntary centers. Public centers, on the other hand, excelled in the amount, variety, and interest value of the space and equipment provided (Prescott et al., 1967, pp. 239 and 347). The data are slim but sufficient to introduce a cautionary note to suggestions of a simple relationship between auspices, physical surroundings, and benefits to children. Untangling and understanding these relations is a critical research issue, with important theoretical implications for distinctions between the human and material components of the child's environment.

POLICY ISSUES AND SOCIAL LEGISLATION

The policy issues of the distant and recent past are still with us, but their contours were sharpened by legislative proposals that appeared in 1971, a year marked by two notable events. On December 7 the Congress submitted the Comprehensive Child Development Program to the President. On December 9 Congress was informed that the President would veto this proposal. In the background, winding slowly through the legislative process, was still another noteworthy legislative package, the Family Assistance Plan. If approved by Congress, the Family Assistance Plan is likely to receive prompt presidential endorsement.

Involved in these respective legislative proposals are radically different presuppositions of the fears and aspirations of the American people, the status of children, and the political and social viability of the family. Briefly, the Comprehensive Child Development program envisaged a nationally coordinated network of child-development programs in which states and localities would be linked directly to federal resources by a National Center for Child Development under the Department of Health, Education and Welfare. Included in this scheme would have been currently operational programs, such as Head Start, to which would have been added a wide range of educational and medical services for children and parents from all socioeconomic strata, regardless of whether mothers were employed. The program would have cost the nation 2 billion dollars in the first year of operation.

By contrast the Family Assistance Plan projects a national network of services for mothers receiving welfare assistance—health, and medical services, child care, vocational rehabilitation, counseling, and social services—which would permit them to obtain and retain employment. Consistent with its intention to promote the employment of mothers (indeed, according to current provisions, the Social Security Act would be amended to require welfare mothers to seek employment even though they have children under 3 years of age), responsibility for the implementation of the overall program would be assigned to the Department of Labor, with provisions for a Federal Child Care Corporation to administer the child-care aspects of the program. It is noteworthy that this legislation defines two types of child-care center: one, a preschool center that would provide child care on a full-day basis for at least five days each week; the other, a child-development center that would be established primarily for educational purposes for no less than five days each week. Costs for these services are estimated at 750 million dollars in the first year.

When we examine the purposes, provisions, and costs of these legislative proposals, it is perhaps enough to marvel that a Comprehensive Child-Development Program emerged at all from the Congress of the United States. Clearly, one segment of the nation's experienced political leadership was able to suggest that the nation needed generous and visible federal provision for the benefit of children and to act as if local constituencies would bless the dollars spent this way.

It is equally clear that another part of our political leadership, the present administration, perceived the public's appraisal of national priorities in a dramatically different way. In his veto message the President scored the "fiscal irresponsibility, administrative unworkability and family-weakening implications" of the Comprehensive Child Development Program. Concurrently, he supported action such as the Family Assistance Plan, "consciously designed to cement the family in its rightful position as the keystone of our civilization", specifically, day care "to enable mothers, particularly those at the lowest income levels, to take full time jobs."*

The President drew further attention to working mothers by supporting increased tax deductions for families when both parents are employed. According to the President, the federal government would, thereby, be assisting parents (presumably not those falling under the Family Assistance Plan) to buy day-care services in the private open market with minimal federal control (e.g., without guidelines and standards set down by the Secretary of Health, Education and Welfare). The President's view of the Comprehensive Child Development Program, in contrast to the Family Assistance Plan advocated by the administration, is that the former would promote communal approaches to child rearing as opposed to the family-centered approach supported by the administration.

Apparently two governmental authorities—the President and the Congress —have interpreted the implications of early childhood programs and the spirit of the American people in vastly different ways. These proposals differ in what they promise; our seasoned political leaders seem to be addressing two different and conflicting services wanted by the people. On the one hand, the electorate is seeking a national commitment to human well-being and, by so doing, it is acknowledging the fragility and tenuousness of individual existence in an inordinately interdependent and complex society. Concurrently, there is a growing fear of the ever tightening grip of distant centralized bureaucratic power.

The Comprehensive Child Development Program affirmed the need for a national support system devoted to human welfare and predicted that this need will not be likely to diminish in the future. Even more, by extending child-development services to children without regard to the economic or employment status of parents, it asserted that the family unit could not effectively pursue its child-rearing functions without community support.

On the other hand, the President acknowledged the family as a political as well as a social institution—an inherently conservative political institution that becomes politically more powerful and more conservative with increasing economic power. The administration's program promised increased autonomy to the family, while ensuring the nation that current difficulties will be confined to families at the lowest economic levels. Presumably, at these economic levels the employment of mothers will not weaken family ties but will serve rather to "bring the family together." In effect, child-care services are presented as a stop-gap measure, justified by a crisis situation. Under these circumstances the institu-

---

* All quotations are from the President's veto message as published in the *Weekly Compilation of Presidential Documents,* December 13, 1971, 1634–1636.

tions and administrative structures created to meet the crisis are expected to wither away when the crisis passes; demands on the national budget presumably would dissolve as the poor become less dependent on community resources and more dependent on family resources. In some degree such an outcome presupposes the emergence of a family able to maintain itself without community assistance.

Thus at issue are fundamentally different views of the kind of family that exists today, and will emerge in the future, and different judgments of whether American families are troubled or serene. At issue, too, are the criteria for determining the need and form of governmental intervention. Is it proper for the government to use a socioeconomic basis for pressing mothers into employment outside the home? Is it proper for the government to assign the development and management of child-care institutions to private business and, further, to subsidize the private sector without establishing federal guidelines and evaluation procedures? By the same token, how can the government distribute astronomical sums to "nonvoting" institutions (whether public or private) without creating a new and unresponsive source of bureaucratic power?

One way of promoting child-care institutions that avoids political controversy is to hide federal support in legislative enactments not primarily designed for children (e.g., according to *The New York Times,* December 19, 1971, the House of Representatives tacked to the burial benefits bill for military personnel an amendment that would provide more federal funds for the "public service employment" of welfare recipients in child-care centers). Our current federal child-development system is characterized by small pockets of programs tacked onto assorted legislative enactments and distributed over several federal agencies. These pockets are haphazard enough (although they may total more than half a million dollars a year) to allay fears of federal intervention and so lacking in coordination that an administrative hierarchy is not likely to coalesce. In the above example explicit provisions for the training of new child-care workers were not specified, provisions for materials and equipment for possibly increased numbers of children were not made, and guidelines for determining the effectiveness of the increased expenditures were not proposed. The amendment seemed to be innocuous and was approved by the Congress and signed by the President without debate or controversy. Generally, these enactments do not attract congressional debate or a presidential veto, and they slip unnoticed into the governmental fold.

In the context of legislative activity the concepts of child welfare, actuarial allocation, and education take on a new perspective. New services may suddenly appear for poor children who might benefit if the services were adequate. At the same time, these services are contingent on the employment of mothers who may not wish to work, whereas the many who do will not find an appreciable expansion in day-care resources. Above all, the many families who would welcome enriched educational opportunities or comprehensive medical services for their children will be disappointed. The irony of 1971 is that the nation has been caught at an intersection of cross-purposes. Actuarial allocation is occurring, but within an exceedingly narrow conception of day care.

3

Beyond the Center

IT IS NOTEWORTHY THAT, AS THE NATION PREPARES FOR another day-care boom, an array of factors—developmental, social, cultural, and historical—is underscoring the need for policies and programs that go beyond day care conceptualized merely as "centers." If child-care programs are to respect the preferences of parents and the existing ecology of functioning institutions, it is necessary to use the actuarial data of current child-care arrangements to do more than demonstrate that relatively few children are enrolled in "center" programs.

THE ECOLOGY OF DAY CARE

"Day care" occupies most of the child's waking day, whether he is at home, at a neighbor's house, or at a center. Early childhood education is about the experiences of children in their homes as well as outside their homes—with their families as well as with strangers. The arrangements made by working mothers offer valuable information about the national ecology of child care: approximately 5 million children unde 6 years of age, or 15% of all the children in this age range, have mothers who work.

Caregiving Arrangements

Among the children under 6 years of age who have full-time working mothers 47% are cared for in their own homes, 37% are cared for in someone else's home, 7% are cared for by their own mothers while they are working, and 8% are in group-care programs. The remaining 1% are receiving other types of care (Low & Spindler, 1968).

A somewhat different pattern of arrangements appears when mothers work on a part-time basis. Approximately 32% of these children are cared for at their mothers' places of employment, 47% are in their own homes, 17% are in someone else's home, and 1% are in group programs.

A surprisingly large percentage of children under 6 years of age are cared for by relatives, including their own mothers. Family ties are preserved for 53% of the children of full-time working mothers and this proportion increases to 80% for the children of part-time working mothers.

Dissatisfaction

Both Low & Spindler (1968) and Ruderman (1968) inquired about the dissatisfaction of mothers with their current child-care arrangements. In the Low and Spindler report 10% of the mothers expressed dissatisfaction and about 32% of Ruderman's respondents expressed moderate to high dissatisfaction. Low-income groups expressed the highest degree of dissatisfaction, particularly when the child was cared for by a nonrelative outside the home or a relative under 16 years of age.

Ruderman (1968) explored the sources of dissatisfaction in some detail. The mothers' most common criticism was that the discipline of the caretaker was too lenient. This concern was tied to the relatively high level of dissatisfaction with out-of-home-care arrangements. The mothers seemed to feel that housework and the presence of other children reduced the amount of care and supervision given their own children.

The mothers' expectations differed according to the kind of arrangement made for the child. Supervision was emphasized in out-of-home care provided by friends and neighbors, but relatively few demands beyond custodial care were made on grandmothers. The strongest expectations that the caretaker would play with the child and engage in teaching activities were expressed when the child was cared for by the father or at a center.

Socioeconomic status (SES) was related to the mothers' assessment of day-care arrangements. Low SES mothers stressed the formal academic training children could receive in a day-care center. Centers were valued for their provision of trained personnel to teach educational and social skills. This emphasis on the acquisition of skills decreased with higher socioeconomic status. High SES mothers were more negative about centers; they emphasized overcrowding, lack of individual care, and excessive structure and regimentation.

Interest in Group-Care Programs

Approximately 49% of the mothers with children under 6 years of age said they would use a group-care program if one were available. Group-care programs were considered more desirable by low SES mothers. Large ethnic differences appeared: 65% of the Negro mothers reported that they would use a center in contrast to 47% of the white mothers (Ruderman, 1968, p. 332). The most interest in group care was expressed by Negro mothers whose children were being cared for by nonrelatives (81%). Although convenience was given as one of the advantages of noncenter arrangements close to the child's home, this advantage is offset for low socioeconomic groups by the poverty, poor housing, and inadequate play space likely to prevail in these neighborhoods.

Preprimary Enrollment

If we considered only the child-care arrangements of working mothers, we would get an inaccurate picture of how many children are actually in organized preprimary programs. Recent data (Nehrt & Hurd, 1968) indicate that 33% of all children between the ages of 3 and 5 are enrolled in preprimary programs. Most of these children are enrolled in kindergarten classes, which accommodate only 64% of the 5-year-olds in the nation. A higher proportion of children is enrolled in preprimary programs at upper than at lower socioeconomic levels. For 3- and 4-year old children the proportion of nonwhite exceeds the proportion of white children. Ethnic differences in enrollment are especially marked in the family-income category of $7500 to $9999 per year: among 4-year-olds 20% of the white children and 45% of the nonwhite childen are enrolled. Judging by relative proportions, preprimary programs have failed to reach children from families in the lowest income strata; for example, among 4-year-olds from low-income families 14% of the white and 26% of the nonwhite children are enrolled in contrast to the 20% and 45% figures noted above. Preprimary enrollment is lowest among children of farm workers (22%) and increases slightly among children of the unemployed or manual/service workers (30 and 29%, respectively). Approximately 4% of the children in nursery schools are attending full-day programs. In absolute numbers more white than Negro children are attending full-day programs (149,000 and 85,000, respectively), but a higher proportion of Negro children in preprimary programs attend all day.

INFORMAL DAY-CARE ARRANGEMENTS

When children are not cared for at centers or by members of their own families, care is provided by an assortment of neighbors and friends. Only an insignificant percentage of these out-of-home arrangements comes under licensing or social-agency supervision. In 1965 only 25 licensed day-care homes were listed in New York City (Willner, 1966). Family day care, as a licensed, supervised arrangement, has traditionally been viewed as a child-welfare service, as an alternative to foster placement or group programs when they were either not available or inappropriate because of special problems (Crawford, 1969; Edwards, 1968; Radinsky and Gordon, 1965; U. S. Department of Health, Education and Welfare, 1968). Supervised day-care homes, however, have not developed to any great extent. Private individuals seem unwilling to bother with complex licensing procedures when it is relatively easy to find children to care for without initiating involvement with private and public agencies. Clearly, the idea has not captured the imagination of either those agencies concerned with family problems (Cauman, 1961) or the potential consumers of services (Emlen, 1970; Foley, 1966). Similarly, since social agencies tend not to use center-type day-care programs (Mayer & Kahn, 1965; Pisapia & Haniwell, 1969), there is no reason to assume that these agencies would undertake in any large numbers the establishment of family day-care homes.

Family Day-Care Mothers

By and large, when children are not cared for by relatives, they are cared for by friends and neighbors under informal contractual agreements. Perhaps of all the arrangements made by working mothers these have caused the greatest apprehension. Data from a study of 242 family day-care mothers indicate that the majority of these women are warm, responsible and mature. In an intensive and imaginative study of informal day-care arrangements Willner (1966, 1969) examined the care giving characteristics of 242 day-care mothers and 360 natural mothers. Mothers, caregivers, and children were interviewed and observed.

Interview questionnaires covered demographic characteristics, child-rearing practices, and attitudes toward the homemaker role. Observers rated the quality of the adult-child interaction on a five-point scale. Mothers were asked questions about how they came to select the day-care home, the nature of the contact with the day-care mother, and so on. In addition, extensive information was gathered about the mother's employment history and the child's day-care history. Although a pioneering study, it faced expected and perhaps unavoidable difficulties; for example, locating day-care mothers was an enormous task, and the group that finally participated in the study may not have been a representative sample. The training of observers was superficial, and the ratings were based on a limited sample of adult-child interactions.

The findings are suggestive, nonetheless, that caregivers were older than the natural mothers, more likely to have intact families, and less well educated.

Slightly more than half of the family day-care mothers had a high school education compared with 90% of the natural mothers. Housing conditions were similar for the two groups, and there were no ethnic differences within the groups, although Negro, Puerto Rican, and white mothers were represented in the sample.

Generally, mothers used family day care because they had no choice. For those mothers who preferred family day care, love, reliability, proximity to their homes, and a homelike atmosphere were the most important reasons given for selecting it. These mothers tended to select a day-care mother whom they already knew or who had been recommended to them by friends or relatives. Approximately 90% of all mothers reported that they got along well. Approximately 76% of the mothers were satisfied with the family day-care arrangement, although 80% said they would switch to group care if given the opportunity. By and large, mothers said they would use group care because it was more reliable. Only 25%, among whom were more Puerto Rican and Negro than white mothers, mentioned intellectual or social advantages. Not one mother mentioned intellectual stimulation as an advantage of family day care. The observers noted that a sizable proportion of the children received no planned activities and little in the way of play materials or outdoor play opportunities. Significantly, 80% of the homes would not have met Department of Health certification requirements.

Enjoyment and satisfaction were most frequently given by day-care mothers as the reason for caring for children in their homes. Willner concluded that the day-care mothers

> possessed many natural attributes for the job; they were warm, they liked children, they preferred to remain at home and do what they knew how to do best, that is, care for children; they were chronologically mature, had experienced success in rearing their own children and liked what they were doing (1966, Chapter 9, p. 6).

Willner, as well as others (Collins, 1966; Radinsky, 1964), notes that mothers often maintain contact with family day-care mothers when the child is no longer receiving care. Another study of 27 family day-care mothers reported that those who ranked highest in quality of care had intact families of their own with children of school age and were above the poverty line economically (Collins, 1966).

Continuity of Care

Extremely relevant (but typically neglected) information collected in these studies concerns the number of care arrangements experienced by the child. In the Willner study more than half the children were less than 1 year of age when the mother went to work. A similarly high proportion of infants receiving day care was found in a Berkeley, California, population studied by Rapoport and Cornsweet (1969). In the Willner study approximately 25% of those under 3 and 34% of those between 3 and 6 years had experienced four or more day-care arrangements. Approximately 75% of these changes were due to changes in the life situations of the adults: mothers stopped working or moved, the day-care mother could no longer provide care, and so on. The remainder had been terminated because of dissatisfaction with the care provided.

The only attempt to follow a sample longitudinally was reported by Emlen (1970). In a sample of 146 mothers he found a median duration of care of six months in a family day-care home at the time of initial interview and a median duration of one year at a subsequent follow-up (Emlen, 1970). Since the investigator reported neither the elapsed time between initial interview and follow-up nor the ages of the children, the findings are difficult to interpret. Using still another index of stability, Emlen (1970) noted that mothers who had worked a year or more made a median number of two arrangements. Altogether, three indices of stability have been used in these studies. None of them, however, takes full account of length of maternal employment, age of children, and the number or duration of day-care arrangements. Some such index would be enormously valuable. Obviously the data necessary to compare the stability of unsupervised family day care with other arrangements are not available. Of particular interest would be studies that examine the specific factors contributing to the stability of these arrangements.

FAMILY DAY-CARE PROJECTS

Several projects have attempted to develop family day care as a viable day-care alternative. The Day Care Neighbor Service represents an interesting approach to family day care (Collins, 1966; Collins & Watson, 1969; Emlen, 1970). Through contacts with central neighborhood women the project created a viable network of day-care "match-making." The women chosen to serve as day-care "neighbors" were already actively involved in neighborhood day care, had intact families of their own, were home-oriented, and interested in children and community projects. The project developers have made the assumption that women with these qualities will intervene to steer consumers away from obviously poor day-care arrangements and will be able to locate and push better ones with minimal consultation from professional workers. Reports of the project do not describe plans for evaluating this assumption or changes in the quality of care made available by this system. Active efforts to improve the quality of care have not been reported, although the project would seem to offer unique opportunities for more substantive educational intervention and evaluation.

An extensive $4.5 million Family Day Care Career program was initiated in 1967 by several New York City agencies. The program is primarily concerned with creating child-care placements for welfare mothers as a means of increasing both in-home and out-of-home employment opportunities. Family day-care mothers are given three days to a week of training in cooperation with New York's Bank Street College and follow-up sessions three times a year. The training program includes "discipline, dealing with separation of mother and child, safety, health, and training practices" (Day Care and Child Development Council of America DCCDCA, 1970, p. 2). Although the training program might include how to stimulate the intellectual growth of children, it received no mention in the published description of the project. The project reaches 4200 children at a cost of about $1700 a year for each child (DCCDCA, 1970).

Family day care has often been advanced as an inexpensive solution to day-care problems. If Willner's report of the poor physical condition of family day-care homes and the lack of play things and educational activities is taken seriously, cost estimates will have to cover renovation or relocation, equipment, and training. The investment may prove worthwhile, but the cost should not be underestimated.

In sum, a wide variety of arrangements is currently made by working mothers for child care. A good many children are cared for by relatives, fathers, and grandmothers. The remainder are cared for by nonrelatives outside their own homes, with only a small percentage in licensed centers. There seems to be little evidence that these existing patterns are in and of themselves harmful and no evidence that they promote or retard the child's development. In general, the children of working mothers fare as well as the children of nonworking mothers (Yarrow, 1964). The quality of care afforded by noncenter, private arrangements might well approximate the quality of care provided in day-care centers, but there are simply no comparative data. Emlen has justly complained that often "with astonishing lack of logic, the worst of private family day care is . . . contrasted with the best of group care in a child development center" (1970, p. 4).

One advantage of group care in centers is that it is open to community scrutiny (Cauman, 1961). Yet visibility is only an advantage if the community exercises its observational privileges (Emlen, 1970). Unfortunately day-care centers tend to receive little public attention and few visitors and are only rarely involved in research or evaluation projects (LaCrosse, 1970). In the long run quality education and care may best be guaranteed by an informed and concerned community. Organized programs are not likely, on the whole, to be much better than the expectations, knowledgeability, and practices of the potential consumer. Higher socioeconomic status of the consumer, however, is not in itself a sign of program quality (Prescott et al., 1967), an indication that any enlargment of the category of consumers using day-care facilities will not automatically produce educational excellence, although it might be justified on other grounds.

Day care is influenced by a great number of people, by the conditions under which families live, cultural differences, child-rearing styles, and social expectations. The child's day, wherever he may be, can be rich in opportunities to develop competence. Projects that are concerned exclusively with the organization and management of services run the risk of ignoring what must surely be the ultimate measure of day-care programs—the improved capacity of children and adults to function effectively in their homes, schools, and communities.

EXPANDING THE CONTEXT OF DAY CARE

Day care has more than one history: a crisis history and a between-crisis history; a societal history and a child-rearing history. Crisis conditions have marked day-care booms. Neither crisis nor between-crisis periods, however, have led to substantive and effective day-care programming. Today's impending day-care expansion carries with it a sense of national emergency mixed with high expectations. There is no reason to expect that, without major reformulation, day care will be more effective today than it has been in the past. Surely some reformulation is needed if we are to respond effectively to the political and social realities that face communities, parents, and children.

A reformulation might call on historical precedence. The early day nursery was in the vanguard of the infant-education movement and could be so today. The plasticity of the very young child, his unique responsiveness to learning opportunities, and the sharpening of individual differences during the preschool years were all concepts articulated at the beginning of the day-care movement more than 150 years ago. They fell by the wayside as fascination with the child as a child was replaced by broader social issues and perhaps by the assumption that material affluence and physical well-being would ensure optimal development.

Most certainly, supplying minimal needs for food, clothing, and shelter ensures the survival of the child. Perhaps there is an anology to be drawn between survival perspectives and developmental theories. One body of developmental theory stresses homeostatic biological needs and drive-reduction mechanisms. The course of developmental outcomes hinges on events that occur when the level of drive is reduced. Such a stress seems appropriate in times of widespread physical privation, when damage to physical and neurological growth must be a central concern.

It seems, however, that the emphasis should change with the spread of affluence. Current developmental theory is more concerned with mastery and competence, with optimal development rather than survival. The new stress draws attention to the child as he is when free of pressing drives and when relieved of hunger, fear, and threat of abandonment.

The satisfied child plays. Indeed, there seems to be a relation between freedom from stress and spontaneous play activity. Play as the basis of infant education dates back to Comenius, but the magnitude of the implications of the child's nonstress activities has received widespread attention only recently. The assertion is not that children are not often angry, frightened, hungry, thirsty, or love-deprived but rather that these negative states interfere with the child's capacity to experience surprise, puzzlement, and other states implicated in the development of competence in cognition, language, and invention. Day-care planning must be deep enough to alleviate conditions that produce fear and deprivation and generous enough to produce those in which children can find pleasure and surprise.

During the first years of life the child acquires the capacity to form strong ties with other people. A critical issue undercutting all the living experiences of children concerns the guarantee that every child will be provided with sufficient continuity and consistency in his human environment so that he can establish stable and predictable relationships with other human beings. Where and by whom the child is cared for may be important only insofar as some arrangements increase and others decrease the likelihood of continuity and consistency. Most actuarial research tends to be cross-sectional, that is, a sample of children and families throughout the nation in one or more cities. That we know little of the longitudinal story of caregiving by parents, relatives, and nonrelatives in day-care centers or nursery schools reflects a general lack of attention to questions of continuity and long-term stability in the lives of children.

The recent attention that has been directed to alternative forms of day care reflects a more general and growing respect for diversity and a willingness to solve problems by coming to grips with those that are experienced by consumers as well as by professionals. Within this perspective the distinctions between relief, rehabilitation, and reconstruction made by Woods (1898) are important. Relief has an emergency character. It is a type of day care that responds to conditions of distress. Relief may be implied when day care is advanced as a service or a utility. It has been closely associated with the physical care of the child. Rehabilitation expresses therapeutic and acculturative day-care strategies. It places emphasis on an external change agent, whether therapist or teacher, and on a competence differential between the change agent and the person being changed. Reconstruction stresses the active participation of the people concerned. It draws attention to the long-term process of constructing a program that meets standards and goals arrived at consensually. It requires continuous revision in the light of interim results and changing goals. A reconstructionist position in day-care planning parallels the view that the child's development is a continuous and active process of proposing, verifying, and changing; that change requires access to problems and to problem-solving resources.

For the most part a long-term strategy for building day-care alternatives has not evolved. At the very minimum such a strategy would require the systematic articulation, evaluation, and revision of alternative ways of enhancing the in-home and out-of-home care of children. If a strategy is to be future-oriented, it cannot confine itself to the assumption that the parents of young children will work longer and longer hours or that parents will play a less and less active role in rearing their children. Parents may have more time to spend with their children, and the quality of care and stimulation in the child's own home may become increasingly important. Indeed, group-care programs represent but one form of day care. Because of their visibility, they might be more profitably developed as sites for observation, training, and research than as primary child-care facilities.

The context of day care is only partly specified by the past and by the policy issues that have grown out of the past. In these chapters we have described the wonder and enthusiasm surrounding the early day nursery and the high expectation that it would lead to new knowledge of the child and innovations regarding his care and education. These expectations were never realized and enthusiasm turned to despair.

Today day care can draw on a substantial body of child-development knowledge to develop long-range and far-reaching programs. In the next context we consider significant developmental systems—social, language, play, and problem solving—which build on the opportunities caregivers provide.

CONTEXT II

THE CHILD

THE DAY NURSERY OF THE EARLY NINETEENTH CENTURY represented a practical extension of the notion that the young child possesses truly remarkable adaptive capacities. Philosophers and reformers alike were attracted to the wonders of the child's mind. By the mid-nineteenth century, attention shifted from the child's mind to his body. New medical discoveries found practical application in the reduction of infant mortality. Day nurseries became increasingly concerned with physical care, sanitation, and hygiene. For infants the ideal setting was one that closely approximated hospital antisepsis; for the older child the ideal was expressed in the training of sleeping, eating, and elimination habits. Later, with increasing numbers of immigrants in the day nurseries, habit training focused less on physical cleanliness and more on acculturation. The earlier, grander thoughts of expanding the child's mind were supplanted by the teaching of vocationally useful skills. As the emphasis shifted from the child to society, child rearing became more a matter of the determined shaping of children by adults. Contributions that the child might make to his own socialization were either ignored or viewed with alarm.

The sense of threat reached its peak as instinct theories and psychoanalytic formulations seeped into the field of early childhood education. For some the recognition of the importance of inborn drives and emotions meant that child-rearing strategies should be directed toward curbing and controlling these impulses. Others, drawing on a combination of psychoanalytic and growth theories, came to a quite different conclusion: the child was viewed as a seething emotional cauldron whose natural growth thrusts were capable of handling developmental crises if adults would but maintain a tactful and discrete distance. The child was seen as an awesome creature, easily warped and often permanently

49

damaged by clumsy and intrusive adult managers. Within the last 10 years a conceptual circle seems to have been completed. This time a grander view of the child's mind is attracting the attention of psychologists, educators, and parents. If, at an earlier time, the tone was one of wonder, today that sense of wonder is enriched by the sense of a mystery waiting to be solved. In 1823 Lord Brougham asserted, ". . . he can and does learn a great deal more before that age [six] than all he ever learns or can learn in all his after life" (in Forest, 1927, p. 49); Bloom summarized his findings by proposing that

> although it is not invariably true, the period of most rapid growth is likely to be in the early years and this is then followed by periods of less and less rapid growth (1964, p. 204).

Both were struck by a similar phenomenon, although the data for one were philosophical, for the other, empirical. If wonder was displaced by awe, today's mood is one of respect and eagerness to understand. Roger Brown states the case for mystery particularly well:

> What made children's language interesting to us and makes it so still are certain mysteries. Probably, there is some dominating mystery behind any program of research that stretches over a period of years. We know the mystery must be there because the pellet-sized presumed truths laid down by a succession of research reports cannot alone account for the researcher's labors (1970, p. 1).

It is of enormous significance that the current revival of interest in early childhood education has abandoned the simple dichotomies of an earlier era—for example, nature versus nurture, mind versus matter—for a more complex, but perhaps more useful, interactionist orientation. Such a perspective seems to underly the increasing emphasis assigned to competence and mastery, to the subtle balance between stability and change that underlies the child's dealings with his environment, and to the interaction between the constraints within the child that determine his status and potential at any moment and the constraints within the environment that reduce and suggest alternatives to where he might go next.

Still another feature of the times is the appreciation of the active role taken by the child in selecting, integrating, abstracting, and changing both the environment and himself. Active engagement is seen as a characteristic of the child but, in contrast to growth theories, not as an explanation of the changes that occur.

In this Context we have selected those mysteries that seem most relevant to program planning in early childhood education. In so doing we are neglecting a large number of issues that might have been included and perhaps ought to have been. This review is not a comprehensive overview of the child's growth and development. At the same time, fundamental problems of structure and change are overlapping and reappear whenever the development of the child is examined.

Each developmental system is permeated with affective themes, with cognitive constructions, with stimulus and response problems, and with cultural and social ecologies. If we have sampled only a few systems, perhaps we can weave into those we have chosen some sense of the texture and richness of these problems and the attributes of child-rearing environments that require our attention and respect.

We have chosen to discuss selected aspects of attachment, language, play, and cognition. Each highlights important aspects of development: attachment assigns special importance to strong feelings and enduring emotional ties to others; play is centrally concerned with creativity and release from the constraints of reality; language stresses communication and provides the child with a means of understanding the intentions, knowledge, and feelings of others; and cognition focuses on the system of categories and relationships constructed by the child to make sense of the world.

Obviously these are sweeping statements. Theoretical as well as categorical issues overlap within these areas—an overlap perhaps made inevitable by our treatment of each area as an independent and distinguishable system. Yet each of these areas bears on and reflects in some way the child's theory of the world.

The "new" child who emerges is neither infinitely malleable nor rigidly predetermined. He lives in a world that is changing, complex, nourishing, and constraining. He brings to this world native talents for dealing with a highly structured environment. His development occurs at the intersection of these opposing stresses, and the problems of greatest interest lie in the interaction of the child with the world about him.

The following sections on "The Child" are not based on the assumption that currently available data offer precise and unambiguous guidelines for day-care programs. We prefer to argue that research dealing with developmental processes serves different purposes. Research, we believe, serves best when it offers conceptual frameworks for (a) defining issues that need to be addressed in program design, (b) indicating alternatives that might be considered, and (c) delineating the margins of safety within which program variations can occur.

Even more, access to information regarding the development of the child characterizes informed caregiving, planning, and program research. In many respects the caregiver, the planner, and the researcher share a similar problem—that of classifying and interpreting the seemingly infinite subtlety and variation to be found in the behavior of children. One day we observed a child-care worker who was "reading" a picture book of animals to a 3-year-old. Playfully, the worker spelled the word "dog." The child was enchanted and insisted that the name of every animal be spelled. Later, the worker questioned the researchers. Why did the child enjoy the spelling so much? Did he know that it was spelling? Did the pleasure come from the rhythmic pattern, or did he like it because it was an addition to a familiar story? Above all, did he learn something? The child-care worker was a high school graduate, the mother of six, grandmother of two, a woman who had never before worked in a formal child-care program or participated in a formal training situation.

We offer this incident merely to underline the point that the attempt to order and understand the behavior of the child is an undertaking that researchers share with people who care for them. We also suggest that the effort is intrinsically fascinating and pleasurable, for it calls on human capacities to recognize interesting phenomena, to ask questions, and to project alternative possibilities. Our model of the informed adult, be it caregiver, planner, or researcher, parallels our model of the informed child. The information of interest is neither a static body of knowledge nor a list of prescriptions, but rather ways of relating and organizing observed events. In a sense, thinking that is closed and fixed and thinking that is vague and fuzzy both work against effective day-care action and inquiry. When the caregiver, planner, and researcher seek fixed answers and pursue closed objectives, action is constricted and the process of inquiry breaks down. The problems simply are too complex and the scheme of human growth too grand for definite, unambiguous answers. In contrast, fuzzy categories, global intuitions, and vague intentions lead to excessively diffuse action and preclude genuine inquiry aimed at detecting relevant phenomena and selecting effective actions.

This reasoning applies to affective as well as conceptual problems. We are arguing on behalf of wonder and delight and for a view of competence in which the roles of observation, playfulness, and reflection have a weight at least equivalent to matters of management, crisis, and manipulation. At the least we would urge that the problem of understanding and enjoying the child as he is be separated from the problem of determining success or failure. A caregiver may not know whether she has been successful in teaching the 3-year-old something when she has spelled out the word "dog," but yet she can derive great satisfaction from the sense of surprise and wonder she experienced as a result of the child's behavior. Most surely, our expectations for 3-year-olds are and ought to be quite different from our expectations for 6-year-olds. An interest in spelling, for example, would not elicit surprise if it appeared in a child of 6. Without the assumptions and information that generate such expectations about children, the grounds for surprise and wonder would not exist. Without the freedom to vary the stimulation we provide for children and without the opportunity to observe the consequences, the unexpected would not occur. Our view of the design of child-care environments thus parallels our view of the child. The problems of greatest interest can be found at the intersection of what is already known and what can be systematically varied.

4

The Child's Social World

DEFINITIONAL ISSUES IN DAY CARE HAVE OFTEN FOCUSED ON the terms "supplement," "substitute," and "complement." In general, these terms refer to alternative ways of representing the relationships between the child's parents and various other caregivers. Yet the problems frequently posed with respect to these relationships have ranged widely over an array of often uncomparable questions. At times the emphasis has been on legal responsibilities; at other times it has been on institutional prerogatives. Educational advantages, caregiving styles, cultural values, attitudes, and the role of the family have also received attention (e.g., Chilman, 1968; Dumpson, 1964; Neubauer, 1965; Wolins, 1965).

Although all are important issues, they do not lend themselves to easy or simple prescriptions. Indeed, whether a day-care arrangement supplements, substitutes, or complements some aspect of the child's life depends on how parental or other caregivers perceive him and how he in turn perceives those who care for him. The regularity of an arrangement, the depth of involvement, and the temporal continuity, consistency, and reciprocity of the relationship all are likely to influence the nature of the ties between the child and other people. This chapter explores several aspects of these social ties and indicates ways in which traditional definitional issues might be recast.

ADULT PERSPECTIVES

Of particular importance to day care is the notion that caregivers may have a general theory of the child, even if it is based on intuition and not explicitly articulated. How caregivers perceive a particular child will depend, in part, on their general theory of childhood and, in part, on the context within which their interactions with the child occur.

Consider, for example, the notion that parents, other relatives, friends, neighbors, and professional child-care workers may define the child's individuality according to different normative systems. On the one hand, the family is likely to preserve a longitudinal or intra-individual perspective. Parents and other family members retain an impression of the child in the process of growth; their feelings, understandings, and behaviors build on experiences with the child at each level of development. They are influenced by their view of the child as he has been and as he might become. Caregivers in a group setting, on the other hand, are likely to adopt a cross-sectional or inter-individual perspective of the child. The child's individuality is likely to be appreciated in relation to other children. In group programs the practices of grouping children and assigning staff according to age level further encourage inter-individual appraisal, whereas the practice of promoting children through a succession of caregivers further reduces the sense of the child's individual growth over time. Presumably, child-care arrangements can combine both perspectives. The Kibbutz nursery, for example, provides relatively continuous group care within a stable, closely knit community. A parent-child center may encourage the participation of parents with children in group programs. Such parental participation is, however, most difficult to achieve in traditional day-care programs; adults who maintain a longitudinal perspective may be notably lacking among the children of working mothers.

In posing the problem of normative perspective, we are suggesting a link between various caregiving arrangements and the constraints that are placed on the way caregivers come to know and feel about a child. It also has been suggested that similar constraints may operate on child-development research and may thereby be important in the determination of the theory of the child likely to emerge from such research (Kessen, 1965, 1966; Kessen, Haith, & Salapatek, 1970). Whether caregivers do construct different theories of the child and whether these theories influence caregiving, nurturing, and educational activities—and ultimately the development of the child—are empirical questions. They become important questions for day care in that significant people in a child's life may perceive him in dramatically different ways. If day-care programming considers the distinctive perspectives of various child-care settings, quite different strategies may be required for optimizing the development of children within these settings. Within the family the central issue may be one of adapting expectations and opportunities appropriately to the child's developing capacities. Within the group the central issue may be one of adjusting rules and routines to accommodate a wide range of individual differences.

Alternative day-care strategies grow out of these considerations. One approach might emphasize the uniqueness of the family in contrast to the group setting and concentrate on the "supplementary" relationship between them. Part-time maternal employment might permit a balance between family and group settings. Another strategy might be to promote both perspectives within each setting; for example, when children are cared for in a group setting, every effort might be made to maintain continuity of caregiving over long periods of time; when children are cared for by family members, these adults might be encouraged to participate with the children in group settings. Presumably environments that share perspectives can be conceptualized as "substituting" for one another.

CHILD PERSPECTIVES

Not only do the people in the child's world build a theory of the child but the child builds a theory of the social world. The child's strategies for the social regulation of his own behavior and that of others grow out of his interactions with significant others (Moore & Anderson, 1969). People become significant when the child cares about what they do, when they come, and when they go. His negotiations with them are invested with intense feelings that persist over long periods of time.

Traditional issues of group care—adult: child ratio, staff qualifications, and group size—all become significant when one asks how children build an effective social world. If, for example, it is proposed that the child's world is built on interactions with significant others, then questions of adult responsiveness, consistency, predictability, emotional involvement, and affective arousal all become relevant. The practical question of the number of people available to the child must be joined by questions of their long-term involvement with him and their skill at responding effectively to him. Although notions of the contribution of these factors to the child's achievement may be too crude and schematic to warrant dogmatic prescriptions, it is possible to examine the grounds for recommending factors to receive special attention in the design of child-care settings.

In the following sections we explore briefly the early development of the child's attachment to others, how features of these ties change, and how separation experiences and other caregiving variables might influence their formation and elaboration. We also consider how the child's ties with others influence his view of himself as a separate social entity. We then consider recommendations for day-care planning that grow out of these questions.

The Development of Social Ties

Attachment has been defined as the affectional tie that the child forms with another individual and is expressed by seeking and maintaining proximity to that individual (Bowlby, 1969). The notion of attachment provides a useful framework for examining the feelings young children invest in their ties with others. The intense emotions that often appear on the departure or return of the mother have led Bowlby to comment:

> No form of behavior is accompanied by stronger feeling than is attachment behavior. The figures toward whom it is directed are loved and their advent is greeted with great joy. . . . A threat of loss creates anxiety and actual loss sorrow; both, moreover, are likely to arouse anger (1969, p. 209).

Although several investigators emphasize the importance of a single mother-figure in the infant's first affectional relationship (Ainsworth, 1962; Bowlby, 1958, 1969), this definition leaves room for early attachments to more than one individual and for developmental changes in the class of attachment objects (e.g., parents, teachers, and peers). Similarly, it allows for changes in the form and purpose of the child's proximity-seeking and proximity-maintaining behaviors and for changes in the situations under which these behaviors appear. Indeed, it is changes in the patterning of situations, attachment objects, and behaviors that index developmental changes in the system of feelings and relationships that constitute the child's social world.

Situational Factors and Distress. Conceptualizations of attachment and its developmental features are based on observations of children in various situations. Some conditions—the departure or return of the mother or the appearance of a stranger, for example—are associated with intense expressions of feeling. Other conditions—when the mother is stationary and the child can move toward or away from her at will—are associated with mild expressions of feeling. As the child explores interesting features of the environment he periodically re-establishes visual, vocal, and physical contact with people who are important to him (Ainsworth & Wittig, 1967).

Factors that place stress on the infant, it is generally assumed, tend to intensify attachment behaviors. Those discussed above—departure of the mother, presence of a stranger, or being alone—may arouse anxiety or fear. Isolation from others, parents, teachers, or peers, is a stressful situation throughout the preschool years and possibly throughout life. Several studies indicate that social isolation increases the effectiveness of social reinforcement in preschool- and school-age children and the tendencies of children to seek social contact (cf. Maccoby & Masters, 1970; Stevenson, 1965).

Internal states, hunger, pain, fatigue, and illness, may also intensify the child's attempt to maintain contact with the mother or some other attachment figure (Schaffer & Emerson, 1964). Moreover, contact with a mother-figure may reduce the child's distress. Thus one interesting aspect of the relation between emotional stress and proximity-seeking behaviors is the possible role of these behaviors in reducing anxiety or emotional tension (Maccoby & Masters, 1970). The important point is that contact with someone with whom the child has formed an attachment may reduce stress not related to separation from that person (Kessen & Mandler, 1961). Several studies have indicated that the presence of a familiar adult in a strange situation modifies stress reactions and supports play and exploratory behavior (Ainsworth & Wittig, 1967; Arsenian, 1943; Cox & Campbell, 1968; Murphy, 1962). These findings support the wisdom of the recommendation that mothers stay with children when they are first introduced to a new day-care setting and also suggest that attachments to people in that setting may help the child deal with new and unexpected events, such as changes in schedules, new personnel, and novel toys (El'Konin, 1969).

The social conditions under which separation distress appears change with age. At first the infant cries when put down. Later he cries on the departure of his mother, and still later he cries when he is left alone or with a stranger (Ainsworth, 1963). Ainsworth reported that in older infants crying was more likely to occur when the child was left alone or with strangers than when he was left with members of his own family other than his mother. In a study of attachment behavior of African Negro babies Ainsworth (1963) observed that no child showed alarm at the presence of a "white-skinned stranger" until 10 months of age but in subsequent weeks all did. Most of these children showed distress at the mother's departure by 9 months of age.

Children also become sensitive to unfamiliar places. The amount and persistence of the distress expressed when separated from the mother may differ if the child is in a strange situation or in his own home (Yarrow, 1961).

Not all proximity-seeking behavior is characterized by intense affect. In some situations children maintain a delicate balance between proximity to their mothers and exploratory activity. Investigators have suggested that children use their mothers as a secure base from which to explore the world (Ainsworth, 1969; Ainsworth & Bell, 1970). In these situations the child can control the distance between himself and his mother. A child will wander away from the mother, explore an interesting object, and occasionally glance toward her or re-establish physical contact with her before wandering away again.

Day care sorely needs to develop a conception of the "benign environment." Each type of environmental arrangement carries with it a set of stresses and restrictions on the kinds of adjustments that are available to children. Observations of children who have been hospitalized, for example, suggest that for some the combination of a strange environment and the mother's absence is intolerable (Bowlby & Robertson, 1955; Robertson, 1958; Schaffer & Callendar, 1959). The stressfulness of the situation may be aggravated when caregivers are changed frequently or when care is impersonal and limited to minimal physical needs. Benign environments, on the other hand, attempt to keep short-term distress within manageable proportions and thereby set some boundaries on the possibility of long-term disturbances. The possible role of significant others as stress-reducers emphasizes the importance of designating such others as a component of a benign environment. In this sense each caregiving arrangement perhaps ought to offer the child people with whom attachments can be formed, that is, caregivers who can be thought of as "substitutes" for one another.

Attachment Objects. In the first year of life the child develops ties to specific people. Schaffer and Emerson (1964) have proposed a three-stage sequence for this development. The first is an asocial stage in which children seek contact with all aspects of the environment. In time they come to single out humans as particularly significant objects and make special efforts to seek their proximity. This marks stage 2, the stage of "indiscriminate attachment," in which protest over separation is not related to the identity of the person from whom they are being separated. Attachment to specific individuals, stage 3, appears between 6 and 9 months of age and becomes more intense in the next three to four months. The first specific attachment object is most commonly but not always the mother. Fathers and grandmothers also have been observed as objects of the child's attachment during this period (Ainsworth, 1963; Mead, 1962; Schaffer & Emerson, 1964). In 30% of the cases observed by Schaffer and Emerson, the principal object of attachment was not the person mainly responsible for physical care; in 22% the principal object of attachment did not participate even to a minor degree in any aspect of physical care.

Yarrow (1967) examined changes in the ability of infants to discriminate the mother and found that by 1 month of age 66% of the 60 infants he studied discriminated social from nonsocial objects and by 5 months all could do so. By 1 month 38% actively recognized the mother and all could do so by 5 months. Although 96% of the infants actively differentiated a stranger at 8 months, only 46% expressed stranger anxiety. In Yarrow's population severe overt separation anxiety first appeared at 5 months of age and characterized the behavior of all infants at 8 months.

In summary, it appears that the elaboration of the child's social world begins with the distinction between people and things. Subsequently, the child actively differentiates specific familiar people and at some later time differentiates familiar and unfamiliar people. The conditions that facilitate these differentiations have not been extensively studied. It is reasonable to expect, however, that specific social discriminations will be more difficult when a large number of different people are providing care or when opportunities for the child to interact with those who care for him are reduced. Once again the implication is that the number and continuity of caregivers and the adult:child ratio (both in the home and in a group setting) are likely to be critical variables in determining the effectiveness of child-care activities.

Typically, attachment to individuals appears after the infant has constructed the schema of a permanent object, and for most children the mother is that first object (S. Bell, 1970). Clearly, the relation between attachment and some other developmental milestone will depend on the criteria of attachment used (Yarrow, 1967). For some children the intense attachment to one figure rapidly attenuates shortly after its appearance. For others intense and focused attachment to the mother persists until almost the end of the third year. A great many young children are upset when left in a strange place among strange people. Such behavior often appears when children are left in day-care centers, nursery schools, or with baby sitters. After the third birthday children find it easier to accept the mother's departure.

A general shift in the balance between focused attachment and seeking new experiences seems to appear during the preschool years. Murphy (1962) studied the different ways children between 2½ and 5½ years of age responded to an invitation to play away from home with a strange adult. Refusal was related to the age of the child. Few of the 2½ to 3-year-olds but almost all of the 5½-year-olds were willing to go with a stranger. Those young children who were willing to go only if the mother came along remained in close contact with her, sitting beside her, clinging to her skirts, and holding her hand during the play period. A decrease in attachment to the mother was also found in a study by Shirley and Poyntz (1941), in which the sharpest drop occurred at about 4 years of age. Cox and Campbell (1968) studied the effects of the mother's departure on two age groups: 13 to 15 and 23 to 37 months of age. The decline in play, speed, and movement during the mother's absence was significant at both age levels, but the effects were greater for the younger children.

The child first seeks to maintain contact with members of his family and with other significant adults; subsequently his social interests extend to peers and to other children. Adults seem to recede in importance, and peers become more frequently sought out for social interchange. Children develop increased skills in dealing with one another, in structuring social play activities (Heathers, 1955), and in maintaining the continuity of social play episodes (Markey, 1935; Smilansky, 1968; Sutton-Smith, 1971a, b). Observations suggest that peer attachments might follow a developmental course similar to that reported for caregivers. The young child plays in "parallel" to others. He seeks proximity but does not single out one child over another. Between the ages of 3 and 5 years children become more selective in their playmates and develop specific, often persisting preferences. Peer-group attachments have not been intensively investigated, perhaps in part because discussions of attachment have focused typically on the relation between the child and a mother-figure. The concept of peer attachments, however, merits a considerably broader application than it has heretofore received.

The conditions that propel a child to seek peer contacts have important consequences for development. The relationship between the family and the peer group has been stressed by Ausubel and Ausubel (1958), who argue that an excessive parental emphasis on obedience and responsibility during the early years may encourage a "precocious independence" which may in some circumstances lead children to transfer their attachments prematurely from the family to the peer group. Often the press of poverty leads to an early attenuation of parental support (Lewis, 1961). In some cultures such transfer is deliberately encouraged (Young, 1970) and in others it is formalized (Bronfenbrenner, 1970), but it is likely to support the social development of the child only when the peer group has the capacity to provide the child with opportunities for success and with models who exhibit behaviors that are needed by the child to function effectively.

Within a few short years the child constructs a world of significant others that is finely textured and complex. We have already suggested that the very early differentiations between people and things, or between familiar people and strangers, become difficult when the child has to cope with so many people that they are all experienced as relatively the same as and uniformly unfamiliar. This can be a significant difficulty because these early divisions of the world establish the foundations of a subtle and intricate system of social relationships which is extended and modified as the child engages peers, neighbors, teachers, and others. Social development may hinge on providing the child with just enough of the right people at the right time.

Attachment Behaviors. The patterns of behavior that become implicated in the syndrome of attachment—looking, following, crying—seem to have their origins in early infant behaviors that serve to maintain contact with interesting or significant events. In a very general sense attachment includes a large class of behaviors that either control the proximity of the child to these events or monitor changes in the proximity of these events to the child. Auditory, visual, vocal, and locomotive systems all are involved.

The precursors of attachment behavior appear early. A growing literature testifies to the rapidly changing capacities of the infant to respond differentially to environmental events, the changing dimensions of these events for him, and the changing nature of the behaviors available to him. It appears, for example, that infants can follow moving objects from birth and that by 2 months a baby can discriminate real distance (cf. Kessen et al., 1970). By 4 months of age a baby will look longer at human faces than at patterns of comparable complexity (Haaf & Bell, 1967).

Bowlby (1958) has proposed that attachment is founded on five "component instinctual responses": sucking, clinging, following, crying, and smiling. The baby initiates contact with the mother when he sucks, clings, and follows, whereas crying and smiling serve to activate maternal behavior. The baby is an active, initiating participant in this relationship (Bell, 1971).

Ainsworth (1963) identified 13 patterns of behavior that mediate attachment. Among them were accommodation of posture to the mother when held, crying when put down by the mother, differential smiling, greeting through smiling, crowing and general excitement, lifting arms in greeting, burying the face in the mother's body, exploration away from the mother, and flight to the mother. These behaviors emerge at different times during the first year. They reflect the increasing differentiation and mastery achieved by the child in regulating his social contacts.

Evidence regarding changes in children's response to stressful situations comes from a study of children aged 3 to 51 weeks who were admitted to a hospital (Schaffer, 1958). The investigator found two major response patterns, one characteristic of infants under 7 months of age and the other of infants over 7 months of age. Members of the older group protested vigorously when separated from their mothers; younger children were quiet and listless. After returning home members of the older group were anxious and overdependent; members of the younger group quietly scanned the environment with little focus and were unresponsive to social stimulation. Thus it appears that at some ages distress may be indicated by unusually quiet, listless detachment as well as by vigorous protest.

There is some indication that between the ages of 3 and 5 years attachment behaviors become further differentiated. Bowlby (1969) has made the point that early proximity-maintaining behaviors do not involve planned intervention with the activities of others. Later, however, the child develops primitive strategies for changing the mother's behavior—pulling, pushing, calling, and asking her to "come here." These primitive plans become more sophisticated, and soon the child can attribute to others the capacity to have their own plans. Eventually the child demonstrates some understanding of what those plans might be and exhibits skill in formulating a course of action likely to effect a change in them (Bowlby, 1969).

One study of the adult-oriented behavior of nursery school children distinguished two behavior patterns that seem to develop differently between the ages of 3 and 5 (Martin, 1964). With increasing age there was an increase in the category "seeks positive attention" and a small decline in the frequency of touching and holding. Behaviors involved in "seeks positive attention" seem to entail a recognition of the values and predispositions of others and the organization of behaviors with respect to these predispositions. Touching and holding, on the other hand, resemble the more primitive contact-maintaining behavior of an earlier age. Support for this distinction also appears in a study by Rosenthal (1965, cited by Maccoby and Masters, 1970).

The active nature of the child's transactions must be kept in mind when designing day-care environments. The child increasingly solicits and elicits behavior from others during the first six years of his life, but in order to develop effective social transactions he may need others who will not only respond but will respond in a way that is predictably contingent on the child's own behavior (Yarrow, 1961).

Factors Influencing the Development and Course of Attachment

Caregiving Behaviors. Several investigators have proposed that a child's capacity to form and maintain human relationships and the quality of the relationships he actually forms are probably rooted in the nature of his relationship with a mother-figure during the first few months of life (Ambrose, 1961). Institutionalized infants who have experienced a low level of interaction with human caretakers during the early weeks of life subsequently show serious attachment disorders (Provence & Lipton, 1962) and are socially unresponsive in comparison with home-reared babies (Rheingold, 1956). Moreover, the intensity of infants' attachment has been related to specific maternal qualities such as responsiveness and to the amount of interaction received rather than to the mere availability of the mother (Schaffer & Emerson, 1964). Mothers who responded immediately when their babies cried and who gave them time and attention had more strongly attached infants than those who were slow to respond or who interacted with them only while providing routine care. Feeding variables (such as scheduled versus self-demand or age of weaning), thought at one time to be particularly important to social development, were not related to strength of attachment. Thus the activities that promote the development of social ties seem to involve more than routine care. When attachments were formed to persons other than the mother, these persons tended to be those who played with the infant and offered him a great deal of attention. The number of people to whom the child forms attachments, then, seems to be a function of the number of people who make stimulating contacts with him.

Several studies have examined variables related to "secure" attachments—attachments that permit a child to strike a balance between the exploration of play materials and contact with the mother (Ainsworth & Bell, 1970; Ainsworth & Wittig, 1967). Maternal behaviors that contribute to such attachments are (a) frequent and sustained contact, especially during the first six months, (b) the mother's ability to sooth the infant's distress, (c) sensitivity to the baby's signals,

(d) interaction that permits the child to derive a sense of the consequences of his own actions, and (e) delight of the mother in the child's company.

Of particular significance is Ainsworth's observation that the mothers of the most securely attached infants were especially well informed about their infants. The likely importance of such knowledge of the child must be underscored. "Knowing" the child, appreciating his sensitivities, and recognizing his capacities would seem to be a precondition for responsive and sensitive caregiving. Frequent changes in caregiving arrangements, or too few caregivers and too many children reduce the likelihood of there being someone who knows enough about the child's individual characteristics to offer tuned-in and knowledgeable care.

Although research in this area fails to deal with many issues and to resolve many others, it does support the notion that routine physical care is not likely to offer the kind of social stimulation necessary to the child if he is to form and maintain close ties with other human beings. The distinction between routine physical care and care that is stimulating and responsive is especially important to the care of infants, in part because it is often possible to gear child-care settings toward the achievement of well-ordered and efficient routines (which yield well-fed and peaceful children) without supplying responsive and stimulating social exchanges. Understaffed group settings (and family settings as well) will surely make it difficult to provide more than routine care, whereas adequate staff does not necessarily guarantee responsive caregiving. The attempt to limit adult:child ratios in group settings is one way of permitting more than custodial care to take place. How the ratio of adults to children influences the quality of care is an important issue in both group and family settings.

In planning training programs and in selecting personnel for day-care programs, it would be helpful to know more about the particular kinds of social stimulation that are important to development. There is some evidence that visual and tactile stimulation, smiling, or contingent reinforcement may be especially important (cf. Chapter 13, Maternal Behaviors). One account of the interaction between the infant's inborn stimulus preferences and the reactions of the mother which is relevant to this question is provided by Robson (1967): first the mother's eyes attract the baby and then the mother responds to the baby's sign of "recognition" with smiles and further stimulation. Robson argues that such eye-to-eye contact initiates a sequence of exchanges that are pleasurable to both mother and baby, thus encouraging future exchanges. Indeed, there is some evidence that more eye-to-eye contact leads to stronger attachments to the mother (Moss & Robson, 1967).

Separation and Caregiving. The concern that frequent or prolonged separation of the child from its mother might have deleterious effects on the child partly accounts for the general reluctance to support group care for infants and toddlers. One aspect of this issue is the possibility that separation per se, an event that is distressful to many children, would lead to disturbances in the child's social and intellectual functioning. Quite another aspect is that children might not have adequate social stimulation, affection, and attention in the mother's absence (Ainsworth, 1962; Bronfenbrenner, 1968b; Yarrow, 1964). Certainly research on the effects of institutionalization and hospitalization, the poor quality of care that characterized the day nurseries of the past, and the difficulty of enacting and enforcing legislative safeguards have contributed to these concerns.

The effects of separation of the child from its mother will differ, depending on the age of the child, constitutional factors, the kind of substitute caretaking provided, and the quality of the mother-child relationship (Yarrow, 1961, 1964). The kinds of separation experiences are many, depending on whether the separation is long or short, single or repeated, regular or erratic. The effects of separation or deprivation may differ according to the behavior systems that have already been organized and those that are in a formative stage (Bronfenbrenner, 1968c).

Children who experience separation from the mother on a regular basis for some part of the day have not been studied extensively. Two available studies (Caldwell, Wright, Honig, & Tannenbaum, 1969; Heinicke, 1956; Heinicke & Westheimer, 1965), however, suggest that arrangements of this kind do not necessarily lead to disturbances in the child's social attachments. In addition, children raised in kibbutzim who undergo far more extensive separation experiences fail to show deleterious effects (Gewirtz, 1965; Rabin, 1958). Yet the literature on institutionalization and hospitalization provides extensive documentation that separation experiences can lead to considerable distress and, if prolonged, may interfere severely with development (cf. Yarrow, 1964, and the World Health Organization's publication, *Maternal Deprivation*, 1962).

Observations by Robertson and Bowlby (1952) of 45 children between the ages of 1 and 4 years in a relatively depriving hospital situation are relevant to this issue. Three stages of response to separation were noted: (a) initial protest at separation and vigorous efforts to re-establish contact, followed by (b) withdrawal and unresponsiveness, culminating for some children in (c) detachment from the mother. The investigators noted that the severity of these disturbances was softened by the presence of an adequate mother-substitute. Once again the data suggest that various caregiving settings ought to be evaluated in terms of the degree and kind of "substitute" or "supplementary" human interaction they provide.

The effects of frequent changes in caretaking arrangements often experienced by the children of working mothers (Emlen, 1970; Willner, 1966) have yet to be examined in depth. With each change the child must re-establish a relationship and rediscover the ground rules that make the behavior of the new caregiver sensible and predictable. Further study is needed to determine how the child accomplishes this task and what factors make it more or less difficult for him.

Several investigators have noted the extraordinary difficulty of providing intensive and stable one-for-one adult-child interactions in group-care settings (Ainsworth, 1962; Coleman & Provence, 1957; David & Appell, 1961; Gewirtz, 1965; Rheingold, 1956; Yarrow, 1961). Independently, Ainsworth (1962) and Yarrow (1963) conclude from reviews of the literature that even when special efforts are made to provide intensive social stimulation the amount and quality of the interaction may not approximate that provided by the mother at home.

In conclusion, the available data do suggest that the fact of separation, or even repeated separation, from the mother may not necessarily be harmful and that the essential variables reside in the amount and quality of care provided for the child in the absence of the mother. Some situations, for example, the kibbutzim and the infant day-care programs reported by Caldwell and Richmond (1968b) and Keister (1970), in which deleterious effects do not appear, provide the child with the opportunity for consistent and responsive interaction with a relatively stable group of caregivers who pay attention to him beyond the satisfaction of his physical needs. The same data also suggest that multiple caretaking which characterizes many of these settings may not interfere with the capacity of the child to form attachments and develop competent social behavior.

Theoretical Issues. What mechanisms account for the specificity of attachment objects and the fact that maintaining proximity comes to matter so much to the child? Theoretical issues are not discussed in any great detail here. More complete reviews of this literature are given by Ainsworth (1969), Zigler and Child (1969), and Maccoby and Masters (1970), and more detailed expositions of currently important positions can be found in Bowlby (1969), Gewirtz (1969), and Cairns (1967). In general these statements attempt to account for a well-documented phenomenon—the tendency for young children to seek out others— and do not necessarily make assumptions about its specific significance for social development.

Some theoretical statements emphasize the biological underpinnings of attachment (Bowlby, 1969), whereas others stress contingent interactions (Gewirtz, 1968a, b) or the associative conditioning of cues (Cairns, 1967). Still others view attachment as a primary need to maintain an optimal level of stimulation (Schaffer & Emerson, 1964a) or as an acquired dependency drive (Bronfenbrenner, 1968b). Despite such diversity, most theorists assume that the perceptual and/or response capacities of caregiver and child are important and that for early attachments to develop at least one stable, long-term dyadic relationship must be established.

Social Planning. It would perhaps be easier for social planners if the existing research suggested a compelling need for children to be raised at home by their parents, since the conditions necessary to ensure the development of the child who is cared for outside his home may be difficult to meet. The likelihood of serious disturbance increases when there are too few caregivers and too many children, when the caregivers are not attentive and responsive (or when they change frequently), and when the parents are unable to spend time with the child and no other stable, continuous caring relationship is available to him. The optimal development of the child who is cared for outside his home is thus highly contingent on a set of subtle caregiving conditions which are not easily monitored. The conditions that favor the formation of attachment in the young child seem to be present in lower- and middle-class homes in England, Africa, and the United States. They are most likely *not* to be present when the child is cared for outside his home unless special efforts are made. The great tragedy of hastily conceived and inadequately funded all-day programs may well be in the creation of deficiencies that might not normally occur.

Our concern for the immediate welfare of the child leads us to believe that his distress signals are important messages to which environments must respond, whether in the form of policy decisions, planning concerns, or caregiving behaviors. Although we do not know the long-term consequences of separation or deprivation, we do know that they can produce acute immediate distress. We maintain that these grounds alone are sufficient for the serious attention of researchers and practitioners alike.

Acquiring a Social Identity

As the child constructs a world of significant people, he finds a place for himself in that world. The child's attachments to others can be thought of as a system through which he receives information about how they feel about him. In some fashion this information becomes translated into feelings about his own worth and competence. The child discovers dimensions that define who he is, and he invests these dimensions with evaluative judgments of good and bad. How children acquire a sense of self has implications for what they will do and what they will try to do; it has implications for the kinds of motivation and expectations that will characterize their behavior and for the kinds of caregiving variables that might influence the self-perceptions they acquire.

During the early years children become increasingly sensitive to the affective tone of the reactions of others to them and from these early social preceptions develop impressions of themselves as people. At first these impressions are highly fluid and change with each situation. As children grow older, these impressions become a stable part of how they conceptualize and feel about themselves (Brown,

1966). Children imitate the behavior of others and perceive similarities between themselves and others (Kohlberg, 1969). Still later, children become able to recognize the age, sex, and ethnic characteristics of other people and identify themselves with them.

The way children feel about themselves is a complex interaction between how they are treated by others and what they learn about the roles, dangers, and opportunities in the world around them. An issue permeating every level of daycare planning concerns the child's development of ethnic identity. These issues are manifested in decisions regarding the ethnic composition of children and adults in group settings, which, in turn, are likely to be influenced by the geographic locations of such programs. For the most part neighborhood centers will mean ethnically homogeneous programs, except perhaps when centers are located in "transitional" neighborhoods. At some point day care must address issues of ethnic homogeneity and specific forms of cultural programming.

Of particular relevance to this issue are studies that show that children become aware of their membership in an ethnic group at an early age and that they place good or bad values on this membership (Clark & Clark, 1950; Goodman, 1962; Horowitz, 1936; Stevenson & Stevenson, 1960); for example, a majority of Negro and white children between the ages of 3 and 5 years chose to play with a white doll in preference to a Negro doll (Clark & Clark, 1950; Landreth & Johnson, 1953). Moreover, a majority of the children of both races thought the Negro doll looked "bad" (Clark & Clark, 1952). Between the ages of 5 and 8 years children assigned the Negro doll to a dilapidated house and the white doll to an attractive home (Radke & Trager, 1950).

A substantial increase in racial awareness appears at 4 years of age (Clark & Clark, 1950; Stevenson & Stevenson, 1960); religious and national awareness appears somewhat later (Goodman, 1952). Although several authors have suggested that membership in a minority group is a predisposing factor in the early development of ethnic awareness (Goodman, 1952; Proshansky and Newton, 1968), even majority group children perceive and respond negatively to ethnic differences during the preschool years (Stevenson, 1967).

A negative self-evaluation may have its roots in the child's early transactions with significant people, beginning well before the child is able to conceptualize group membership (Dai, 1955; Spurlock, 1970). The injustice and tensions of the world outside the home are communicated to the child by the behavior of his parents and other family members (Davis, 1968; Hess, 1969). If the child is continuously exposed to feelings of anger and hopelessness, it will be difficult for him to develop positive feelings about himself. Perhaps the more attached he is to the adults who care for him, the easier it will be for the child to perceive himself as others appear to perceive him in their direct, daily interactions. When adults belittle the child's attempts at mastery or fail to indicate their pleasure at his success, the child is likely to become less willing to incur the risks of venturing forth. When adults set standards too high or react with angry impatience at the child's failures, the child will come to expect failure from his efforts (Zigler & Child, 1969). Proshansky and Newton (1968) suggest that it may be especially important for children who belong to a stigmatized socal group to experience warm, stable, and satisfying relationships with adults. The implications of this view are that such relationships cannot be replaced during the early years by verbal concepts or by information stressing the positive values or contribution of the ethnic group to which the child belongs. If the child does not feel that he is valued *personally* by the people who matter to him, he is not likely to acquire positive self-evaluation by identification with a group, no matter how positively that group is perceived.

These alternatives are not mutually exclusive, although their relative importance might depend on the age of the child. Thus before the child is able to conceptualize ethnicity a culturally oriented curriculum is not likely to be of value: quality of his interactions with people who are important to him might be the more crucial factor. On these grounds we suggest that day-care programs that fail to consider the child's experiences in his home will be ignoring a part of the child's world that has enormous meaning and significance to him. We also suggest that the characteristics of the people who work with children should receive more attention than they have in the past. Many of the obvious cues to ethnic identity—skin color and language style—vary considerably within ethnic groups. If day-care programs are to consider "ethnic matching," the thrust would be toward day-care environments that are social and cultural substitutes for the child's own home. If, on the other hand, programs are to consider "ethnic diversity," the thrust would be toward day-care environments that complement without replicating or negating the ethnic characteristics of the child's background. It may be that positive and intensive encounters with people from his own as well as other ethnic backgrounds will counteract or qualify the impact of pervasive societal racism or cultural and religious prejudice. The complications, subtleties, and importance of the child's ongoing transactions with people argue strongly that the interpersonal competence and stability of those who care for him, regardless of their ethnic characteristics, must be an issue in the development of child-care programs. Yet no quick and easy way of evaluating these dimensions of caregiving has appeared.

Culturally oriented program content will be most valuable to the child if it is tuned to the level of his conceptual ability and complements the cultural values of the home. Intensive cultural programming might have its greatest value for adults—parents and staff. The respect and admiration that adults feel for their own and other ethnic groups might enhance their competence as caregivers and, more importantly, as citizens.

THE PEOPLE IN A DAY-CARE SETTING

To Substitute, Supplement, or Complement

We have discussed how the young child develops ties with others and how these ties can change during the first six years of life. We have suggested that social ties and self-identity develop as caregivers respond to the child's needs and as he responds to the stimulation they provide. When care is given by a small, stable group of people, such ties can be reciprocal. Caregivers can come to know and feel affection for the child, just as the child can come to feel secure and at ease in their presence. These factors might be particularly important for infants, relatively less important for older children. The infant is not likely to benefit from the presence of other children, whereas the older child may have much to gain from the companionship of peers. Thus for infants optimal caregiving environments may be thought of as having a "substitute" relationship with one another. As children grow older, however, and develop an interest in peers and older children, a group setting may best supplement and extend their opportunities for social development.

Questions for the Long Haul

Long-range day-care planning must concern itself with two different but equally important classes of questions. On the one hand, there are developmental questions that deal with defining the conditions under which children establish social ties with adults and other children. Specifically, how many caregivers are appropriate for children of different ages? How does the number of caregivers and quality of caregiving influence the number and depth of attachments formed? What is the role of continuous care from the same individual and the effects of discontinuous care? How does the size and age spread of the peer group influence the formation of peer relationships?

On the other hand, there are operational and policy questions. How can day-care arrangements be designed to limit the different people who care for the child to some optimal number? How can the turnover of caregiving figures be controlled? How can the ecologies of day-care arrangements be designed to ensure sufficient and appropriate opportunities for the social involvement of the child?

In raising these questions, we are assuming that one aim of day-care programs is to enhance the child's ability to construct a world of differentiated social attachments and a set of effective strategies for regulating his own behavior and the behavior of others within that world. Therefore criteria of the effectiveness of programs might be the extent to which these aims have been achieved. We are also suggesting that program aims and criteria will and should change according to the ages of the children served.

Issues to Start With

Although research in day care has still to address these and other important issues, notions regarding attachment and its development have several implications for defining what should be of concern in designing and implementing day-care programs.

1. Program planning for out-of-home care might consider provisions to support the stability of caregiving settings. The Illinois report, which indicates that almost as many day-care facilities are closed as are opened every year, should be a source of concern (Illinois Department of Children and Family Services, Perspectives, 1969). In addition to encouraging new facilities to open, existing facilities should receive the support needed to develop stable operations. Special provisions might also be made to increase the continuity and stability of caregivers within settings. For center programs enough personnel should be available so that the children can see some of the same people every day. For family day-care programs stable substitute arrangements should be made in the event that the day-care mother is unavailable. Above all, conditions that lead parents to seek out-of-home care should be re-examined. Ultimately the welfare of children might best be ensured by tying the work schedules of parents to the needs of their children.

2. The people selected for out-of-home programs should like young children, should be warm and responsive, and should be able to give generous quantities of time and affection. The selection and evaluation of a child-care staff is a crucial day-care issue, but even competent caregivers will be unable to function effectively if they are expected to care for too many children. Current guidelines (e.g., *Federal Interagency Day Care Requirements*, Sugarman, 1968) summarize the experience of day-care practitioners which might serve as a baseline for examining the influence of group size, adult:child ratio, and selection criteria on the interpersonal environment of the child.

3. Every effort should be made to create those conditions that help people feel enthusiasm and satisfaction with their contribution to the growth of children. Wolins (1969a) has argued that factors such as these distinguish successful from unsuccessful institutional programs. Child care in the United States is sorely in need of higher status. Attractive personnel policies and salaries and less tangible factors such as the respect and admiration of the community might encourage experienced and talented people to enter and remain in the child-care field.

Day-care programming also might recognize explicitly the importance of enthusiasm and satisfaction in the homes of children. Parents and other family members need the same positive feelings about their caregiving activities as paid professionals. We have argued that care provided within the family is likely to have the greatest continuity throughout the child's life. Therefore it is important that efforts be expended toward improving the capacity of parents and other family members to function as caregivers. The potential of the extended family for providing stable, continuing, and quality care needs more attention than it has ever received.

4. In view of the many uncertainties and ambiguities, long-term strategies that explore various alternative day-care arrangements are necessary. One such strategy might focus intensively on the family, another perhaps on central community facilities. Within these overall partitions programs might examine the effects of continuity, consistency, and responsiveness on children's development. It might be expected that various child-care settings would differ with respect to these variables. How they differ and how they influence the ties children form with others are problems that must be addressed by continuing research and evaluation efforts.

SUMMARY—DAY CARE AND THE CHILD'S SOCIAL WORLD

In this section we have examined some aspects of the child's social world: adult perspectives of the child and the child's view of others and himself. We have argued that adult perspectives will differ, depending on the circumstances of their contact with the child over different periods of time. In examining the child's construction of a social world, we drew special attention to the literature on attachment. This literature documents important changes in the child's sensitivity to social situations over time and emphasizes the role of attachment figures as stress reducers. It was suggested that during the first six years of life the child reaches out to an increasingly varied group of others and simultaneously develops remarkable competence in regulating his social contacts.

On both theoretical and empirical grounds there is support for the view that responsive and stable caregiving is needed if specific attachments to others are to develop. Even more important is the suggestion that interactions that go beyond good physical care—playful attention and pleasurable and direct social stimulation—are major factors in this development. These findings appear in studies of children in their own homes and in various child-care institutions. We also suggested that the child's early social experiences might influence his self-perceptions and that at these early ages societal stresses are transmitted to the child by the adults who care for him.

We suggested that the literature dealing with the child's social world offers clues regarding the factors that should be of concern in designing, implementing, and evaluating day-care settings. To the list of traditional concerns (such as the adult:child ratio in group settings) were added several new concerns; for example, the total number of caregivers in the daily life of the very young child, their stability, knowledgeability, and responsiveness; the balance between the family group and the peer group; and program features likely to promote a positive self-identity. Last of all, we proposed a long-term strategy for program development that would explore alternative day-care settings and attempt to enhance the ability of each to optimize the child's social development.

5

The Mystery of Language

A CONFLICT THAT HAS BEEN BREWING FOR A LONG TIME IN day care is beginning to surface. At the very time when the consensus is that day-care programs must pay specific attention to language development, pressure is also growing to find answers to the disconcerting questions why, how, and for what purpose.

What, exactly, is the role of language in the homes, factories, businesses, and schools of a technological society? Are we to accept Jensen's notion (Jensen, 1970) that the extraordinary demand for language skills in the schools of today is an arbitrary, capricious middle-class preference, reflecting the origin of the school as an institution designed to meet middle-class needs? To accept this proposition is to set "middle class" equivalent to "technological" and to confuse verbal habits with verbal skills (Labov, 1970). Without unduly glorifying language, it may be more helpful to treat it as a form of human adaptation which grows more important as human technology becomes more sophisticated and complex. One way of looking at this relationship has been offered by Bruner, Olver, and Greenfield (1966):

> Note first that when a society grows more complex in its technology and division of labor, there are two deep changes that must necessarily occur. First, the knowledge and skill within the culture comes increasingly to exceed the amount that any one individual can know. Almost inevitably, then, there develops a sharp disjunction between the worlds of the child and of the adult. . . . Increasingly, then, there develops a new and moderately effective technique of instructing the young based heavily on *telling* out of context rather than on *showing* in context. The school, of course, becomes the prime instrument of this new technique but by no means the exclusive one. For, in fact, there is also

73

a great increase in telling by parents, again out of the context of action, for there come to be fewer spheres in which learning *in situ* can be practiced. . . .

In more evolved technical societies, then, the very nature of the learning situation *requires* a contingent dialogue between parent or tutor and the child, for once one is out of the task context in which learning occurs directly one can no longer point or "let the situation carry the meaning (pp. 62–63).

But language is more than the adult "telling" and the child "listening," although such asymmetrical communications surely characterize most classrooms. Language has enormous implications for the child's intellectual activity in that it offers a way of symbolically probing and exploring phenomena, a way of asking questions and posing possibilities to himself and to others, that otherwise might be inaccessible to him.

Language also is more than a device for sharing information. In most cultures language fulfills critical social and interpersonal functions. It is used to initiate, maintain, direct, and terminate social contacts, to convey (as well as to disguise) feelings and sympathies, and to amuse and entertain.

From these questions of utility emerge problems of defining the linguistic and nonlinguistic skills that are essential for the transmission of information, for symbolic manipulation, and for social regulation. In addition to grammar, semantics, phonology, and pragmatics, we need to consider the roles of attention, motivation, and interpersonal adaptiveness.

When a child acquires language, he finds out what it is used for and how it is used. He learns that words relate to categories of objects and actions and that they can be put together into utterances that convey a host of intentions, dispositions, and propositions. It is likely that each of these aspects of language is learned concurrently and that what is learned about one part influences what is learned about another. The process begins well before the child produces anything that sounds like language to a mature speaker. How children arrive at this competence, how their mastery is determined by their endowment as human beings and by the language environment available to them during the early years are questions of social, educational, and scientific concern.

There is still a third problem that contributes to the unrest in early childhood education. Just as language serves important cultural, intellectual, and social functions, it is also constrained by the very functions it serves. Cultures place different values on language functions. There are social rules about what can be said, to whom, and under what conditions. Even more important are the general principles that govern the rules of discourse—how one talks to certain people is determined in part by these rules and in part by the perception of their status, needs, and limitations.

What ought to be the goals of language programs? What exactly does the child acquire and how can one best account for individual variations in performance? How can programs be designed to ensure each child a high degree of culturally relevant competence? In the sections that follow we discuss these issues as they are related to the uses of language and to language programming in day-care settings.

THE COMMUNICATIVE FUNCTIONS OF LANGUAGE

Language may be used to express feelings, thoughts, and intentions toward others and toward oneself. Interpersonal communications may be used to express feelings, to control the behavior of others, to maintain social contacts, to convey or receive an organized body of information, or to elicit information. Eventually the child learns to use the forms that are appropriate to particular occasions and settings, and he learns how to formulate a diverse and fairly subtle repertoire of information and intentions. Children develop a theory of speaking and listening that deals with the appropriateness of language to time, place, and setting (McCaffrey, 1970).

Use and Acquisition

Cultural and social issues weave through the ways in which children meet language in the course of communicating with parents, teachers, and peers. M. M. Lewis (1951) has suggested that the infant's expressive sounds—that is, sounds of discomfort and comfort—represent the earliest use of language. At first these sound patterns may not be used intentionally, but eventually they help to control the behavior of others. The instrumental functions of language have been amply demonstrated in studies of operant conditioning with infants (Rheingold, Gewirtz, & Ross, 1959; Weissberg, 1963) and with older children (Ballif, 1967; Reynolds & Risley, 1968). These studies highlight the importance of caregivers who respond relevantly and contingently to the child's utterances.

It is important, however, to distinguish between the control function of language, through which the child obtains goods, services, and attention, and the social function of language which serves to identify or communicate feelings and to maintain or intensify contact with other human beings.

Infants respond differentially to pleasant and unpleasant sounds. Within these classes sound patterns become differentiated, and the infant begins to interpret the emotional meaning, intonation, contours, loudness and softness, and other features of the sounds he hears. There is some evidence that infants prefer the mother's voice to the voice of a stranger (Friedlander, 1970) and the mother's intact voice to a distortion of it (Turnure, 1969). The child's first theory of language function might be that language serves simply to enhance the participation of significant others in expressive and pleasurable interchanges.

Recent evidence regarding the early word acquisitions of children suggest that there may be two quite different patterns, depending on the way mothers use language with their children (Nelson, 1971). One emerges from interactions that are heavily invested in references to things. Children exposed to these interactions produce a preponderance of object names in their early speech. Another pattern emerges from interactions oriented toward sociability. These children learn expressive phrases such as "hi there" and "go bye-bye."

Bernstein (1970) has suggested that communication codes may have fundamentally different orientations, toward means on the one hand, when language is applied to concrete, specific, and closed outcomes, and toward ends, on the other, when language is used to explore open-ended, speculative, and ambiguous propositions. There is some empirical evidence that children's language will differ in reality situations and in dramatic play situations (Cowe, 1967; Marshall, 1961). Further, there are differences in the amount of fantasy and instructional language mothers use when playing with their children (Baldwin, 1969; Baldwin & Frank, 1969).

Parent Talk. The functional underpinnings of language acquisition are highlighted when attention is given to the language adults use when they speak to children. Observers of the language exchanges between parents and children have frequently commented on the prevalence of nursery talk (Ervin & Miller, 1963; M. M. Lewis, 1951). Some of this interchange has been described in great detail (Casagrande, 1948). Before the child shows any real consistency in his use of sounds, he is frequently engaged by adults in standardized, highly intonated word-action sequences (bye-bye, where's baby, pat-a-cake, peek-a-boo). Certain objects are given invariant labels (daddy, cookie) in highly inflected and well-patterned ways. It is not clear whether these early forms serve to introduce the child to syntactic, semantic, phonological structures or whether they simply show the child that language is a pleasurable social event.

Adults may also select the words they use to name things for children according to special rules and criteria. Roger Brown (1958) has pointed out that children learn that things have names but that the same object can have many names. The household pet can be called "dog" or "Bowser," but rarely do mothers call it "animal" or even "poodle." Furthermore, people use the same word for a great many things—many different dogs and kinds of dogs are called "dog." Parents manage somehow to transmit to children the names and categories agreed on by their cultural and social community. What factors enter into the naming decisions parents make?

Brown proposed a "utility theory" of naming in which parents give the child the most common name for any particular object. Parents seem to develop an informal naming curriculum that considers both the number of different objects the name will refer to and the frequency with which these objects are likely to be encountered by the child.

Yet parental judgments seem to consider other factors as well. Often a special "nursery" name might be given at an early period and the common name substituted later (e.g., tick-tock and then clock). A piece of pie might be called a "cookie" and a soft drink might be called "juice." We know relatively little about the naming techniques of parents and very little about how these techniques hinder or facilitate language development. Yet the teaching of names for things is a major focus of many current early education programs and should be considered in day-care programs, whether the language curriculum is formal or informal.

Cultural variations in language usage are likely to be keenly felt by young children. Cultures tend to have highly formalized vocabularies of special baby words. These words tend to designate biological functions (defecating, urinating, sleeping, eating), body parts (penis, feet, toes), affective states (approval, disapproval, fondness, warning), familiar objects (including animals and people), and familial relationships (Casagrande, 1948). When day-care groups are composed of children from different backgrounds, uniform "naming" conventions for the entire group are frequently established.

Teacher Talk. When children attend school, they come into contact with still another kind of talk—teacher talk. Teachers use fairly subtle cues to signal shifts from one aspect of an instructional sequence to another. Teachers and pupils follow rules of pedagogical discourse in which information is structured and presented, questions are formulated and posed, and answers are given. Language in the classroom involves complex functions such as fact stating, explaining, defining, interpreting, and justifying (Bellack, Klieband, Hyman, & Smith, 1966; Wilensky, 1965). The role of instructional language in promoting overall language mastery (as distinct from the mastery of subject matter) has not been examined, even though a good deal of the child's verbal interaction with others is governed by adults' intentions to convey information to him that is not specifically linguistic. It may be that instructional language does not and ought not to be thought of as serving a language acquisition function; instead its primary role might be seen as imparting information within the realm of language already acquired by the child (Carroll, 1967). Perhaps instructional settings can best promote new language knowledge by the co-occurrence of nonlinguistic information (objects, pictures, and actions) with new language elements. A teacher might be interested primarily in telling a child about a baobab tree— where it grows, how it grows, and its uses. In the course of this instruction children might incidentally learn the word "baobab."

Peer Talk. In the ordinary course of growing up children spend a good deal

of time interacting with peers and siblings. On the surface it would seem that
this kind of interaction would facilitate language development, since the level
of complexity will be matched and interest will be high. Children surely do
engage in active conversation during play (Marshall, 1961; Similansky, 1968),
and dramatic play in particular is likely to produce mature language behavior
(Cowe, 1967). A study of nursery school children by Marshall (1961) indicated
that the most frequent use of language to communicate suggestions, agreement,
and hostility occurred during dramatic play rather than during reality contacts
with peers. Furthermore, the use of this language in play increased with age,
whereas in reality situations it did not. On the other hand, Smith (1935) observed
that children produced longer sentences during face-to-face interactions with
adults than with peers. Peer talk was characterized by simple negatives (no) and
reduced imperatives (gimme). Complex and compound declarative statements and
questions were more likely to appear in conversations with adults. Similar findings
have been reported by Cowe (1967). Children do learn peer language, but the
peer language they learn represents a small and limited part of the total language
system.

Perhaps these conflicting data can be reconciled by viewing language development as a series of shifts between subsystems of the total language system
that children sample as they move from one social context to another (Riegel,
1966). Each subsystem serves to introduce the child to some functional, semantic,
or syntactic aspect of the total system. Babytalk, parent talk, peer talk, and
teacher talk all illustrate selected features of the total language system. In the
course of growing up children hear and deal with different kinds of talk, and
as a result they learn more than one way to speak.

Speech Environments. What kinds of talk are likely to benefit the day-care
child? Most research and language curricula place a premium on adult talk for
a number of reasons: (a) partly because this talk is most likely to be explicitly
directed toward the child (Friedlander, 1970); (b) it is the talk most likely to
have tuitional purposes; and (c) it is the talk most likely to be tuned to the
communication intentions of the child (cf. Flavell, 1967, and McCarthy, 1954,
for discussions of egocentric speech in children). Yet peer talk is also a significant
part of the child's ordinary language environment and may provide invaluable
opportunities for the symbolic use and elaboration of language.

Contexts and Codes

Children not only hear and use different kinds of language, they also experience
it in contexts that place different demands on the amount and kind of information
that must be expressed. Some contexts demand scrupulous attention to the

completeness of the verbal message—for example, when telling a stranger on the telephone how to reach one's house. Other contexts require far less emphasis on the linguistic coding of the information—for example, when speaking face-to-face with an old friend about perceivable objects and shared experiences. The language behavior of children eventually becomes sensitive to these contextual requirements. How this sensitivity develops and its implications for language performance is important in the design of day-care environments.

Low Context Settings. One of the most extensive series of laboratory studies of the communication behavior of young children was reported by Glucksberg and his colleagues (Glucksberg & Krauss, 1967; Glucksberg, Krauss, & Weisberg, 1966; Krauss & Glucksberg, 1969). In general, 4- and 5-year-old children were either unmotivated or unable to communicate information about novel visual patterns to other children and to adults. A kindergarten child might say "It goes like this" and trace the design with a finger when asked to describe the design to a listener who could neither see nor be seen by the child. Feedback from adult listeners, such as "I don't understand what you mean," or "Tell me more about it," did not improve communicative effectiveness. Skill in communicating was found to improve with age.

Age differences in the communication skills of children have been extensively studied by Flavell and his associates (cf. Flavell, 1967). In one situation children were taught to play a game without verbal instructions. The children then attempted to teach the game to an adult who was blindfolded and to another adult who could see. One of the game rules was that the child was not allowed to touch any of the game materials while instructing the adults. As expected, the communications of eighth-grade children were more effective than those of second-grade children. The most interesting finding, however, was that, as age increased, the content of the instructional messages to the sighted learner was increasingly different from that of the messages to the blindfolded learner. The older children used a greater number of different words, for example, when the adult was blindfolded than when he was sighted, whereas the younger children failed to respond to such differences in the information needs of the learner.

Flavell's data also suggest that the verbal communications of preschool children are highly elliptical and insensitive to contextual requirements. Yet even here some qualifications may be necessary. One group of investigators has reported that the language used by Head Start children to describe a picture was more elaborate and complex in the absence of the picture than in its presence (Brent & Katz, 1967, cited by Cazden, 1970).

High Context Settings. Ellipsis is a form of communication that tends to occur in situations in which much of what is being discussed is immediately present or presumed to be understood by the speakers. In elliptical communications relevant information is deleted from the verbal message. The parent says "spoon," and the child must decide whether the adult is asking for a spoon, urging the child to use a spoon, or labeling an object. Holzman (1969) argues that ellipsis is a pervasive characteristic of naturally occurring parent-child discourse. Elliptical communications present the child with a problem: in order to be understood, these communications require the child to process concurrently the adult's language and intentions in the light of the situation. Although the verbal content of messages between adults and children is often extremely reduced, we do not know whether these reductions facilitate or hinder language development. Special types of ellipsis (holophrastic and telegraphic speech) seem to be the child's first style of communication, both with respect to speech and comprehension. One might speculate that adult ellipsis, matched to the child's language knowledge, is a poor technique for imparting new language information to the child. When the objects under discussion are present, however, they may convey information of immediate practical significance within the child's limited verbal attention span.

Social Codes. Several investigators have suggested that social relationships regulate the verbal options that speakers select. The notion is that the form of the social relationship acts selectively on the principles by which individuals select material from an intact and complete language system (Bernstein, 1965, 1966, 1970; Labov, 1966).

According to Bernstein (1965), the social structure not only determines the pragmatic rules acquired by the child but the nature of the social structure is itself transmitted by these rules. Bernstein (1965, 1966) found social-class differences in the communication codes used by 16-year-old boys. The code used by lower-class boys was highly restricted verbally; communication was found to depend on tacit understandings, intonation, gesture, and facial expressions. In the more elaborate verbal code used by middle-class boys there was greater individual variation in the mode of expression and more complex and differentiated kinds of words and sentence organization. The communications of lower-class children were also found to be more context-bound when compared with the communications of middle-class children.

Several implications of these different codes for describing mother-child interactions have been explored in a series of studies by Hess and his colleagues (Hess & Shipman, 1965, 1966, Hess, Shipman, Brophy, Bear & Adelberger, 1969). Using an all-Negro sample of mother-child pairs, these investigators found that the strategies used for controlling the child varied with social class, as did the teaching styles used in an experimental situation. Middle-class mothers were more likely than lower-class mothers to use personal-subjective statements that considered the individual qualities and inner states of the child and less likely to use imperative statements that arbitrarily imposed rules and status-bound normative values. Middle-class mothers also tended to use relatively more instructive than imperative statements. In the teaching situation mothers of higher socio-economic status were likely to exhibit behavior that was initiatory and varied rather than reactive and repetitious. Further, lower-class mothers tended to produce language that was more restricted and contained shorter sentences than did that of middle-class mothers. These dimensions were generally related to the language performance of the children. Unfortunately, the Hess and Shipman studies do not make it possible to separate maternal characteristics that are controlled by the behavior of the child from those that are enduring, stylistic characteristics of the mother (Bee, Van Engeren, Streissguth, Nyman, & Leckie, 1969).

It is necessary to pose a parallel question for the children: to what extent is their performance limited or enhanced by the adult teaching styles to which they are exposed? It may well be that for particular children the teaching style used by lower-class mothers is more effective than a middle-class style. The issue has enormous significance for the design of day-care programs, for personnel training and selection, for parental participation in day-care programs, and, above all, for attempts to change the teaching styles of lower-class parents. It may be, for example, that the restricted language of certain mothers is appropriate to their children's language skills; that imperative adult statements are more likely to offer unambiguous guidelines for the child's behavior (Johnson, 1935b), that elliptical, reduced sentences in high context settings effectively communicate information, or, conversely, that unnecessarily complex statements will distract a child who has not mastered these forms.

Once again, the question facing day care has to do with the way in which children come to master the requirements and implications of verbal com-munications in diverse settings. An adult language style adequate in a setting that contains visual props may not be adequate in a setting that requires more explicit language coding. Similarly, children who perform well when props are available might perform poorly when they are gone. Day-care programs need to consider the importance of language skills in both kinds of setting.

The views of Bernstein (1965, 1966) have not gone unchallenged, however. Evidence is accumulating that the restricted language behavior of lower-class children may be situation-specific. Social-class differences in stylistic features, in the number of words spoken, in the degree of connectedness of the utterances, and grammatical features depend on situational factors such as the topic being discussed, the presence of peers, the informality of the situation, and status dif-ferences (cf. Cazden, 1970); that is to say, lower-class children may *possess* language codes as equally elaborate as those of middle-class children. The major difference between groups may be in their perception of the language require-ments or inducements of social situations (Williams & Naremore, 1969).

The language of children in natural settings is also highly responsive to features of the activities or materials they are using. One study indicated that children in a kindergarten setting produced more mature language during house-keeping and discussion activities and less mature language while playing with blocks (Cowe, 1967).

Labov (1970) has argued that none of the standard tests adequately measures the language capacity of lower-class black children. It may also be the case that standard tests do not adequately reflect the competence of children in general. This issue poses critical questions for the understanding of social-class, ethnic, and developmental differences in child language and for designing settings that will promote language development. The message for day care is simply this: day-care programs will have to consider language functions and capacities well beyond current assessment categories. The language competence of children can be mapped only by their performance in an array of situations and such a mapping can occur only in day-care and test settings that encourage verbal com-munication.

PROGRAM STRATEGIES IN DAY CARE

Language development has long been a source of fascination for parents, baby biographers, linguists, philosophers, and educators. Stress on language develop-ment has increased as evidence has accumulated that significant numbers of children are not developing adequate language skills. Yet it is remarkable that virtually every child learns to speak with remarkable ease and with a high level of competence. One of the basic issues in the formulation of day-care programs stems from these contrasting observations: virtually all children acquire amazing language dexterity, yet many may show serious language deficiencies, even when situational factors are taken into account.

This issue may be roughly expressed in the distinction between language-remediation and language-acquisition program strategies. Such a distinction is a helpful way of contrasting decisions involved in the formulation of compensatory, instructional programs with those involved in the design of child-care environ-ments. In the former case the emphasis is on first identifying what the child does not know and then teaching it to him. The technology of instruction de-veloped for this purpose need not duplicate or be derived from the conditions that ordinarily optimize language development (Bruner, 1966; Cazden, 1968). In contrast, when planning child-care settings—especially for children under 6 —the conditions that ordinarily optimize language development must be examined if for no other reason than that these settings encompass what happens to a child during many waking hours of language activity. The issue is whether 20 or 30 minutes a day of intensive language teaching can adequately span the universe of language-learning opportunities that might ideally occur during a child's day.

Moreover, in the case of remediation the assumption is made that some natural language environments are depriving and fail to offer children appropriate information for adequate language skills to develop. Therefore programs must be designed to ameliorate or, in the case of day care, to prevent anticipated language impoverishment (Bereiter & Engelmann, 1966; Deutsch, 1965). In the case of an acquisition strategy the assumption is made that language environments typically considered depriving are really just different and that children who grow up in these environments master fundamental language elements. Differences among children that appear when language skills are assessed are not necessarily related to basic language competence but rather to situational, motivational, or stylistic differences (Baratz & Baratz, 1969; Labov, 1970). Programs that accept the latter assumptions would stress conditions that support the child's use and exercise of his current language capacity in the communication style most comfortable to him—both by providing caregivers who share his particular language patterns and situations in which language interactions are nourished.

When young children are involved in programs based on "deficiency-remediation" assumptions, attempts are made to identify or predict inadequacies in the child and to guarantee that opportunities relevant to the repair or prevention of these inadequacies are provided. In contrast, "difference-acquisition" assumptions attempt to optimize general communication opportunities and incentives in an environment quite similar to that of the child's ordinary experience. Each of these approaches leads to different, although not necessarily incompatible, program strategies for day care, and each strategy produces its own special problems.

Language Acquisition Strategies

A language-acquisition approach to day-care programming stems from the notion that children have or develop natural aptitudes for learning language and that adults employ natural strategies to facilitate this learning. Such a model proposes that children select and organize language information according to their level of competence and that caregivers who effectively facilitate language development do so by appropriately "biasing" the information available to the child. An approach of this kind is essentially concerned with optimizing the child's competence and less concerned with establishing the minimum condition for the acquisition of a skeletal language structure. When day-care programs choose the "acquisition" route, they have to consider the ways in which children ordinarily develop language skills and the ways in which adults ordinarily contribute to this development as well as the situations and settings that depress or enhance different types of verbal learning and communication. Neither of these issues has significance, however, without a full appreciation of what children acquire when they acquire language.

What Do Children Acquire? Perhaps the central issue for an acquisition approach to language development entails an appreciation of what children acquire when they acquire language. Obviously, they learn to comprehend and speak words and sentences and to articulate the sounds and intonation patterns that constitute words and sentences. More generally, and perhaps more significantly, children acquire the capacity to generate a seemingly infinite number of meaningful and situationally appropriate messages, many of which they have never heard or spoken before.

The child's first words appear at about the age of 12 months. It is not until about six months later that he takes the next giant step. New words appear at an amazingly rapid rate. A common observation is that these early words are used to convey more information than the words themselves contain. The child might say "cookie" as he hands his mother a cookie, as he looks at a cookie, or as he points to a cookie far away, apparently asking to have it. The child's communications are supported by gestures, objects, and other features of the context.

When the child is between 18 and 24 months of age, the first two-word combinations appear. Children seem to progress from predominantly one-word, to two-word, and then three-word constructions. Although group curves often appear continuous, individual children show steep rises, plateaus, and small regressions (Cazden, 1969a; Nelson, personal communication; Riegel, 1966).

Some features of language acquisition during these early years have been intensively studied. Early word combinations, negation, and questions are but a few of the child's grammatical accomplishments that have been analyzed (see Bellugi & Brown, 1964; Brown, Cazden, & Bellugi, 1969; McNeill, 1970; Smith & Miller, 1966, for discussions of child grammar).

Far less attention has been given to the words themselves. Children seem to learn the form-classes of words at a very early age. By the age of 4, they know that the nonsense word in the expression "a niss" is a count noun and that in "to niss" is a verb. The little words "a" and "to" are not only differentiated but they signal the class membership of words that follow them (Brown, 1958). Investigators have estimated that the 6-year-old child has mastered about 7500 different morphemes which he can combine into approximately 23,700 different words (Carroll, 1964). Yet far too little attention has been given to the fascinating manner in which the child accomplishes this feat, how such a prodigious lexicon is organized, and how words manage to appear when they are needed (cf.

McNeill, 1970; Mowrer, 1960; Skinner, 1957, for different approaches to this problem).

Although the child's acquisition of language is rapid, there are individual differences in rates of acquisition and also differences in patterns of development; for example, the two-word productions of some children are highly regular, whereas the two-word productions of others are not (Bloom, 1968). Most important are the differences in the ways children *use* language (Berstein, 1970; Cazden, 1966). These differences have critical implications in any attempts to assess language competence and to develop day-care strategies that will promote this competence.

Ultimately, acquisition programs have to make judgments regarding individual differences that hinder the full exercise of language and the features of environments responsible for producing these differences. Children may require very little encouragement or information to get started, yet the richness, diversity, and flexibility of their language repertoires may hinge on fairly specific language-learning opportunities. If day-care programs decide to adopt the strategy of promoting development through "natural" environments that provide optimal language stimulation, it will be necessary to examine the ways in which the child's natural language curriculum facilitates language growth.

Natural Adult Strategies. Studies of mother-child or adult-child interactions have drawn attention to relationships between the language behavior of care-givers and children. Emerging from these studies is some sense of the techniques adults naturally use which might facilitate language development.

Mothers tend to employ simpler constructions when they speak to children than when they speak to adults, yet the complexity of the mother's language remains somewhat greater than the child's (Baldwin & Frank, 1969). This is supported by observations of mother-child interactions in Mexico, Samoa, Kenya, and California (Slobin, 1968). Cazden (1970) has presented evidence that older children also adapt their speech to the capacities of younger children.

One analysis of the language exchanges between mothers and children suggests that mothers frequently expand children's telegraphic utterances (Cazden, 1965, 1968). The child might say "dog bark" and the mother might respond, "Yes, the dog is barking." If, in fact, the child has not mastered the elaborated form, expansions might provide him with extremely useful information in a situation already tuned to language communications. Cazden tested the notion that expansions would be a particularly helpful language-teaching strategy. The children who participated were attending a day-care center in which the adult: child ratio was 1:30. One group received 40 minutes a day of individual sessions with an adult who expanded all sentences; another group received an equal number of sessions with an adult who spoke an equivalent number of well-formed sentences that were not expansions; a third group received no special treatment. Contrary to predictions, the children who received the *nonexpanding* language stimulation gained the most on measures of language such as sentence imitation, mean length of utterance, and noun-phrase and verb-phrase complexity. An examination of the language used by adults in this condition revealed a rather regular pattern. Although the adults were forbidden to expand the sentence grammatically, they did expand the meaning of the sentences; for example, when the child said "Dog bark," the adult responded with a related idea: "Yes, he's mad at the kitty." Cazden suggested that these responses promoted the child's language by introducing new ideas and more complex grammatical elements. This interpretation is supported by data provided by Bloom (1968), which suggest that even though children speak in two-word sentences they really understand and work from fully formed sentence structures. Thus Cazden's expansion group would have received little information about language that they did not already have. These findings tend to support the notion that the force operating toward grammaticality may be the occasional mismatch between the child's view of how words are put together—his theory of grammar—and the language data he receives (Brown, 1970). These implications are so significant in day-care programs that they are urgently in need of further elaboration and additional research.

Who ordinarily speaks to children and what characterizes the language children are likely to hear? In a recent study of the language environment of middle-class children, the investigator (Friedlander, 1970; Friedlander, Cyrulik, & Davis, undated) placed time-sampling tape recorders in the homes of two 12-month-old infants. The data indicated considerable differences in the amount of speech brought into the home from people not in the immediate family. In both families, however, mothers constituted the greatest source of language directed at the infant. Approximately 70% came from the mother, 20% from the father, and the remainder from guests. Reflective expansions, reduction, and reinforcement of utterances did not constitute a major feature of the infant's language environment. Tutorial modeling, imitation, questioning, and word play were, on the other hand, frequently observed. Comparable data are not available from lower-class homes or for day-care settings but they would make a useful contribution to an understanding of the way in which language problems are presented to children. The language environment of lower-class disadvantaged children has been described typically as inadequate along one or more dimensions: amount, quality, salience, appropriateness, or relevance of language stimulation. Because it is likely that the lower-class child and the child in group-care settings will be cared for and spoken to by many individuals (and because of the possibility that these speakers will interact with them in different ways), a description of language ecologies would contribute substantially to an understanding of language development in these children.

Adults do not appear to exert explicit pressure on children to use proper grammatical construction, for they respond quite relevantly to badly formed sentences and seem to have little difficulty comprehending incorrect grammar (Brown, 1970). The notion that adults in natural settings systematically give approval to well-formed sentences or selectively reinforce grammatically correct utterances has not yet received support from extensive analyses of mother-child communications (Brown, 1970; Friedlander, 1970; Friedlander et al., undated).

Although there is no doubt that the warmth and responsiveness of caregivers to the child's speech contribute to his language performance, there is little evidence that reinforcement of particular forms can account for the acquisition of grammar. Studies of reinforcement effects on infant vocalizing have demonstrated that contingent smiling, touching, and vocalizing increase the vocal outputs of infants (Rheingold, Gerwitz, & Ross, 1959; Weissberg, 1963). Generally the vocal activity of children with one mother-figure excels that of children with six to eight mother surrogates (Rheingold & Bayley, 1959). Mothers at home talk more and produce more infant vocalizing than caretakers in institutions (Provence & Lipton, 1962; Rheingold, 1960, 1961). Cazden (1966) concluded that reinforcement might operate to increase vocalization at the babbling stage but that there was nothing to support the contention that it aids the child's *grammatical* progress. It has been frequently demonstrated that contingent reinforcement increases vocalization at later stages of development (Ballif, 1967; Hart & Risley, 1968; Reynolds & Risley, 1968; Salzinger, 1967). In all these studies the children initially possessed the desired language forms; reinforcement merely affected when and how language was *used*.

Yet active tuition in the form of reinforcement and correction may also facilitate the acquisition of words and word meanings. Cazden (1968) has argued that adults are more likely to correct semantic than grammatical errors in child speech. However, even vocabulary acquisition may require more than simple reinforcement for correct forms and usage. Soviet research in this area (Razran, 1961; Slobin, 1966a,b) seems to suggest that word acquisition is also facilitated by factors such as language variability or complexity, novelty, and a playful, role-playing setting.

Salience and Relevance. In many respects the view of the child as organizing and constructing a coherent world out of interactions with a world that is itself coherent and structured has had a major impact on current thinking about children's language learning; for example, attention is now being given to the ways in which settings and situations constrain, sustain, direct, and in general account for considerable portions of the child's language learning and behavior. Some records indicate that a 3-year-old child is bombarded with 30,000 words a day on the average (McCarthy, 1954), but most surely only a small part of this language is "heard" by the child.

Several investigators have pointed to the value of settings characterized by one-to-one interactions between a child and a mature language user for learning relational words (Palmer, 1969b), phonology (Irwin, 1960), and grammar (Cazden, 1968). How might these interactions facilitate language growth? If variables such as the amount and complexity of language stimulation are tied to the salience of language events, signal:noise ratios may have an important role in the child's detection of language information (Cazden, 1966; Deutsch, 1964; Friedlander, 1970). Although there may be a great deal of language in the child's surroundings, if he is not listening or attending or if the language is more complicated than he can possibly understand, he will not be able to learn from it. It may be that one-to-one interactions set limits on what adults will say. If adults adjust their language to the level of the child's production and to topics that are of interest to him, he may be able to use most of the information being provided and be better able to derive new language structures and functions.

Changing the Language Environment. In the last section we discussed how aspects of the language behavior of those who speak to children might influence language growth. In general the data suggest that adult communication geared predominantly to a grammatical expansion of children's utterances is not likely to promote language development. A program strategy oriented toward language acquisition is thus faced with a critical dilemma: namely, how can the language of adults be modified so that it provides a highly individualized, moment-to-moment sensitivity and responsiveness to what children are saying? One possibility is that acquisition-type programs involving out-of-home care might have to stress the selection of people who already possess this sensitivity. Another possibility is continuous in-service training based on the analysis of taped adult-child interactions. Still another is the scheduling of one-to-one activities such as reading or story telling which encourage language interaction. Ultimately, however, adults in day-care settings must become instant analysts of child language. This may require considerable familiarity with the speech patterns of individual children, time in which to explore their language capacities, and a setting that is conducive to language exchange.

This brief review has ignored many important and interesting issues in language acquisition. We have not, for example, dwelt on the distinction between language production and language comprehension. As a result we may have given some support to the sentiment that language learning does not begin until the child begins to speak. The error of such an implication is highlighted by recent studies of infant auditory perception. It has been found, that infants begin to discriminate the phonemes /p/ and /t/ between 11 and 28 weeks of age, /i/ and /a/ between 5 and 15 weeks, and /b/ and /g/ between 20 and 24 weeks (cf. Friedlander, 1970). Observers of infant language development seem to agree that comprehension precedes production (Fraser, Bellugi, & Brown, 1963; Friedlander, 1970; M. M. Lewis, 1951).

Language Remediation

Remediation strategies derive from the highly reliable finding that children from disadvantaged environments perform less well than children from advantaged environments on indices presumed to reflect grammatical, phonological, and semantic competence. Differences appear in mean length of utterance, subject-verb agreement, use of tenses, noun and verb inflections, grammatical complexity, and fluency (cf. Cazden, 1966; Engelmann, 1967; John, 1963; Karnes, Hodgins, & Teska, 1968; Loban, 1963; Whiteman & Deutsch, 1968). These findings are based on a variety of tests and test situations: the Stanford-Binet, the Illinois Test of Psycholinguistic Ability (ITPA), taped records of spontaneous or elicited speech, and so on. Still other studies point to phonological difficulties among children from disadvantaged backgrounds (Brodbeck & Irwin, 1946; C. Deutsch, 1964; Irwin, 1948a,b; Templin, 1958) as well as differences in speaking, listening, and communication skills (Eisenberg, Berlin, Dill, & Frank, 1968; Krauss & Rotter, 1968; Peisach, 1965).

A large number of studies have reported differences in vocabulary size and word comprehension between high and low socioeconomic groups (Carson & Rabin, 1960; Deutsch, 1965; John & Goldstein, 1964; Karnes et al., 1968; Whiteman & Deutsch, 1968). All reported differences favor the middle-class groups, and these differences tend to be maintained when social class and ethnicity are not confounded (Lesser, Fifer, & Clark, 1965).

Differences and Deficiencies. Of greater interest here are studies that explore qualitative features of obtained differences. John and Goldstein (1964) reported that lower-class Negro children had particular difficulty on the Peabody Picture Vocabulary Test with words such as "digging" and "tying"—that is, words that label particular kinds of action. These investigators suggest that such words differ from object-reference words in that there is less stability in the relation between word and referent. They argue that the process of learning the meanings of action words is facilitated by a learning situation in which there is active participation with a more mature speaker. Such a position is not unreasonable since actions have special intentional and temporal components (e.g., the act of "tying" implies an intention, it has a beginning and an end, and its topological anatomy involves a complex sequence of events).

The responses of lower- and middle-class children have been compared on word-association tasks. In these tasks the child is given a stimulus word such as "deep" and asked to produce a response word. In general young children give words such as "hole" or "down" (syntagmatic responses) or idiosyncratic words in response to these stimulus words. Older children tend to offer response words that preserve the grammatical class and perhaps the relationship implied by the stimulus word. In response to the word "deep" they might say "shallow" or "wide." If the stimulus word is a noun such as "giraffe," younger children tend to offer descriptive associations such as "neck," whereas older children tend to give the names of other animals or category labels (i.e., "animal").

John (1963) equated first-grade Negro children on their ability to name objects. On a word-association test high socioeconomic children gave more category labels and paradigmatic responses for nouns than low socioeconomic children. On a sorting task in which pictures represented objects from four categories high socioeconomic children sorted more consistently according to category than did low socioeconomic children.

Yet Entwistle (1970) has reported more paradigmatic responses for black inner-city than for white suburban first-grade children when the stimulus words were pronouns and adjectives (although by third grade the inner-city children lagged behind). These findings regarding the early semantic organization of children may reflect important differences in the way language is spoken and learned in different subcultural groups.

Several studies have explored differences in the nature of word organization. These studies generally assume that words are organized more efficiently by a generic classification scheme than by a functional scheme, although the merits of that assumption have not been examined. Carson and Rabin (1960) equated groups varying in social class on their ability to match a picture to a word. The children were then asked to define the words. Definitions were scored according to the level of organization they represented: categorical (a wagon is a vehicle), synonym (a cart), essential description (a thing with four wheels), essential function (you ride in it), and vague functional description (it bumps into people). Northern white children used fewer functional definitions than northern Negro children, who used fewer of these definitions than southern Negro children. Spain (cited in Cazden, 1966) explored three levels of categorization in definitions elicited from children differing in age and socioeconomic backgrounds. Functional definitions remained the dominant mode of response for disadvantaged children at all age levels. Descriptive definitions increased with age in both groups, but generic descriptions rose most sharply for the middle-class group.

These studies and others suggest that there may be differences among socioeconomic groups in the organization of their lexicons. Yet there are critical methodological limitations to research in this area; for example, attempts to equate groups on comprehension are far too rare. Explorations of children's word organization might also be helped if words were selected from the child's own vocabulary. Conclusions are further limited by the restricted number of test and situational formats that have been employed. Moreover, too many studies confound ethnicity and social class. That ethnicity and social class may have different implications has been underscored in a study by Lesser, Fifer, and Clark (1965). Whether children from different ethnic or social backgrounds simply know different words or whether they have different rules for organizing their words are questions that have considerable significance for language remediation efforts in day care.

It is currently a matter of considerable controversy whether lower-class children exhibit deficiencies or simply differences in language behavior. Several researchers have advanced the argument that lower-class children do not learn standard English, but some dialect or variant, such as Negro, Appalachian, or Brooklyn dialect or a modification of a language other than English. Negro dialect is the most frequently cited example of a variant that codes most of the distinctions in English, but in a different way, using different rules for tenses and calling on intonation patterns and other legitimate linguistic devices that convey to another dialect speaker all the subtleties of standard English (Labov, 1970). If so, the grammatical deficiencies of Negro children would be largely a result of language measures that count all deviations from standard English as errors (Baratz, 1969; Cazden, 1969a). The most dramatic evidence of this position appeared in a study that presented Negro and white children with two sets of materials in a simple recall task. The semantic content was identical: one set was in Negro dialect, the other in standard English. Performance, measured as errors in recalling the stimulus sentences, revealed that white children were as deficient in the recall of dialect as Negro children were in the recall of standard English (Baratz, 1969).

Other studies also cast doubt on the notion that lower-class children have difficulty with basic grammatical structures. In one study children were asked to give a meaningful word for a nonsense word in a nonsense sentence. The only clues to the part of speech were signaled by word endings or by word endings and position. Older children performed better than younger children, but social-class differences were not found (La Civita, Kean, & Yamanioto, 1966). Similar findings with a similar task are reported by Shriner and Miner (1968).

Although the literature on social-class and ethnic differences in language functioning casts doubt on current conceptualization of language deficiencies, the safest assumption for day-care planners may be that the amount and kind of language information available to children will vary and that some child-care settings will fail to optimize language development. Areas of functioning likely to be adversely affected are semantic development, communication in low-context settings, and phonology (Baldwin & Frank, 1969; Krauss & Rotter, 1968; Slobin, 1966a).

Remediation Strategies. Early-childhood intervention programs generally concede that language is an area in need of special educational effort. Most programs plan language experiences that introduce new words and expose the child to well-formed sentences, varied constructions, parts of speech, and so on. Remediation programs have taken two tacks. Some programs have stressed intensive enrichment (M. Deutsch, 1968; McAfee, 1967; Weikart, 1967), whereas others have stressed structured, formalized teaching (Bereiter & Engelmann, 1966).

When intervention programs apply a "verbal bombardment" rule (Weikart, 1967), the assumption is that the personnel in such programs are themselves proficient and enthusiastic language users. If such is the case, one can be fairly certain that in some way or other children will receive substantial exposure to a great many language elements. The outcome may be less certain when personnel are not themselves spontaneous and fluent language users. The extent to which programs will be able to make effective use of paraprofessionals, near-peers, teenagers, and mothers may well rest on careful analyses of the conditions that promote the language use of caregivers. Effective intervention might require more specific and more limited intervention techniques that do not place excessive demands on the intervention agents. Other enrichment-type programs have attempted to provide guidelines for those who work with disadvantaged children. In these programs caregivers are urged to use sentences (say "This is a giraffe," not "a giraffe," in response to a child's question), category labels ("This animal is a giraffe), and descriptive words rather than nonspecific terms ("behind the door," "the giraffe" rather than "there," "that," "it," and so forth) (McAfee, 1967).

A specific remediation technique is illustrated by programs that apply operant conditioning procedures to alter children's verbal behavior (Hart & Risley, 1968; Reynolds & Risley, 1968; Salzinger, 1967). One such study attempted to increase the rate of adjective-noun combinations (size and shape) of disadvantaged children attending a traditional preschool. Time in school, intermittent teacher praise, and social and intellectual stimulation had not been effective in changing the low rates of using adjectives of size and shape. Although effective teaching increased the combinations of color and number adjectives with nouns in the teaching situation, it was ineffective in changing rates of usage in the children's "spontaneous" vocabularies. By making access to preschool materials contingent on the use of adjective-noun combinations significant increases were found in the spontaneous vocabularies of all the children (Hart & Risley, 1968). Thus operant techniques seem to be able to increase the use of language information already available to children without demanding extensive language behavior on the part of adults. Other studies, however, suggest that reinforcement situations may have to be more complicated if the goal is to impart language skills that generalize to many situations (Weiss & Born, 1967).

Highly structured language programs have been developed by Hodges, McCandless, and Spicker (1967), Gotkin (1963, 1968), Karnes et al. (1969), and Bereiter and Engelmann (1966). Spicker and McCandless reinforced language behaviors such as speaking in complete sentences, calling adults by name, and social forms such as "please" and "thank you." Gotkin's language games stress the encoding and decoding of complex instructions such as "Put a blue circle on the two boys drinking milk," whereas Karnes's program stresses the use of words in conjunction with the concrete manipulation of materials.

In the Bereiter and Engelmann program both the content and the method of presentation are carefully prescribed. The program content developed directly out of the assessment of children's language performance. According to Engelmann (1967), 4-year-old disadvantaged children tend to omit articles, prepositions, conjunctions, and short verbs; they do not understand the function of *not*; they cannot produce plurals nor use the pronoun *it*; they do not use tenses to describe past, present, and future, and do not understand many of the common prepositions and conjunctions. More generally these children have difficulty describing their own actions and, more seriously, they do not realize that two or more words can describe one object.

Language drills were developed to remediate these deficiencies. In the Bereiter-Engelmann program teaching sessions are carefully planned. Little is left to chance or to the natural style of the teacher. Indeed, it appears that the focus of the programming is as much the teacher's behavior as it is the child's. The particular set of language materials received by the child may be less important than the relatively high language output that the materials are able to generate from adults. Unfortunately the effects of this program have not been assessed in terms of changes in the *spontaneous* language behavior of the teachers or the children (The Bereiter-Engelmann program is described in greater detail in Chapter 17).

Although operant procedures and highly structured programmed materials reduce pressures on the teacher for complex language processing, the language program proposed by Blank and Solomon (1969) seems to increase these pressures. These authors view the language difficulty of lower-class children as a lack of a system necessary for thinking. They emphasize the use of language "to organize thoughts, to reflect on situations, to comprehend the meaning of events, and to choose among alternatives" (1969, p. 47). Realizing that these goals could not be built into any one set of activities or materials, the investigators trained the teachers to apply specific verbal interaction strategies across situations. Teachers were trained to tune into children's statements, to control their responses, and to initiate activity. They were taught how to add concepts, label objects, change the pace of the teaching interaction, review activities, and so on. Interactions occurred in one-to-one sessions with the children. Teachers trained in these techniques proved to be extremely effective in enhancing children's competence. An important consideration, however, is the extent to which such a complex strategy can be used by individuals who lack a substantial set of language and teaching skills or who do not easily engage children in language interactions. This clearly is an empirical issue for which no data currently are available. Moreover, it is a crucial issue for day care as programs attempt more and more to involve in teaching roles people with varying skills.

Quite another approach to language remediation comes from the Soviet Union. The problem arises from assessments of young children attending state nurseries which indicate that "insufficiencies of group upbringing have an especially unfavorable influence on the development of the speech of children" (Lyamina, quoted by Slobin, 1966b, p. 131.) Children raised in state nurseries seem to have particular difficulty in semantics and phonology, even when the ratio of well-trained upbringers (who apparently spend a great deal of time with the children) is about one to three.

Soviet developmental psychologists have concentrated on formal training devices closely tied to the systematic study of the variables associated with semantic or phonological development. The Soviet approach contrasts markedly with American efforts in that basic and applied problems are dealt with simultaneously. The research style is clearly formative and perhaps reflects both the Soviet disapproval of mass testing and their interest in the identification of specific language variables.

In one study children 19 months of age were taught the word "book" under three experimental conditions. Group I saw a single book and heard a single sentence containing the word "book"; Group II saw a single book and heard 20 different sentences, whereas Group III saw 20 different books and heard one sentence. Learning, as measured by the children's ability to select a book from a pile of objects, was greatest for the varied language group and least for the single book–single sentence group. Indeed, the acquisition of meaning may be facilitated more by variety in language than in objects; the object may already be familiar and "understood," leaving the child with the task of analyzing and applying the linguistic information (Razran, 1961).

Still another study explored the role of sentences that required the child to deal with an object in varied ways ("Feed the doll," "Rock the doll") in comparison with sentences with primarily designative functions ("Here is the doll," "Where is the doll?"). The word "doll" was presented 1500 times to each of 10 infants, 20 months old, under either one or the other of these conditions. The children who had acted on the object during training were more successful in selecting a doll from an array of objects than those who had heard the word "doll" in sentences that did not promote varied activities. Other Soviet studies have examined how other characteristics of objects might enhance word acquisition. In general the names of unfamiliar or unexpected objects are learned more easily than the names of familiar objects. (See Slobin, 1966b, pp. 363–386, for abstract of several Soviet studies.)

The Soviet assumption appears to be that the most effective remediation effort with young children requires concentrated one-to-one interactions with a highly trained adult under highly controlled conditions. Yet one might wonder about the 1500 presentations needed to teach the word "doll." How disadvantaged were these nursery children and how many presentations of a word do children actually receive in natural optimizing language environments? Whether or not Soviet nurseries attempt to manipulate these variables systematically in the natural setting is not reported.

The Problem of Assessment. Remediation programs have assessment problems that are in many respects similar to those faced by acquisition programs. In acquisition programs the burden of assessment is placed on the individual adult, focused on an individual child, and concerned with the interpretation of particular instances of the child's language behavior. To the extent that remediation programs attempt to design specific instructional materials, they must search for general characterizations of the language deficiencies of a presumably representative sample of target children. Although materials might be applied on the basis of individual diagnosis, the remediation possibilities are constrained by assessment techniques and available materials. The peril facing formal assessment is that children's actual competence may be underestimated. In view of the growing body of analysis and evidence that suggests that language performance is highly sensitive to situations and that lower-class children in particular will find typical test situations troublesome, underestimation of language competence may lead to curricula that "teach" the child what he already knows. Even more serious, prehaps, is the restriction of highly structured programs to fairly narrow aspects of language. The danger is that the overall language environment will remain depriving.

Problems of assessment highlight differences between acquisition and remediation as day-care program strategies. In general, acquisition programs must stress the general verbal competence and sensitivity of the adults who speak with children. Remediation programs, in contrast, concentrate on the competence of children with respect to readily measurable and presumably teachable features of language.

QUESTIONS FOR DAY CARE

In this brief examination of issues concerning the language competence and performance of children we considered how children use language as they acquire it, the kinds of language subsystems they are likely to meet in the course of social activity, and some specific demands on language use made by particular social requirements. We also contrasted two program strategies open to day-care planners on the assumption that it might be possible to combine elements of acquisition and remediation strategies.

Children generally learn more than one way to speak. They learn the language patterns of peers, adults, and teachers. Presumably children who speak dialects have mastered most of the essential features of standard English. Children from foreign-language homes often learn to speak one language at home and another outside the home. There is considerable anecdotal evidence that under favorable conditions children can easily master two quite different language systems (Leopold, 1949). Depending on the wishes of the families concerned, day-care programs might be bidialectical or bilingual (cf. Cazden, 1969a; John & Horner, 1970). We would urge only that children have contact with capable speakers of whatever language is used.

Not all children exhibit adequate language skills in the diverse settings that demand them. Several investigators have argued eloquently that differences must not be confused with deficiencies (Baratz, 1969; Cazden, 1970; Labov, 1970), yet by the same token different languages can be understood, spoken, and used inadequately. (By "inadequacy" we mean language competence insufficient for competent functioning in a particular society). Presumably a skilled dialect speaker has a large language repertoire and most likely a good part of that repertoire consists of standard English forms and diverse functional categories.

Although day care can seek programming strategies from those developed for use in compensatory programs, its burden is far more awesome. Bernstein (1970) has noted the folly of giving compensatory education to children who in the first place have not received an adequate educational environment in their schools. The Soviet experience suggest that group care can be an inadequate environment with respect to language development. Perhaps day care requires a double strategy—acquisition and remediation—to ensure that the language environments of day-care settings are not less adequate than those to which children would ordinarily be exposed.

The hard knot to untie is this: although we know that children learn language, we do not know how to teach it. The language curricula developed over the last few years have explored ingenious ways of teaching particular components of language. Yet these curricula represent but a small fraction of what children ultimately learn in benign and facilitating environments. Moreover, we do not know very much about the consequences of these programs beyond the limited test performance of children. We do not know, but need to know, how intensive and selective language programs promote langauge behavior in a range of communication contexts.

There are, however, some preliminary guidelines for day-care programs:

1. In general, one-to-one interactions seem to support language growth. Day-care programs can provide opportunities for these interactions to occur.

2. What is said in the course of these interactions is important. Grammatically focused reflexive expansions or other restricted adult responses are not likely to promote development, whereas relevant extensions of children's ideas may introduce new grammatical and semantic forms.

3. Packaged programs may be helpful for caregivers who do not possess a broad language repertoire or who do not use language effectively with children in informal situations.

4. Language should be used in diverse settings that illustrate the complex functions of language. Occasions for instructional, explanatory, descriptive, expressive, social regulatory and control language that offer opportunities for further language applications and language learning can be deliberately created and conscientiously monitored.

6

Play Reconsidered

A PROFOUND CHANGE IN THE EDUCATIONAL PHILOSOPHY OF group day-care programs occurred during the thirties and forties. This change was manifested most dramatically in the increasing attention given to play. Eventually the materials and equipment of model day-care centers began to resemble that of nursery schools. These materials—blocks, cars, trucks, child-size play cribs, stoves, sinks, dolls, dishes, dress-up clothes, paints, clay—reflected the stress given by early-childhood educators to imaginative and dramatic enactments or constructions growing out of the child's real-life experiences (Read, 1950).

Today the trend in early childhood education is away from play and toward structured activities, which, if not explicitly academic, are often justified by their presumed contribution to intellectual or verbal growth (Frank, 1968). The new "no nonsense" look in early childhood education emphasizes planned activities and materials structured to demonstrate physical attributes (e.g., size, form, color, spatial, and topological relationships) and processes related to the organization of attributes (e.g., matching, discriminating, seriating, classifying, attending), often in the hope of advancing more general features of intellectual competence (e.g., conservation or quantification). In contrast, attention to play has been associated typically with an emphasis on socioemotional development as distinct from cognitive development (Dreyer & Rigler, 1969). Even more decisively negative has been the representation of play as at best an inefficient way of influencing any aspect of development (Bereiter & Engelmann, 1966).

These criticisms of play-oriented early childhood programs reflect specific concerns regarding (a) the unobtrusive teacher role advocated in this programming, which may amount to detached (though benign) neglect in the hands of the unskilled or the untalented, (b) individual differences either in the ability of

98

some children to use play effectively or in the needs of others for remediation, concerted preparation for academic learning, or well-structured activities, and (c) the pervasive lack of clarity regarding the function of play in development.

Indeed, these criticisms reflect existing realities. On the one hand, justifications of play have often been little more than eclectic lists of all "good" things. The functions of dramatic play proposed by Read (1950) serve to illustrate the tendency to assign sweeping affective (and, incidentally, diagnostic and therapeutic) functions to play: "Play makes children feel less helpless (p. 284) . . . . Disturbing experiences are often acted out (p. 285) . . . . Play offers an opportunity to drain off negative feelings (p. 287) . . . . Many kinds of feelings are revealed in play (p. 288)." Others have assigned equally sweeping intellectual functions to play. Frank (1968) considered play an activity "which is actually the most intensive and fruitful learning in the child's whole life cycle (p. 435) and a way of learning by trial and error to cope with the actual world (p. 436)."

The following comprehensive list of the possible functions of play was offered by Hartley, Frank, and Goldenson (1952):

> Through this activity the child is given an opportunity to (1) imitate adults; (2) play out real life roles in an intense way; (3) reflect relationships and experiences; (4) express pressing needs; (5) release unacceptable impulses; (6) reverse roles usually taken; (7) mirror growth; and (8) work out problems and experiment with solutions (p. 27).

On the other hand, the eclectic stance toward play represents an attempt to state as positive values those everyday conceptions of play that are *not* related to the satisfaction of homeostatic needs, *not* identified with required tasks, and *not* oriented toward end products that have social or economic value in the adult world. Perhaps the most prevailing positive description of play is that it is spontaneous and fun and, given half a chance, children would play all the time. We would suggest that it is precisely these latter characteristics that lend urgency to discussions of the function of play.

PLAY AND EDUCATION

Comenius, perhaps, was the first to point out the possible significance of play in the education of the child and in so doing drew attention to the child's continuous activity and his spontaneous and concentrated engagements with objects. Comenius perceived the child's interest in objects as the foundation for later achievements. In learning how to read, for example, the child requires contact first with real things, then with the pictures of things, and then with the words for things. Later, from similar observations of the child's fascination with objects,

Pestalozzi reached quite different conclusions: the child learned about the abstract physical attributes of things by contact with them. The implication of these two definitions of an "object" are profound. To Comenius objects were the things of daily use—cups, leaves, boxes and sticks—and therefore the child's early learning grew out of his use of things. To Pestalozzi objects were expressions of attributes—circles, squares, and rectangles—and these attributes could be systematically taught. For the education of the young child the distinction underscores the difference betweeen informal activities presumed to have functional significance and structured lessons presumed to demonstrate a specified principle. Later the theme of function was sounded by Rousseau, who heralded the "free" child in a natural environment, whereas Hall (1921) sparked the notion that environment could be designed to match the child's natural interests. Modifications of the attribute theme have also appeared. The Pestalozzi lesson was teacher-oriented, but although in the same tradition, the Montessori lesson was material-centered: Pestalozzi, and Froebel, worked with supervised structured groups, whereas Montessori stressed structured materials with individual choice and freedom.

The theme of play as social education has also been stated. Isaacs (1930) considered play as offering the child his "first effective social education." In sociodramatic play the child must recognize others and their fantasies. In order to sustain a dramatic play episode the players must reach some consensus regarding how roles can be constituted, how they can be changed, and the activities that appropriately define each role. Some observers have noted that play has a special set of instigating and maintaining signals. Communications such as "let's pretend" are recognized by children as young as 2 years of age as invitations to suspend "reality" functions, to cross the boundary between real life and fantasy (Sutton-Smith, 1970, 1971c). In addition, once play is started, there are preservation and integration techniques used in social situations to keep the play boundary from breaking down: humor, changing of themes, assimilation of disruptive events to the play theme, and so on (Smilansky, 1968; Sutton-Smith, 1970, 1971b, c). Soviet psychologists and educators, in particular, have called attention to the tension between "pretend" and "real" social regulation in children's play.

A re-examination of the function of play is dictated in part by the swing of the early childhood pendulum to formal education. This issue has special urgency for day care, not merely because day-care programs will cover a long day of group living for some children but also because day-care planning can cover a range of child-care environments far broader than group programs. When considering the span of the child's total day, the educational potentials of diverse settings become matters of vital interest.

In particular, we have focused on the aspect of child's play characterized by "as-if" and "let's pretend," a mode of play distinguished by symbolic, imaginative activity. Our attention to this aspect of play is partly practical—it is the mode of play which, when looked at from an adult point of view, often seems to display what the child does not know without promoting new knowledge. Pretending to be a tiger is clearly not equivalent to a lesson in zoology; but even more seriously the child's pretense that a mud pie is a hamburger may run counter to adult desires to teach him that mud is earth (a mixture of silicates and carbons) and that hamburger is meat (ground, shaped into patties, and cooked). It is symbolic play, then, that is likely to seem frivolous and remote from the acquisition of social or physical knowledge. Even more, pretend play can raise disconcerting questions. Should children pretend to be babies (shouldn't they rather practice more mature, not less mature roles)? Suppose a boy decides to play mother and a girl decides to play father? Suppose dramatic play episodes contain enactments of cruelty to animals, death, or domestic conflict? These questions so seriously disturbed Dewey (Dewey & Dewey, 1919) that he stressed play oriented toward "projects" growing out of planned group experiences (a trip to the docks, the market, and so on) rather than play organized by children around their personal lives.

Our interest in symbolic play has been further heightened by theoretical arguments that this form of play may, in fact, have special significance for the development of cognitive and social structures. Clearly our emphasis on symbolic play will lead us to neglect for the moment those spontaneous problem-solving activities in which the child deliberately explores and manipulates the physical features of objects to achieve specific outcomes—a ball to bounce, blocks to pile, or a round piece to fit into a round hole (cf. Millar, 1968, for comprehensive coverage of the play literature). The problem-solving mode is discussed in Chapter 7. In contrast, when we deal with symbolic activity, we are specifically concerned with the child's capacity to suspend the immediate "pull" of real objects, real people, and real situations. In the following sections we discuss the development of symbolic play, research bearing on the influence of materials and adults on play activities, and alternative views of the functions of play.

THE DEVELOPMENT OF SYMBOLIC PLAY

Perhaps the most detailed structural description of symbolic play has been offered by Piaget (1945), although its major features have been noted by others (Bühler, 1935; El'konin, 1969). According to Piaget, play has its origins in the infant's repetition and exercise of sensorimotor schemas—shaking a rattle or kicking a cradle gym. Other investigators have similarly noted the infant's delight in objects that are recognizable (Hunt, 1965; Schultz, 1970) and pleasure in practicing actions that are well established (Bühler, 1935). Piaget emphasizes the child's deliberate intention to "pretend" as a hallmark of the transition from repetition for pleasure to symbolic representation.

> As for symbols, they appear towards the end of the first year. . . . For the habit of repeating a given gesture ritually, gradually leads to the consciousness of "pretending." The ritual of going to bed, for instance (laying down one's head and arranging the corner of the pillow with the hundred and one complications which every baby invents), is sooner or later utilized "in the void," and the smile of the child as it shuts its eyes in carrying out this rite is enough to show that it is perfectly conscious of "pretending" to go to sleep (Piaget, 1932, from the 1965 edition, p. 32).

By the age of about 18 months the actions appropriate to one object are deliberately and playfully used on another. The body adjustments that partly replicate familiar activities are seen by Piaget as transforming the meaning of the objects immediately involved in the transaction. It is as though by temporarily suspending some of what he knows about how these objects function in actual life the child becomes able to create wonderful jokes about the real world.

Piaget's observations of this early behavior are important enough to present verbatim:

> OBS. 64 (a). In the case of J., . . . the true ludic symbol, with every appearance of "make-believe" first appeared at 1; 3 (12) in the following circumstances. She saw a cloth whose fringed edges vaguely recalled those of her pillow; she seized it, held a fold of it in her right hand, sucked the thumb of the same hand and lay down on her side, laughing hard. She kept her eyes open, but blinked from time to time as if she were alluding to closed eyes. Finally, laughing more and more, she cried "nene" (Nono). The same cloth started the same game on the following days. At 1; 3 (13) she treated the collar of her mother's coat in the same way. At 1; 3 (30) it was the tail of her rubber donkey which represented the pillow! And from 1; 5 onwards she made her animals, a bear and a plush dog also do "nono."
> OBS. 65 . . . at 1; 6 (28) she pretended to eat and drink without having anything in her hand. At 1; 7 she pretended to drink out of a box and then held it to the mouths of all who were present. These last symbols had been prepared for during the preceding month or two by a progressive ritualisation, the principal stages of which consisted in playing at drinking out of empty glasses and then repeating the action making noises with lips and throat (Piaget, 1945, from the 1962 edition, pp. 96–97).

In symbolic play the child repeats and organizes his activity in terms of a well-mastered scheme and deliberately applies the relationships demanded by one scheme "inappropriately" to alter the relationships implied by another. Piaget classified the components of symbolic play that appear between the ages of 18 months and 5 years in the following manner (in all but the classification of collective symbolism, the examples are taken from Piaget's observations):

(1) *a. Projection of symbolic schemes to new objects*

OBS. 75 (a) At 1; 6 (30) J. said "cry, cry" to her dog and herself imitated the sound of crying. On the following days she made her bear, a duck, etc., cry. At 1; 7 (1) she made her hat cry.

At 1; 8 (25) she took a spoon and fed her doll, digging the spoon into an empty bowl. The same day she used a shell, which she put to her mother's mouth and to her doll's. At 1; 9 (28) she put a shell on the table and said "sitting," then she put it on top of another, adding delightedly: "Sitting on pot."

At 1; 11 (0) she made a giraffe drink out of a little pan: "You've finished, Muoom" (the mushroom painted on the bottom of her own bowl). She put a doll to bed in a pan, then covered it with a postcard: "Baby blanket . . . cold."

OBS. 75 (b). At 1; 6 (2) L. fed her doll and put it to bed. At 1; 6 (4) she laughed as she dandled a spoon as if it were a doll (Piaget, 1945, from the 1962 edition, pp. 121–122).

b. Projection of imitative schemes to new objects

At 1; 8 (2) she pretended to be telephoning, then made her doll telephone (assuming a head-voice). On the following days she telephoned with all kinds of things (a leaf, instead of a receiver) (Piaget, 1945, from the 1962 edition, p. 122).

(2) *a. Identification of one object with another*

At 1; 9 (0) she saw a shell and said "cup." After saying it she picked it up and pretended to drink (cf. obs. 65, but here the thought preceded the action). The next day, seeing the same shell, she said "glass," then "hat" and finally "boat in the water." (Piaget, 1945, from the 1962 edition, p. 124).

b. Identification of self or body with other people or things

At 2; 7 (4), having seen a little boy who said "I'm going home," she went in the same direction, said "I'm going home," and imitated his gait. . . . At 2; 7 (23) she was a cousin of her own age.

At 2; 8 (5) she crawled into my room on all fours, saying "miaow." . . . (Piaget, 1945, from the 1962 edition, p. 125).

(3) *Symbolic combinations*

At 3; 6(9) she collected small handfuls of pine-needles to make an ants' nest. There was the pillow, the blanket, the quilt, the sheets, a hole for the baby, a table, a chair, then the mother and a cousin; there was some macaroni in the cellar. "The ants (there weren't any) sit down here (she sat down herself). Granny comes." Then an imaginary character came in. The next day the game was played again, but it all become a cats' house. (Piaget, 1945, from the 1962 edition, p. 128).

(4) *Collective symbolism—sociodramatic play*

Julie walks over to Sally and Teddy and says to Teddy: "You are going to play with me 'cause I'm your friend. I gave you peanuts." Sally: "Shall we play house?" "You be the mommy and Teddy and me will be the babies," answers Julie. "You must have your supper now," says Sally. Teddy, "I don't want any supper." Julie, "But, baby, you must eat 'cause you'll be hungry." Julie finds a dirty popsicle stick on the ground and gives it to Teddy. "This is your spoon, baby." Julie, "I'm such a good baby, mommy, take me and baby brother for a walk." She says this in a tone imitating a baby as she walks with a mincing step.

The three arrive back at the plank and Julie says: "Are we going to the movies?" Sally says, "All right, if you babies get dressed quick." The three pretend to change clothes and walk to the step. They sit in a row. Julie is in the middle. They all stare ahead of them for a minute as if there were a screen. Julie bobs up and says, "All right, it's all over now." (Hartley, Frank & Goldenson, 1952, p. 97)

Symbolic play thus contains features quite distinct from pleasurable straight-forward repetition or practice. Further, at these early stages the features are quite distinct from exact replicas of reality, although Piaget does maintain that the roles mimed by the players and the object constructions (e.g., block structures) that are used in some dramatic play activities tend to become more exact and detailed as the child becomes more sophisticated intellectually.

A normative study of play by Markey (1935) involving 54 children ranging in age from 22 to 50 months, used categories quite similar to those proposed by Piaget. As might be expected, the total amount of symbolic play increased with age. Of greater interest were shifts in the types of play activity that appeared at different ages. Children 3 years of age and under showed a predominant interest in the make-believe use of materials and personifications (roughly similar to Piaget's first two categories). After 3½ years of age these early forms became relatively less common, as make-believe situations, construction activities, and dramatic play entered the symbolic play repertoire. Markey also noted that the younger children typically engaged in imaginative activities related to the specific materials before them, whereas the older children more frequently engaged in complicated make-believe involving relations and themes. The older children en-dowed unstructured materials with functional meanings dictated by the play theme and combined materials in complicated ways. The 2-year-olds, for example, used sand with digging toys, but older children used it as a make-believe lubricant for a make-believe train (a tricycle). Of particular interest in the development of play are changes in the way language is substituted for absent objects and pro-posed happenings.

To summarize, symbolic play is generally characterized by a set of variations that develop from spontaneous to premeditated transformations of the functions of objects and the roles of people. During the early stages of play the child derives pleasure from reproducing familiar activities or recognizing familiar events. As symbolic schemes are constituted, they are projected to new objects, functionally different objects are identified with one another, and the child identifies himself with others. Eventually these symbolic operations are combined, and subsequently they can be maintained in shared group enactments. In general, when taking an "as-if" stance toward objects or people, the child's relationship to language and to social and physical objects acquires a distinctive personal flavor.

PROMOTING PLAY

What features of cultures, people, and settings promote play? Although play has traditionally been treated as an inevitable developmental accomplishment, symbolic play does not flourish in all cultures, even though symbolic competence is universal; play is sensitive to different materials and settings and, of course, not all children play the same way.

Cultural and Socioeconomic Factors

Play, particularly symbolic or sociodramatic play, may not be so ubiquitous as many observers of children have supposed. Cross-cultural studies provide some evidence that fantasy and imitative play are almost completely absent in some cultures and immensely rich and varied in others (Whiting & Child, 1953). Similarly, the notion that play and games are used by cultures to initiate children into the power relationships of that culture—the "conflict enculturation" theory of play—is based on evidence that play forms may be sensitive to cultural pressures and conditions (Sutton-Smith & Roberts, 1970). Although the amount and content of fantasy and imitation appearing in play may be related to the narrowness or richness of the lives of people, it also is necessary, however, to consider the impact of specific variables such as child-rearing practices (Baldwin, 1949; Sears et al., 1957), cultural definitions (Sutton-Smith & Roberts, 1970; Whiting & Child, 1953), and material riches on the appearance of particular play forms.

In an intriguing recent study of sociodramatic play Smilansky (1968) explored some of these issues. Advantaged and disadvantaged Israeli kindergarten children were observed in similarly equipped classrooms during free-play periods. The most startling finding was a difference in the play behavior of the advantaged and disadvantaged children—sociodramatic play, for example, occurred in 10%

of the observation periods in disadvantaged classrooms and in 78% of the observation periods in advantaged classrooms. Informal observations of disadvantaged children in this country suggest similar socioeconomic differences (Mattick, 1965; Pavenstedt, 1965).

Further comparisons between the play samples collected for each group revealed differences in all aspects of play examined: advantaged children were more likely to engage in imitative role play, make-believe, and verbal communication. The advantaged children played more sociodramatic games at any one time and play was organized in many small groups that sustained the play for relatively long periods of time. The play of the advantaged children was not connected with special toys but instead involved diverse real-life roles and elaborated episodes. In comparison, the play groups formed by disadvantaged children broke up quickly; the children manipulated toy replicas of real objects but rarely wove these objects into elaborated themes. Little pretending occurred without the aid of object props. Smilansky suggested that the disadvantaged children might lack either the information around which to organize play episodes or the techniques for initiating and maintaining episodes.

The symbolic play of children is likely to be influenced by cultural and socioeconomic factors. Although conditions that produce these differences are not clear, we discuss in a later section how play patterns in group settings may be modified. As day-care programs begin to consider the value of play in the lives of children, attention to individual differences such as these becomes necessary.

Themes and Techniques

In a subsequent phase of Smilansky's study an experimental procedure was designed to separate two factors that might have contributed to the difference between advantaged and disadvantaged groups. Smilansky hypothesized that the disadvantaged children might lack either the concepts and knowledge necessary for dramatic re-enactment or the techniques for initiating, elaborating, and maintaining "as-if" sequences. In one type of training teachers taught specific play themes to the children in an intensive enrichment program. In a second type of training they taught play techniques by intervening in on-going play sequences. These interventions, which followed a careful diagnosis of the play deficiencies of each child, might suggest a role, an elaboration of a theme, an interaction with another child, or a make-believe with an object. A third group received both theme and technique training and a fourth group received no special remedial attention. The results were dramatic. Technique and theme-and-technique groups changed, but the most dramatic change occurred in the theme-and-technique group. Smilansky interpreted these results as supporting the notion that symbolic social play is optimized by a set of facilitating techniques learned from other children or adults.

An alternative possibility, of course, is that teacher intervention influenced motivational rather than structural variables. The teachers may have been reinforcing play when participating in it, much as mothers have been observed to reinforce playfulness when interacting with their children (Marshall & Shwu, 1966). Whichever interpretation is preferred, the study draws attention to the importance of playful interactions between adults and young children.

Smilansky's study helps clarify types of adult behavior that might facilitate dramatic play in day-care settings. Her findings suggest that children can learn play techniques and that they might use new information in dramatic episodes if they also receive specific technique training. These findings are highly relevant to group day-care programs, since they suggest that play in these settings can be promoted by sensitive and knowledgeable adults.

Situational Factors—Materials and Settings

Several studies have examined the role of equipment, materials, and spatial organization on children's play and on the behavior of adults with regard to play. Some early studies were concerned with the influence of particular kinds of materials—for example, blocks versus clay—on the play behavior of nursery school children (Hulson, 1930a; Hurlock, 1934; Updegraff & Herbst, 1933; Van Alstyne, 1932). One study found that when pairs of children played together clay promoted more imitation than blocks (Updegraff & Herbst, 1933). Another study reported that children played longer with toys that were more complex (Moyer & Gilmer, 1955) or more novel (Gilmore, 1965). More recently a study of 5-year-old children demonstrated that a greater variety of fantasy themes are elicited by unstructured than by structured toys (Pulaski, 1970). The complex dramatic enactments of Smilansky's advantaged children also seemed to thrive on unstructured materials, whereas the play of disadvantaged children revolved primarily around toy replicas of real-life objects. How the characteristics of materials and the capacities of children influence play behavior is not well understood. The available evidence suggests that (a) children respect the structure objects provide and (b), when well-established symbolic themes are available, children will impose forms and representations on ambiguous or "raw" materials as these representations are called for in the course of play.

That the child's pretend behavior is a function of his developmental level and the characteristics of objects is suggested by the observations of Piaget (1945) and Markey (1935). Early play symbols deal with such things as the motions of drinking out of a familiar cup and the motions of sleeping on a familiar pillow. Later, the actual real-life use of familiar objects becomes less constraining and play symbols are applied to both familiar and unfamiliar objects. Eventually play variations encompass the child's own familiar behaviors and the behaviors of others, until, finally, in sociodramatic play, variations deal symbolically with role enactments that the child may never have experienced directly. The objects (things and people) that nurture fantasy thus seem to change with age. For older children enactments and elaborations are limited by highly structured environmental features but are enhanced by those that are less structured. As Markey has noted, relatively unstructured things are used in relatively complex symbolic combinations with various role representations.

Three implications for day-care settings emerge from these considerations. If children's play is to be promoted, (a) the kinds of physical materials in day-care settings may have to differ for children of different ages, (b) the rules for older children may have to be flexible enough to permit materials to be used in several ways, and, above all, (c) children may need contact with other children for the full exercise of their symbolic powers.

A rather large body of research, although not directly concerned with symbolic aspects of play behavior, deals with dimensions of stimulation associated with the interest, attention, and emotional expressions of young children. These dimensions have been described as surprise (Charlesworth, 1969), complexity (Munsinger & Kessen, 1966), and discrepancy from a familiar pattern (Kagan, 1968). The implication is that day-care settings will have to pay careful attention to the number and kinds of materials available to children, giving as much to the possibility that they may be excessively stimulating, complex, or novel as to the possibility that they will fail to invite exploration and manipulation.

There are also more general ways in which the equipment, materials, and spatial arrangements of child-care environments influence play behavior. In an early experimental study of the influence of play equipment on play behavior Johnson (1935a) introduced and withdrew equipment from the outdoor play area used by nursery school children. When the available play equipment was reduced, there was less bodily exercise, more play with sand and dirt, more game playing, more undesirable behavior, and more social interaction. An increase in outdoor equipment reversed these trends. An observational study of day-care centers further supports the notion that space and equipment exert important influences on the behavior of people (Prescott et al., 1967). In this study the "quality of space," that is, the variety and complexity of materials and the degree of organization was related to the behavior of teachers and children. High-quality space was associated with teacher behaviors that were concerned with creativity. High-quality space was also positively associated with child behavior that reflected interest and involvement. These findings must be interpreted with considerable caution, since many other factors (e.g., size of center and teacher qualifications) were also associated with these behaviors. Therefore the effect of space per se is difficult to determine.

Another recent observational study examined the behavior of nursery school children in different play activities—that is, while using the art, book, doll, block, and game areas (Shure, 1966). The observers recorded participation (relevant, irrelevant, absent), affect (positive, negative, neutral), constructiveness (constructive, neutral, destructive, no contact), and social participation (unoccupied, solitary, solitary-some, onlooker, parallel, associative, cooperative). The block area was the most densely occupied (772 appearances by 143 children), whereas the book area was the least densely occupied (205 appearances by 47 different children). Relevant participation was highest in art and lowest in blocks; constructiveness was highest in art and books and lowest in blocks; single-child participation occurred most often in blocks and games; and complex social interaction occurred most often in the doll area. The investigator did not explore particular parameters of these settings—for example, the effect on observed behaviors of size of area, teacher participation, or the amount and kind of materials available. Yet when these results are placed beside the observation of Hartley et al. (1952) that symbolic and sociodramatic play varied with the materials being used, the direction future research might take is clear.

Prescott et al. (1967) examined the impact of program format and in so doing made an important distinction between "free-choice" and "free-play" formats. In a free-choice format children choose among activities prepared by the teacher for special purposes; in a free-play format all activities are always available and there is little teacher preparation or selection. The free-choice format was notably high on teacher encouragement and low in restriction: teacher leadership was active and directed to individual children and the tempo of play was relaxed. In the free-play format teacher encouragement was relatively low and restriction high and the tempo was relatively tense. This format was also high on noncommunicative teacher activity and care of physical needs. Once again adult involvement and planning emerges as an important variable in child-care settings, although symbolic play was not examined in this analysis.

Emotional State

The general consensus is that play is most likely to occur when the organism is free from strong biological drives (Berlyne, 1960; R. W. White, 1959). Even though the clinical literature suggests that the content of play often expresses anxiety and aggression, play is disrupted when children are under stress (Erikson, 1950; Peller, 1954). Conditions that frustrate the child (Barker, Dembo, & Lewin, 1941) or (in the case of the young child) separate him from his mother interfere with exploratory and manipulative play behavior (Ainsworth & Wittig, 1967).

One study examined the interaction between levels of anxiety and the toys that children prefer (Gilmore, 1965). Gilmore hypothesized that children would rather play with state-relevant toys; that is, anxious children (children who were hospitalized) would like toys in keeping with what they were anxious about (such as stethoscopes and thermometers), but nonanxious children (children who were not hospitalized) would like novel toys. Anxious hospitalized children did indeed prefer toys with a medical theme, but all children preferred novel toys.

These and other findings suggest that factors that place children under stress are likely to disrupt or substantially alter play activity. Stress factors in natural settings have not received nearly enough attention, although many of the variables studied by Prescott et al. (1967), Johnson (1935a), and Jersild and Markey (1935) highlight the importance of possible stress-producing factors such as crowding, inappropriate play equipment, and inadequate supervision.

But why should symbolic play be promoted at all? Two recent arguments of considerable theoretical importance attempt to deal with this question. One view focuses on the cognitive implications of play, the other deals with its social implications.

SENSE AND NONSENSE

In general, the relation between the objects and the symbols of play seems to change with age. The earliest symbolic play builds around objects that have clear and obvious functions and the child's symbolic activity involves deleting or ignoring some of these functional attributes. The child's symbolic adventures quickly grow bolder and soon more drastic violations of functional rules occur. The child begins to attribute deliberately outrageous possibilities (i.e., a seat, glass, cup, hat, or boat in the water) to objects whose actual functions may be vague (e.g., shells). To objects whose individual functions may be clear (e.g., tablecloth, fur collar, toy monkey, or hands) he may assign a common function (i.e., things to sleep on) which alters their customary functional significance. One game is about "what things can a shell be," the other, "how many things can you sleep on."

Of considerable importance is the observation that children consider such propositions funny. When playing these games, they seem to know that some standard rule is being violated. The child seems to create a joke by deliberately generating incongruities between what he knows a serious world to be and what he thinks a silly world might be (Piaget, 1945; Shultz, 1969).

That symbolic play is fundamentally concerned with the creation of incongruity has been argued by Sutton-Smith (1967, 1971b, d).

... whereas much of life is given over to removing disequilibria and acquiring some physical and psychological homeostasis, the intentionality of play may be, by

contrast, to test out what occurs when one upsets these customary balances . . . .
Language and logic systems are structured to make sense. Whereas it may be
that play and games are structured to make nonsense out of ordinary expectations
(Sutton-Smith, 1971b, p. 300).

It is the open-ended quality of play that led Sutton-Smith (1971b) to offer
play as a paradigm for divergent thought processes. In so doing he proposed a
status for play that contrasts markedly with psychoanalytic notions in which play
is seen as the way the child "draws off some of the excess emotional energy
which has become dammed up behind neurosis" (Lowenfeld, 1931, p. 226) or
as an expressive vehicle in which children "assign to themselves roles which
express basic problems . . . use play to disguise genuine conflicts and tensions
. . . to relax tension" (Slavson, 1948, p. 320). Psychoanalytic views of play
reflect a primary concern with affective structures and pay little attention to
the way play itself works. Studies of play in the past have often reflected this
diagnostic-therapeutic orientation to play. Hartley et al., for example, summarized
the purpose of their observational study of play in the following statement: "All
in all we were interested in two main aspects of dramatic play: what it can tell
the teacher about the child and what the teacher can do to help the child utilize
it fully in working out his own problems" (1952, p. 22).

A similar disregard for the special contribution of play appeared in Piaget's
work. From Sutton-Smith's point of view Piaget is concerned with those thought
processes by which the child's conceptions move into closer harmony with features
of the environment. Following the Piagetian frame of reference, several investigators have drawn attention to cognitive change which results from the child's
capacity to recognize and reduce discrepancies between external events and conceptual schemes (Charlesworth, 1969; Kagan, 1971). In the Piagetian paradigm
the direction of change is toward equilibrium and consistency. Symbolic play,
a supreme expression of deliberate distortion and disequilibrium, thus appears
to be contrary to adaptive thought.

In what way may "disequilibrium on purpose" represent divergent thinking?
Consider for a moment what happens when the child juxtaposes the functional
characteristics and the physical properties of objects. A cup, a glass, a hat, a boat,
and a seat can be represented by a shell. Although these objects seem to have little
in common by way of use, they may have much in common by way of attributes
such as shape or topology. The child interchanges postcards and blankets; pillows,
fringes, collars, and monkey tails; himself, a toy bear, a duck, and a hat. His
actions and words seem like "speculations" about the features of these objects
that might make them interchangeable, even though they are not interchangeable
in the "real" world of covers, pillows, and children. In grouping these objects,
functional and physical classifications are allowed to diverge to the point of ab-
surdity. The child seems to violate deliberately the expectancies generated from

one classification scheme as he creates them from another. To do this he needs only to reorganize what he already knows. His accomplishment does not involve adjusting what he knows to *new* information but rather realigning, stretching, and reclassifying *old* information.

Play as divergent thinking also seems to carry with it an affective mode, perhaps best expressed in the word "wonder." As a verb wonder takes no object (I wonder if, I wonder whether) and requires an animate noun for a subject. As such it contrasts with the affective mode indicated by other words that have often been associated with the detection of externally imposed incongruity. Surprise, for example, which often occurs when expectations are violated by unexpected events (Charlesworth, 1969) requires an animate object. In contrast, wonder is tentative and speculative—an examination of alternatives and a reflection on the possibilities.

Evidence of a relationship between play and divergent thinking is slim but worth considering. In a study of the play behavior of disadvantaged children Sigel and McBane (1966) found a relationship between the inability to categorize in representational terms and play impoverishment, minimal role playing and block play of low elaboration. Furthermore, play behavior in children correlates highly with information-seeking skills (Maw & Maw, 1965, cited in Sutton-Smith, 1967) and creativity (Lieberman, 1965).

In a recent study Sutton-Smith (1967) argued that in play the child might increase the range of associations to objects, since anything can be combined with anything else for a novel result. In this sense play creates the optimal conditions for the discovery of new relationships. In play there is a temporally and intentionally close relation between analysis, activity, and effect—conditions considered by some theorists to be optimal for change (Gewirtz, 1968a, b). That play might present optimal conditions for exploring new relationships is supported by a number of findings. Sutton-Smith showed that a greater variety of functions were attributed to toys that were more frequently played with; others have reported that games were more effective than workbooks in facilitating the learning of identical content (Humphrey, 1965, 1966); and still other research shows that a playful atmosphere (in contrast to a task-oriented atmosphere) elevates scores on a test of creativity (Wallach & Kogan, 1965).

Unfortunately, at present the role of play in the development of thinking remains very much an open question. Serious analysis of play is in its infancy and is by far the least well understood of all the behavior systems dealt with here. Nonetheless, the theoretical underpinnings of its implications for intellectual development have been advanced.

These implications suggest that in day-care settings play and structured activities are not interchangeable. Divergent, open-ended symbolic activity is neither task-oriented nor conveniently translatable into right and wrong answers.

Early childhood programs have become more sophisticated in their specifications of conditions necessary to convergent thinking than those necessary to divergent thinking. Day-care programming can, with planning and forethought, contribute to restoring a balance between these two aspects of development.

PEOPLE—WHO ARE THEY?

Several authors have given stress to the role-playing and role-learning aspects of play, especially as it develops in the older preschool child (El'konin, 1969; Kohlberg, 1969). Role playing is more easily discussed when specific examples are available:

Doris is playing at the carriage. Janie, "I wanna play with you." Doris, "only if you are the little sister." When she has completed fixing the carriage to her satisfaction she tells Janie, "You're little sister. Hold here and help me push the baby. Now walk." Doris has arranged the carriage with a broom across it. Janie takes the broom away. Doris pulls her back ordering, "stay here," and then, "no, no, no." They walk along, Doris pushing the carriage and Janie holding on at the side. The teacher greets them: "Hello! Nice baby you have." Janie, looking at Doris, says, "You play with me." But Doris quickly answers, "No, she's just the little sister." Rickie yells for no apparent reason and Janie still standing beside Doris imitates him. Doris hits her on the head. She offers no resistance. They walk back across the room, Janie holding on. Doris orders her, "Now turn, we have to go to the store." Janie says, "I wana go to the park." She is told by Doris, "Well, you can't." Janie finally says, "I don't wanna play," but is told by Doris, "Well, you have to," and she continues (Hartley, Frank, & Goldenson, 1952, pp. 29–30).

Harvey was playing with Karen, his twin sister. Karen began to push the carriage. Harvey said, "Let me be the baby, Karen," and started to talk like a baby. He got into the carriage. Karen pushed him around the room as he squinted his eyes and cried. She stopped the carriage, patted his shoulder, saying, "Don't cry, baby." He squirmed around, put his thumb in his mouth, and swayed his body.

Josie came to the carriage and wanted to push Harvey. He jumped out and hit her in the face. She walked away almost crying. He went to her, put his arm around her and said, in a sympathetic manner, "Come, you be the baby, I'll push you in the carriage." She climbed in. He ran and got the dog and gave it to her saying, "Here, baby." She smiled and began to play with the dog. He went to the housekeeping corner, got a cup and held it to her mouth. He smacked his lips, looking at her, smiling. He pushed her around in the carriage. Karen ran to him and said, "Harvey, let me push the carriage, I'll be the mamma, you be the daddy." Harvey said "O.K.," and reached his hand in his pocket and gave her money. He said, "Bye, baby," waving his hand. He went to the shelf, took a hammer and a bed, then sat on the floor and vigorously nailed spokes in it. Karen pushed the carriage to where he was. She said, "What are you doing, Harvey?" He said, "I'm making a bed." He looked at Josie and smiled (Hartley, Frank, & Goldenson, 1952, pp. 70–72).

Harvey ran to the carriage and said to Karen, "Come on, mother, take the carriage and teddy bear out." Karen said, "Harvey, you be the mother, I'm the baby." She climbed into the carriage and he pushed her into the gymnasium. Karen was crying like a baby. He stopped and gave her a stick for a bottle, then left her in the carriage and went to the wagon. He filled it with blocks and pulled them saying, "Peep, peep," jumping up and down. When he ran by Karen, she called, "Mamma, mamma." He stopped abruptly, ran to her and gave her a piece of paper, pushed her for a minute, and went back to the wagon. Later he passed the carriage again. Karen was screaming "Give me a pencil." This time he did not stop. . . . (Hartley, Frank, & Goldenson, 1952, pp. 71–72).

For the most part role playing in dramatic play has been seen as contributing to the child's development of a more mature social identity. Kohlberg (1969) has argued that role playing is the way the child builds a world of shared social relationships. Imitation, which invariably is a part of role playing, stems from the child's admiration for the competence of another and his desire to achieve comparable competence. The child's competence is confirmed when his performance is admired by adults. The child's call of "look at me" when he portrays the adult behavior expresses his expectation that admiration will be forthcoming. It is thus by mastery-motivated imitative processes that the child expands and elaborates his first major division of the people world—the division between self and others.

Although Kohlberg is more concerned with social development than with play, it can be proposed (as Soviet psychologists in fact have done) that symbolic play is primarily concerned with social objects and that it is especially sensitive to human activities—the relationships between people and things and between people and people. Play, with its rules and structures, is thus a category of socializing in the same sense that, for Sutton-Smith, play is a category of thinking. As a social phenomenon, play reflects the child's social sensitivities on two levels, one ". . . the plane of the relations between children dictated by the roles assumed, [and the other the] plane of the real relationships between children" (El'konin, 1969, p. 175).

What conditions make role playing possible? El'konin and Kohlberg share the view that a certain independence or differentiation from adults is necessary. El'konin has suggested that the child wishes to be independent but also wishes to participate in the activities of adults and that these contradictory tendencies are resolved by taking on the role of the adult and producing adult activities (El'konin, 1969). As we have seen, a different mechanism (which hinges on the child's interest in adult activities, his desire for competence, and the admiration of adults) has been offered by Kohlberg. For play to be developmentally progressive, however, both investigators assume that adults constitute the major role-playing models.

How well does this assumption conform to observations of children's play? A list of the roles played by children in the records we have reproduced indicates that they play mothers and fathers, specific adults (a charwoman), specific children (a little boy, a cousin), animals (a cat), babies, and siblings (a sister). Children play the roles of real and imagined characters—people, creatures, and animals. These roles do not seem confined to powerful or nurturing figures and do not necessarily deal with power relations. During the early stages at least children seem to re-enact activities that appear to them to be generally "neat," fascinating, strange, and wonderful, and they find these activities in the world around them. Furthermore, children do not always look to others for admiration; their play sometimes is self-sustaining (R. W. White, 1959). As children grow older, play themes become more serious, yet even here roles can be adopted and changed with remarkable fluidity. Children enact the roles of those who are more as well as less competent than themselves; for example, Harvey, the child in the above record, plays mother, father and baby. At the same time, there are constraints—no one but Karen can play the role of mother when he is the baby, and, when Karen abandons the baby role to call for a pencil, Harvey, as mother, can ignore her. Fluidity is therefore bounded, and children make fine distinctions —for Doris, Janie is the sister, not the baby. For children who have played together a great deal (e.g., the twins, Harvey and Karen) role transitions are smooth and effectively communicated. In addition, children display different techniques for maintaining role continuity—Doris commands, Harvey uses props.

When observational records of sociodramatic play are examined, we find the following features which theoretical formulations need to consider:

1. Children play the role of others who are more or less different from themselves; these others can be older or younger, human or infrahuman, real or imaginary. In the sociodramatic play of older children roles seem to explore complementary relationships: mothers, fathers, babies, siblings; cops and robbers; animals and animal keepers.

2. Early enactments seem to represent particular others, whereas the enactments of older children seem to represent classes of social others; for example, the class of fathers, mothers, or babies.

3. The role characteristics children select for re-enactment may be quite discrepant from the characteristics of particular people they know; a child might role play a "mother" with characteristics quite discordant with the real mother. A large clinical literature (Hartley et al., 1952; Peller, 1955) suggests that children's role playing can reflect wishes as well as realities.

4. Role play is both fluid and constrained. There are identifiable techniques for clarifying roles and for maintaining role continuity, and external sources of reinforcement typically are not evident.

El'konin argues that "the logic of the actions performed by a child in a game or at play exactly reproduces the logic of adults in that the introduction of the smallest amount of arbitrariness is rejected by the players" (1969, p. 177). In apparent contradiction, he also argues that "in the make-believe relationships the children are practicing acquiring and mastering new forms of social relationships which are transferred to real relationships" (p. 176). El'konin's problem is to suggest how violations of adult logic (which is implied by the term "make-believe") also can reproduce adult logic exactly. Even more, El'konin must conjure with how a "new form" can emerge from a presumably fixed copy. One possible resolution would be to underscore the word "play" in the expression "role play." If play is represented as a paradigm for divergent thinking, it can easily encompass social as well as physical relations. Sociodramatic play, then, would be a way for children to generate and pose possible hypothetical questions and alternative answers about complementary social relationships: What would it be like if I were a mother, a father, a baby, a sister, a charwoman, or a cat? What would be appropriate for me to do? What would be my responsibilities and my privileges? Although children explore the possibilities suggested by their own experiences, group play can survive only when the partners can reach some consensus regarding the critical characteristics of these roles and the boundaries of the possibilities. Notice in the episode of Janie and Doris that Doris proposes, Janie counterproposes, Doris rejects the counterproposal, Janie proposes again, and Doris again rejects the proposal. Play continues after Janie apparently accepts Doris' insistence that one boundary of a "sister" role involves a direction of the authority from "mother" to siblings.

Indeed, the observations of sociodramatic play and information on the real home lives of the children suggest that when pretending the child is able to explore a range of relationships from the possible to the improbable, from the congruous to the incongruous. Hartley et al. note that the twins, Harvey and Karen, have an incompetent mother and a conflict-ridden home life, whereas Doris has a domineering mother and Janie is prone to tantrums. In play Harvey and Karen can explore the range of competent nurturing and Janie can explore the possibility of submission to authority. The primary function of play (e.g., divergent thinking) need not change in the course of development, whereas the level and complexity of the relationships explored in play may undergo important transformations. Sociodramatic play would have its major focus on the extraction of interpersonal social dimensions and the examination of how they might be combined and regulated. Although new possibilities may never be transferred to real life (Janie's real mother may never become assertive), situations might appear in which such transfer is possible. The affective mode of role play is "wondering," but the child wonders about his social rather than his physical world.

There is a growing body of evidence suggesting that, whatever the process and whatever the nature of the actual accomplishments of play, play influences the child. El'konin (1969) cites Soviet studies indicating that obedience to a rule inherent in a role increases in comparison to obedience to a rule external to a role. In one study the actions that followed from a role were in conflict with actions that were attractive to the child. The role-related rule resisted the pull of momentary desires. New words may be more easily learned in role-playing situations than in task-oriented teaching situations (Slobin, 1966a). Other studies in a different vein have explored the influence of models on the beliefs or the behaviors of children (Bandura, 1967; Kohlberg, 1969). The question for play, however, is not learning from models but rather whether enacting the role of the model has an influence beyond that of merely observing a model.

Clearly much of the foregoing discussion is speculative. It is a case, however, in which speculation is used to inquire whether there is a place in day-care programs for a form of child activity whose value is speculative and whose primary significance to the child might be for future rather than for current behavior. Obviously much additional research in this area is needed, and at present we could not even assign any probabilities to the likelihood of its probable usefulness. Yet to ignore the place of play in day care is to load a major part of the burden for socialization and cognition on the environment and to locate the force for change outside the child. In this discussion we have stressed the symbolic level of play more than actual child-child interactions. Peer relations and influences are discussed in Chapter 16.

PLAY IN DAY-CARE SETTINGS

We have argued that a serious re-examination of the functions of play may provide a necessary redress of the swing toward formal, organized activities in early childhood programs. Perhaps the play form likely to seem least relevant to academic or socially desirable performance is symbolic play, yet it is this form that may have major implications for the child's conceptions of physical and social realities in its relation to divergent thought processes. Our discussion drew attention to the development of symbolic activity, variables likely to influence this activity, and theoretical formulations of the significance of various kinds of symbolic play activities.

If play is to flourish in day-care programs, the significance of several factors must be appreciated. We have visited many day-care centers that seemed to provide the basic stock of play materials, yet the children wandered aimlessly about or used the materials sporadically and briefly. In other programs limited equipment and materials were available, and in still others the child's predominant contact with materials was during highly structured, frequently teacher-directed group activities. In the latter centers play was treated as a "transitional" period between lunch and rest or between one group activity and another. If play is to be used as a serious part of day-care programming, it will be necessary to note carefully the kind, quality, duration, and persistence of the play that occurs and to arrange deliberately an environment in which play can flourish. Special consideration should be given to the following factors:

1. The arrangement of materials may be as important as the kinds of materials that are available. Some arrangements invite involvement. Others may invite conflict and chaos.

2. The kinds of materials and equipment available to the children of different ages should be examined. If the children are quite young, realistic materials may be used more productively than abstract materials. For older children unstructured but suggestive materials may be more useful than realistic miniature reproductions.

3. Adults may have to be active in the development of symbolic and sociodramatic play techniques. Some children may have to be offered experiences from which play themes can develop (e.g., the opportunity to observe people functioning in real-life roles); others may require help in the acquisition of play techniques.

4. Stress may depress or disrupt play activity. Some children may have so much to cope with at home that little can be done to promote play without attention to the family situation. Other children may find aspects of an out-of-home setting stressful. Too many children, too little space, too little variation in the day, too little opportunity for quiet, privacy, and rest are all factors likely to interfere with children's play, and these factors may be equally relevant for in-home as out-of-home settings.

5. Although there is no research regarding the influences of older peer models on play behavior, older children who do play effectively may enhance the play behavior of younger children. Day-care and early education specialists have tended to advise homogeneous age groupings. Perhaps play is one area in which mature behavior would be enhanced by mixed age groups.

7

The Problem-Solving Child

TO BORROW A METAPHOR FROM ULRICH NEISSER, THE CHILD in some ways is like a paleontologist constructing a dinosaur out of a few bone chips stored in memory. In the manner of the paleontologist, the child goes on to build a world of objects and creatures that exist in space, are caused into being, and survive over time. But the child does not come to this task with a polished set of specialized tools provided by the careful tutelage of others. The mystery of the child is how the tools he starts with, which seem so limited, are still of such power that within a few years he can build a world equivalent in many respects to that possessed by adults. Those who study children have attempted to understand the nature of this basic equipment and how it becomes transformed and elaborated.

Activity is a first principle and has been accepted in some form by investigators with vastly different orientations. However, it is necessary to distinguish between the active motor behavior of the child—seeking, touching, looking—from the active nature of the processes engaged in selecting, analyzing, storing, and recovering information picked up in the course of this continuous activity. The methodology of the child differs in one important respect from that of the paleontologist. He is as much an experimenter as he is an analyst.

We are advancing an image of the child as theorist, prone to problem defining and problem solving.

> For the child as theorist, his environment serves two chief functions, particularly the environment of other human beings. It is a source of problems to be solved (or of new data that require modification of existing theories) and it is a verification system. Thus, an 18-month-old child will begin to make proposals about the nature of his language, presumably on the basis of an interaction between

119

certain biological givens and his experience of a natural language. Those proposals of his are either accepted by the surrounding verification system or they
are refused (sometimes in subtle ways) and he is put to the task of revising his
theory of the language. . . . In fact, one way of conceiving the variations in
early care . . . is exactly by specifying the nature of problems posed for the child
and the range of solutions acceptable to his caretakers (Kessen, 1970, pp. 8–9).

In earlier chapters we sketched some of the problems posed and solutions
tendered by the child as he constructs theories of language and social relationships. We also suggested that a good deal of his ordinary activity brings him
into contact with things, that some part of his contacts with things is governed
by "pretend" and make-believe, whereas another part is subsumed by increasingly
systematic manipulation and exploration.

From an image of the child engaged in comprehending the physical world
emerge several questions of importance to day care. What exactly is the child's
theory of the physical world at any given time? How does he use what he
knows? How does he revise his knowledge? Spanning all of these is the
question: How do environments bridge the gap between the child's naïveté and
the categories or concepts deemed important by adults? In this chapter we consider the uncertainties and opportunities of day-care programs, the implication of
developmental sequences for program design, motivational components, and how
these issues bear on the problem-solving competence of children in day-care
settings.

UNCERTAINTIES AND OPPORTUNITIES

Organized systems of stored information are generally called "cognitive structures." By organization is meant the regular and controlling interrelations between
parts of this information; information refers to aspects of experience retained
for future use.

Before discussing the development of cognitive structures it might be helpful
to describe some of the strategies and dilemmas faced by researchers who wish
to determine how these structures change and by caregivers who wish to promote
the child's conceptual capacities.

Observation

Perhaps the first step in any inquiry is observation. Many authors have commented on the "blooming buzzing confusion" experienced by the infant, but
too few have noted the similar confusion attending a serious effort to understand
developmental change over the first six years of life. In the study of the child

the observation of spontaneous behavior has been an invaluable starting point for systematic exploration. Systematic study of the child always hinges on presenting the child with a "problem," that is, some event that engages his activity. Observations of the child in natural settings have helped to define problems that are likely to be useful, although they change dramatically between birth and 6 years of age. By that time the child can identify problems presented by an array of different people—peers, teachers, relatives, and parents—and different things—liquids and solids, pencils and paper. To resolve them he calls on a host of differentiated and refined strategies.

A key element in problem-solving competence is knowing how to interpret the constraints and requirements of a variety of situations. The child, for example, soon learns that in some situations choices are available; in others they are not. Some situations call for active participation and some can be ignored. Some situations impose an external goal, such as arriving at a correct solution; others entail no goal other than that which he himself proposes. The child, by the age of 6, has developed a complex and articulated "theory" of the demands, expectations, and options of a variety of situations and this theory increases the predictability of daily events.

Interpretation

When we attempt to interpret the behavior of children, the contrast between the 6-year-old, the 3-year-old, and the infant is startling. Suppose we wanted to find out whether a child could distinguish between a square and a triangle. The infant might not respond to the difference because he had failed to discriminate between these shapes. On the other hand, the failure might arise from the lack of adequate measures to detect the differentiating responses that he did make. Failure to find discrimination in the 6-year-old might be for these reasons, but, in addition, he might have chosen not to respond or he might have been acting on a set of notions regarding the task that were irrelevant to the intentions of the investigator. Failure in a 3-year-old might be dependent on any of these reasons and, in addition, he might have been immersed in a game of fantasy and not at all concerned with a problem-solving task. Often the performances of children underestimate their competence in the problem of interest to the adult while revealing their competence or willingness to decipher the purpose of the task. To the extent that a child resembles an adult, adult guesses about his behavior are likely to be accurate. To the extent that the similarity is superficial, these guesses are likely to be woefully wrong and difficult to revise. For those engaged in child research and child rearing children constitute a never-ending, problem-defining, problem-solving situation.

A pertinent series of studies has been reported by Ricciuti (1965; Ricciuti &

Johnson, 1965). Infants between 12 and 20 months of age demonstrated that they could classify objects—beads and clay balls—into two groups. Some of these children, retested when they were 40 months old, could still group beads with beads and clay balls with clay balls but they did other things, too. Some paired objects from different classes, whereas others made designs and patterns. Thus it might appear as though they could classify objects better when they were younger. Certainly, a simple count of "correct" sortings would indicate that such was the case. More importantly, there are no theoretical grounds to expect that these identical objects and instructions would be understood by the younger children to mean "group them" and by the older children to mean "mess around."

Understanding the differences between children of different ages presents an enormous challenge to those who want to understand the child. In the case of the individual child the burden rests on adults in the day-care setting who know enough about his typical behavior to guess correctly. In general, it rests on adults who know what to expect of children of different ages and who can entertain appropriate alternative hypotheses about the meaning of specific child behaviors.

Day-care programs need more than a nodding appreciation of these issues. Whether the problem is the daily, ongoing interactions between the child and objects or whether it is the design of a structured curriculum, the child is devoted to making sense out of a puzzling and surprising world. Froebel's concept of "opportunities" nicely conveys the notion that puzzles and surprises are biased by adults. In one way or another adults in day-care settings will bias the problems available for solving and will inform the child of solutions that are acceptable.

Complications

Let us consider a particular problem likely to be given to a day-care child. Most early childhood educators agree that the relationship of "over" and "under" are important concepts for the child to understand (McAffee, 1967; Palmer, in press). Furthermore, although a child cannot ordinarily master this concept until he is 4 years old, with special training he can do so at an earlier age (Palmer, in press). What does a concept-training procedure look like? The teaching adult might tell the child to find or put things "over" or "under" other things, describe the spontaneous placements of objects "over" and "under" other objects, or engage the child in dramatic role playing. Yet the actions related to the words "over" and "under" have peculiar characteristics; for example, children who can follow the direction "Put the block under the table" may not be able to follow the direction "Put the block under the ring" when the ring is lying on the table (Soklin, 1959, cited by Slobin, 1966a, p. 145). Apparently coordination of the actions and concepts involved in picking up one thing in order to place another thing under it presents substantial difficulties. Similar difficulties appear when a child is given a ladder with a red block in one slot. If the child has a blue block in his hand, the instruction, "Make it so that the red block is under the blue block" will be hard for him to follow (Huttenlocker & Strauss, 1968). According to Huttenlocker, children need to be able to do two things. In the first place they need to be able to conceptualize the final state of affairs intended by the message; second, they need to unravel the instructions and the actions required for the final state to be achieved.

What, then, constitutes mastery of the concept? If we are to follow Huttenlocker's suggestion, we might define mastery as the ability to conceptualize the relationship in such a way that it can guide and coordinate complex as well as simple actions. As concept-training curricula become formulated for day care, it will be necessary to examine what, in fact, the child has mastered and what else he might master with respect to concepts and relationships.

Any day-care program that is to begin with the child's available and effective capacities will have to face the problem of goals, methods, and assessment. Attention to what the child can do must be supplemented by an appreciation of what he cannot do but might be able to do if the conditions relevant to improved performance were provided. Problems in the assessment of intellectual and language ability are similar. A variety of situations is necessary to map what the child knows, and a variety of opportunities is necessary if the child is to expand that knowledge.

SEQUENCES AND PREREQUISITIES

One significant innovation in early childhood education has been the explicit attention now given to the sequential, ordered nature of development. Some developmental sequences are logical: a child cannot throw, roll, or drop an object until he can grasp it. Other sequences are empirical: children do, in fact, seem to understand concepts such as "open" before they understand concepts such as "rough" (Palmer, in press). Still other sequences have a theoretical status: children represent the world motorically before they represent it symbolically (Bruner, Olver, & Greenfield, 1966).

Whatever the status of a given developmental sequence, specialists must consider the knowledge or skill prerequisites for a given task—that is, the competence needed to make a new problem solvable. Presumably the child and the curriculum should come together in such a way that there is a match between the child's acquired level of competence and situations that permit and demand an extension of that competence. Let us define a curriculum as a guide for adults that indicates (a) the kind of problems children might be asked to solve, (b) ways of interpreting the solutions children offer when problem-solving opportunities are provided, and (c) ways of verifying the appropriateness of a problem with respect to the child's ability.

Sensorimotor Development

Information is organized by the infant in the course of his active encounters with the world—looking, hearing, and sucking during the first few days, head turning, reaching, shaking, dropping, pushing, and pulling later on. These response systems express and constitute the early organization of intelligence. The sensorimotor period, which covers roughly the period from birth to 15 months, is one during which these systems become elaborated, refined, and coordinated.

Early in life the end points of the infant's activities are dominated by the features of the objects he contacts. Soon the child is freed from fixed end points, and it becomes possible for him to submit the objects around him to interventions in which the consequences of his actions are systematically varied. The first sign of the infant's ability to initiate planned activity appears at 6 months of age. The development of prehension nicely illustrates these changes.

Bruner (1969) has suggested that the eyes, the hands, and the mouth are tied into the development of visually directed reaching. The eyes come to negotiate systematic shifts in attention from one object to another with appropriate adjustments of the head, eyes, and body position. The hands begin to grasp objects, move them through space and then to the mouth. The mouth itself begins to open in anticipation of an object being brought toward it. According to Bruner, the full development of visually guided reaching begins with the freeing of the sequence from subservience to the mouth as a final resting place for objects. It is then that the acts of reaching, shaking, dropping, grasping, looking, and listening can be combined to produce new complex actions and experimentations with objects.

Bruner's analysis is based on the careful study of films made while infants were engaged in responding to objects. The analysis involved a painstaking dissection of the child's actions as they changed with age.

B. L. White (1969) has studied the same phenomena in a large number of infants who were raised from birth in an institution. His studies had a twofold purpose: to obtain longitudinal data regarding the normal developmental sequence of reaching and to determine whether modifications in rearing conditions would accelerate or otherwise alter the natural developmental sequence. His observations revealed that prehension develops in an orderly fashion. At first infants simply hold the object in their hands. Later they hold and view it, and still later they view the object and hold it in one hand while exploring it with another. Moreover, he discovered that the development of infants who are given different kinds of enrichment experiences (such as extra handling and interesting objects to view and grasp) was substantially accelerated in comparison with infants who were not exposed to such conditions. Prehension was achieved at 89 days of age by the experimental group but not until 147 days by the control group.

The issues raised by Bruner and the data provided by White are essentially compatible. The level of prehension reached by the child reflects the organization of his ability to respond to spatial features of the environment. Acts of prehension, in turn, contribute to the refinement of that organization and no doubt facilitate the location of permanent objects in space. When the infant can free the manipulation of objects from the terminal demands of stimuli or responses, he has acquired the freedom to subject objects systematically to hypotheses about how things work. He can now drop a variety of objects, in a variety of ways, and observe their trajectory; whether they plop or bang, bounce or burst, disappear or reappear. What is meant by a developmental period (or in this case a subperiod) is just these dramatic changes in the qualitative nature of the child's behavior. Something new has been added to the rules that the child applies to his transactions with the world. One new rule might be " I wonder what would happen if . . . ?"

The development of prehension is sensitive to the child's previous opportunities to deal with objects. We are also suggesting that, once arrived at, prehension may contribute to further growth. In combination, the argument says that day-care programs which hope to support the development of infants during these early periods will have to tolerate a substantial amount of dropping, touching, pushing, and pulling and furthermore will have to promote opportunities for the child to engage in such activities.

We have presented the development of prehension in some detail because it conveniently illustrates several important issues in the relationship between the problem-solving child and the problem-posing environment:

1. The child comes to recognize that "out there" something of interest has happened—for example, in the case of prehension, that there is something that may be "graspable."

2. He exhibits some intention to verify his hypothesis—that is, he tries to grasp the object.

3. In the process of verification he selects appropriate operations (i.e., visually guided reaching) with a monitoring system that permits him to correct and redirect his activity.

The important point is that almost all children, unless they are reared in extremely depriving environments, acquire prehension during the first half year of life. Yet it does not appear as a full-blown skill; rather it is preceded by gradually emerging intentions and increasingly coordinated, precise operations. Other behaviors appear concurrently with the mastery of prehension, and these constitute a new repertoire of possibilities. How then might the problems posed by the environment influence the child when such a universal developmental accomplishment is involved? We suggest that other areas of knowledge are correlated with the child's early attempts to grasp objects. These objects can vary in size, shape, texture, coldness, distance, and perspective, in how they look, feel, and taste; and, of course, they vary, depending on whether they are detachable, graspable things or pictures of things. Thus in the process of reaching for things the child must deal with their inherent properties and adapt his efforts to these characteristics. In brief, if given the opportunity, the child will encounter a complex and significant array of problems and, once prehension is achieved, the knowledge gained from old encounters will be reorchestrated and deepened. In general, then, we are suggesting that the universal acquisitions of children are accompanied by related achievements that are sensitive to the context in which developmental propensities are exercised and that define the breadth and richness of the child's constructions. How the richness of environmental contacts within a given level of competence influences the child's progression to subsequent levels is not clear. Moreover, it may be that progression is not so much an issue as the type of classifications achieved within a level, the problem-solving style elaborated, or the motivational systems exhibited.

One might ask what features of the environment are likely to capture the attention of young children. What objects are likely to encourage exploration and manipulation? Recent studies offer some clues. In general, the objects and events that invite attention present problems that are somewhat novel or more complex than those the child has already experienced (Kagan, 1968). A similar phenomenon appears in word learning (cf. Mallitskaya, abstracted in Slobin, 1966, p. 375) and in complex intellectual functioning (Munsinger & Kessen, 1966). Findings such as these are important to the selection and presentation of objects to children in day-care settings. Objects to look at and handle need to be in plentiful supply and selected according to their capacity to stimulate rich exploratory and manipulative behavior in the children for whom they are intended.

Although institutionalized children show sensorimotor retardation by the time they are 7 months old, there is no evidence that lower-class children are any different from middle-class children at this age (Uzgiris, 1967). Developmental retardation in babies seems to be associated with child-rearing conditions outside the home which deny them sufficient opportunity to have active contact with people and things. Another cause, perhaps, is severe object deprivation (cf. discussion by Meers & Marans, 1968, of infants reared at Metera). Children from lower-class homes begin to show a developmental lag by 10 months of age and by 15 months are responding in a manner similar to 11½-month-old children from middle-class homes (Uzgiris, 1967).

The child-care environment of young children can be depriving. Although the separate contribution to development of people and things is not clear (Bronfenbrenner, 1968b; Cairns, 1967; Casler, 1961; Greenberg, Uzgiris, & Hunt, 1968), it is safest to assume that each source of environmental stimulation makes a different contribution to development. The physical environments of day-care settings require careful planning and evaluation.

Objects and Classifications

Observations suggest that infants develop sensorimotor concepts but that the objects fitted into this kind of organization lose their substance when they are no longer in actual contact with the child. An important developmental achievement appears when the child recognizes the permanence of objects (Piaget, 1936). Befort this time, when an object moves out of sight, the child will not attempt to locate it. If he drops an object out of his crib, he will look at the hand that once held it. Gradually the child begins to anticipate the future position of objects. He looks over the edge of his crib as he drops the object out of it. He can identify his bottle when he sees only its back. Soon the child begins to search actively for an object that has moved out of sight. At first his search is haphazard; later it is directed toward the place where the object was last seen. Finally the child can find the object when it has been moved to successive locations. Initially he gives up if it isn't in the first place he looks. Later he seems to adopt the strategy, "if it's not here, it must be somewhere else."

As with prehension, object permanence gives the child a valuable conceptual tool. With the freeing of objects from the boundaries of immediate time and space, the child is in a position to develop schemes for classifying the multiple phenomena of the world.

In the years from 3 to 5 the child refines his concepts of space and spatial relations. He moves from classifying figures according to topological features (open-closedness) to the use of form (circle-square). Although at 3 years of age big and little are nominal, absolute classes, by 5 years of age size can be dealt with as a system of relationships along a continuum (Flavell, 1970a). It is only later that the child is able to analyze components of size such as long and short, fat and thin (Sinclair-deZwart, 1969), and to conceive of objects in a series as being quantitatively related to one another (Fein, in press).

During the preschool years children have difficulty sorting objects according to multiple characteristics (red, square, and long). The conservation literature is too vast to discuss here, but the child's inability to conserve relationships during the preschool years is thought to reflect the global nature of his notions of amount and size. When, for example, liquid is poured from one container to another that differs in shape (thinner and taller or shorter and wider), the child judges the amount of liquid to have changed. His judgment is often based on the height of the liquid in the new container in comparison with the old. It is during the elementary school years that the child begins to understand that the amount must be constant, since nothing was added or taken away, or that the difference in the height of the new container is compensated for by a difference in the width, thus discounting as irrelevant the absolute level of the liquid (cf. Bruner, Olver, & Greenfield, 1966; Elkind & Flavell, 1969; Flavell, 1970a).

Although in spontaneous activity young children seem to classify objects according to function, when asked to sort groups of objects or pictures, they tend not to use such a scheme. Their groupings are more likely to be "thematic" or "complexive" (Bruner, Olver, & Greenfield, 1966). A thematic grouping is one that places a banana with a monkey because monkeys eat bananas. A complexive grouping is one that displays multiple criteria: a red house and a red barn might be put together because they are red, but a cow joins the group because he lives in the barn. A functional grouping would place bananas, pears, peaches together because they are fruit or because they are things to eat. The failure of preschool children to use functional groupings in such tasks has been widely replicated (cf. Flavell, 1970a).

Piaget has argued that the child's predilection for complexive, inconsistent groupings reflects his difficulty in monitoring and planning his behavior. The child loses track of how he started and rapidly abandons his tentatively developed strategy. His classifications seem to be strung out in time in such a way that the relation between the first pair of objects does not necessarily govern relations between the next two or between the second and the third. Preschool-aged children who try to order a series of sizes work with pairs erratically related to other pairs. On the other hand, the results of the study by Ricciuti and Johnson (1965) suggest a word of caution. The child from 3 to 5 years of age is at the height of his interest in symbolic play. There is no reason to suppose that fantasy will not enter the child's behavior in these relatively unstructured, gamelike situations. They are, indeed, the very situations that encourage a disregard for the formal organization of objects on behalf of highly imaginative reconstructions.

The implications for early childhood education parallel the implications for research. Although concept-teaching games have been developed for preschool children (Gotkin, 1968), games and play situations in which there are few constraints on open-ended thinking may not be the best situations for ensuring that the child will be exposed to a specified set of concepts. A broad range of situations may be needed if the conceptual competence of the child is to receive adequate mapping and nurturing.

The preschool child, however, never ceases to challenge simple characterization. One series of studies presents unusual challenges. Children were shown an ordered set of 10 sticks varying in size. They were told to take a good look so that they would be able to draw the series later. Drawings made after one week were easy to predict from what is known about children at the various ages tested. The 3- and 4-year-olds drew a set of lines of equal size; slightly older children drew lines of two sizes, big and small; the oldest children drew a small series of lines of different sizes. The surprise came when the children were retested six months later. They improved in their ability to draw the original model without having had any opportunity to see it again. At each age group they moved to the next highest level of reproduction (Piaget, 1968). A subsequent study confirmed this effect and supplied some evidence that improved motor coordination was not an important factor (Altemeyer, Fulton, & Berney, 1969). Although these findings have interesting implications in any attempt to describe how information is received, stored, and applied by children, they have implications as well for those who would design optimal day-care environments. At least the data suggest that children note and code remarkably subtle features of the environment long before they can put them to use. We are reminded here of Flavell's distinction (Flavell, 1970b) between production and mediation deficiencies and the possibility that cognitive comprehension as well as language comprehension might march ahead of production. At least one implication of this relation for day-care programs would be that a curriculum designed exclusively to meet the child's productive capabilities, that is, his surface behavior, is likely to be redundant with respect to what he understands.

Several programs created over the last few years have dealt with the child's cognitive development during the preschool years. Some of them fit into a Piagetian framework and offer children experiences in classifying and relating objects to one another and exposure to concepts of number, time, and distance. Other programs have been oriented toward the skills and concepts that children will need for successful school performance (cf. Chapter 17 for an analysis of preschool programs). The trend, however, is toward programming based on the assumption that children acquire knowledge and knowledge-producing skills in a sequential manner—that some competencies are prerequisite to others (Palmer, in press). The source of order in the curriculum often comes from the order observed in the child. Prepared programs such as these can strengthen the ability of caregivers to offer enriched experiences to day-care children. Indeed, a prepared curriculum perhaps serves its most useful function in helping adults to organize and plan systematic and appropriately stimulating problem-solving situations.

Yet even within the area of the planned curriculum distinctions can be noted. "Discovery" methods may be as effective as directed teaching (Palmer & Rees, 1969). Whereas Gagné (1967) has adapted the notion of hierarchical organization to tightly sequenced programmed instruction, Gotkin (1968) would loosen the links between highly structured materials and the child's interaction with these materials. Any attempt to impose a too mechanical, one-for-one correspondence between features of the child's mind and those of the environment as a program of instruction may, in the end, reduce the range of strategies and combinations available to the child; for example, a hierarchical organizational scheme is one that adults have but do not always use. The argument that higher-order skills depend on lower-order skills may be difficult to refute, but creative problem solving may rest as well on unusual selections and combinations of those skills. Defining a problem may be a first step toward solving it, and skill at defining problems may depend on the opportunity to encounter a great many more than programmed materials can possibly provide. Perhaps the most important concepts children acquire during the early years are those that concern the properties of problems and the classification of problems into useful categories—probability, analog strategy, heuristic, and algorithmic problems. Programmed materials seem to be at their best when they deal with algorithmic procedures and factual material, thereby leaving many significant problem areas for the child to discover on his own.

LANGUAGE AND COGNITION

Much research and many educational practices make assumptions about the relations between language and various aspects of intellectual functioning. Several early childhood programs, such as those developed by Deutsch (1968), Blank and Solomon (1969) and Bereiter and Engelmann (1966), justify language training by representing concepts as equivalent to words, problem solving as directed by covert verbal behavior, or logic as a function of verbally coded propositions.

There are many who would assign to language a powerful and central role in the amplification or modification of man's intellectual capacities. Bruner, Olver, and Greenfield (1966), Luria (1961, 1969), Vygotsky (1962), and Whorf (1956) have presented some of the arguments and some of the possibilities. Studies by the Kendlers (Kendler, 1963), Reese (1962), Rohwer (1966), and Kohlberg, Yaeger, and Hjertholm (1968) have explored some of the implications of these propositions for the development of children. It should be noted that most of the discussions of the relation between language and nonlanguage systems have concentrated on language and thought, although clearly there are other options—for example, affective systems (Luria, 1969) and fantasy systems (Luria & Yudvitch, 1959). The speculations of Whorf and Bernstein, which focus on the reciprocity between language, thought, and culture, are more concerned with questions of cognitive content than of cognitive structure.

Several meanings have become attached to the concept of verbal control by various investigators (Beiswenger, 1968). It has been proposed as a factor in the control of attention, self-instruction, redirection of ongoing activity, conceptual labeling to facilitate learning or remembering, covert rehearsal, or the planning of sequential behaviors.

The notion that descriptive or referential labels contribute to the distinctiveness of stimuli has received extensive exploration (Spiker, 1956; Reese, 1962). A rather large literature testifies to interest in the notion that verbal representations of abstract physical dimensions facilitate discrimination learning and transfer. Recent studies by Flavell and others (Daehler, Horowitz, Wynns, & Flavell, 1969; Flavell, 1970b) have stressed the distinction between words used as labels for objects and words used to mediate problem-solving behaviors. On the other hand, there is a growing body of data that suggests that a linguistic system is not a necessary condition for the development of conceptual classifications and concrete operations, although language might facilitate the rate at which these abilities are acquired. Furth (1966) has been an active advocate of the view that intellective processes such as those proposed by Piaget do not depend on the development of a conventional language system. Intensive studies of deaf children seem to suggest that the ability to classify, conserve, and seriate does not require language.

Once again, research seems merely to generate uncertainties for day-care planners, but if day-care programs are to search for firm theoretical and research foundations it will be necessary to re-examine what is being done and why— even when current practices seem to be working. In the case of the relationship between language and intellectual functioning research findings add a necessary cautionary note: children who do not speak very much may think effectively, have extensive problem-solving capacities, and hold fairly sophisticated theories of the world. If the task of conceptualizing day-care settings and cognitively oriented curricula becomes more complicated as a result of these findings, we can only hope that more effective programming will follow from an appreciation of the difficulties in analyzing the competence of children.

STARTING, STAYING AND SHIFTING

Notions of how activity in children is initiated, how it is maintained, and how it stops have undergone a major change in the last decade. The shift was signaled in a classic paper of R. W. White which argued on behalf of untying motivational constructs from biological drives. White noted that children seem to repeat actions out of sheer functional pleasure, that they seem to derive pleasure from the mastery of problems, from the development of skills and proficiencies, and from effective interactions with the environment.

There is a competence motivation as well as competence in its more familiar sense of achieved capacity. The behavior that leads to the building up of effective grasping, handling, and letting go of objects, to take one example, is not random behavior produced by a general overflow of energy. It is directed, selective and persistent, and it is continued not only because it serves primary drives, which indeed it cannot serve until it is almost perfected, but because it satisfies an intrinsic need to deal with the environment (White, 1959, pp. 318–319).

Competence motivation may underlie the child's desire to imitate effective and highly regarded adults (Kohlberg, 1969) and may sustain the child's exploratory and manipulative behavior. Explicit recognition of these motivational resources has appeared in preschool programs of Sprigle et al. (1968) and Montessori (1967). O. K. Moore's autotelic responsive environment (1966) and elaborations of these ideas (Nimnicht, McAfee, & Meier, 1969) rely heavily on notions of intrinsic motivation.

Motivational constructs, such as competence and mastery, deal primarily with the anticipated or realized consequences of behavior—the ongoing interaction between activities and products. Quite another set of constructs has been proposed to deal with the way in which exploratory, attentional, or investigative behaviors are instigated. It is here that factors of affective arousal such as surprise or novelty (cf. Berlyne, 1960; Charlesworth, 1969) and notions such as violations of expectancies (Charlesworth, 1969) or discrepancies from established schemas (Kagan, 1968, 1969) are important. The overlapping ground among these proposals is that the state of the child—both his current situation and his developmental level—will determine to some extent the degree to which he will be "turned on" by environmental happenings.

The implications of motivational constructs which call on nondeficit conditions in the child to account for a heightening of his interest and point to behavior-linked conditions that maintain and direct this interest are important to day care in two respects. In the first place these motivational systems may not be able to operate when children are physically deprived or fearful. In the second place they may be overwhelmed by environments geared to external rewards and punishments. Hunt (1967b) has commented on the noticeable difference between school children governed by an external reinforcement system (i.e., in the form of tokens earned for school-valued performance) and children working for pleasure and satisfaction. The former group was preoccupied with the accumulation of tokens, whereas the latter group was fascinated by the material being studied.

The expectation of failure seems to inhibit independent problem-solving behavior, and the anticipation of success seems to promote such behavior (Turnure & Zigler, 1964). A child's criterion of mastery can be directly and explicitly determined by adults, by the child himself although transmitted by adults, or by the intrinsic satisfactions accomplishments offer. The child's interest in reading, for example, might be promoted by social approval, by the child's wish to do what adults do, or by the pleasure he derives from the rhythms of language or the contemplation of distant events. Some specialists have argued that it does not matter how the child arrives at a skill so long as he develops it (Bereiter, 1968; Bereiter & Engelmann, 1966). Others have expressed concern that skills initially supported by external rewards will fail to develop the internal supports needed for their continuation in later life (cf. Maccoby & Zellner, 1970). There may well be equally effective though different paths to the same ends. On the other hand, different paths might entail such radically different processes that the end results would be only superficially similar.

Programs that depend on surprise, novelty, and incongruity will need to consider the purpose and appeal of toys, materials, and projects that invite activity and participation. Programs that rely on external sources of reinforcement will have to consider the organization and systematic scheduling of reinforcements with respect to behaviors and the transition from external to internal supports. As goals and criteria are formulated in day-care programs, distinctions between different notions of what arouses and what maintains behavior must be appreciated.

PROBLEM SOLVING IN DAY-CARE SETTINGS

Between birth and 6 years of age the child develops an impressive theory of the world out of some small set of strategies which helps him to elaborate and extend early fragments of experience. How this happens has not been clearly explicated, yet certain general statements do emerge. Cognitive development is likely to be facilitated by an environment that offers challenges, that beckons and permits investigation, and that has sufficient variety, flexibility, and manipulability. Yet the sheer amount of variability in the world is probably not so important as the amount of variability in relation to the child's conceptual competence. The active child can be trusted to select much of what he needs—but only if the number of choices is not so overwhelming that he is always searching but never finding. Clearly, there is a delicate relationship between the problems available for solving—the problems that are developmentally essential to solve— and the individual child as he is at any moment in time. The child is not static nor is the environment most suitable for him. At the very least an appropriate material world requires adequate material resources from which to draw and the appropriate intervention of tuned-in adults.

We do not yet know much about the grand scheme, nor do we know about the kinds of problem children encounter as they progress through a rich and stimulating environment. Studies of the natural ecology of problems—that is, the kind and number of problems children find in various day-care settings—are long overdue. These studies are necessary if flexible and effective day-care environments are to be designed. Cognitive competence can be but partly represented by facts and well-established routines for arriving at correct answers. It also implies dealing with problems that have no obvious precedents, no clear external source of feedback, and no absolute solutions.

Systematic attempts to introduce specific concepts and to present specific problems can be part of a day-care program. Many effective programs have already been devised and evaluated (cf. Chapter 17). Structured materials, however, are likely to reach only a small part of the child's conceptual and problem-solving potential. The difficulty arises when we attempt to represent the child's current level of competence: our assessments too often examine only superficial features of performance. We tend to infer too much about too little from a small sample of tasks. When programs are geared to improve performance based on these indications of ability, the danger that children will be taught only a few production routines increases. If children can already deal with the concepts being taught, the program will be offering material that is too close to the child's current ability to produce significant cognitive change. On the other hand, if children are expected to deal with material that is too far ahead of their ability, they are likely to experience frequent failure that will discourage further efforts.

A substantial literature demonstrates that children growing up in physically and psychologically impoverished environments will obtain low scores on intelligence tests and show deficits in other areas of functioning. Clearly, not all poor performance in test situations reflects cognitive deficits. Affective, motivational, and stylistic factors, as well as matters of problem definition and comprehension, can produce behaviors that appear to be dysfunctional (Kagan & Kogan, 1970). Yet day-care planners would be safest to operate from the assumption that insufficient or inappropriate learning opportunities limit the ability of children to perform intellectual tasks.

In this chapter we have discussed some of the issues related to the cognitive development of children in day-care settings. We have explored the need for observation, problems in interpretation, and complications that develop in determining the objectives of planned programming. We have also indicated how natural developmental sequences and the child's status at any given time determine what he is capable of understanding. Issues of motivation and cognition also were discussed. The following suggestions summarize the implications of this discussion:

1. Child-care workers should have ample opportunity to observe children. Observations should be directed toward specific aspects of behavior and be used

in evaluating a child's abilities. Whenever possible, program planning should start from an appreciation of the abilities children already have.

2. Formal assessment is also necessary, especially if structured curriculum materials are to be used. One way of preventing structured materials from locking children into inappropriate levels of activity is to examine what they can do under the most favorable conditions, how they do it, and where the boundaries of their competence might be.

3. Every effort should be made to achieve a balance between activities that are structured and those that are open ended. The toys, materials, and activities in a day-care setting should invite exploration, manipulation, and engagement.

4. Careful attention must be given to limiting problems to those that children can solve, either on their own or with moderate guidance from adults. The adults who work with children must be able to share the pleasure children derive from the solution of these problems, even though they may not have high status in an adult system of values.

5. Consideration must be given to the role of adults in supporting children's behavior. Whether stress is placed on the intrinsic features of the environment or on the external systems of reinforcements, decisions of selection and modification must be made by those who work in child-care settings.

We would extend our image of the problem-solving child to include the problem-solving adult. If adults are to work effectively with children, they require an organized system of information and ways of defining problems, searching for problem-relevant procedures, and verifying hypotheses so that inaccurate information can be discarded and new theories can emerge Perhaps the first step in evolving a strategy for the training of caregivers is to comprehend in depth the theories they already possess and the operations and verification systems they already use.

8

The Changing Child

THE CHILD DESCRIBED IN CONTEXT II BECOMES ATTACHED TO
people—he plays, he speaks, and he thinks. These aspects are a part of his status
as a growing human being. By this we mean that there are universal characteristics of human development brought about by the interaction of species-specific
biological givens and environmental universals. Human beings construct cultures
that differ vastly in the way in which human capacities are valued and nurtured,
but the range of variation likely to appear is itself determined by combinations
of universal dimensions. Moreover, within each culture there are differences in
the extent to which individuals satisfy culturally defined expectations. Here, again,
it is not unreasonable to suppose that certain general principles of intracultural
variation are expressed in the course of human development.

Many of us have become so accustomed to reducing environments to the
technology of a managing and engineering world that we balk at concepts that
pose "natural" human environments. Obviously, cultures have ways of managing
children's development. Yet, although it is urgent to recognize humbly our own
culturally biased myopia, it would be equally myopic to refuse to recognize that
the range of variation present in human societies tells us something about the
constructive and adaptive propensities of the human species. To give but one
example from the material we have covered in preceding chapters, it is legitimate
to wonder whether a structured language-teaching program can simulate (or
substitute for) the central language problem posed for children in "natural"
environments. In our concluding discussion of the child we highlight briefly
some theoretical images of the changing child—images devised to capture universal principles of human development.

Of all the systems discussed, attachment has been most closely identified with theories of association which assume that the child changes as inherent drives find satisfaction and as secondary drives appear. The construct of dependency was developed within the context of this kind of formulation (Sears et al., 1957). Recent ethological positions have stressed the biological function of attachment behaviors in ensuring the infant's survival. By examining the activators and terminators of a behavioral system, ethological positions direct attention to events that control, elicit, and release the behaviors of both caregiver and child. The cries, smiles, vocalizations, and eye-to-eye contacts of the infant are seen as actively influencing the responses of those who are tuned into these behaviors by virtue of their biological heritage. It is only one step, but a giant theoretical step, from this position to the view that changes in attachment behavior depend on contingencies established between the responses of children and caregivers. Within a contingency system, the child is credited with the power to reinforce caregiving behavior and thus, in part, to determine his own social development (R. Bell, 1971; Gewirtz, 1969).

But the child not only responds to, modifies, and invests feelings in social objects, he also acquires a large and complex array of social behaviors with surprising rapidity and efficiency. Features of the behavior of others, their social roles, language, social styles, and preferences, appear in the child's behavior with a veridicality that boggles any simple-minded rules of change. In particular, learning theories, which generally tend to be tied to responses already acquired by the child, have difficulty coping with the dramatic and sudden expansions of his social repertoire. One solution to this dilemma is to introduce a new process of change to those already elaborated by the theory. Several theorists in the associationist tradition have introduced imitation as a mechanism by which novel, complex behaviors can be readily acquired (Bandura, 1967; Miller & Dollard, 1941).

Imitation is generally recognized as an important phenomenon of childhood. A substantial body of research demonstrates the effectiveness of modeling in promoting aggression (Bandura, 1967), language (Bandura & Harris, 1966; Cazden, 1966), moral judgment (Bandura & McDonald, 1963), and choice behavior (Turnure & Zigler, 1964). Children constantly pick up substantial chunks of behavior simply by watching others. Inevitably it will reflect the behavior of those seen on television (Eron, Huesman, Lefkowitz, & Walder, 1972), in school, on the street, and at home.

As the focus moves from clearly social areas to language, play, and cognition, the role of social agents diminishes. For some aspects of language a speaking model alone may not be sufficient. The child acquires a meaning system that reflects his conceptions of objects and of how words are used in relation to them and to social situations.

In general, cogntive-developmental formulations view the child as progressing through a series of successive structural organizations. Heretofore these theories have been more adept at describing the organizations than at describing how they change. The work of Piaget has contributed to a uniquely cognitive, structure-based statement of change. In this view change occurs when there is a discrepancy between the child's scheme for organizing incoming information and properties of objects that resist organization. One way the child deals with discrepancy is by revising and changing the scheme. Another way is by avoiding, dismissing, or withdrawing from the noncomprehensible information. Cognitive theorists have proposed that the latter occurs when discrepancies are too large. The child will ignore or withdraw from whatever has no meaning or drastically violates the meaning he has constructed. On the other hand, when information bears some formal similarity to what is already understandable, the child will initiate transactions directed toward assimilation. These transactions are assumed to be inherently pleasurable, and the reduction of discrepancy that results is assumed to be intrinsically reinforcing (Hunt, 1964b, 1966).

Views of cognitive change and reinforcement methods might be compatible to the extent that the emphasis of cognitive theories on the active engagement of the child with people and objects is supported by reinforcement contingencies which promote that end. The stance taken by reinforcement theorists is "specify what you want the child to do and we'll increase the likelihood that he will do it." In contrast, the stance of a cognitive-developmental approach is "if you want the child to achieve mature conceptual forms, here are the things he ought to be doing."

Caregivers contribute to cognitive change when they mediate between the child and new information. Adults who are tuned to the quality of the child's thought are able to offer him an array of "opportunities" for activity and engagement based on an accurate appraisal of his current status. The task of appraisal places heavy demands on caregivers in several respects. The task is to view the child's transactions with the world as informal test situations which provide clues to his organization of knowledge. In these test situations errors can be as revealing as responses that conform to adult standards. In addition, caregivers need to have at their disposal a set of materials, activities, and possible "experiences" that can be matched to the level of the child's ability. A curriculum is just such a set of experiences, developed for adults who work with children. This curriculum contrasts markedly with the collection of "gifts" and "opportunities" prescribed by Froebel or with the specific skills taught by highly structured programs. Froebel presented an invariant and restricted sequence fitted to a conception of the child's mind as static, preformed, and lacking sense-making, change-inducing rules. Contemporary programs are more sophisticated and quite effective within the range of objectives they project. Yet the cognitive child described in incongruity, complexity, and discrepancy theories needs more room than this to grow in.

Perhaps the most powerful change-inducing rule that a cognitive theory based on discrepancy could attribute to children is the ability to create discrepancy rather than merely to respond to whatever happens along. This function is a crucial change mechanism, any ability of the child to create discrepancy locates within him a change process of vast potential significance. A new complication is added to the role of caregiver. The challenge is to provide the child with techniques and opportunities to manipulate symbolic transformations of objects and relationships and the themes or contents that add variety to these manipulations.

Today's pendulum is well to the left of maturational theories of development. Yet it seems clear that some form of maturational statement is called for. The error of the past was one of suggesting that maturation was itself an adequate explanation. On the contemporary scene there are serious attempts to formulate a theory of maturation that will identify genetic processes such as "thresholds," "mutations," or systematic stresses that appear during the life-span. Borrowing from biological theory, Riegel (1966) has offered the notion of ontogenetic mutations as a model of language development, that is, changes brought about in the genetic code as a function of age changes in thresholds. McNeill (1970) poses a similar mechanism when he suggests that the child progresses from a sentence dictionary to a word dictionary. In this scheme the change occurs when the processing and storage capacity of the sentence dictionary is overloaded and when the child has reached a level of biological maturity that makes another kind of organizing principle possible. Some maturational formulation seems necessary to account for the sudden dramatic changes that occur during a person's lifetime. There is, however, a crucial difference between maturation used globally to "explain" development and a set of constructs that illuminates maturational processes.

All that is known about children suggests that they are remarkably robust. They can survive enormous deprivation and environmental press (Freud & Dann, 1951; Skeels & Dye, 1939). The settings in which children live and the potentials they bring to them become increasingly important as society demands more than that they merely survive. These factors become paramount when the community elevates the value of human capacities to conserve the past, to formulate plans for change, and to revise those plans when outcomes are unsatisfactory. Such capacities become increasingly important in the management of daily living in a complex, rapidly changing society.

Children have become recognized as active agents in the modification of social and interpersonal relations and as active seekers of knowledge and understanding. Whether these capacities will be inundated by fear of failure, anger, and apathy or whether they will develop the refinements and selectivity necessary for problem solving in complex situations depends on three consequential factors which need to be considered in future plans for child-development research and day-care programs. The first is the evolution of more elegant and sophisticated theories of development supported by the analysis and specification of major environmental variables. But research and theory have not, nor will they ever, provide infallible guides to child care and educational practice. The best they can do is to carve out some of the possible pathways, relevant dimensions, alternative strategies, and likely consequences.

The second factor is the dissemination of current knowledge to those engaged in the child-care enterprise. It will always be up to those who rear and educate children to choose wisely and discriminatingly among several alternatives.

The third factor is the design of applications. Programs can attempt to capture the essence of one or another developmental theory and call on the best of the available evidence to generate formulas in support of program practices. In the transition from theory and hard research to action much more must be known about the natural organization and distribution of crucial developmental variables. Who speaks to children, when, how, and under what circumstances? How are natural adult teaching styles distributed among siblings, peers, parents, and professional child-care workers? What are the problems posed by those who care for children and what solutions will they accept?

Information of this kind seems essential if the gaps between the child, the family, and extrafamilial child-care institutions are to be bridged. Theories of application are strategies for arranging caregiving ecologies so that they will maximize the occurrence of variables crucial to the child's development. Features of natural ecologies can be selectively provided, that is, manipulated, in the best tradition of research design and implementation.

Perhaps the first step of a maturing science, a maturing pedagogy, and a maturing movement for social reconstruction is the identification of the uncertain, an openness to alternative procedures, and a willingness to inquire about relative effectiveness. Surely such a spirit will reflect and be reflected in a view of the child as on open-ended, inquiring, and experimenting organism capable of both impressing and distressing those who know him well.

CONTEXT III

THE FAMILY

9

Perspectives

BEYOND THEIR MORE OBVIOUS RELATIONSHIPS TO CHILD DE-
velopment, issues in day-care are also inextricably linked to fundamental questions
regarding the role and function of the family. Historically, day care has been
perceived alternately as a cure and a cause of family disruption; politically,
legislation has often floundered on the respective powers of family, church, and
state; professionally, day care has uncomfortably occupied an ill-defined position
midway between the family social worker and the educator. Too often the family
enters discussions of day care in a loose, polemical, or sentimental way to be
disparaged or eulogized or to be posed as an alternative to day care rather than
as part of its definition. The concept of day care we are proposing in this book,
which focuses on the child's interacting with his environment, makes necessary
a rational assessment of family roles, functions, and structures. This assessment
can be discussed from three points of view: day-care models, factors influencing
development, and dimensions of diversity among American families.

DAY-CARE MODELS

Central to our discussion of family structures and functions is the assumption
that diverse and innovative day-care models can emerge from an appreciation of
family variability. In advocating diversity in day care, we do not mean a set
of nonoverlapping and isolated institutions; rather we are referring to a range of
structural and functional variations in day-care resources and allied services.

   For example, let us suppose that a substantial number of children have
large families whose members live in the same neighborhood. Indeed, census

surveys suggest that the children of working mothers are often cared for in the homes of nearby relatives. We might generate models of day care that are based on the assumption that this type of arrangement, either now or in the future, might be desired by parents and might be advantageous for children. We might even go so far as to assume that parents who have no local kin (such as the isolated nuclear family) might prefer an arrangement with similar characteristics, (i.e., informality, nearness). Again the data suggest that parents often seek these arrangements because of their advantages rather than as an undesirable alternative to centers. Two issues arise: (a) how can various caregiving arrangements be compared and (b) how can supportive day-care models be generated?

At least two dimensions of comparison emerge from developmental studies: continuity over a lifetime and continuity from one situation to another. From the child's point of view his contact with a relative is likely to persist over time even if the arrangement itself is terminated, whereas continuity is less likely when the caregiver is not related. The mothers interviewed by Willner (1966) often reported that in informal day-care arrangements friendships between themselves and caregivers continued even though the arrangement was terminated. If, however, we use a scale of lifetime continuity, a kinship arrangement would generally rate higher on this dimension than an arrangement with a friend, neighbor, or institution.

Situationally, arrangements with relatives and neighbors are likely to be quite similar to one another, and to the child's own home (in contrast to "center" care). They are also likely to be similarly impoverished or similarly enriched. It is exactly here that a day-care *model* differs dramatically from a *natural* form of day care. Models devised to accommodate naturally occurring forms can concurrently match and enrich; for example, funds (through loans or grants) could be provided to day-care mothers and to families for educational materials or for child-related home improvements (e.g., a safe, attractive, outdoor play space). A special service "center" for these families might offer child-development programs such as part-time preschools, adult education, health care, a source of qualified "substitutes" when caregivers are unavailable, a toy library—the possibilities are unlimited.

Interesting possibilities also arise when we consider family functions; for example, the census data suggest that fathers often care for the children when mothers work. Again we might consider day-care models that support these kinds of parental sharing and that support fathers in a caregiving role. Cooperative nurseries might encourage volunteer parent services in exchange for concentrated educational and group experiences for the children on a two-or-three-day-a-week basis.

Innumerable programming possibilities suggest themselves, yet continuity need not be a criterion in their development. Centers, by their very form and organization, maximize discontinuity, and if discontinuity is deemed desirable (if, for instance, parents want day-care programs that resemble the school rather than the home), day-care centers could serve that function. Traditionally, center programs have tried to establish at least some minimal continuity between the child's life at home and at the center by encouraging parental participation. Such participation has for the most part, though, been difficult to achieve. Participation requires time, and working parents have little time to give. Staff members rarely live in the child's neighborhood; centers are closed on weekends, and there is little opportunity for informal visiting or social exchange among adults. Even when parents are included on the board of directors, it is questionable whether they are "participating." Many of the factors that vitally influence the lives of the children appear at the level of daily implementation, several levels and many options removed from the policy-making group. The problem is clear: parental participation is, at the outset, bounded by the structure of a day-care service. The form and potential of program components inevitably are constrained by the framework in which they occur.

FACTORS INFLUENCING DEVELOPMENT

A second assumption behind our discussion of the family is that studies of the family offer clues to the attitudinal, physical, and interpersonal variables that optimize children's development. Much of our knowledge of child rearing comes from these studies. We know that a child's behavior and development are influenced by his contacts with his physical, social, and cultural environment. We also know that the family is the provider and mediator of much of this environment. The family contributes a physical setting for the child (including toys, games, and playmates) as well as love and approval, experience in living with people, language models, and living habits (Bossard, 1948). Clearly, the family has an immense effect on the child's cognitive development (Hess, 1969) and on his achievement in school (Coleman, 1961b) and is at least partly responsible, as well, for his emotional development and social competence. Details of how particular aspects of family life influence the development of children are indispensable in designing programs for their care, for although these variables are extracted from study of the family they are likely to generalize to other settings. To illustrate, the importance of toys and physical materials in a day-care center is likely to be equivalent to that which has been discovered in the home. Teachers and caregivers in a day-care setting share many characteristics and roles with mothers, fathers, and other relatives. Generalizations about favorable adult:child ratios, applicable to day-care personnel, may be formed on the basis of observations of different sized families. The influence of older siblings can be useful in considering a policy of heterogeneous grouping in an early education program, if not throughout the child's entire school career.

A substantial part of the literature that illuminates the influence of family factors on the development of children is based on social-class comparisons. By and large, studies of social-class differences indicate that on measures of intellectual and verbal performance, on indices of motivation, self-esteem, school achievement, and so on, affluent children do better than poor children. In order to place these studies in perspective, it is necessary to recognize that those who design assessment procedures and thereby define the human qualities worthy of consideration, continuously and unavoidably introduce their own values and viewpoints. Of necessity, abstract conceptualizations of human competencies are expressed in particular tasks, materials, and instructions in the context of specific situations. Weaving ubiquitously throughout the process, from conceptualization to implementation, are ample occasions for the introduction of biases—middle-class, cultural, personal, theoretical, and historical biases. The arguments of Labov (1970) and others with respect to language apply to the many variables that have entered into social-class comparisons: variables represent conceptualizations of the world constructed from experience; they are operationalized via situations; situations mean different things and call forth different behaviors in different people. Soon we find ourselves in a conceptual corner. On the one hand we become deeply committed to the a priori assumption that there *are* social-class differences, and on the other we come perilously close to affirming that anyone who conceptualizes and operationalizes these differences is, by occupational definition, bound to introduce a negative bias. By what rational process, then, can we reach some consensus about "reality"?

Obviously the problem is easier to pose than resolve. There are at least three minimal conditions for the survival of a "reality-seeking" enterprise: (a) that biases be acknowledged and clarified, (b) that schemes for contrasting biases, for sharpening and summarizing distinctions, be formulated, and (c) that there be an agreed-on procedure for verifying the implications of biases. When these conditions are absent, there is little basis for adjudicating alternative constructions of reality.

From the viewpoint of day care social class is an exceedingly peculiar variable. Social mobility in the United States has endowed a substantial segment of today's middle class with a working-class background. Day care in the last century focused on the poor Irish, Jewish, Italian, Polish, or Swedish immigrant whose grandchildren are among today's affluent. In examining social-class differences, it is necessary to ask how easily people shed the burden of poverty. If social values change over generations, how much does the change cost in terms of intellectual and emotional functioning? Although ready to dismiss the "melting pot" as an American fantasy, we may, in reaction to the apparent unfairness of the biases in social science research, too readily create a parallel fantasy—that social classes do not differ, that differences do not reflect or influence people's capacity to function, or that the ways in which people differ are trivial when compared with the ways in which they are similar.

We can consider the possibility that the competencies required for optimal functioning are not the same for all eras and societies and, within specific societies, for all situations. Although the ability to gather and use information can be thought of as a general capacity required in all life situations, effective strategies change as problems change. The problems of the hunter are not the same as those of the farmer; successful strategies for the baker might not work for the plumber. Problems change with changes in tools and materials, with changes in the organizational structure of society (e.g., raising food for a family is not equivalent to feeding a city), and with changes in task requirements (listening to a story is not the same as writing one).

The notion of "effective" child-rearing practices always contains assumptions about utility, that is, about the competencies needed to deal with a "real" world, however that may be conceived. Quite different child-rearing practices may be "effective" when the poor and the foreign within a technological society are expected to make it on their own than are "effective" when the community affirms a willingness to supply helpful resources. Although attachment to other human beings can be thought of as a necessary component of emotional and social well-being, one kind of attachment relationship might be needed when the world beyond is truly dangerous and hostile and quite another when that world glitters benignly with useful information and unlimited opportunity. Day-care programs are most likely to be challenged when they project a "reality" too discrepant from the world comprehended by the families they serve.

The "utility" assumptions underlying the many measures used to study the family—parents and children—are not always clear. Although a substantial quantity of data is available, the data require more critical analysis than they have received and more than we can accomplish in the following discussion, if the kinds of competencies that may have been assessed are to be classified. Investigators (cf. Hess, 1969) have used a variety of methods (ranging from naturalistic observations to laboratory studies) to study a number of different tasks in various settings. In our report of findings we indicate the kind of competence index used (e.g., IQ, school achievement, self-esteem) by the investigator, even though we may not necessarily concur with his choice or with his measurement procedures. Occasionally we indicate our reservations about the generality of the conclusions drawn from these studies primarily to illustrate the types of issue that might be raised throughout the research.

An examination of the literature suggests that many of the variables associated with effective parental functioning appear even when social class itself is *not* an issue. Social class is a gross category; within social-class groups there is enormous variation; middle-class children can fail and poor children can succeed. Affluence is not a precondition for effective functioning and poverty is not a precondition for failure.

One inescapable difficulty in interpreting research dealing with family variables is a result of the correlational nature of this research. Correlations merely reveal factors that "go together" in some way. In the natural world factors do cluster, but not every factor in a cluster plays a role in determining the outcome; for example, family size and the absence of the father are related to poor performance levels on standard tests and various other indices of adjustment and achievement. Both factors, however, are also related to the economic security and well-being of families. Teasing apart these factors is a major challenge for research, one that often poses overwhelming methodological problems; for example, if poor families are more likely than wealthy families to rear children born out of wedlock, it may be extraordinarily difficult to find a sample of family-reared, father-absent children that does not contain a disproportionate number of poor children. The problem of conceptualizing population characteristics is awesome. In the case of "father-absence," how should the presence of other males in the household (uncles, grandfathers, teenage brothers) be evaluated? What about the working hours of "father-present" groups? Should we develop a special category for fathers who rarely see their children? These and other pertinent questions have not been posed. The current status of research in this area must be seen in the light of what has been ignored.

Our confidence in research findings increases when different projects in different parts of the country, using different sampling techniques, measurement instruments, and theoretical perspectives, report similar results. Although the replicability of phenomena does not provide a guide for interpretation, it does draw attention to phenomena which merit further analysis. With respect to day care, it reveals issues that require care and caution.

DIMENSIONS OF DIVERSITY

It is not uncommon today for day-care planners to advise respect for the life style, attitudes, and values of families. Often, however, the substance of diversity is not specified. The question, "How different *are* families of different ethnic or economic subcultures?" is often addressed, when a more productive question might be, "*How* are they different?"

As we indicated earlier, the attempt to specify dimensions of difference frequently leads to social-class comparisons, and typically these comparisons are accompanied by evidence of a poor prognosis for lower-class children. At this point planners are faced with a painful policy issue: can a responsible program establish practices that conform to parental practices but provide a less than optimal environment for children, as our current knowledge would define such an environment? This question appears most often when programs develop educational plans and formulate strategies for discipline and control. It is for this reason that a hard look at the evidence—its implications and limitations—is essential, even at the risk of seeming to promote social-class stereotypes. To the degree that American families differ profoundly in their values, attitudes, and child-rearing practices, and to the degree that these differences reflect socio-economic stratifications, the achievement of social integration will require careful thought and preparation. In the following examination of diversity among families we are trying to answer questions of vital relevance for day-care planning:

1. What are the functions of families in American society and how can day care optimize the capacity of the family to fulfill these roles?

2. What are the structures of American families and how can day-care programs respect and build on these structures?

3. What are the physical environments of children and how do they enhance or depress development?

4. What are the values, attitudes, and goals of parents in regard to children and their education? How can day-care programs satisfy their hopes and aspirations?

5. What can day-care planners learn from examining different methods of child rearing used in American homes?

6. What universal dimensions of caregiving are illustrated in the behaviors of mothers toward their own offspring and how may such dimensions be applied to broader day-care arrangements for children?

10

Forces Affecting Family Functions and Structure

ACCORDING TO THE "ORTHODOX" POSITION OCCUPIED BY SOCI-
ologists in recent decades, the family has experienced a great erosion of functions
as a result of the demands placed on it by the urban and industrial way of life
(Kay, 1965; Smelser, 1965). Smelser describes the typical argument associated
with this position as unfolding in three phases. The first involves an image of a
"traditional" family (a "farm family" or a "frontier family," perhaps). This
image, he alleges, is often romanticized; it is rarely documented by historical research. The traditional family is viewed as having been economically self-sufficient,
embedded in a network of extended kinship ties, and under the inescapable
authority of the father. It provided status, economic support, education, religion,
recreation, protection, and affection (Ogburn, 1953; Kay, 1965).

The second phase involves some sort of "shock" imparted to this traditional
family by the development of a commercial-market structure, by the development
of industry, or by the development of cities—usually a combination of all three.
The effects of this shock have been to draw one or more family members into
the labor force, to make the family more socially and geographically mobile, and
to place the family in an anonymous social environment.

The third phase of the argument involves the image of the "modern" family
that emerges after the shock. The most fundamental of these changes—imposed
mainly by the demands for mobility—is the individuation and isolation of the
nuclear family. The extended kinship group has been replaced by the nuclear
family. No longer do three generations live and work together; families are now
two-generation affairs. Concurrently, average family size has decreased from the

150

"traditional" 12, with 66 sets of personal relationships, to a "modern" four with only six sets (Bossard, 1948). Simultaneously, the relations between parents and children have undergone a vast transformation. The father who now has to leave the household for employment in a separate establishment loses many of the economic-training and supervisory functions he previously enjoyed with his children. Often, Smelser claims, this decline in economic authority is thought to have spread to a decline in general authority. The former relations of distance and respect between father and child have now become relations of intimacy, affection, and equality. The mother has become the crucial agent in early socialization.

Nevertheless, in spite of the concentrated relations between mother and children in the early years, this period is short-lived. The nuclear family in an urban-industrial environment loses control of its children very early to educational institutions and the peer group and, eventually, permanently to the labor market.

> Scholars and the general public alike tend to view such trends with apprehension and dismay. The loss of parental control, one hears, threatens the moral fiber of the society. To this loss of authority, one also hears, it is possible to assign much responsibility for social evils such as delinquency, illegitimacy, teen-age drinking (or, more currently, drug abuse), school dropouts, and so on. Behind such claims, one suspects, lies a sort of diffuse fear that as a society we are "losing control" of the dangerous explosive forces of childhood and raw youth (Smelser, 1965, p. 69).

Having expounded this orthodox viewpoint, however, Smelser proposes a re-examination of this supposed trend in the family role. He advises caution in accepting any pronouncement of the precipitous decline of parental authority—a symptom he claims is typical of periods of many types of social change, not merely of social decline. He illustrates his caution with a citation from "the most famous observer of our society":

> The distance which formerly separated a father from his sons has been lessened; and paternal authority, if not destroyed, is at least impaired . . . . The relation of father and son becomes more intimate and more affectionate; rules and authority are less talked of. . . .

This from the pen of Alexis de Tocqueville in 1832.

Smelser suggests four related but distinct trends in modern social authority over children and youth. Together they do not add up to a general decline of parental authority but rather to a much more complicated picture. His discussion has great relevance for the issues of day care.

The first trend Smelser describes is indeed a relative decline in some aspects of parental authority. The clearest example is the decline in parent's economic training and control functions. Educational institutions and training programs have assumed this aspect of the parental role.

A second, concomitant trend, however, is the relative increase in other aspects of the authority of parents, particularly during the first two to four years of the child's life. The modern parent probably has more exclusive guardianship —hence more authority—over children in these years than in the past, when the extended family, the neighborhood, and the community figured more prominently in infant care. The modern child, being less surrounded on an everyday basis by uncles, aunts, adult neighbors, and domestic servants, probably relies more exclusively than before on its parents as authority models.

Smelser's third trend of authority over children is that more in an absolute sense is being demanded of children. Before the development of a formal educational system the child probably received little training in literacy. With the development of educational institutions, however, a new authority—control over the acquisition of reading and writing skills—has been imposed on the child. Such a development means more than the family now sharing what it formerly controlled exclusively; it means a new type of authority has emerged. In the future, as technology and specialization increase and are transmitted primarily in the schools, one might perhaps expect that this authority will increase its domain, diminishing further the authority of parents and leading to an even greater experiential chasm between parent and child.

A fourth related trend is the dispersion of authority over children. After the child's first few years of intensified and concentrated relations with its parents, a time period that is being increasingly shortened by the current emphasis on earlier and earlier "formal" education or institutional care, the child moves into contact with an ever-widening range of authorities: the baby sitter, the nursery school teacher, followed by a complex of teachers, den mothers, scoutmasters, camp counselors, church youth-group leaders, and peer-group leaders. Not only are more skills and roles being demanded of the young but a greater variety of persons and agencies are doing the demanding.

Smelser concludes that, taking these trends together, the challenge to the family in modern times seems less the decline of parental authority than the possible *discontinuity* between the various types of authority imposed on the child. This challenge, we assert, is not only of concern to the family but represents a fundamental issue which must be considered in planning for day care. Smelser concludes that as society becomes more complex, heterogeneous, and mobile the main social problem becomes not so much the absolute amount of parental authority but the relations between parents and other authorities.

Smelser, of course, has dealt largely with the trends and concerns of the American middle-class family. For the children of lower- or working-class families discontinuity is even more likely. Besides industrialization and urbanization, three other types of movement have had a special impact on roles in these families: immigration, migration, and social mobility. The trend over the years has been for black Americans to migrate from the South to northern industrial cities and for Indians to migrate from their noncompetitive societies to fast-paced cities in the West. Mexicans and Puerto Ricans have made a double leap from countries with different languages and cultures and from agrarian to industrial economies (Herzog, 1967). Concurrently, there has been a tendency for individuals to move socially—usually upward under the aegis of education—from positions of their parents in the stratification system.

These three movements—cultural, economic, and social—have had tremendous impact both on the particular families concerned and on American society as a whole. They have created immediate problems of economic, social, and psychological adjustment for adults and children alike. Adults tend to be influenced by the traditions of their own culture, whereas children are more receptive to the culture of their new setting. Migration and immigration have aggravated threats of discontinuity for the child, since the authority structure, values, and attitudes of these families, on whom demands have been imposed by predominantly native American teachers, employers, and other authorities, have been discontinuous in varying degree. Similarly, the socially mobile individual is likely to experience standards of authority very different from those of his origin. As a result of these movements, there has been a growing diversity in the mainstream culture and closer contact between people of different beliefs, behaviors, and family structures. Although social-class characterizations are becoming increasingly difficult to make, differences between the middle class and the "culture of poverty" are inescapable and must be incorporated into any programs of child care proposed.

Another tragic by-product of migration and immigration has been the unemployment and poverty that almost invariably accompany such change. Since such moves are made most frequently by young adults, the problem is especially one for families with young children. It is an unfortunate fact that 48% of nonwhite families with children under 18 are poor (Herzog, 1967). Unemployment is particularly common among young male migrants, and it peaks just at the age when they are likely to be fathers of young children. It is much easier for an uneducated female to get a job, albeit menial (Herzog, 1967), and this creates another problem: working mothers of young children.

To be sure, day care does not provide a balm for poverty and unemployment. It can, however, relieve some of the pressures by providing mothers who must work with adequate care for their children and by assisting in the acculturation process by helping both adults and children to learn the new language. It is, however, of the utmost importance that all day-care services and early education programs *respect* the diverse cultural backgrounds these families represent, even while they are offering entrance into the mainstream of American culture. To do otherwise is to aggravate the conditions of change for both parents and children.

Industrialization and urbanization have created stresses on the family far beyond those discussed by Smelser. Urbanization has generally reduced the physical domain of the family; the world of the child has become his apartment or his block. In rural areas the child was or is cared for by the community (Hunt, 1967b); but, ironically, although there are many more people to be met in cities, there are fewer opportunities for meaningful *human* contacts between individuals (Bronfenbrenner, 1969). This is true for adults and for children. It is a problem that could be alleviated by careful planning of child-development programs to include meaningful participation by adults and children.

By creating a densely populated environment urbanization and centralization have also made necessary a certain minimal level of conformity to social norms. It has made the rights of the individual versus society an increasingly complex and crucial question (Chilman, 1966). One technique for achieving the conformity which seems necessary may be group settings for child raising. What is needed in our urban society, however, is an awareness and consideration of the feelings of diverse others—not blind conformity to social norms. This can be achieved in a day-care setting only if day-care personnel themselves respect and take into account the diversity with which they are confronted. The need for intimate, interactive relations between day care and the family is apparent.

Two final pressures which have influenced the family's role in the socialization of its children should also be mentioned. One is the force created by "expert opinion"—specifically about child rearing and the role of parents. The impact of expert opinion in the past has been mentioned in Context I of this book. One quite recent effect was the increase in permissiveness which released the child from strict parental control. This trend peaked in the 1950's. Now, since expert opinion is even more available—even though often controversial—and is made salient by the mass media, it may well become more influential.

One current theme revived from the past focuses on the incompetence of parents—particularly lower-class parents—to raise their children, a criticism coupled today with excessive demands for competence among parents and children. The family is no longer held responsible merely for the moral, social, and emotional development of its children. Now, with the spotlight on the inferior school performance of ghetto children, the role of the family in promoting the child's intellectual development and his motivation to succeed is receiving attention as well. Certainly such criticism has not increased the confidence of parents in their own abilities and may be, in part, responsible for their increasing willingness to relegate child care to the institutions of the establishment. Only recently has there appeared in the literature the hint of a balancing force of acceptance of the child-rearing methods of the poor and the black (Baratz & Baratz, 1969; Young, 1970).

Yet, whether these families are seen as deficient, damaging, or even just different, they are still generally considered depriving (Hess, 1969).

The last force on the family to be mentioned here emerges from the growing attention of social and political groups to day care. Women's groups, for example, have challenged the rigid sex-role structures present in American society and represented within the modern American family. Whether these proposals for day care emphasize communal child rearing or "universal child care for all children 24 hours a day" (e.g., Yale Day Care Committee Report, 1970), a change in the child-rearing functions of families is often implied, even though the elimination of role differences and inequities is their major target. At least two related questions might be considered. Are rigid role structures a necessary part of family life? Do day-care services necessarily eliminate them? Eastern European observers have noted that although working mothers become less occupied in caregiving activities, they typically retain major responsibilities for other housekeeping chores. The sex-typed role of the woman thus would remain unchanged, but a potentially rewarding part of it has been passed on to others—typically women.

The care of the children of working mothers may not be an issue around which the role of women can be redefined. This issue concerns an exceedingly narrow sphere of equalization (employment) and accepts what might be a most damaging source of inequity, that is, the notion that socially useful employment is that for which contemporary society provides monetary rewards, power, and status. Such an assessment of social usefulness is quite consistent with contemporary political realities; although often romanticized, the child-rearing enterprise has yet to become a high national priority. A national basis for role redefinition may require a focus on the dynamics of child rearing *in* the home in which attention is given to the roles of all adults in the family, and in which program design is aimed at enhancing the contribution of these adults to a better life for children.

This discussion of the role of the family in present-day America leads to a compelling conclusion. The family is having a difficult time. Not only is more being demanded of children, but more is being demanded of parents (Parsons, 1965). Lower-class families are condemned as ineffective (Hess, 1969); middle-class—"democratic"—families are as often blamed as praised for reducing the role of parental authority, thereby increasing the child's susceptibility to the social environment of his extrafamilial peers and insulating him from adult traditions (Bennis & Slater, 1968). There is pressure from many directions to abandon traditional family roles and turn child raising over to day-care institutions.

In the face of these mounting pressures we cry "Wait!" There is no evidence that the solution to the problems of the family lies in group care of children per se. Certainly the stresses now confronting public education provide no support for this conclusion. One should examine completely the potential strengths of families before disparaging, abandoning, or replacing them. We must differentiate clearly between diversity of culture and deficiencies in competence. Interventions should be accommodated to families as they are and to cultural and philosophical differences as they exist. The family today may not be rich or strong or stimulating enough to provide an optimal environment for a child's development. Yet a reasonable solution may be to help it, not destroy it.

11

Diversity in Family
Functions and Structure

DIFFERENCES BETWEEN FAMILIES IN AMERICA ARE CONSIDERED
here in the framework of social class or ethnic membership only because in the
past researchers have almost invariably investigated differences according to such
classifications. Class divisions are not fixed, determinative, or invariable; they
merely provide statements of probability that a given type of behavior is likely.
Change over time, mobility within classes, and individual variation within groups
all lead to considerable variability. Reliable data on which to base conclusions
and programs can come only from direct observation of the particular sample
of families with which one is concerned.

Included in the discussion of family differences that follows are research
findings related to the apparent influence of certain family variables on the child.
It is important to note at the outset that this influence is not unidirectional.
The parent or physical setting is only one side of an interaction with the child's
innate predispositions and natural tendencies. It is always difficult and frequently
impossible to assign a causal direction to these parent-child relationships.

The Moynihan Report (1965) outlines and documents the prevalence of
"problems"—broken marriages, female-headed families, large families, illegitimate
births, dependence on public assistance—among the blacks, the poor, and in the
cities. Families seem to be suddenly "crumbling" at a disastrous rate. Yet not
everyone agrees with this conclusion (Chilman, 1966; Herzog, 1967). In fact,
the increase in broken homes has not been acute over the last 25 years, but instead there has been a gradual, wavering rise. Although divorces have become
more common in the lower class, Peterson (1965) suggests that they may occur

only because of an increased use of legal facilities. He further indicates the possibility that a rising divorce rate may represent a more law-abiding population. Whereas, previously, disruption would have been accomplished by separation or desertion, today it is accomplished by legal means. Similarly, the rate of illegitimacy has been rising steadily; there has been no sudden upsurge (Chilman, 1966; Herzog, 1967). Indeed *some* families—the "hard-core poor"—are frequently dysfunctional, disorganized, and pathological (Lewis, 1965; Pavenstedt, 1965), but they are only a small minority. Most lower-class families fall within the range of normal functioning, and it is with these "normal" families that we concern ourselves.

Gans (1967) states that social-class differences reflect responses that people make to the opportunities, incentives, rewards, deprivation, prohibitions, and pressures they encounter in society and the natural environment. The task of the lower class is to evolve a way of life that will reduce insecurity and enhance power (Cohen & Hodges, 1963); the structure of the lower-class family reflects this attempt.

The lower-class, particularly the urban, black family, is characteristically female-based, with a "marginal" male who is not always present or dominant (Lewis in Herzog, 1967; Moynihan, 1965) and who has little to do with child rearing (Cohen & Hodges, 1963). Parental sex roles in lower-class families are apparently segregated (Gans, 1967), although it is interesting that black mothers report more joint decision making than whites (Ruderman, 1968).

Research indicates that the absence of a father-figure in the home may not only affect the behavior of the child directly but may also influence the mother in the direction of overprotectiveness (Bronfenbrenner, 1961). These influences are often associated with problems for the children, particularly boys, of motivation, self-esteem, susceptibility to group influence (Bronfenbrenner, 1970), sex-role identity, need gratification (John, 1964a), independence, and assertiveness (Bronfenbrenner, 1961). However, Chilman (1966) suggests that social development in families in which parents are in conflict may be worse than in a fatherless home. There does appear to be consensus that a *harmonious* two-parent home is better for children—and parents—than a one-parent home (Herzog, 1967).

The data are far from complete: parents divorce and remarry, fathers leave and return, children are exposed to these disruptions at different ages, and a variety of social and emotional supports may or may not be available. Studies that examine the finer details of disruption and adjustment and move on to examine more carefully the contribution of fathers to the development of children are needed.

A second characteristic of the lower-class family is its tendency to be larger than families of other social classes. According to the Department of Labor Statistics, large families are 24% poorer than small families. Large family size, too, tends to be detrimental to the child's development, especially when it is confounded with poverty. Among the poor the children of large families have been found to be lower in reading achievement (Whiteman & Deutsch, 1968). In Head Start programs psychiatrists have observed that the more frequently a family has moved, and the larger the number of siblings in it, the more likely it is that the young child will be "disturbed." It is pertinent to record, however, that 75% of the Head Start children examined (all from poor families) were within normal psychic and developmental limits (Hotkins, Hollander, & Munk, 1968). The extensive literature on birth-order effects is also relevant here. This literature indicates that younger siblings are often inferior to first-borns in achievement, language development, and intellectual endeavors (e.g., Jensen, 1968; John, 1964a).

In our discussion of social-class diversity it is important to note once more that there are, as well, *intraclass* differences between families which raise methodological issues beyond that of the possible middle-class or cultural biases of assessment instruments. If we propose to treat behavior as a joint function of situations and capacities, and if it is capacities which we wish to assess, conclusions based on narrow and limited assessment formats are open to question (Cole, Gay, Glick, & Sharp, 1971). Accurate assessment is not the only issue. When we find that the younger children of large poor families perform poorly in a variety of assessment situations and we fail to pose a critical intermediate question, we find ourselves lacking a necessary basis for the development of day-care programs. We are left knowing what children *cannot* do in various situations, but we know nothing about what they *can* do in other situations; we know something about deficits but nothing about strengths. The penalty of partial data is that they deprive educational planners of clues to the kinds of situations that encourage optimal functioning. As long as children function at a less than optimal level, planning for their continued growth is futile. More comprehensive data might indicate, for example, that the later borns of large families function better when they have the opportunity to help younger children or when they are alone with an attentive adult. Unfortunately we have too little insight in regard to situational opportunities or demands and thus lack guidelines for program design.

Returning to our examination of social-class-related differences in family structure, we find that not only are the immediate families of the lower class generally large but they are usually set in a network of relationships—the extended family. Membership in the group may be based on kinship, neighboring, or adolescent peer groups. Most often, however, it consists of relatives who live nearby (Cohen & Hodges, 1963). The extended family, as well as the immediate family, is often female-based and consisting of female relatives (Bradshaw, 1968, Gans, 1967). The extended family is the strength of the lower class: it reduces insecurity and operates like a good insurance policy. It offers food, shelter, baby care, clothing, and protection (Riessman, 1962). The extended family also allows related and different-aged children to spend a lot of time together and for young children to be cared for by siblings (Bradshaw, 1968). The advantages to the parent are obvious and perhaps there may be some advantages for the children. Bossard (1948) suggests that such an environment is healthier for child development than a parent-child environment. The extended-family environment is more understanding and more interesting, competition is more protected, and the older children provide more education for the younger ones. It is not entirely beneficial, however, for this exposure to other children may occur at the expense of a continuous close relationship with a single adult or with the loss of interaction with adults generally. Furthermore, since the extended family usually places responsibility for child rearing in the hands of a number of adults with somewhat different expectations (Bradshaw, 1968), the child may become confused in regard to authority and acceptable behavior (Wortis, Bardach, Cutler, Rue, & Freedman, 1963). "Multiple mothering" in itself is not necessarily detrimental to a child's development or attachment (Ainsworth, 1963; Caldwell et al., 1963; Gardner, Pease, & Hawkes, 1961; Gardner & Swiger, 1958; Gewirtz, 1965; Rabin, 1958; Schaffer & Emerson, 1964a; Yarrow, 1963; Yarrow & Goodwin, 1965), nor does intermittent short-term separation impair the mother-child relationship or the child's development (Yarrow, 1961). However, a constant shifting of mothering figures may result in a number of "child custodians," none of whom develops a close and dependable relationship with the baby (Marans & Lourie, 1967). This would be detrimental, but it does not appear to be typical of an extended family.

Another characteristic of the lower-class urban family is that parental control and emotional support tend to be cut off early in the child's life (as early as 5 or 6 years), as the parents lose confidence in their ability to control him. Such early independence allows conditions outside the home which are not planned or guided by the parents to affect the child at an early age (Lewis, 1961). This phenomenon points up the essential need to involve lower-class parents in the care of their children and to attempt to bolster their abilities and their confidence with day-care and educational programs.

It has often been suggested that these characteristics of the lower-class family structure are part of a "universal culture of poverty" shared by poor blacks and whites throughout the country. Although few data are available on the rural poor, the existing data suggest that this is not so (Chilman, 1966; Young, 1970). A recent extensive observational study of a southern black, small-town community (Young, 1970) revealed that 38 of 41 households were headed by men in respected rather than marginal roles. Granting that the sample was biased in favor of stability because it included only families with 3-to-6-year old children, this study suggests that matrifocality may not be so prevalent as inferred by available census reports.

Young also notes the importance of the *extended family* over three or four generations. In her sample, however, ties occurred in the male as well as the female line. They were based exclusively on kinship, for there were no communal activities with neighboring groups. Although there were many illegitimate births and marital breakups, the family was not dysfunctional. Whether headed by a man or a woman, these families provided secure groups for child raising. Illegitimate children were accepted by all, as were the multiplicity of fathers or male providers that characterized most families. Continuity for the child was provided by a single continuous, permanent, mother-figure and stability by the maintenance of ties over three or four generations. Babies in these families were constantly played with, teased, and carried about by everyone in the family. Starting at 15 months, the child was included in the children's gang. By age 3 he had transferred dependence from his mother to the gang, and the mother's role in direct rearing receded.

As distinct from the lower class, the "working class" consists of skilled and semiskilled blue-collar workers and their families. The family structure is basically similar to that of the lower class. These families, too, are large. Regardless of ethnic membership, they accord a dominant role to a family circle that is larger than the nuclear family and based on social relationships among relatives. The extended family of the working class, however, does not need to serve the "insurance" function it has in the lower class. Instead it has a more social purpose (Gans, 1967). As in the lower class, the child's peer group is an important agent of socialization (Gans, 1967). Finally, in the working-class family as well parents assume clearly differentiated roles. Mother, father, and siblings are all involved in family life (Pavenstedt, 1965), but child rearing is the woman's work —at least according to the fathers (Kohn & Carroll, 1960).

The next step up the social-class ladder belongs to the middle class—the "mainstream culture" of American society. Individuals in the middle class derive most of their emotional and social gratification from the small nuclear family. The family is child-centered. Friends and institutions help and support the parents in child raising (Gans, 1967; Ruderman, 1968), but few relatives are available and generally parents are isolated in rearing their children (Mead, 1963). The peer group does not assume significance until the child is going to school, and, since families are generally smaller, siblings are not usually instrumental in child-training activities.

In the middle-class family, as opposed to the lower class, the parents' roles are not sharply differentiated (Kohn & Carroll, 1960). Although the father participates somewhat less than the mother in matters of discipline, he uses the same methods (Clifford, 1959).

One further class distinction has been made by some sociologists (Gans, 1967). The "professional class" is at the top of the American stratification system. Its dominant family structure, like that of the middle class, is nuclear, but at this socioeconomic level there is even greater emphasis placed on the independent functioning of its members. Individual development and self-expression is fostered by mothers early in the lives of their children; consequently the professional-class family may be termed adult-centered (Gans, 1967). No studies of differences in family structure seem to have been made between this and lower classes, but we may assume that there are no radical departures from structures characteristic of the middle class.

This description of family structure provides only a bare outline of aspects of the family in different subcultural groups. Unfortunately, more complex data are not readily available, particularly for the upper classes. Middle-class subjects have been commonly studied in the psychological laboratory, but seldom have they been observed, as families, in the home. Numerous studies have examined the overall effects of subculture on child development. Unfortunately, these studies have confounded such variables as physical environment (stimulation, toys, overcrowding), maternal variables, health and nutrition, and parental attitudes toward family-structure variables. No attempt appears to have been made to study the effects of family structure per se. Investigations of this kind would contribute to a proper foundation for adequate day-care programming.

IMPLICATIONS FOR DAY-CARE SERVICES

The children of lower-class families have generally been considered the most likely and deserving candidates for expanded day-care facilities. The preceding examination of typical family structures within different social classes, however, suggests that this expectation may not be well founded. By offering parents new avenues of involvement with their children, by increasing options for career-minded mothers, and by exposing children to peers of different backgrounds and to adults other than their own parents, day care, broadly interpreted, can become a resource for working- and middle-class families as well. Moreover, in the lower class the typical role of relatives in rearing and caring for children in extended families indicates that the need for care outside the home may not be so urgent as are opportunities for educational stimulation inside the home. Once again, the issue of day-care models need not hinge on treating *services* as equivalent to *arrangements*. Surely, with sufficient ingenuity, it should be possible to develop programs that would enrich the lives of children wherever they may be.

When group care *is* desired by lower-class families, it is especially important that the parents be involved in the program, since it has frequently been observed that parents in these families lose "control" of their offspring at an early age. If programs are to promote genuine parental involvement, traditional conceptions of day care may need to be revised; for example, it may be necessary to offer evening meals to parents and children in order to provide a social setting for communication and interaction between them and caregivers. Planned opportunities for involvement may be especially important when both parents work full-time.

In extended families, in particular, an area of further concern is maintaining consistency of care among those who share responsibility for child rearing. Once the viability of the extended family is acknowledged, the challenge is to design programs that take into account the special features of these relationships. Communication between relatives about different child-rearing practices may be as difficult (or more difficult) than communication between friends or professionals. Available and sympathetic "others" (e.g., child-development counselors) might provide a neutral setting in which problems could be discussed.

Fears about the development of social attachments in young lower-class children have been expressed both by those who would provide a mother-substitute in day care to compensate for presumed deficiencies in mothering at home and concurrently by those concerned that day care will hinder or harm a child's attachment to his own mother. The observation that, in fact, the presence of a single mother-figure is usually stable and continuous in lower-class families suggests that such fears may be premature or overemphasized. Since a maternal figure is available, it is the quality of her caregiving and interaction that will determine the strength and adaptiveness of the infant's attachment, regardless of social-class status.

Mothers of any social class may be incompetent, unresponsive, or overprotective. In small nuclear families, typical of the middle class, the problems of social achievement resulting from inadequate caregiving may be even more acute, since the mother is likely to be the *only* attachment object and social model available. Perhaps for such isolated mother-child dyads the "neighborhood" model of day care would be appropriate. The presence of concerned and qualified adults in home or out-of-home day-care arrangements can advance the child's social development, whether he lives in a slum or a suburb.

A strong father figure is also beneficial to the social development of children. The absence of such a single salient father-figure or the possible dilution of his impact because of long working hours dictates that the role of the male caregiver be given attention. Male as well as female models, in central and permanent roles, have an essential place in day-care arrangements at home or at a center. They play a part that becomes increasingly valuable, especially for young boys, as the children grow older. Involving fathers in the care of children may demand profound readjustments in employment practices and social attitudes.

The question of favorable adult:child ratios is another issue that arises from an examination of research in family structure, in particular its size. It appears that children in large families often suffer as a consequence of their limited contact with adults. Although it is the quality rather than the quantity of caregiving by parents that most affects children's development, too many youngsters in the family can place impossible demands on even the most skillful and responsive caregiver. Similarly, caregiving and careful program planning in a day-care setting can provide excellent care for a number of children; yet here, too, a minimum adult:child ratio can be reached beyond which adequate care is impossible. Although no definite estimate of this minimum ratio can be provided, as a first approximation a ratio equivalent to that found in a large family (1:6) might be considered as a guide. This estimate, however, precludes the contribution of the father and other relatives and assumes that the family is free of social and economic stress. Minimum feasible adult:child ratios will depend on the competence of available caregivers and the financial resources of the program. "Optimal" adult:child ratios cannot be stated with certainty, either. The size of the average nuclear family suggests that a ratio of 1:2.4 might be appropriate; yet this estimate would neither include the contribution of the father nor would it take into consideration the relative skill of the mother. Identifying "optimal" with the nuclear family also implies that the nuclear family provides a structurally ideal setting for children. Actually, similar adult:child ratios occur when several generations occupy a single household or when communal living arrangements are established. It may well be that the optimal ratio cannot be stated as a factor of "one" neuter gender adult; for example, 3:15 (two adult males and one adult female for every 15 children), might be a more helpful statement. The solution or, more accurately, solutions to the optimal adult:child ratio question can be determined only by careful research that considers how many people are available, what these people do, and how well they do it.

12

Physical Environments

FAMILIES DIFFER IN THEIR PHYSICAL SETTINGS, AND THESE differences, too, are often associated with social class. Unfortunately, as in research on family structure, there have not been enough longitudinal investigations to draw firm connections between socioeconomic conditions, specific aspects of the physical environment, and the effect on parents and children. Fowler (1962), in his review of the effects of environment on intelligence, concluded that available studies were too broad to be useful in determining antecedent-consequent relationships. In this chapter, however, we discuss briefly the data that are available and indicate some possible relationships. The use of socioeconomic classifications in this discussion serves to guarantee a broad sampling of physical environments, since the financial resources of a family are likely to set firm limits on housing, play space, and play materials as well as on opportunities and dangers.

Lower-class homes have at times been described as overstimulating, understimulating, and inappropriately stimulating by various authors—each with some truth in his analysis. Lower-class homes frequently are "understimulating" to the children growing up in them. Whether, as a result of economic pressure or personal preference, many ghetto homes are austere, without decoration (C. P. Deutsch, 1968), and lacking in cultural materials associated with development of school readiness—namely books, toys, and games and paper and other school objects (Deutsch, 1963; Gordon, 1965; Lavatelli, 1968). Young (1970) describes the preschool children's environment in her southern black sample as totally human. Children are exposed to and play with no physical materials. In studies involving all social classes such material understimulation has been shown as detrimental to child development. Fewer books in the home has been associated with lower reading-readiness scores in grade 1 (Milner, 1951) and with lower verbal scores in grade 5 (Bing, 1963). Fewer toys at home has been found to be related to less frequent and shorter play periods in 10-month old infants (Tulkin, 1969). These data bring to mind the early studies of institutionalized infants and children in perceptually barren circumstances, without opportunity for motor development, and lacking toys and physical stimulation, who were seriously retarded in mental and motor development (Bakwin, 1942; Dennis, 1960; Goldfarb, 1945; Roudinesco & Appell, 1950; Spitz, 1946, 1965; Spitz & Wolf, 1946). Some reviewers (e.g., Casler, 1961, 1968) have suggested that perceptual stimulation was the essential missing ingredient responsible for the retardation of these orphans. Yet it is generally believed that it is not simply the amount of stimulation, above a certain minimum cut-off, that is critical for a child's development (Bronfenbrenner, 1968a; Tulkin, 1969; Yarrow, 1961) but the conditions under which the stimulation is given, particularly its mediation by a human caregiver. Dennis' twin study (Dennis, 1938, 1941) is often cited as evidence of the view that the amount of perceptual stimulation is not of paramount importance. When given only a small amount of tactile, vestibular, auditory, and visual stimulation, the twins developed "normally" as infants. Unfortunately conclusions about potential or optimal development cannot be inferred from these results. Enrichment interventions carried out by White (1966) do suggest that it is possible to accelerate development in infancy by increased sensorimotor stimulation.

It appears that a variety of stimulation is essential to the optimal development of a child's intellect. Perceptual monotony (noise or white hospital walls) has been found to lead to a decrease in infant vocalization (Schaffer, 1958) and significantly lowered activity (Wolff, 1966). The variety of toys, not the number, has been related to an infant's later exploration (Rubenstein, 1967).

Although the lower-class home lacks books, playthings, and school-related objects there are some aspects of stimulation in it that appear to be sufficient. In particular, there are concrete object-oriented tasks and chores. Investigators have suggested that the latter are related to the normal development of arithmetic and quantitative concepts in older children (Deutsch, 1960; Gordon, 1965; John, 1964a).

In some respects the lower-class home is even overstimulating. It is often noisy, disorganized, and overcrowded (Deutsch, 1963; Gordon, 1965); it is usually more cluttered than a middle-class home (C. Deutsch, 1968); and the TV, radio, or record player is always turned on (Hess, 1969). These characteristics may not be conducive to optimal learning or development. Studies have reported relationships between crowding and reading difficulties (Hess, 1969); high noise level in the home and verbal learning (Jensen, 1968) and the learning of auditory discriminations (Deutsch, Katz, & Templin in John, 1964a; Jensen, 1966).

From these proposed characteristics of lower-class homes it is impossible to construct a single image of what the homes are like or to apply to them simple unitary descriptions. There are different material symptoms of poverty, ranging from the emptiness of a tar-paper shack to the clutter of a slum apartment. There are different dimensions of stimulation which may be deficient or excessive. These characteristics are important if they reflect a discontinuity between sources of physical stimulation and the needs of children.

The most critical stimulation for optimal development appears to be mediated by, as well as provided by, the human environment—usually by the parent (Ainsworth, 1962, 1964; Yarrow, 1961). The parent mediates stimulation for the infant or child in a number of ways. One way is by influencing the amount and nature of the practice the child gets in discriminating among stimuli. In this regard C. P. Deutsch (1968) notes that in the lower-class family there is less labeling and teaching of discriminations. Provence and Lipton (1962) suggest another way that caregivers mediate the child's stimulation. They claim that personal relationships affect the way in which a baby relates to objects. "A toy is just a toy"— unless it is invested with positive feelings by virtue of its association with the loved human attachment object. The mother can also mediate stimulation by her restriction or indulgence of the child's play and exploration of materials. Bing (1963) has found that although the number of toys a child had before school age did not relate to his nonverbal ability in fifth grade the freedom he was given to play with these toys and to explore the environment did distinguish between children of high and low ability. Similarly, the mother's use of home resources has been related to her child's reading readiness and achievement (Hess & Shipman, 1965).

Perhaps the most influential and critical form of parental mediation of stimulation occurs in the sphere of language. That a child is likely to be restricted to *hearing* only certain language forms—in these days of a TV in every home—is clearly absurd. TV watching has, in fact, some beneficial effects on the size of children's vocabularies (Schramm, Lyle, & Parker, 1961), but the most important influence of the child's linguistic development seems to be the human adult. The child's acquisition of language appears to be fostered by demands on him for communication (Williams & Naremore, 1969), reinforcement for this communication, and a rich and varied adult-language model. The sheer amount of verbalization in the home is apparently not so important to the infant's development as distinctive vocalization, directed toward the baby, uncontaminated by irrelevant activities, and at an appropriate level for the baby's age (Gordon, 1969a; Kagan, 1968, 1969); for example, "mealtime conversation" is one aspect of language behavior that has been compared in different families. Despite their avowed desirability by lower-class mothers (Ruderman, 1968), family conversations around the dinner table are less frequent, more restricted in range of vocabulary, use of imagery, and encouragement of child participation in lower-class homes (Bossard,

1948; Keller in Cazden, 1966; Milner, 1951). In other studies such aspects of mealtime conversation have been correlated with children's reading achievement in the first grade (Milner, 1951) and reading achievement (Whiteman & Deutsch, 1968) and written verbal ability in the fifth grade (Bing, 1963).

Once again it is necessary to note that all human children learn to speak and understand language; they learn phonological, grammatical, semantic rules. Nonetheless, some children perform less well than others on tests of language ability. Although some portion of the difference undoubtedly reveals more about the format of test situations and questions than the competence of children, another portion may reflect genuine differences in the ability to use standard English constructions. There are, for instance, language-object relations that pose special problems for most people (e.g., it is more difficult to follow the direction "put the saucer on the cup" than "put the cup on the saucer"). There are "little" words such as "with," "on," "in," "at," "for," and "by" that subtly determine the meaning of a sentence but are easily missed by inattentive or unskilled listeners. Especially in the classroom, whether traditional or informal, important messages are often housed in complex, subordinated, qualified, or incomplete utterances. Deficits in the ability of children to use language in a wide variety of communication settings are genuine liabilities. Conditions that restrict communication opportunities may contribute to these deficits. Group-care programs that fail to consider these conditions may promote deficits that would not occur in the child's own home; home-based day-care programs (e.g., in which an educational consultant visits the home) that fail to recognize the absence of responsive language interaction may be unable to expand the child's opportunities for verbal communication.

Systematic visual stimulation (controlled exposure to abstract visual forms) improved the scores of lower-class children in a discrimination test involving such forms. Their gains were greater than those of middle-class children and more than those produced by simple exposure to pictures (Covington in C. Deutsch, 1968b). This suggests that systematic stimulation may be lacking in the lower-class home and that this deficiency can be counteracted, at least in part, by deliberate teaching.

Another dimension of physical stimulation is its responsiveness to control by the child. This may be the optimal kind of stimulation and the most important aspect of the physical environment in an infant's development (Hunt, 1967a). Sadly, we have no studies that have considered this factor specifically. Such studies could provide exceedingly valuable data about optimal physical environments and how to achieve them.

This discussion of the physical environment of different families provides certain suggestions for day-care programming, whether at home or at the center. Unstimulating homes can be supplemented with toys and books. Systematic and deliberate exposure to materials may be important to children from "deprived" homes. Children from noisy, overcrowed homes can benefit from a day-care program that makes possible quiet times to be alone. The importance of the physical environment to the child's development is clear. The challenge before the day-care planner is the provision of *appropriate* stimulation, whether care is provided by parents, neighbors, or professionals, in homes or at centers.

The roles of adults as mediators of physical stimulation requires more intensive analysis than it has received, since it appears that stimulation provided by the physical environment is most effective if mediated by an adult. A caregiver assumes this role when defining a "plaything"; are playthings only those things that are labeled "toys" or are they things that attract and stimulate the child's activities such as pots, spoons, and daddy's shoes? A caregiver also assumes this role when responding to the child's verbal communication: is the response of the adult relevant to the message communicated by the child? Moreover, the adult mediates stimulation when making decisions about inviting people into the home or when deciding to take the child for a walk. Some group-care programs discourage causal visitors from interacting with the children, whereas others promote interactions of this kind. Each program makes decisions about the role of people in the child's world, decisions that influence the amount and quality of physical stimulation. Every caregiver functions as an "administrator" when negotiating the pattern of events, people, and things that make up a child's day. In addition, caregivers function as initiators of stimulating contact and as responders to contacts initiated by the child. One part of enhancing the material resources of the home and day-care center involves the way in which caregivers preceive the value to children of these resources.

13

Values, Attitudes, Goals

ACCORDING TO MANY SOURCES AND STEREOTYPES, THERE ARE
a number of differences in the value systems of different social classes. At the
lowest end of the social scale, it has even been claimed, parents have no values
(Pavenstedt, 1965). Although this may be true of pathological families, it does
not seem to be among normal, even lower-class, families. Indeed it is apparent
that these stereotypes have overemphasized and inflated the differences between
classes. Evidence suggests that there is a common core of basic human values
that all subcultural groups embrace. Happiness, honesty, consideration, obedience,
dependability, manners, self-control, popularity, neatness, and cleanliness are all
valued to a greater or lesser extent in all social classes (Kohn, 1959b). Parsons
(1965) concludes that the lower classes are not characterized by value commit-
ments basically different from those of the higher groups.

It is tempting to dismiss a list of this kind as hopelessly simplistic, to argue
that the term "obedience," for example, means far too many things to different
people and that people are not likely to agree on the proper label for a given
instance of behavior. It is surprising, therefore, that there is remarkable consistency, clarity, and agreement in the use and meaning of many common descriptive adjectives, including those listed above (Anderson, 1968). At least there may
be an idealized definition of these terms accompanied by widely shared semantic
rules. Moreover, it is revealing that one of the most nationally painful and disturbing attacks on dominant American values occurred when young people chose
to be visibly dirty, sloppy, deviant, loose, irresponsible, disobedient, dishonest,
and angry.

Apparent differences in the relative *emphases* placed on these values by
different families may be the result of exigencies in the environment. The middle

and lower classes may share a common set of values. Their value hierarchies may not be identical, however, because salient and emphasized values depend on what is important and problematic for the individual. The lower classes, because of their economic circumstances, are concerned with problems of housing, income, occupation, and daily survival. The upper classes, somewhat more remote from such concerns, can take "neatness" and "cleanliness" for granted, since they are, for them, so easily attained. Therefore they can afford to, and do, emphasize values such as consideration and other abstract ideals. Differences in occupational demands may be reflected in different class-value emphases (Kohn, 1959b). The lower classes, by virtue of their social circumstances, especially their employment, may have to be concerned with rule following. The occupations of the upper classes generally require self-direction.

Apparent differences in the stated values of different groups may also result from a "value stretch." Since the lower-class or minority-group member cannot attain middle-class or majority goals, he develops an alternative (lower) set of values and aspirations *as well as* the general values of society. Thus he has a wider range of values to which he is less committed (Rodman, 1963). In a questionnaire given by a professional-class psychologist he may give just the lower value—or not. Most members of the upper classes also have dual sets of values; *they* call it "realism" when they settle for the less lofty (Herzog, 1967).

Values apparently differ also according to dimensions of urbanization and religious and ethnic membership, but few studies have investigated these differences separately from those associated with socioeconomic status (Kluckholm, 1958; Kohn, 1959b). Findings suggest there may be real differences in value orientation, depending on cultural divisions. Also missing are data on the "new generation" of radicals as parents, which might reveal other "true" differences in values.

There is general agreement that the goals of poor parents for their children are similar to those of middle-class parents (Chilman, 1968). According to Lewis (1961), what lower-class parents say they want for themselves and their children conforms to middle-class standards, but they lack the knowledge to achieve this goal.

Differences between families in attitudes and feelings are associated with their relative positions and conditions in society. The apparently common feelings among the lower classes of distrust, low self-esteem, inefficiency, passivity, fatalism, and orientation to the present (Chilman, 1968; Herzog, 1967) have been interpreted as adjustment to frustration and unpredictability. According to some investigators, the working-class tendency to perceive and structure social relationships in terms of power may follow from a position in society that offers few opportunities for a voice in the decisions affecting daily life (Herzog, 1967). These feelings of the parent may influence the child. In one study fathers' feelings of powerlessness were negatively correlated with the flexibility of the thinking of their sons at age 11 (Busse, 1967). Parental satisfaction with the father's job correlated positively with the son's academic performance (Honzik, 1967).

Three examples of family values, goals, or attitudes of special interest for our purposes in this book are discussed in greater detail in this chapter: (a) the value of education, (b) attitudes toward children and the role of the parent in child rearing, and (c) the goals of child rearing. Differences among families may be especially important to group-care programs aspiring to cross social-class boundaries. If socially integrated programs are to emerge and if genuine parental participation is to be realized, it will be necessary to acknowledge differences and to seek accommodations.

The dimensions of differences discussed in this section should be viewed as tentative hypotheses for which some empirical support has been found. Too often findings are based on single interviews conducted by strangers and outsiders; it is still rare to find "inside" reports based on long-term contact with families or to find several independent sources of information in a single study (e.g., interviews with different family members and systematic observation). These become serious research deficits when sensitive issues are involved. One danger, of course, is posing questions or creating situations that force people to respond in ways they ordinarily would reject. Consider the following interview question: how would you punish your child if he broke your best vase? It might take considerable courage for a parent to fly in the face of such a demand to say, "Well, I might not punish him at all." It might require a subtle grasp of standard English to appreciate the implications of the construction, "how would you . . . if . . . ," or considerable social independence for parents not to select the answer judged most acceptable to the interviewer.

VALUE OF EDUCATION

Some researchers have considered the lower classes "anti-intellectual" (Cohen & Hodges, 1963; Reissman, 1962) a trait that may, in fact, be pervasive *throughout* all social classes in present-day America (Hofstadter, 1963). Most evidence, however, suggests that all parents place high value on education for their children, although for different often nonintellectual reasons.

To members of the lower class, education is important for getting a job, for coping with daily problems, and for satisfying an interest in science (Reissman, 1962). They want education (Gordon, 1965; Lewis, 1961; Reissman, 1962; Wortis et al., 1963) but do not know how to achieve it (Lewis, 1961). They feel powerless and view the school as distant and formidable (Hess & Shipman, 1966). Associated with the parents' feelings of powerlessness are children's low reading scores and marks in first grade (Hess, 1969). Lower-class mothers also like day care: they are attracted by its formal training, by the opportunity it provides their children to acquire educational and social skills (Ruderman, 1968). Heterogeneity is found, however, in the lower class in the value placed on education; for example, whether or not parents took the initiative in enrolling their children in Head Start might be an indication of the importance to them of education. In homes in which parents did enroll their children it was found that there were also more books and more space. The children in these families had IQ and verbal scores equivalent to those of a middle-class sample and significantly above those of the Head Start children who were "recruited" (Holmes & Holmes, 1966). In the working class education is important as a means of earning more money (Gans, 1967). Yet for members of this class, too, schools are unapproachable (Hess & Shipman, 1966).

For middle-class adults education is a means of achieving job satisfaction and status, whether in a man's career or in a woman's role as mother (Gans, 1967). It is the professional class that places the highest value on education. Children of this social class go to school longest, since they are able to afford the luxury, and consider education an avenue toward personal development (Gans, 1967). Upper-class parents realistically aspire to a greater amount of education for their children. This aspiration, it turns out, is correlated with the child's reading achievement in school (Whiteman & Deutsch, 1968). Parental pressure for academic achievement, regardless of socioeconomic status, was similarly associated with high reading ability (Honzik, 1967). Upper-class mothers, however, are *not* enthusiastic about the contribution of day care to the education of young children; they perceive it as overcrowded, lacking individualized care, and excessively structured (Ruderman, 1968).

ATTITUDES TOWARD CHILDREN

Parents in the lower classes try to raise the social level of their children; they are not satisfied with their "culture" (Gans, 1967). They like children; according to Young (1970), children are the most important part of their lives. They also like caring for children, more than do mothers in the middle class (Ruderman, 1968) although they may not be as accepting of the child as are middle-class parents. Young, black, lower-class, expectant mothers expressed punitive or unaccepting attitudes toward aggression against parents, toilet accidents, refusal to eat, crying, talking, and naughtiness (Gutelius, 1970). The lower-class parent is described as a controlling, limit-setting authority (Garfield & Helper, 1962; Kohn & Carroll, 1960; Wortis et al., 1963), whose role it is to direct and guide the child (Kohn & Carroll, 1960). They are also more inclined to utilize the services of day care or the extended family to help in raising their children (Ruderman, 1968).

The middle and professional classes view the role of the parent as supportive rather than limit setting (Kohn & Carroll, 1960). These parents tend to be warmer, more accepting, more encouraging of autonomy and cooperation, more permissive, egalitarian, and affectionate (Bayley & Schaefer, 1960) and more democratic (Baldwin, Kalhorn, & Breese, 1945; Bronfenbrenner, 1958). They are not likely to use day care as a resource for child training (Ruderman, 1968). Parents in these classes follow expert child-rearing advice more quickly and readily than those in the lower classes, although lower-class parents also follow expert opinion when possible—in the laboratory (Walters, Connor, & Zunich, 1964) and over long periods of time (Bronfenbrenner, 1958). There may be several reasons for the "slowness" of the lower classes. Lower-class parents may be too concerned with problems of housing, income, and occupation to be able to afford the luxury of studying the latest methods and theories of child rearing. More importantly, the status of "expert" may be awarded to experienced members of the family rather than to remote professionals. A profitable exchange of information about children may require close interpersonal relationships and a recognition of family-life realities. The working-class life style and circumstances— lack of education, greater attachment to extended family—may be conducive to their retaining familiar methods. Finally, the experts' advice has generally been predicated on middle-class values. For families who know that their children must become self-supporting practical achievements may carry more assurance than the abstract competencies proposed by experts.

GOALS OF CHILD REARING

It has already been mentioned that the goals of all parents for their children are *basically* the same but have different emphases (Bronfenbrenner, 1958; Kamii & Radin, 1967). Lower-class parents stress being liked by adults, being neat and clean (Kamii & Radin, 1967; Kohn, 1959b), honest, and sex-typed (Kohn, 1959b). When asked what they would teach their children before they went to school, one sample of lower-class, black, teen-age expectant mothers mentioned obedience, manners, honesty, name and address (Gutelius, 1970). Half of these girls also mentioned the value of language stimulation, educational material, and experience outside the home, which demonstrated the heterogeneity of goals even within this restricted sample. There has been some suggestion that social classes differ in child-training goals with respect to aggression and impulse control. A survey of the literature, however, suggests that there is no fundamental difference in parents' goals for these behaviors, even if there are differences in disciplinary practice that may lead to variations in child behavior. Lower-class parents do not encourage or permit aggression or sex play (Gutelius, 1970; Wortis et al., 1963; Young, 1970), but they do value the child's fighting back if molested (Wortis et al., 1963).

For the working class the goals of child rearing are obedience, neatness, cleanliness, and compliance with authority (Kohn, 1959b). These parents want their children to be good and nice (White, 1957), to work for good grades and to please the teacher (Pavenstedt, 1965), and to follow the rules of respectability (Kohn & Carroll, 1960). These goals may prepare the child for authority at school but not necessarily for abstract learning or for mutually enjoyable interaction with other people (Hess & Shipman, 1969).

Middle-class parents want their children to be considerate, self-controlled, internally guided, curious, happy (Kohn, 1959b), and dependable (Kamii & Radin, 1967). The child should decide for himself (Kohn & Carroll, 1960); he should be "well adjusted" (White, 1957). These parents expect more from their children (Bronfenbrenner, 1958) and seem to get it (Crandall, Dewey, Katkovsky, & Preston, 1964).

It is too early, of course, to have data to describe the values and child-rearing goals of young radical or hippie parents. One might speculate that they would be different from those of any traditional social-class group. The current emphasis of these youthful groups on "doing your own thing" could be reflected in an emphasis on the goal of child autonomy. Certainly there is a move in Women's Liberation toward less sex typing and less compliance with accepted authority which could also be reflected in child-rearing goals. Perhaps, too, increasingly greater emphasis will be placed on the goals of flexibility and accommodation as necessary characteristics of Protean Man.

SUGGESTIONS FOR DAY-CARE PROGRAMMING

This discussion of values, attitudes, and goals in different social classes has great relevance for day care if the premise that programs and clients must make sense to one another is accepted. There is comfort in the observed consensus that parents from all classes share the same *basic* values and goals for their children. However, one should not rest on this consensus and plan programs without further consideration of parental attitudes.

The discussion suggests that parents from different social strata may want different emphases in educational programs for their children. Middle-class parents may favor a loosely structured program; lower-class parents are more likely to prefer a more structured approach. Middle-class parents may urge creativity and social skills; lower-class parents will probably emphasize the three R's. These desires should be respected, for it appears likely that parents have a good idea what programs their children will find most compatible and helpful. Parents often evaluate a preschool program in the light of the demands and expectations of the neighborhood elementary school and the need to reduce unmanageable discontinuity for their children. If the implications of studies of the child and the impact of the environment are to be translated into day-care programs, alternatives must be developed that consider parents' values and attitudes and the likelihood that they are changing and will continue to change.

This discussion of parental values has also indicated some of the benefits of involving parents in day-care programs: (a) so that they may gain the knowledge and skills necessary for achieving their own goals, (b) so that schools and similar institutions will become perceived by these parents as approachable, and (c) so that parents may become aware of, appreciate, and understand the characteristics and development of their children.

14

Child-Rearing Practices

MORE FREQUENTLY DOCUMENTED THAN VARIATIONS IN VAL-
ues have been differences in child-rearing practices favored by families of different social strata. This is not surprising in view of Lewis's (1961) contention
that the lower class shows greater conformity to middle-class standards in what
they *say* they want than in their actual child-rearing behaviors. Child-rearing practices, as well as expressed value hierarchies, are adaptations to prevailing circumstances. The behaviors of lower-class parents, as they interact with their children,
are often pragmatic adjustments to internal and external stress and deprivation
(Lewis, 1961). Such factors as the number of children in the family, their close-
ness, the physical space available, the safeness of the neighborhood, the adequacy
of sanitation, as well as values conditioned by occupational circumstances or educational experiences affect the family's child-rearing practices (Becker, 1964). Consequently class-linked differences in child-rearing practices do exist, although it
has been noted that such differences seem to be diminishing (Bronfenbrenner,
1958).

Early studies of child-rearing practices concerned themselves with traditional
socialization issues: feeding, weaning, and toilet training. No socioeconomic differences have been found in feeding and weaning (Littman, Moore, & Pierce-
Jones, 1957; Maccoby & Gibbs, 1954; White, 1957; Wortis et al., 1963), nor has a
relationship been observed between feeding method and child characteristics
(Ainsworth & Bell, in press; Chodorkoff, 1960; Hernstein, 1963; Orlansky, 1954;
Sears, Maccoby, & Levin, 1957) or between flexibility of feeding or weaning and
child behavior or development (Ainsworth, 1963; Orlansky, 1954; Schaffer &
Emerson, 1964; Sears et al., 1957). Some social-class differences in toilet training
have been observed (Sears et al., 1957), but in more recent studies they have not
been consistent (Littman et al., 1957; Wortis et al., 1963).

177

The most completely investigated aspect of child-rearing practice is that of discipline. Since this is such an important issue, relevant to a discussion of differences among families and of appropriate planning for day-care programs, we discuss it here in some detail.

DEGREE OF CONTROL

Bronfenbrenner (1958), reviewing studies of social-class differences in child-rearing practices, points out the trend from 1920 to 1950 in all social classes—but most marked in the middle class—toward greater permissiveness. Such permissiveness applied to feeding, toilet accidents, sex aggression, freedom of movement, tolerance of child's expressed needs, and punishment. Before 1938 the emphasis in child training was on a "by-the-clock" regularity, and parents were concerned with winning the struggle with the child for domination. About that time the child came to be considered harmless and mildness was advocated in all areas. According to the experts then, giving care and attention to the baby's demands would make him less demanding later. The "peak of permissiveness" was reached in 1950, with the middle class continuing to show more permissiveness (e.g., Sears et al., 1957). Since then, according to Bronfenbrenner (1958), a note of conservatism has crept into the opinions of experts and the middle class. Middle-class and lower-class differences are disappearing; perhaps in the future they will even meet half way. As recent research indicates, however, they have not met yet, and perhaps, as the present "freedom-advocating" generation of college students become parents, they will not.

A subtlety that many studies of parental control have apparently missed (Becker, 1964) is that it is not just "restriction" or "permissiveness" per se that is important to the child; warmth and hostility are also involved. Future researchers should be careful to separate these two dimensions and to examine the degree of parental control in the context of the emotional relationship between parent and child. When this is done, the issue of discipline becomes even more complex. Young (1970), for instance, describes child rearing in a small black community as a complex interplay of permissiveness and regulation, indulgence and frustration, carried out on a deep level of interpersonal involvement.

When these dimensions are separated, as far as it is possible, there is evidence that restriction-permissiveness can be considered globally (Becker, 1964). Contrary to certain popular beliefs, there is evidence also that lower-class parents are generally not restrictive (Bradshaw, 1968; Williams & Scott, 1953; Wortis et al., 1963; Young, 1970) except about sex play and aggression toward parents or siblings. In fact, they are less restrictive than working-class parents about cleanliness, noise, and manners (Bradshaw, 1968; Wortis et al., 1963). There is no difference between social classes in parents' restriction of children's aggression toward other children (White, 1957). In the lower-class family aggression is encouraged and boasted about—as a game—during the baby's first year (Bradshaw, 1968; Young, 1970). Beyond that age cooperation is encouraged, and by age 3 aggression is controlled (Young, 1970). The middle-class parent is still the most permissive (especially compared with the working class) about demands for attention, sex behavior, aggression toward parents, table manners, neatness, orderliness, noise, bedtime rules, and general obedience (Becker, 1964).

According to Becker's review, results of studies that investigated the effects of degree of control on children support the common-sense supposition that restriction leads to inhibited behaviors and permissiveness to uninhibited behaviors. Parental restrictiveness in the first three years of the child's life is associated with greater conformity, less aggression, less dominance, less competition with peers, more dependence on adults, less mastery behavior, more inhibition (Becker, 1964), less play behavior (Tulkin, 1969), retarded motor development (Williams & Scott, 1953), and lack of initiative (Antonovsky, 1959). Becker concludes that restrictiveness, although it may lead to well-controlled, social behavior, also tends toward fearful, dependent, submissive behaviors, to dulling of intellectual striving, and to inhibited hostility. Permissiveness may foster outgoing, sociable, assertive behaviors and intellectual striving but tends to lead to less persistence and increased aggressiveness.

Restrictiveness among children 3 to 6 years old, on the other hand, is associated with socially approved aggression in boys, but for girls, with aggression, less mastery behavior, and dependence (Becker, 1964). This finding illustrates the difficulties often encountered when global variables are applied too lightly to varying age and sex groups and conditions.

In the present case findings may be reflecting different kinds of restrictive behaviors or different kinds of prohibitions. It may well be that researchers and informants apply the same (or different) labels to different (or highly similar) kinds of child behavior; for example, the aggressive behaviors of boys and girls might be topologically quite similar, although they bring approval to boys and are criticized in girls.

Missing in this research is a serious analysis of the specific restrictive and permissive techniques parents use, the occasions that bring them about, emotional components of these situations, and the clarity and consistency of the rules by which restrictions are imposed and permissions are granted. To the degree that analyses of this kind are lacking, a dimension such as "restrictiveness" will cover too much variability and will be impossible to translate into program elements. Even more, overly inclusive categories interfere with the emergence of theoretical formulations that must consider how general trait characteristics (such as restrictiveness) are linked to other characteristics of the person and critical features of the environment, how linkages develop and how they are modified. Indeed, it is the absence of elaborated theoretical constructions that creates insurmountable obstacles to effective implementation. To the degree that abstract notions are insufficiently operationalized we will lack the rules on which implementation depends.

The reported relationships between restrictiveness and cognitive development further illustrate these problems. Restrictiveness has been found to be detrimental to performance on IQ tests, language maturity, and nonverbal ability (Baldwin, Kalhorn, & Breese, 1945; Bing, 1963; Kagan & Freeman, 1963; Marge, 1965; White, 1969). Apparently it has also fostered high achievement in school (which could be a side benefit of inhibition and conformity) and verbal ability (Bing, 1963; Drews & Teahan, 1957; Milner, 1951). Freeberg and Payne (1967) concluded in their review of the effects of restrictiveness on cognitive development that controversy still exists. Perhaps, too, this is because in this research as well variables have been confounded: the age and sex of the child, the emotional context of the disciplinary action, the mode of restriction (social versus physical), and so on. In any case, more research is demanded before generalizations on the *effects* of restrictiveness are clear.

Granting independence to the child appears to be generally beneficial for his development. Such independence has been associated with high IQ scores in 2- and 3-year olds (Bayley & Schaefer, 1960), competent nursery school behaviors (Baumrind & Black, 1967), reading achievement at 7 years (Rau et al., 1964), high differentiation at 10 (Witkin et al., 1962), flexible thinking at 11 (Busse, 1967), and high achievement at 15 and 16 (Shaw, 1964). Once again, independence can be encouraged in different ways, at different ages, and under different circumstances.

METHOD OF CONTROL

Discipline in the lower classes is more likely to be physical (Becker, 1964; Bronfenbrenner, 1958; Herzog, 1967), severe (White, 1957), and harsh, unpredictable, and authoritarian (Chilman, 1968), although it is not necessarily extreme (Young, 1970). Lower-class parents are more likely to use "power-oriented" techniques of control: appeal to status, imperatives, normative control (Olin, Hess, & Shipman, 1967), deprivation and ridicule (Becker, 1964; Bronfenbrenner, 1958), threats (Hoffman, 1960), punishment and power assertions (Bayley & Schaefer, 1964; Hoffman, 1960; Sears et al., 1957). Parents in the upper classes, by comparison, are more likely to favor "love-oriented" punishment techniques: withdrawal of love, isolation (Becker, 1964; Bronfenbrenner, 1958), and show of disappointment and guilt-arousing appeals (Becker, 1964). They more often give rewards (Kamii & Radin, 1967) and praise (Maccoby & Gibbs, 1954; Wortis et al., 1963). Upper-class methods of control are also based more frequently on cognitive-rational appeals: parents give instructions rather than commands (Olin et al., 1967); when they do give orders, they are accompanied by consultation or explanation (Kamii & Radin, 1967); parents use reasoning to control their children (Becker, 1964). Like the trend toward greater permissiveness, a concurrent trend has been observed in the direction of greater emphasis in these latter methods (Bronfenbrenner, 1961).

In general, research has revealed that these two contrasting methods of control have differential effects on children's behavior. The former complex of techniques, seen most commonly in lower-class homes, appears to be related to aggression, hostility, power assertiveness (Becker, 1964; Hoffman, 1960), lower reading achievement (Hess, 1969) and a tendency for the child to be externally motivated (Becker, 1964).

Research does not, however, lead to a clear-cut generalization regarding the advantages—from the child's or the parents' point of view—of either of these disciplinary methods. It is not a simple good/bad dichotomy. Complexity is increased by differential occurrence and effects according to the sex of the parent and the sex of the child (Baumrind, 1967; Becker, 1964; Bronfenbrenner, 1961). Bronfenbrenner discusses these issues at length. Girls are exposed to more affection and less punishment than boys and at the same time are subjected to "love-oriented" discipline of the type that encourages the development of internalized controls. Furthermore, girls are especially susceptible to the detrimental influence of overprotection, whereas boys are more likely to suffer ill effects from insufficient parental discipline and support.

What is more, data suggest that the "risks" experienced by each sex during the process of socialization tend to be somewhat different at different social-class levels. The danger of overprotection for girls is especially great in lower-class families, whereas in these same families boys are in greater danger of suffering from inadequate discipline and support. The upper-middle-class boy, unlike the girl, exchanges one hazard for another. Since at this upper level the more potent "psychological" techniques of discipline are likely to be employed with *both* sexes, the boy, too, presumably runs the risk of being "oversocialized," of losing some of his capacity for independent aggressive accomplishment, leadership, and competitiveness. Finally, differential effects of discipline according to the child's sex are complicated by differential treatment of the child associated with the parent's sex. Research (Bronfenbrenner, 1961) reveals a tendency, most pronounced in the lower classes, for each parent to be somewhat more active, firm, strict, and demanding with a child of the same sex, and more lenient and indulgent with a child of the opposite sex. This is unfortunate, according to Bronfenbrenner, since both responsibility and leadership are fostered by the relatively greater salience of the parent of the same sex.

The emotional context introduces further complexity into the already clouded issues of degree and method of control. There is a tendency for parental hostility to be associated with the power-assertive and physical methods of control and for warmth to accompany psychological methods (Becker, 1964). Baumrind (1966) compared three types of parental control, combining degree, method, and context in her classificatory scheme. "Authori*tarian*" parents set standards of conduct, demand obedience, and are stern and often punitive. "Authori*tative*" parents control but do not restrict their children; their directives are given in a rational, issue-oriented manner. The "permissive" parent is nonpunitive, accepting, affirmative, and reasoning and allows the child to regulate his own behaviors. Baumrind discovered that firm yet mild discipline, which was not associated with punitiveness or a lack of warmth—the authoritative style of control—did not lead to conformity or dependent behavior. Yet it was, indeed, beneficial for child behavior (self-assertiveness) and achievement (especially verbal). Coopersmith (1967) similarly found that definite and enforced limits were associated with high self-esteem, freer self-expression, creativity, independence, social acceptance, and confidence. The parents who set these limits, although demanding, were accepting of their children and did not utilize drastic forms of punishment.

Aversive stimulation may not be so effective as positive reinforcement in eliciting desired behavior in the operant conditioning laboratory. As Baumrind (1967) suggests, however, the conclusion does not follow that punishment as typically used in the home is ineffective or that its use could not be made more effective. To the child permissiveness may imply acceptance and approval of behaviors permitted, as in Siegel and Kohn's (1959) demonstration that the presence of a permissive adult increased the incidence of children's aggressive behaviors.

CONSISTENCY

Generally it has been believed that parents in the lower social classes are less consistent in their disciplinary behaviors than those of higher socioeconomic status. This inconsistency is apparent, whether one is considering behaviors of the same parent at different times or the two parents in the same family (Chilman, 1966). Inconsistency may arise from several sources. Lower-class parents do not appear to follow a "theory" of discipline; they punish according to the inconvenience of the immediate consequences (Kohn, 1959a). The particular behaviors punished thus include disobedience, fighting, sex play, breaking rules, and other generally nonacceptable behaviors (Kohn, 1959a; Wortis et al., 1963). By contrast the upper-class parent punishes mainly the child's loss of self-control. He bases his conscious decision to punish or not to punish on his judgment of the child's intent. Inconsistency of discipline, between father and mother or in the behavior of a single parent, has been associated with more aggression and crime in the children thus disciplined (Becker, 1964). Even power-assertive techniques of control may be effective in inhibiting aggression if they are given consistently over a sufficiently long period (Becker, 1964).

In sum, it must be emphasized that the consequences of disciplinary practices cannot be fully understood except in the context of the warmth of the parent-child relationship, the consistency of discipline and emotional relations, the role structure of the family, and the social and economic conditions under which a particular family unit is living. We would also reiterate the need for realization of the complexity involved in this issue. The dimensions of the sex, age, and individual sensitivity of the child, the sex of the discipliner, the temporal placement of the punishment, the severity, and the method of control must all be considered.

DISCIPLINE IN A DAY-CARE SETTING

When large families share a single dwelling, the methods of control must be subdued and unobtrusive (Whiting & Whiting, 1960). So, too, in day care discipline should be an unobtrusive component. In a well-managed program in which caregivers are trained to anticipate children's moves its overt use need occur only infrequently. When, however, discipline must be employed, the preceding discussion of child-rearing practices contains several relevant suggestions for policy.

The various disciplinary methods and styles observed in different families are important to keep in mind if one is attempting to maintain continuity of authority. A middle-class child is more likely to have been exposed to a permissive, low-key, indirect disciplinary atmosphere at home and will probably adapt well to this mode away from home. Children from the lower classes who are accustomed to more restriction, more physical punishment, and more power-oriented control, on the other hand, may not fare so well in a situation of complete freedom. Their parents may be right when they complain that discipline in day care is too lenient (Ruderman, 1968). Since research has not convincingly demonstrated that permissiveness and love-withdrawal are good for the child's development and that restrictiveness and power are bad, home practices may justifiably provide an initial guide to day-care practices. Research has produced evidence of the benefits to be derived from consistency of disciplinary practices; this may apply to consistency *between* home and day care as well as *within* each.

Eventually, however, the solution to the issue of discipline may lie in a third alternative of control. Our discussion of discipline has suggested that a balance between restrictiveness and permissiveness, limit-setting and acceptance, a policy of firm yet mild discipline, and an "authoritative" method of control, besides providing a compromise for middle-class teachers in a ghetto setting, may also be the most effective and satisfactory method of controlling most children. Furthermore, in a program for children from more than one social class such a policy may be the only one acceptable to all parents. With this or any other disciplinary policy it is essential that punitiveness and hostility be avoided and that discipline be administered in a context of warmth and positive emotion.

Finally, this discussion of child-rearing practices has indicated the importance of considering children as individuals. Different children respond differently to various methods and degrees of control. Such differences have been observed with children of different ages and different sexes. If, for the moment, we accept the findings on their face value and suspend the many necessary qualifications, girls may be generally more susceptible to detrimental effects of overprotection and restriction; boys may suffer ill effects from insufficient discipline and support. Such differential effects of discipline can also be related to more subtle individual differences between children. The best method of discipline takes such differences into account, while seeking an optimal and consistent balance between freedom and control.

15

Maternal Behaviors

PERHAPS THE MOST PRODUCTIVE APPROACH TO THE STUDY OF family characteristics and corresponding individual differences in children has been to look beyond the broad patterns of child-rearing practices to specific behaviors of parents, particularly mothers (Ainsworth & Bell, in press; Orlansky, 1964). Clearly, a mother's behavior is shaped partly by the influence of the economic, social, and cultural community in which she lives and by her position in it. There is also some evidence of a relationship between socioeconomic status and maternal characteristics (Maccoby & Gibbs, 1954; Tulkin, 1969; Wortis et al., 1963). In this area, even more than in those already discussed, however, the categories of social class and race are indeterminate and gross overgeneralizations. A mother's behavior is also greatly affected by her child: his response patterns, innate predispositions, and individual sensitivities and vulnerabilities—differences in infants that seem to be related to genetic inheritance and appear soon after birth. They include such behaviors as smiling (Brackbill, 1958), attachment (Freedman, 1965), cuddliness (Schaffer & Emerson, 1964), sensory threshold, autonomic response patterns, motility, perceptual response, sleeping and feeding patterns, emotional tone, and reactions to bathing, discipline, and play (Chess, Thomas, & Birch, 1959; Thomas, Chess, Birch, Hertzig, & Korn, 1963). These innate tendencies of infants influence their mothers' behavior; mother-child interaction is a reciprocal relationship. Generally researchers have concentrated on the mother-to-child direction of influence, but exceptions (cf. Bell, 1971; Blauvelt & McKenna, 1961; Clarke-Stewart, 1972; Escalona, 1965; Moss, 1967; Robson, 1967; Sander, 1964, 1969; Sander & Julia, 1966; Yarrow, 1963) have convincingly demonstrated the reciprocal nature of this relationship.

It has been claimed that deprivation is a function of the environment created in the home by the ·mother rather than a general socioeconomic condition

(Weikart & Lambie, 1968). This applies not only to the physical environment she provides but the psychological environment created by her own behaviors. Maternal behaviors may be the most crucial environmental influence on a child's life and future; they may be the most critical and universal dimensions of child rearing. The generalizations suggested by study of the effects of maternal behaviors are applicable not only to relations between mothers and their own children but to teachers and their pupils and to day-care personnel and their charges. Therefore a consideration of the effects of maternal behaviors on children is critical in any discussion of day care.

"CUSTODIAL CARE"

Scientific investigation of the effects of "mothering" began when observers were struck by the severe developmental retardation of children in institutions. Here infants who received no individualized care beyond feeding, diapering, and being kept warm were found to be profoundly retarded or damaged in physical, social, emotional, intellectual, and, especially, language development (Dennis & Najarian, 1957; DuPan & Roth, 1955; Goldfarb, 1945; Pringle & Tanner, 1958; Provence & Lipton, 1962; Roudinesco & Appell, 1950; Schenk-Danzinger, 1961; Spitz, 1946). Researchers also found, however, that if a baby were given individualized attention from a mother-substitute he might develop naturally even in somewhat depressed environmental circumstances (Bakwin & Bakwin, 1960); Freud & Burlingham, 1944; Freud & Dann, 1951; Rheingold, 1956; Skeels & Dye, 1939). From such studies it was apparent that more is necessary than caring for the baby's physiological needs, at least after the first six months. "Custodial care," whether it occurs in the home, orphanage, or day-care center, is not enough to guarantee the optimal development of any child. The extent of the deficit will depend on the duration and intensity of privation, constitutional vulnerability, and age of the child.

EMOTIONAL BEHAVIOR

Once studies of institutionalized children had focused attention on the importance of "mothering," investigators began to examine the processes involved in the mother-child relationship as it occurred in natural families. One aspect of this relationship that received considerable attention was the emotional one. Although agreement is not unanimous (cf. Crandall et al., 1960; Stewart, 1950), a large number of studies presented evidence of a positive association between maternal warmth and affection and child performance, or the converse, a negative relationship between maternal rejection or coldness and child behavior.

This relationship has been found in the area of children's cognitive development; expressed warmth and affection, loving treatment, and a high degree of involvement with the child, at home or in the laboratory, were associated with accelerated intellectual development, (Bayley & Schaefer, 1964; Caldwell, 1967; Dave, 1963; Stern, Caldwell, Hersher, Lipton, & Richmond, 1969; Wolf, 1964; Yarrow, 1963), high academic achievement (Dave, 1963; Hess, 1969; Milner, 1951; Wolf, 1964), high verbal ability (Bing, 1963), high need for achievement (Rosen & D'Andrade, 1959) and flexible thinking (Busse, 1967).

Positive maternal emotion has also been associated with social initiative (Yarrow, 1963; Yarrow & Goodwin, 1965) and greater involvement with mother (Clarke-Stewart, 1972; Stern et al., 1969). Similarly, the mother's warmth and involvement affects the child's play behaviors. Initiative in play (Antonovsky, 1959), exploration and manipulation (Yarrow, 1963; Yarrow & Goodwin, 1965), higher ability to cope with stress (Yarrow, 1963), and belief in internal control (Katkovsky, Crandall, & Good, 1967) are all associated with the mother's expression of love. Rejection, coldness, or no overt expression of affection from the mother appears to have undesirable consequences for the development of children (Baldwin et al., 1945; Clarke-Stewart, 1972; Hernstein, 1963; Lewis, 1954; Milner, 1951; Spitz, 1951; Wittenborn et al., 1956).

TOGETHERNESS

Some investigators have examined the proposition that the sheer amount of time the mother spends with her child, in whatever activity, will be a critical influence on his development. Results of this research indicate, however, that the amount of contact per se, beyond a necessary minimum, is not a critical dimension (Bee, 1967; Rheingold, 1960). What does seem important is the context (caretaking versus play) and quality (responsive and loving, versus disciplining or rejecting) of the interaction. Studies which have found a positive relationship between amount of maternal contact and child development have confounded this with other variables such as emotional tone, quality of interaction, and immediacy of mother's response (Ainsworth, 1963; Chodorkoff, 1960; Geber, 1958; Maccoby & Masters, 1970; Schaefer, Furfey, & Harte, 1968; Schaffer & Emerson, 1964; Walters & Parke, 1965). When maternal availability has been separated from maternal responsiveness, no differences in infant attachment appear to be associated with availability (Clarke-Stewart, 1972; Schaffer & Emerson, 1964). Stolz (1960), reviewing the literature on children of working mothers, reported no differences between these children and others whose mothers did not work, which also implies that availability of the mother is not necessarily critical. Differences in amount of interaction do tend, however, to be associated with other significant characteristics of the mother-child relationship. Usually mothers who give "better" care also spend more time with their children (Ainsworth & Bell, in press; Chodorkoff, 1960; Moss, 1967).

TOUCHING, TALKING, TEASING . . .

According to Schaffer and Emerson (1964), different mothers favor different modes of interaction: personal, which can be physical contact (touching) or non-contact (talking, looking) and impersonal (toys, food). If an infant is given physical contact with his mother which is gentle, firm, close, and frequent, it seems to have a beneficial effect on his early motor development, his physical attachment to his mother, his capacity to handle stress, and his intellectual development (Chodorkoff, 1960; Dennis, 1938, 1941, 1960; Dennis & Najarian, 1957; Goldberg & Lewis, 1969; Provence & Lipton, 1962; Yarrow, 1963). Such handling may be appropriate to very young children only, however; as the child matures, such contact may become restrictive (Ainsworth & Bell, in press).

Eye-to-eye contact between mother and infant has been found to stop the baby's crying (Wolff, 1969), to lead to stronger attachment to the mother, and possibly to greater social responsiveness (Moss & Robson, 1967).

Deliberate stimulation of the infant by the mother, visually and vocally, appears to be advantageous to the infant's development (Clarke-Stewart, 1972; Moss, Robson, & Pederson, 1969; Stern et al., 1969). Early perceptual and physical stimulation provided by the mother has also been found to lead to higher IQ scores (Chodorkoff, 1960) and more exploratory behavior (Rubenstein, 1967). This stimulation is especially effective when it occurs in the context of play. Infants who receive the benefits of a high degree of playful stimulation from their mothers at home were more socially developed (Walters & Parke, 1965), performed better in auditory and visual laboratory tasks (Tulkin, 1969), and were superior in intelligence, exploration, and ability to cope with stress (Yarrow, 1963; Yarrow & Goodwin, 1965).

One aspect of maternal stimulation that is of critical importance to a child's optimal development is the mother's verbal behavior toward him. Verbal stimulation by talking or reading to him when the child is young has been associated with more frequent infant vocalizaton (Goldberg & Lewis, 1969; Wolff, 1969), distinctive vocalization to the mother's voice (Tulkin, 1969), language competence (Clarke-Stewart, 1972), and language maturity (Marge, 1965). If the mother provides opportunities for the child to enlarge his vocabulary and to use a variety of sentence patterns, the effect on nonverbal performance measures is beneficial (Dave, 1963; Wolf, 1964). In an experimental setting (Cazden, 1965, 1966) it has been found that an adult model (like the mother) who provides rich and varied verbal stimulation is more effective in increasing a child's language development than an adult who expands the child's own sentences. Responding to the child's utterances is one way of reinforcing his language behavior. Reinforcement also occurs when the mother responds to the child's early questions or directly tutors him in word and sentence productions. Bing (1963) has found that such verbal responsiveness is associated with high verbal ability in the fifth grade. Punishment for poor speech or deliberate speech coaching, on the other hand, is associated with low verbal performance in the child (Bing, 1963; Marge, 1965).

SENSITIVITY AND RESPONSIVENESS

In all the research that has attempted to analyze "mothering" it is the "quality" of maternal contact that stands out most consistently as advantageous to optimal child development. "Quality" of maternal contact has different definitions. The most recent and popular emphasizes sensitivity and responsiveness. The "sensitive" mother is "tuned in" to her child's needs, wishes, and intentions; she can read his signals and she knows what will meet his needs and satisfy his desires. The "responsive" mother responds immediately and contingently to the signals of her child. To these maternal characteristics have been attributed decreased crying (Aldrich et al., 1945; Caudill, 1969; Stewart et al., 1954) and happier vocalization (Caudill, 1969). They have been associated with optimal attachment, balanced with exploratory behavior (Ainsworth & Bell, 1970; Clarke-Stewart, 1972), better overall emotional development (Robertson, 1962), greater verbal ability (Bing, 1963), cognitive development (Lewis & Goldberg, 1968), and intelligence (Clarke-Stewart, 1972; Weikart & Lambie, 1969). Lewis and Goldberg suggest that the sensitive and responsive mother creates in her infant a generalized expectancy that his behavior can affect, perhaps control, his environment. This motivates him to produce and utilize behaviors and skills not reinforced in his experience. Such an expectancy is essential to optimal development.

As children get older, but still before school age, specific maternal teaching strategies become important to the child's cognitive and social development. Apparently such strategies often differ for mothers of different social classes, though not of different races. In the laboratory, at least, middle-class mothers rely less on physical feedback; they motivate the child rather than threaten him and reinforce correct responses with praise rather than giving negative feedback or negative reinforcement for errors. They provide more orientation to the task and use more specific and complex language but give less specific suggestions than lower-class mothers (Bee et al., 1969; Hess, 1969; Walters, Connor, & Zunich, 1964; Zunich, 1962). Children who are exposed to these different teaching strategies differ in their immediate performances during the task being taught, in other problem-solving tasks, in intelligence test scores, in persistence, and in later reading achievement (Hess et al., 1969), and in distractibility (Bee, 1967). The teaching strategy described as characteristic of the middle-class mother is associated with superior child performance in all these measures. According to Hess, if a mother does not inject sufficient cognitive meaning into her interactions with her child, she may structure the interaction so that he not only fails to learn but develops a negative response to the experience and to all cognitive learning experiences.

"MATERNAL CHARACTERISTICS" APPLIED TO
DAY-CARE PROGRAMMING

The characteristics discussed in this chapter have been attributed to "mothers." They represent much more, however, than a description of how mothers behave with their own children. They apply equally well to the behavior toward children of teachers and other adults; they may be considered important and universal dimensions of child rearing. An ideal day-care program, in fact, may be equivalent to what an active mother does with her children.

The key generalizations and applications to be derived from this discussion are the following:

1. "Custodial care" is not sufficient for a child's optimal development.

2. The amount of adult contact per se is not so influential as the quality of that contact.

3. A caregiver should express warmth and positive emotion toward the child.

4. Physical stimulation is beneficial for the infant. Visual and verbal stimulation are more important for the older child.

5. Stimulation available in a context of play is most desirable.

6. The sensitivity and responsiveness of an adult caregiver may be the most powerful influence on the child's progress.

7. Cognitive teaching strategies of parents or other adults influence the child's intellectual development and academic achievement.

These generalizations can form the core of a day-care program in its treatment of children, its training of personnel, and its guidance of parents.

16

The Family: Summary and Recommendations

IN THIS *CONTEXT* WE HAVE DISCUSSED IN SOME DETAIL THE tenuous yet critical role of the family in American society. We have mentioned historical and current forces—urbanization, industrialization, immigration, migration, social mobility, expert opinion, and mass communication—pressures that have molded the family's role. These forces have been responsible for a lessening of parental control over children and at the same time have placed a greater emphasis on the parents' roles as motivators and teachers of their children; they have created a necessity for conformity, yet at the same time have thrown into closer contact families who represent great diversity in values, goals, and behaviors. We have attempted in this chapter to illustrate the diversity represented by the American family circa 1970.

Families vary in structure. Such variation is present even among well-functioning families. A family may be matrifocal; it may consist of an extended kinship group; it may be a smaller nuclear unit. All can function adequately. Each type of family structure has its own peculiar advantages and disadvantages. A family without a father present may be better for the children than an inharmonious two-parent family. An extended family may provide needed help for the parents in child raising and also allow the child to be exposed to more variation among adult figures, but it can lead to confusion for the child and inadequate attachment if there is a constant shifting of mother-figures, none of whom has developed close and dependable relations with the child. Multiple mothering in itself is not necessarily detrimental to the child's development. The extended family does provide continuity and stability, and it may be characterized by consistency and warmth. The small family may be especially responsive to change, which in these times may be its great advantage. On the other hand, it may be too vulnerable and unstable. It may require special types of community support.

Since American families represent diverse structural forms, each of which has strengths and weaknesses, we would recommend that day-care planners define program aspirations in terms of varying family structures and not solely in terms of the problems that are present when parental care cannot be provided. It is not clear that even specialized child-care institutions can function effectively if their purposes are narrow and if they recognize only a small part of the parent population. A full-time working mother may not be able to participate in a child-development program, but her sister, who cares for the child, might be an enthusiastic participant. The *central* mission of a day-care model is not to promote a particular caregiving arrangement but rather to conceptualize a set of procedures needed to develop optimizing environments in the home, playground, center, and school. We can conceive of a day-care model that could be realized with an office and several telephones and a "natural" child-care staff of hundreds who would work with children in homes and neighborhoods, learn about children in local high schools and colleges, and utilize parks and playgrounds, museums, movie theaters, stores, and firehouses. A day-care model deals with what happens when a caregiver, a child, and a resource come together. Any particular model can have an unlimited number of concrete realizations, and it can include components that consider the special features of different types of caregiving arrangements.

Physical environments provided by families vary enormously. These are the source of perceptual stimulation that is critical for optimal development of the child. Stimulation from such environments can be too much or too little; worse, it can be confusing, unresponsive, inappropriate, or unsystematic. The most critical aspect of stimulation appears to be its mediation by adults. It would not be an effective intervention in understimulating homes merely to deliver a box of toys and books to the door. It would not be effective even if the rats and roaches were exterminated and the walls freshly painted. Since effective stimulation must be mediated by adults, the parents must be interested and available, involved and knowledgeable.

The values, attitudes, and goals espoused by different families may, superficially, appear to be diverse. Fundamentally, however, they are probably more congruent than is evident on the surface. Happiness, honesty, consideration, obedience, dependability, self-control, popularity, neatness, and cleanliness are valued to some extent by all American parents. Particularly misleading are the variations associated with social-class divisions. Apparent differences have resulted from the environmental exigencies and social circumstances that make some goals unavailable or irrelevant and result in greater emphasis on those that are attainable. Basically, families of different social classes are in agreement. Furthermore, this agreement appears to be increasing and will continue to do so if ameliorative programs have their desired effect on social mobility of parents and if the value confrontations of the last few years lead middle-class parents to a more decisive and authoritative defense of these values. Fundamental differences present in groups of different ethnic or ideological subcultures have not been studied.

Among individual parents attitudes toward children vary from rejecting to accepting. The role of the parent may be perceived as limit setting and restrictive or affection-giving, supportive, and permissive. Some parents emphasize the child-rearing goals of neatness, cleanliness, obedience, rule-following, and respectability. Others are more abstract in their demands for internal standards, curiosity, and consideration. The trend that has been observed toward greater consensus may be true of parents at different socioeconomic levels, but current differences between the old and the new generations do not promise eventual total agreement. If young social radicals and reformers have any influence, the goal of neatness and cleanliness may be on the wane. Similarly, rule following and respect for society's authority are devalued in the new generation. Higher value is accorded spontaneity, joy, and pleasure, and the child's "doing his own thing" is of central importance. In these youthful groups there may also be a less utilitarian view of the child. Children are not a necessary component of status; they are not seen as a useful means of keeping parents together or as a way up the social ladder; such parents have no dynastic aims. Even if these parents become more conservative as they grow older, their children will have been reared according to these youthful ideas.

A generally valued goal among all parents is that of education for their children. Parents differ in the reasons they have for holding this value: it may be to get a job, to cope with daily problems, to earn more money, to gain status, to allow children to compete effectively or to develop individually. Parents also differ in their ideas about where this education should be obtained: at home, in the community, in "free schools," or in the educational establishment. The three R's appear to be a fundamental prerequisite. Generally, however, educational values imply a desire for competence, for growth and development, and for "moving up," whether personally or socially.

What happens if family and professionals differ about the needs of children and the goals of programs? Clearly the question may never be raised if the parents' involvement in a program consists of only a few minutes in the morning when the child is delivered and a few minutes in the evening when the child is picked up. When differences do appear, is the day-care worker to abandon years of training and firm beliefs about children out of respect for the possibly less informed desires of parents? Fortunately, professionals disagree on enough issues so that diversified day care can offer options to parents. Even more, the professional has an obligation to share with parents the basis of a program design. A

necessary prerequisite to meaningful parental participation is a thorough ground-
ing in what the program hopes to achieve and how it proposes to implement its
aspirations. Once the die is cast on the side of parental participation, programs
incur an obligation to create an educational experience for parents as well as for
children.

A crucial area of divergence of parental opinion and practice involves the
issue of discipline. Some parents utilize power-oriented techniques; some favor
"love-oriented" or psychological techniques; most use a mixture of both methods.
Some parents are extremely restrictive; others are totally permissive. Most are
somewhere in between. The issue of discipline is an extremely complex one. It
involves differential behaviors, effects, and interactions determined by sex, age,
and individual differences in parents and children; it must, furthermore, be
viewed in the emotional context in which it occurs. It appears that excesses in
the direction of too much discipline or too little should be avoided. A compromise
of firm yet mild discipline, appropriately and lovingly administered, might be a
possible way of incorporating the assets of both positions. Since the most critical
aspects of discipline is that it be consistent, this compromise solution may also
be necessary to provide consistency for the child between his home and out-of-
home setting.

Individual characteristics of mothers or primary caregivers may be the most
critical influence on the child's development. Such differences are not constrained
by ideological conviction or economic circumstance. They may, however, be somewhat modified by training. Studies of inadequate mothering, usually in institutions, have demonstrated that "custodial care" is not enough for the child's development, especially after the first six months. Research has revealed, moreover,

that mere quantity of maternal contact will not necessarily optimize the child's
development either. It is the quality of the interaction that is critical, particularly
the mother's consistent and evident warmth, her sensitivity and responsiveness,
her particular language behavior, and her mode of teaching cognitive strategies,
directly or indirectly, to her child.

The mother or other caregiver provides a complex and variable stimulus—in
some settings probably the most interesting and salient stimulus object in the
child's environment. She is also a responder and thus provides controllable stimulation, meets needs, and reinforces behaviors. The immediacy, contingency, and
accuracy of her responsive behavior is essential to the child's optimal development.
This is so not only in the narrow context of the efficacy of reinforcement for
increasing desired behaviors directly, or even indirectly by adding to the adult's
power as a model and teacher, but also more broadly by permitting the child
to control his environment. Moreover, the caregiver is a designer of "settings"
or experiences, a mediator of stimulation. Such stimulation can be material, perceptual, social-communicative, or achievement-oriented. A mother's role is not

simple, because it changes as the child grows older; for example, physical handling early in the child's life appears to be beneficial. After the baby is about 6 months old, however, there appears to be a shift so that a large amount of physical handling at this age is detrimental to development. At a later age, too, the mother assumes greater importance as a teacher. Her teaching of language and cognitive strategies is important to the child's performance in school. The characteristics and behaviors of mothers which we have emphasized are equally applicable to the preschool teacher or day-care worker.

Throughout this section on the family we have attempted to discuss possible relations between the family and the child and the family and out-of-home care of the child and to suggest ways in which knowledge of the family can be utilized in day-care programming. Day care can help families under pressure; it can help to achieve the educational goals of parents and children, it can foster their feelings of competence, and it can strengthen relations between them. It can do so only if day-care personnel are aware of and can deal with the varied problems with which they are faced, only if they recognize the differences between diversity of cultures and deficiency in competence, and only if they provide the warmth and consistency that are the successful modifiers of deprivation. Conversely, the family can help day care by providing enthusiastic support, labor, information, and a balancing force of individuality.

CONTEXT IV

EDUCATION

A GRADUALLY GROWING FORCE, ACCELERATED BY THE ADVENT of Sputnik and the war on poverty, has recently culminated in an explosion of projects focused on the early education of the child. Until a few decades ago the psychological-educational scene in the United States was dominated by beliefs in fixed intelligence and predetermined development. The dicta of Darwin, Gesell, Dennis, and Hall held sway. Even John Watson, the complete environmentalist, advised leaving the child until he had matured before redistributing his response repertoire. Consequently, unless one wanted to "tune up" the child's social skills or "tone down" his emotions by offering him the privilege of attending nursery school, starting school at age 6 was considered quite early enough.

Eventually, however, research data accumulating and ignored since Skeels and Dye's (1939) classic intervention study, had to be interpreted as indicating the great importance of early experiences. Results of research, such as that of Hebb (1949), Riesen (1947), and Thompson and Heron (1954) with animals, that of White, Castle, and Held (1964) with institutionalized infants, and Kirk (1958) with retarded children, revealed inescapably that early deprivation of sensory experience is deleterious, that provision of enrichment at a young age can accelerate development. Moreover, these studies were instrumental in creating the realization that cognitions as well as emotions can be shaped by early experience. Concurrently, developments in orthodox conditioning experiments began to demonstrate that learning need not be motivated by homeostatic need, painful stimulation, or even acquired drives, but sometimes could be attributed to such motives as "curiosity" or "exploration" or to a desire for increasing complexity (White, 1959). This made it even easier to justify providing early learning environments for very young children. Bloom's (1964) widely quoted, if misleading, statistic that 50% of a person's mature intelligence develops in the first four years of life provided a final, empirically based push toward educating the preschool child.

At the same time, in the spirit of Kennedy liberalism, white middle-class America woke up to the plight of its poor and black compatriots. Negro and lower-class Americans, beyond their obvious disadvantages in the labor force and in living arrangements, were apparently losing out right from the beginning of elementary school. An "obvious" solution to this problem was to provide poor children with enriched experiences before entering school. In 1965 Project Head Start, sponsored by the Office of Economic Opportunity, after an all-too-brief period of intensive planning, burst on the country. Head Start has been the most extensive and prominent preschool education project attempted. It is certainly not the only one, however, and in this Context we describe some of the variety available in well-designed and carefully implemented early education projects.

Some say that Head Start—in fact that compensatory education—has failed (cf. Elkind, 1969a; Jensen, 1969). There are many answers to this controversial accusation. One emphasizes the importance of adequate and appropriate evaluation of early education projects, a requirement in which some think Head Start has been remiss (e.g. Campbell & Erlebacher, 1970). A second response focuses on younger and younger children; perhaps intervention at age 4 or 5 is already too late. A third answer, related to the first, insists that nationwide Head Start cannot be considered a unitary program and that knowledge of the effectiveness of compensatory education depends on careful analysis of separate components— teachers, samples, curricula, goals. Another perhaps more searching answer takes the form of a string of questions. What exactly was Head Start designed to achieve? Is it being faulted for failures that were not part of its intentions (White, 1970)?

Each of the issues implied in these "answers" to the current dilemma of compensatory early education is also discussed in this section. We can promise no definitive answers to the questions raised. What kinds of teachers are most effective? What is the best program for ghetto children? How many children should participate in a class? What is the optimal ratio of teachers to pupils? What goals are most appropriate? We have, however, included relevant published data that bear on these questions. They are the most positive and "hopeful" data available. They demonstrate the effectiveness that small, carefully planned and monitored projects can have for the education of young disadvantaged children.

It is our feeling that education is an essential aspect of the multidisciplinary context of day care in the 70's. In the Context that follows three aspects of educational designs are discussed: variations in program dimensions, implementation factors (physical settings, teacher variables, peer-group influences, individual differences), and evaluation. Whether one is concerned with early education per se, with compensatory education in particular, or with the application of educational principles to all-day care of young children in homes or in centers, these educational features demand consideration.

17

Programs

ALL EARLY EDUCATION PROJECTS HAVE TEACHERS AND SPACE and equipment and, of course, children, but it is the way in which components are integrated that constitutes the "program." A great number of diverse preschool programs are in operation in the United States. They differ in ways that are externally obvious: duration, size of group, population served, and age of children. Here we have chosen to discuss the less obvious but perhaps more fundamental and significant theoretical dimensions along which they vary. It is our feeling that a close examination of the subtle assumptions and theoretical biases on which programs are based will be a valuable exercise for anyone interested in the welfare and education of children. Before any program for children is established, evaluated, or replicated it should receive such scrutiny from its prospective implementers or assessors. Whenever possible in our discussion the results of formal evaluations have been included, although too few attempts to compare programs along such dimensions have been made.

There are, to be sure, areas of general agreement and basic similarities between programs. All agree that education is worthwhile, that a child should enjoy the program and experience success within it, and that he must be motivated in order to learn. All agree that economically disadvantaged children can learn under the "right" conditions, although definitions of "right" naturally vary. In all programs, whether based on Skinnerian principles of programmed learning or Piagetian stages, there is agreement that sequencing of lessons or materials is essential.

Another area of consensus is the importance of individualized approaches. In some programs attention to the child is entirely individualized, as in tutoring

199

(Gordon* [home program]; Painter; Weikart and Lambie [home program]; Skeels and Dye; Montessori). Moreover, in group settings some programs make an initial diagnosis of an individual child's level and then plan his individual program accordingly (Deutsch; Glazer and Resnick; Spiker, Hodges and Mc-Candless). Even in programs in which children are taught in groups, grouping is usually homogeneous according to the child's initially assessed ability (Bereiter, Engelmann and Becker; Costello; Sprigle). Frequently, too, within group settings such as nursery school or day care, special effort is taken to provide occasional individualized help, attention, and guidance on a one-to-one basis (Blank and Solomon; Caldwell and Lally; Kirk; Nimnicht, Meier and McAfee). This consensus regarding individualization has three implications: different children profit most from different types of program; any program, to be effective, must start from where the individual child is; individual attention is beneficial to any child and essential to the "hard to reach" (Costello, 1970b).

In order to examine the fundamental dimensions differentiating programs let us view each dimension as a continuum (Figure 1). Ideally, the best treatment of these dimensions would involve sending a blank set of rating scales to each program inventor and asking him to rate his own program. At the same time a trained rater would be sent to observe each program in operation to make an objective rating. Unfortunately, we were unable to carry out such a project. Therefore our placement of illustrative programs on these dimensions is based solely on published descriptions with the realization that if program developers were asked to do their own placing our educational map might look quite different. Indeed, we hope that program dimensions will become so carefully and systematically formulated in the future that the characterization of any given program would cause little controversy.

At the outset we must explain that these dimensions are not necessarily independent or unidimensional. We believe, however, that they are useful in conceptualizing important distinctions between programs.

CONCEPTION OF THE CHILD

Perhaps the most fundamental dimension on which programs differ relates to the issue of "what is a child?"; that is, how much potential does the child possess

---

* In the discussion of programs that follows programs are generally referred to by the name(s) of their principal investigator(s), undated. References of program descriptions are indexed in the bibliography under these authors' names. We are also indebted to Maccoby and Zellner's summarized descriptions of different *Follow Through* models and to the program descriptions in the 1968 AIR Evaluation Report by Hawkridge, Chalupsky, and Roberts (republished: USDHEW, *Preschool programs in compensatory education* 1 [*It Works*]).

already? Must certain environmental conditions be imposed on him in order to ensure his optimal development? This dimension has been discussed by Caldwell (1967), Zigler (1968), Elkind (1969b), and Kohlberg (1968). It looks like an updated and applied reformulation of the old environment-heredity controversy. The extreme positions are no longer mentioned, however, and the dichotomy has become a continuum or, perhaps more accurately, a trichotomy. The difference between maturational and environmental theories is no longer in the exclusive recognition of either innate or environmental causal factors in development but rather which set of factors is considered the source of basic patterning.

At the extreme left of this scale, influenced by Rousseau, Gesell, and Freud and espoused by some traditional nursery schools, is a position that seeks to enliven the educational process from the inside out by means of freeing the child's emotions, fantasies, and drives. It is a position which assumes that the child is driven (intrinsically motivated) by powerful forces to grow and learn: the "thrusts" for companionship, physical competence, independence, and understanding (Law, 1964). These thrusts will inevitably lead to absorption of an education from the environment in which he finds himself. The main role of the nursery school teacher is to teach the child to control his (antisocial) impulses and to provide the environment in which these thrusts may be fulfilled. The pedagogical environment should create a climate that allows inner "good" (abilities and social virtues) to unfold and permits inner "bad" to come under the influence of the inner good. It should be an "enriched" environment which allows for self-expression, creativity, and a "readiness" that will develop spontaneously. Programs that hold this maturational position are child-centered and present-oriented.

At the opposite end of this dimension is the environmentalist position. This approach to education originated in the work of Locke, Thorndike, Skinner, Fowler, and Berlyne and presently finds support in the programs of Bushell, Etzel, Baer, and Risley, Ulrich and Wolfe, and Bereiter, Engelmann, and Becker. These educators adopt Bruner's hypothesis that any subject can be taught effectively in some intellectually honest form to any child at any stage of development, but they fail to acknowledge Bruner's qualification: that a child's developmental level determines the teaching procedures and materials likely to be most effective and the level of understanding he can attain. This is the environmental mystique: that the intellect is plastic and trainable, an environmental product. In this goal-and-future-oriented view the child is seen as under environmental control. The direction of education in these programs is from the outside in. It is important that the child gain cognitive and moral knowledge and that he learn the rules of the culture. This can occur only if he is given information by direct instruction. Environmentalists admit that for the child to accept this knowledge he must be motivated. Motivation as well as information, however, may be imposed extrinsically. Consequently these programs employ direct, external reinforcement, faith-

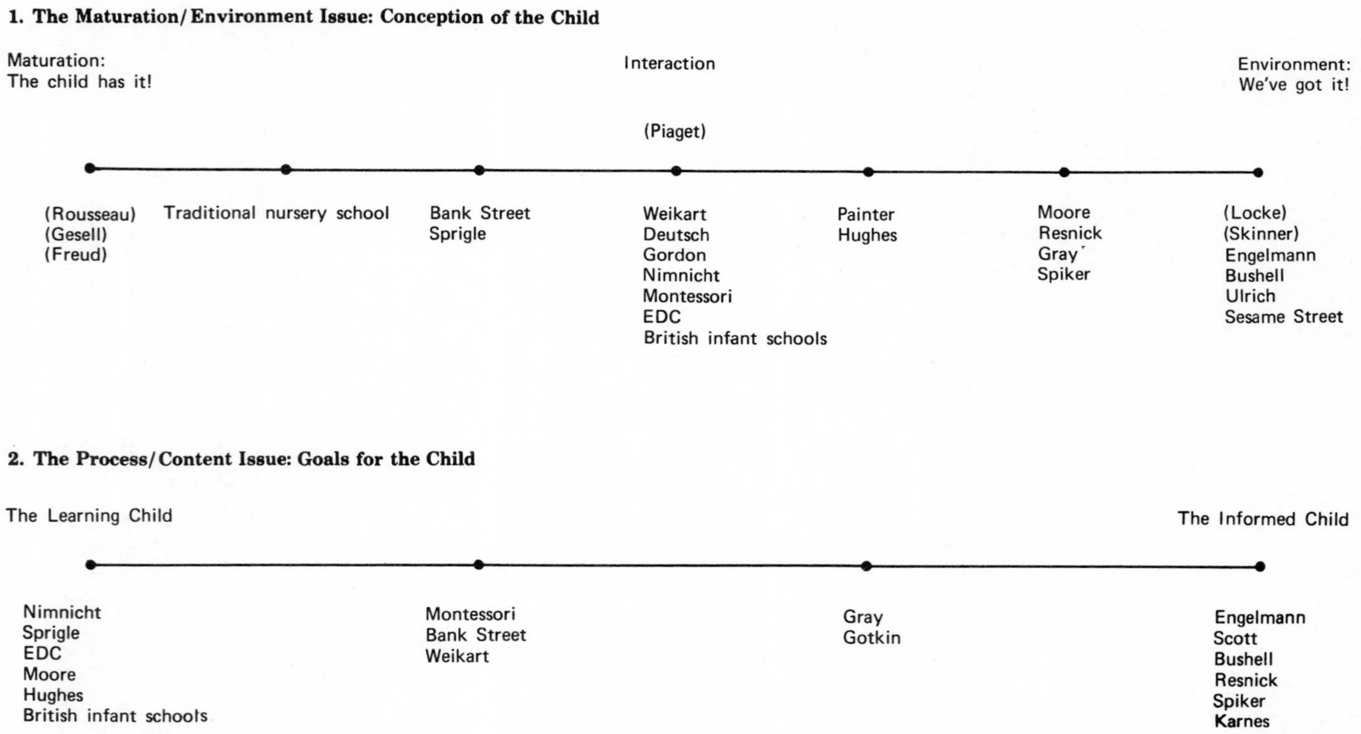

1. The Maturation/Environment Issue: Conception of the Child

Maturation:
The child has it!

Interaction

Environment:
We've got it!

(Piaget)

(Rousseau)
(Gesell)
(Freud)

Traditional nursery school

Bank Street
Sprigle

Weikart
Deutsch
Gordon
Nimnicht
Montessori
EDC
British infant schools

Painter
Hughes

Moore
Resnick
Gray
Spiker

(Locke)
(Skinner)
Engelmann
Bushell
Ulrich
Sesame Street

2. The Process/Content Issue: Goals for the Child

The Learning Child

The Informed Child

Nimnicht
Sprigle
EDC
Moore
Hughes
British infant schools

Montessori
Bank Street
Weikart

Gray
Gotkin

Engelmann
Scott
Bushell
Resnick
Spiker
Karnes

Figure 1. Preschool program dimensions. Programs are labeled by the name of the person or institution most commonly associated with them. More complete listings of associated investigators are given in the text. Names in parentheses refer to persons whose thinking has been associated with the position indicated on the scale.

3. The Hard/Soft Issue: Aspect of Development Emphasized

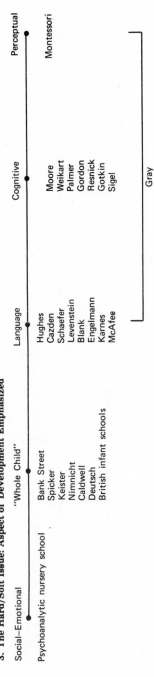

Social–Emotional	"Whole Child"	Language	Cognitive	Perceptual
Psychoanalytic nursery school	Bank Street Spicker Keister Nimnicht Caldwell Deutsch British infant schools	Hughes Cazden Schaefer Levenstein Blank Engelmann Karnes McAfee	Moore Weikart Palmer Gordon Resnick Gotkin Sigel	Montessori

Gray

4. The "Depth of Solution" Issue: Level of Education Attempted

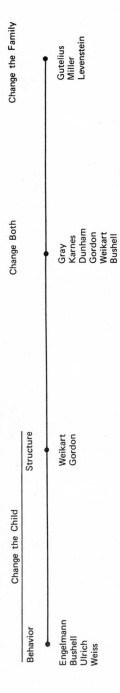

Change the Child		Change Both	Change the Family
Behavior	Structure		
Engelmann Bushell Ulrich Weiss	Weikart Gordon	Gray Karnes Dunham Gordon Weikart Bushell	Gutelius Miller Levenstein

5. The Degree of Structure Issue: Program Techniques

Unstructured   Highly Structured

Keister	Bank Street	Nimnicht	Montessori		Karnes	Engelmann
Skeels	EDC	Gray	Moore		Painter	Gotkin
Traditional	Robinson	Hughes	Weikart			Spiker
nursery school	British infant schools	Sprigle				Deutsch

6. The People/Things Issue: Amount of Adult–Child Contact

Teacher–Centered   Materials–Centered

Engelmann	Bushell	Deutsch	Bank Street	Resnick	Nimnicht	Stern
Hughes		Gray	Caldwell	EDC		Moore
Rheingold						Montessori
Skeels						

fully administered according to the principles of instrumental conditioning. Food, praise, feedback, tokens, dramatic change of pace, novel teacher reactions, and children's preferred activities are all used as incentives to motivate the child's learning. Negative reinforcement such as scolding, more work, loss of reward, or isolation may also be used. According to these educators, there *is* no distinction between intrinsic and extrinsic motivation. By a process of gradually reducing tangible external reinforcement and continually using the least powerful reinforcement that is effective, the child can be taught to want to learn. Therefore they see no reason for waiting for this motivation to develop naturally. Children exposed to these techniques are able to work progressively more independently. Such programs have generally been successful in effecting IQ and achievement test gains (Bereiter & Engelmann, 1968; Etzel, 1970; Ulrich, Wolfe, & Bluhm, 1968).

Between these two extremes lie the majority of preschool programs, which approach to greater or lesser degree an interactionist position. The "truly" interactional approach owes its impetus to Jean Piaget. It is not equivalent to a watered-down amalgam of maturational and environmental approaches and most accurately probably should not be placed on the same continuum. The interactionist position maintains that favorable cognitive and affective structures are natural emergents from interactions between the child and an environment in which such interaction is allowed or fostered. Educators espousing this view believe in the child's potentialities, his inherent motivation to learn, and his ability to develop competence when provided with a suitably stimulating environment. By means of adaptive actions on objects, classes, and relations between classes during transactions with the environment the child proceeds through stages of structural reorganization. The best conditions for this reorganization entail an optimal balance of discrepancy and match between behavioral structures of the child and structures of his environment.

The child, in this view, is intrinsically motivated. Mastery of new tasks and reduction of incongruity are intrinsically gratifying. Thought processes occur spontaneously when proper "nourishment" is available and do not require specifically directed experiences. Learning involves a continuous process of searching for increasing complexity, increasing novelty, and successive cognitive matches. It must be directed by the child, since only he knows his optimal level of complexity. Providing the opportunity for the child to make these matches is the role of the teacher in such a program.

The interactionist account assumes that structural change depends on experience. The effect of experience, however, is not conceptualized as the reinforcement of responses; rather the effect of training is determined by the child's cognitive categories. This position acknowledges that experience is necessary for the child's stages of development to take the shape they do, as well as often assuming that generally more or richer stimulation will lead to faster advances through the stages.

An interactionist position characterizes the Montessori Method. This program offers the child an opportunity to interact individually with an environment that is specially structured to provide experiences of increasing complexity. It is founded on the assumption that a stage in development is reached in which the child seeks out new experiences, an activity that becomes rewarding in itself. It emphasizes that learning for its own sake should never be replaced by performance for reward or punishment. The Montessori approach differs from Bruner's in a significant way: Montessori defines subject matter and the child's task according to the child's developmental level (e.g., at one level the task might be to order things on the continuum of size, brightness, or weight, whereas at another the task might be to order quantities); Bruner attempts to teach the child an adult conception of the subject matter (e.g., the theory of numbers), regardless of the child's developmental level. At the same time Bruner would have teaching methods take into account the system of representation (enactive, iconic, or symbolic) which the child can use at any particular time. He thus combines a developmental view of the child's competence with an adult definition of the child's attainable knowledge.

An interactionist approach to preschool and infant education is also seen in the programs of Weikart, Deutsch, Gordon, and Nimnicht and in the Leicestershire infant schools. These programs have been successful in improving intellectual functioning as measured by IQ tests. Furthermore, children given special Piagetian training in object relationships, although they gained only five IQ points, were significantly superior in logical operations (Lavatelli, 1968b).

A position between maturational and interactionist emphasis would be accorded such programs as the Bank Street Nursery schools (Biber, Minuchin) and the Learning to Learn program (Sprigle, Van De Riet). Although they accept Piagetian views in some form, these programs lean toward emphasis on the child's innate drives. The Learning to Learn program is based on the assumption that every child has a drive toward maturity, increased competence, mastery, and that conditions for change are present. However, it is also founded on acceptance of Piaget's key tenet that stable and enduring cognitions of the world come about only by active commerce with the world on the part of the knower. The Bank Street philosophy has roots in the ideas of Freud and Gesell, modified by the shift in psychoanalytic thinking to functions of the ego and by the work of Piaget. Bank Street educators maintain that motivation develops from the intrinsic pleasure and satisfaction of learning, especially when learning is grounded in the real experiences of living and supported by a special kind of relationship between children and teachers.

The programs of Painter at University of Illinois and Hughes in Tucson,

Arizona, are interactionist, yet give more weight to the influence of the environment. Hughes's philosophy is that the child does not have to be forced or even asked to learn. If the environment is sufficiently interesting, it will, of itself and without any prodding from the teacher, "demand" that the child learn. Painter, also acknowledging the importance of interaction to the child's development, employs implicit reinforcement to assist the learning process by sequential presentation of material and activities from least to most preferred.

The programs of Moore, Resnick, Hodges, Spicker, McCandless, and Gray give still more emphasis to environmental factors; Spicker, Hodges, McCandless, and Resnick use external rewards; so does Gray's Early Training Project at DARCEE, George Peabody College. This last program has been observed to be comparatively high in active teaching, direct academic requests, verbal instruction by the teacher, and recitation by the children as well as in the frequency of contingent positive reinforcement such as praise and knowledge of results (Miller & Dyer, 1970). The "responsive" aspect of Moore's environment and its most famous representative, the talking typewriter, also provide reinforcement. This reinforcement comes through immediate feedback, whereas its "autotelic" aspect permits the child to select from among the available instructional devices those encounters that suit him.

THE PROCESS/CONTENT ISSUE

Related to one's conception of the child is the opinion of what the child should become. This is the issue of "school orientation" versus "human orientation" or, from a slightly different angle, the issue of "content" versus "process." The two extremes can be described as the desire for an informed child versus the goal of a learning child. Concurrent with the view that the source of basic patterning is the environment, there is a belief that the acquisition of specific, usually academic, content by children can and should be the goal of education. This position also usually entails the belief that the child should be a success in the school system as it exists. Those who attribute more of the basic patterning to the child, however, frequently believe that the *process* of learning is more important than specific content, and they attempt to create programs that will further this goal of education. Their aims for the child generally include individual autonomy and self-actualization rather than normative goals focused on academic achievement. Potentially this view, by proposing the importance of individual achievement, is more likely to permit diversity of outcomes, including those that are racially or ethnically influenced. By the same token it has always alarmed those who realize that social mobility through education is often contingent on normative achievement indices.

Content emphasizers have devised early-education programs that base their curricula on "the three R's." The Bereiter-Engelmann-Becker program, perhaps the most extreme example, deliberately teaches the skills that are being tested: basic academic concepts in language, arithmetic, and reading. In Karnes' Ameliorative Program, another content-oriented intervention, lessons are given in mathematics concepts, language arts, reading readiness, and science-social studies. The purpose of Project Homestart (Scott, 1967), similarly, is to develop skills with a formal school end, even though this is a home-visitation program that starts as early as age 2. School-appropriate behaviors also are taught specifically in Bushell's program in Kansas and Resnick's in Pittsburg. Bushell uses systematic reinforcement to teach the child skills he will need to compete effectively in school: knowing when to talk and when not to talk, to stay with assigned tasks, and to respond appropriately to praise, as well as the conventional subjects: language, reading, writing, and mathematics. In Spicker, Hodges, and McCandless's program, in addition to language skills, the child is taught to take turns, to call the teacher by name, to brush his teeth, to wash his hands after toileting, to answer in complete sentences, and to say "please" and "thank you."

An intermediate position on this continuum can be attributed to Weikart, Gray, Gotkin, Montessori, and Bank Street. The Perry Preschool Project (Weikart, Kamii, and Radin) is concerned with subsequent academic and social adjustment in school. It teaches language, impulse control, and task orientation. Teachers are urged, however, to treat children as autonomous individuals who can make choices for themselves in an effort to assist development of the child's self-concept and his capacity to learn and solve problems. Moreover, this program may be shifting toward less and less concern with formal academics (Weikart, 1971).

Although it emphasizes school achievement, there is no deliberate coaching for tests in the DARCEE Early Training Project (Gray). The goals are to develop achievement aptitudes (cognitive skills, perceptual discriminations, language, and attention span) and attitudes (motivation, persistence, interest in school-type activities and materials, and identification with achieving role models). These achievements are intended to lead to successful learning not only in school but at home and in the community as well. The content of Gotkin's Games is as specific and academic as that found in the Bereiter-Engelmann-Becker program. Gotkin, however, seeks to emphasize the fun involved in the process of learning.

Although the Montessori *environment* is highly structured, the schedule and the selection of models or materials is not. Here the learning process of discovery is emphasized. Graded materials permit the child to grow as his interests lead him from one level of complexity to another; self-correction is built into the materials. The child educates himself; the teacher is just there to help on request. Freedom permits the child to create for himself situations from which he can learn. Yet Montessori programs are not at the extreme left on this dimension, since they do not explicitly emphasize "process" over "content," except in their goals of attention and concentration. Furthermore, the materials available to the child are limited and offer mainly perceptual experience rather than the opportunity to understand or the logical operations to develop. The concentration is on formal learning of practical skills, sensory concepts, reading, writing, and arithmetic.

Traditional nursery school programs, particularly those formulated by Bank Street educators, have always stressed self-actualization, free choice, and "discovery." However, since they do not focus on the learning process per se, they, too, are given an intermediate position on this dimension. The child in nursery school is encouraged to experiment, dramatize, improvise, and create with the diverse materials available. He is stimulated to start searching, and his spontaneously initiated activities, including play, are responded to as potential learning experiences by nursery school teachers. Yet, besides such encouragement of self-development, the nursery school has recently incorporated a specific content emphasis. Language and cognitive skills, in particular, are formally taught, although still in the context of the child's own activities and communications. Moreover, the child is taught school-like routines; he is taught to follow directions in a group and to respect authority, and an attempt is made to inculcate attitudes conducive to harmony between individuals.

At the extreme on this dimension are those programs that emphasize the *process* of learning. They do not favor teaching the child specific content. Some would even be against such teaching at a preschool age on the basis that to focus on training for specific skills is to teach the child a body of information whose meaning to him is full of subjective distortions (Smock, 1968). This is based on the realization that the young child's mode of thinking and his experience of reality are different from the adult's.

Several different approaches have in common the primary goal of a learning child. As its name suggests, the Learning to Learn program was conceived and developed on the premise that the primary objective of early childhood education is to help the child learn to learn. This program does not make a frontal attack on language, perceptual development, readiness skills, or exposure to a variety of rich experiences; it is *not* just preparation for first grade. It emphasizes the foundation of basic concepts on which the child will build later learning. The child is led from dependence on manipulation to internalization of experiences, words, and ideas. Sprigle has articulated the basic principles underlying this program:

1. The child must be an active participant in the acquisition of knowledge and be given a major share of the work in what he learns.

2. The child must receive feedback that the application of his knowledge has made a contribution to himself and someone else.

3. The internal satisfaction and feeling of adequacy that develop from the knowledge that he can cope with and master his environment stimulate the child's growth toward independence and achievement.

4. Learning becomes more meaningful to the child when it is in the form of a problem that challenges him and sparks his curiosity. The emphasis is placed on the process of problem solving and not on the accuracy of the solution.

5. The verbal symbols, concepts, skills, and attitudes learned will more readily become a part of the permanent repertoire of intelligent behavior if they are immediately useful and helpful in the child's everyday world.

6. The child must be exposed to opportunities for the interaction of multiple sensory and other activities and the accurate labeling and communication of the information received.

7. Learning experiences for the child take on value not in mere exposure but in their timing, continuity, and the ways in which they are structured.

Another approach to the contentless curriculum is advocated by the Educational Development Center (Armington, EDC), which is based on the open classroom of the British infant schools (Barth & Rathbone, 1969; Cazden, 1969b; Featherstone, 1967; Hull, 1964; Plowden Report, 1967a). A major emphasis in this approach is self-development for teachers, students, and programs. The fundamental aim is to have the child assume the responsibility for his own learning. Children are encouraged to initiate activities, to be self-directing, and to become intensely involved in their interests. Typically, many different often interdisciplinary activities are going on. The flexible time schedule permits children to learn according to their individual rhythms of engagement and disengagement. The theme of self-management also finds expression in a social environment of cooperation in which children work together and learn from one another. The environment is characterized by openness and trust: open space, open time, open curriculum, open self, open choice. Furthermore, what the child learns in this environment is functional, relevant to his own needs and interests rather than to those of the program directors. Learning usually occurs by experimentation with carefully selected materials rather than in textbooks or readers or by rote learning or memorization. Children are encouraged to face uncertainty and change, to tackle complexities they have not been taught how to manage, to be unafraid of being wrong, to be open and honest, to challenge ideas, to respect others, themselves, and the environment, and to accept responsibility as a part of freedom.

The teacher is seen as a responsive, insightful human being who likes children. She enters into their growth, not as someone who directs or is a sideline spectator, but as a guide who is constantly involved, and whose objective is to get the child involved in things relevant to him.

A third program that emphasizes the process of learning has been adopted at the New Nursery School in Greeley, Colorado, and in other projects started by Glen Nimnicht. The purpose of these programs is to develop individuals who have the ability to solve problems on their own and the confidence to attack them. They attempt to promote the formation of concepts essential to later learning by enhancing the child's intellect, his sense of autonomy, and his self-concept. The classroom environment is structured so that as the child explores it freely he will make interrelated discoveries about his physical, cultural, and social world; for example, by experimenting with the electric typewriter, the child learns to read and write; at the same time he is learning to find answers to problems by himself. Two main concepts in this program, which have been adopted from O. K. Moore, are *autotelic* and *responsive*. An autotelic activity is self-rewarding and does not depend on rewards or punishments that are not related to the activity itself; for example, the words the child learns are important to him. They allow the learner to reason things out for himself and free him from dependence on authority. Furthermore, the environment in which these activities take place is responsive to the child. It is responsive to what he is interested in learning and gives him immediate feedback from his problem-solving attempts. The teacher, too, is responsive to the child. She guides him, helps him find answers, but avoids giving them to him. When she thinks it is appropriate to teach a particular concept or fact, she does so by making use of and elaborating on what the child is interested in. Moreover, the program is basically self-pacing, in accordance with another suggestion made by Moore.

In Marie Hughes's program there is also less emphasis on the items taught and the transmission of specific content than on "learning to learn." Here, too, the teacher is at the service of the child. She does not insist that he perform as she directs. Language is made available, but not taught; for example, children write and record stories about the Dewey-like projects they undertake. Content is relevant; reading and writing are functional.

At least limited support for the success of *all* these programs has been found in evaluation research. Bereiter and Engelmann (1968) raised the IQ scores of disadvantaged preschoolers 17.14 points in the first year and 8.61 points in the second. This was a decidedly superior outcome compared with the IQ score changes effected in a nursery school control group. The effectiveness of direct teaching of specific content has been demonstrated as well in Karnes' Amelioration program (Karnes et al., 1969) and the Perry Preschool Project headed by Weikart (1968). Gains thus induced are evident in measures of intelligence, verbal ability, and achievement. According to Weikart (1967), success in improving language, IQ scores, and quantitative skills depended on how much deliberate effort had

been made to teach these skills. In a comparative study of his own program
with Bereiter-Engelmann's and a traditional nursery school, Weikart (reported
in Hunt, 1969b) found that after one semester of preschool experience the gains
in IQ scores made under the Bereiter-Engelmann program were substantially
the largest; the gains under Weikart's program come next; and those of the
children in the more traditional preschool program were the smallest. By June
of the year, however, the mean gains for the various programs had essentially
evened (33, 28, and 28.5, respectively). These data are not conclusive, since
there was no teacher control or replication and because not all other program
comparisons concur. There is, however, a suggestion that even when the dependent measure is the IQ score, one cannot conclude that specific academic content
is the only or necessarily best way of improving scores. Support for the position
comes from the reported success of programs at the other extreme of the continuum. Sprigle (Van De Riet & Van De Riet, 1969b) obtained IQ gains of 14
and 19 points (compared with kindergarten or no-treatment controls whose IQ's
dropped 7 and 2 points in the same time). Nimnicht (1967) also reported significant gains for his subjects in IQ score, self-image, and readiness. Weikart's
most recent conclusion (1971) regarding the results of his comparative program
evaluation is that it is the teacher's competence rather than the specific academic
content or theoretical approach of a program that determines its effectiveness.

Although standardized measures of "learning to learn" are not available,
subjective impressions of the effectiveness of the approach of the "left" *are* favorable. Featherstone (1967) observed that, although the children in British infant
schools may not have been getting spectacular scores on standard achievement
tests, what they did know, they knew well and that knowledge included such
essential cognitive operations as conservation and seriation. Similarly favorable is
Hunt's (1967b) observation that the children in Marie Hughes's program were
"turned on" to their projects and classmates and were eager to talk about them.
This contrasted with the attitude of children in a reinforcement-content-oriented
program, who were interested in talking only about how to win prizes with tokens and not about curricular matter at all.

THE "WHOLE" CHILD

Different program innovators have chosen to emphasize different aspects of child
development. The dimension of "the whole child," too, is related to our discussion, since it affects what the specific content of a program will be. At the "soft"
end of this dimension the child's social and emotional behaviors receive a great
deal of attention; at the "hard" end his perception and cognition are emphasized.

In the middle might be placed those programs that attempt to focus on "the whole child."

The best example of a purely perceptual emphasis is found in strict Montessori programs. Like Hebb (1949), Maria Montessori hypothesized that simple sensory learning transfers to complex perceptual tasks. Consequently the program she devised emphasizes sensory concepts in reading, writing, and arithmetic. What the Montessori program lacks are interpersonal, affective, aesthetic, and play experiences.

The most popular current approach to early education places emphasis on cognition and language. This is especially applicable to programs that intervene in the lives of disadvantaged children. Some programs that stress cognition are like Weikart's Piagetian-based preschool project, which does not enrich or extend, but in carefully programmed sequence teaches temporal relations, spatial seriation, classification, and symbolism. O. K. Moore's responsive environment also encourages development of cognitive elements, such as the discovery of relations and new experiences in the physical, cultural, and social world. Ira Gordon's Florida project is oriented toward the Piagetian theory of cognitive development. The children learn to seriate, to classify, and to name. Tasks related to Piagetian stages are progressively sequenced and demonstrated in a variety of contexts in class and at home; for example, a systematic attempt is made to enumerate all the ways in which the toys and objects in the classroom can be used and the child is then helped to discover and explore the alternatives himself. Results indicate that these methods are successful in improving cognitive performance (Gordon, 1969a; Weikart, 1969; Weikart & Wiegerink, 1968).

Two short-term cognitive studies should be mentioned to illustrate the range of programs that emphasize cognition. Palmer and Rees (1969) found that two hour-long concept-training sessions a week were sufficient to increase the scores of 2- and 3-year-olds in intelligence, language motivation, and classification tasks. Classificatory training (Sigel & Olmstead, 1967) was responsible also for increasing the frequency of grouping responses and the ability to form and articulate classes. Equivalent sessions of verbal interaction or role playing given to comparison groups of children had no effect on these responses. Miller (1969) summarizes a review of short intervention studies with the generalization that when limited intervention objectives in psychomotor and cognitive areas are clearly delineated and intervention techniques are specifically designed to accomplish these objectives significant gains can be obtained over a short intervention period.

DiLorenzo (DiLorenzo, Salter, & Brady, 1969) was responsible for a four-year comparative study of eight different preschool programs in the State of New York, all of which were the same length and included free play, snacks, outdoor activities, rest period, and group activities. In three of them special cognitive additions were incorporated. One involved individual work with reading readiness; a second, Bereiter-Engelmann language drills or small group discussions; the third utilized a combination of the Edison Responsive Environment (Talking Typewriter), modified Montessori materials, and games of Language Lotto. This study revealed significant differences between the disadvantaged children in these eight programs and children in a no-treatment control group on the Stanford Binet, the Peabody Picture Vocabulary Test, the Illinois Test of Psycholinguistic Abilities, and the Metropolitan Readiness tests—*only* in the programs with cognitive additions. For middle-class children, however, nursery school-type programs did increase IQ scores (cf. Miller and associates, 1970). None of these programs was effective in improving self-concept or physical development.

Programs emphasizing language development are currently in vogue, (e.g., Cazdan; Hughes; Schaefer, Furfey, and Harte; McAfee; Karnes; Levenstein; Blank and Solomon; Bereiter, Engelmann, and Becker). Their diverse approaches to teaching language include expansion or modeling of language, the talking typewriter, the Language Master, language games, and operant conditioning. Each of these techniques has improved children's language behavior to some extent, usually more than the programs that have no specific language emphasis (Blank & Solomon, 1969; Karnes et al., 1969). Evaluation results suggest that systematic verbalization from an adult which demands reciprocal verbal interaction from the child is most effective in improving language and IQ scores (Bereiter & Engelmann, 1966; Blank & Solomon, 1969; Karnes et al., 1969) and later achievement, particularly in reading (Karnes et al., 1969).

A popular approach to early education, traditionally the domain of the nursery school, is the attempt to foster development of the "whole" child. Although at one time nursery school programs may have been directed almost exclusively toward the child's social and emotional needs, their goals now include promoting personal, social, motor, intellectual, and language development. Current nursery school objectives include meeting organic needs and establishing routine habits, developing large muscle and manipulative skills, and teaching control and restraint. They attempt to foster in the child the development of self-possession, security, and self-confidence; they provide an environment in which to learn to play, to get along with others, to understand adults, to respect the rights of others, to share, to speak well, to be creative, and to learn and utilize cognitive strategies (Sears & Dowley, 1963). Children's activities in nursery school include music, story, and art activities, play in the doll corner, and use of the housekeeping center, the block area, and outdoors.

Other approaches similarly concerned with the development of "the whole child" would be those of the New Nursery School, Caldwell, Deutsch, and the British infant schools.

Current preschool programs do not often focus solely on the child's emotional needs. One such "therapeutic" program, in which teachers acted as mother figures, was compared with a conventional nursery school program by Strodtbeck (1963). In both programs children made intellectual gains, but the gains were much greater in the conventional program. In general, nursery school appears to benefit social rather than intellectual development. Children who attend nursery school made gains in initiative, independence, self-assertion, self-reliance, curiosity, interest in the environment (Walsh, 1931), and sociability (Hattwick, 1936); they also evidenced fewer undesirable infantile dependent and nervous habits (Hattwick, 1936; Joel, 1939; Kawin & Hoefer, 1931). Furthermore, later sociometric ratings of children from "good" nursery schools were higher than those of children who did not have that experience (Allen & Masling, 1957; Bonney & Nicholson, 1958). Apparently, however, the effectiveness of nursery school enrichment is limited. Nursery school had no significant benefit for children who already came from privileged homes (Olson & Hughes, 1940), and differences between nursery school and control children diminished after the first year (Jersild & Fite, 1939).

Investigators have attempted to compare the relative effects of programs that differ on this dimension of emphasis. Cox (1968) found that a Montessori program was more beneficial than a traditional nursery school program in personal-social responsiveness, associative vocabulary, and test scores on the Binet, the PPVT, and Caldwell's Preschool Inventory. This was true for both lower- and middle-class children. Dreyer and Rigler discovered in their comparison that

> Montessori children responded to the emphasis in their program upon the physical world and upon a definition of school as a place of work; Nursery School children responded on their part to the social emphasis and the opportunity for spontaneous expression of feeling (1969, p. 415).

Montessori programs have also been associated with increased verbal ability, greater independence, self-confidence, readiness for first grade, improved interpersonal relations, and learning ability (Fleege, 1967), especially in lower-class children (Stodolsky & Jensen, 1969). They have not been found to improve creativity, sensorimotor coordination, or learning attitudes (Fleege, 1967). Even when modified by the additional enrichments of expression and dramatic play and family social services, they have not always increased cognitive development (Stodolsky & Jensen, 1969). Moreover, when Miller and Dyer (1970) compared controlled replications of four different preschool programs (Montessori, traditional nursery school, DARCEE [Gray], and Bereiter-Engelmann-Becker), traditional and Montessori programs were least effective in all measures. The other two programs were more successful in producing cognitive gains (in IQ, arithmetic, sentence production) and persistence. The comprehensive DARCEE program was generally the most effective and was associated with the highest gains in resistance to distraction, inventiveness, achievement, independence, and verbal-social participation.

"DEPTH" OF EDUCATION

A fourth dimension of program variation is the depth or level of educational attack. An intervener may attempt to change the overt behaviors of the child—academic, verbal, or social—or he may attempt to build structures within the child—cognitive, affective, or social. Let us hasten to add that the poles of this dimension ("surface" and "deep") are not equated with "bad" and "good": it is not clear that the mission of education is psychotherapy or that deep structures (e.g., cognitive or linguistic) are amenable to environmental interventions.

Operant conditioning techniques have often been demonstrated to effect the first kind of change. Problem behaviors can be eliminated, basic skills "shaped up" (Ulrich, Wolfe, & Bluhm, 1968). The Juniper Gardens Preschool program at the University of Kansas (Bushell, Etzel, Baer, and Risley) is based largely on these techniques. This program uses systematic reinforcement procedures to teach children the skills they need to compete effectively in school: the social as well as the academic role of the student. An effective system of reinforcement makes a preferred activity contingent on improved academic or social behavior. Typical preferred classroom activities, it might be noted, include recess, snack, art, and stories. For maximum effect reinforcement must be provided immediately. The immediate delivery of a story, however, would terminate rather than strengthen the behavior on which it is contingent. Consequently, in this program a token economy has been instituted in some classrooms. Tokens (along with praise) can be dispensed at once, contingent on appropriate behavior, which can then be exchanged for preferred activities when they are available. At Juniper Gardens the teacher's role is that of behavior modifier; parents, too, are hired to function in this role. In lessons on classroom management mothers have learned to manage pupils by using positive reinforcement and to provide good social learning experiences in group situations.

The level of change to which the Bereiter-Engelmann-Becker preschool program aspires is similarly behavioral. Children are taught verbal rules: the right answer in the acceptable form. This program does not attempt to tap the potential power of the child's language ability. The curriculum, however, is carefully planned to facilitate the acquisition of generalized response systems that will apply to whole sets of problems; for example, the children learn the sounds that letters stand for and are able to read words they have never seen before, or, by learning that an average is a fulcrum and that each is equivalent to an equal sign they can generalize to multiplication, average, and lever problems. Paying attention to a task is also regarded as a generalized response set that can be reinforced and learned. The use of reinforcement is a key element of this program. Children are praised or smiled at for correct performance, for there is a conscious effort to make these social reinforcers contingent on the accomplishment of academic tasks.

The success of the Bereiter-Engelmann-Becker program in changing the behaviors it attacks has been amply demonstrated. Another attempt at behavior modification of language (Weiss & Born, 1967) suggests an important distinction between speech and language, if language is taken to mean understanding and generating novel utterances. In this experiment, although a child could be trained in specific language patterns, his language behavior did not generalize beyond the training situation. Conditioning approaches can be contrasted with a "deep" solution in that any changes brought about in the child's behavior can be extinguished by changes in reinforcement contingencies; if "new" behaviors do not come to control positive reinforcements outside the school setting, achievements will vanish.

Preschool programs with a thrust toward building cognitive structures in the child are generally based on Piagetian concepts. In these programs learning is more than acquiring a response; education is more than changing behaviors. This approach to intervention is found in the programs of Weikart and Gordon. Rather than trying to teach specific responses by reinforcement, teachers set the stage for concept acquisition by equilibration, acting only to call the child's attention to dissonant information and asking him to justify his response. The materials presented can be assimilated in a sensorimotor way: one does not just show a child a square and tell him it is a square; one has him trace it with his finger or walk around it on the floor. The perceptual stimulus is woven into his actions; the child operates on it. Sequencing from simple to complex is also crucially important if the child is to be moved along through the stages of cognitive development. It has been possible to accelerate logical intelligence by inducing cognitive conflict, by training the child to recognize that an object can belong to several different classes at once, by demonstrating a gradual transformation in visual stimuli so that the effect of change in one dimension is to produce change in another, and by demonstrating reversibility (Smock, 1968). Kohlberg (1968) suggests that speeding up structural cognitive change is extremely difficult to achieve, but that it is likely to have long-range general effects; teaching behaviors is easier but unlikely to have permanent developmental effects. Changes that are universal, progressive, or irreversible require a "deep" solution; an associationist approach is sufficient to account for and produce situation-specific behavior changes.

Certain early-education programs, in attempting to influence the behavior or development of children, have taken an indirect approach by working with the family. These programs have taken two forms: the social service model, which focuses on emotional problems within the family, and the parent-education model, which may be concerned only with the mother's interaction with her children or which may be conceived more broadly as providing means for parents to climb the career ladder. Hunt suggests that the first model of intervention has failed. Professional psychotherapy-like counseling has not proved nearly so effective as illustrative demonstrations combined with explanation and participation.

> Attempting to modify the child-rearing practices of parents by means of professional talk alone fails. Perhaps this should not surprise us inasmuch as one of the chief characteristics of such parents is their lack of facility of linguistic communication. On the other hand, these same parents of poverty can learn improved ways of child rearing from opportunities to observe the ways of relatively expert teachers and to observe the effects of the experts' approaches on the children's behavior, especially when these effects are then explained in language which they can understand. Moreover, these parents are able to communicate through demonstration and take these improved practices in child rearing to their neighbors [1969b, p. 30.]

Ira Gordon's infant stimulation program is an attempt at maternal education. Instruction by demonstration is given to the mother in the home by the parent educator. She is shown specific sequences of stimulation exercises for her infant. The goals of this program include not only the improvement of the infant's development by maternal stimulation but also an increase in the mother's competence and self-worth. The program has successfully affected the development of infants as measured on the Griffiths Eye and Hand and Hearing and Speech scales. Although no evidence of improvement in their self-esteem has been found, these mothers have increased their belief in internal control (Gordon, 1969a).

Phyllis Levenstein's project is another that attempts to influence child development by the mother. Toys and books are brought to the home, and techniques for eliciting and modeling language by means of these materials are demonstrated. The IQ scores of children whose mothers were so trained were found to be superior to the scores of others who received no visits or with whom material gifts were left but no training in verbal interaction was attempted (Levenstein, 1970). Similar efforts to change the mother's interaction with her infant have been successfully made by Parkman-Ray and Bayer (1969) and Gutelius (1970). The latter's study also included cognitive stimulation techniques, encouragement of exploration, and discussion of topics in education and child psychology. Karnes et al. (1969) also found that home training of mothers for two hours a week over 11 weeks was sufficient to show a significant increase in the IQ and language scores of their 4-year-old children.

Another version of this approach was taken by Miller (1968). Mothers of preschool-aged children were given training in stimulation techniques; diffusion effects were then assessed by examining the younger siblings in these families. Children whose mothers had been given this training were superior to children whose older siblings attended a preschool program, to children who had been directly exposed to a stimulating home visitor, and to a no-treatment control group. This study demonstrates the potential power of parent education and involvement.

Some programs, of course, have attempted to intervene both directly by providing preschool experience for the child and indirectly by working with their parents. Gordon's program is one example; another is Dunham's Project Know-How in which a comprehensive educational program includes both mothers and fathers. In Weikart's program home training is given in addition to the classroom curriculum. The mother is seen typically as having command of the language and concepts necessary to teach her child but needing to be encouraged to *use* her skills. The teacher therefore suggests tasks for the mother to present to her child and adds ways in which she can teach him more effectively.

Another program with a multifaceted approach is Gray's Early Training Project. In the center setting behavior modification is used to shape up adequate school behaviors, and nursery school materials are utilized to induce positive attitudes toward academic tasks and achievement. The importance of mother-child interaction to the child's development is emphasized in parental education during home visits.

Programs that focus on the family have been responsible for increasing the child's development, as we have mentioned (Gordon, 1969a; Gutelius, 1970; Karnes et al., 1969; Miller, 1968). The benefits of this approach, however, have a broader application. Hunt (1969b) notes that more than half the mothers in a replication of Gray's Early Training Project subsequently completed high school, or enrolled in courses to upgrade their vocational skills. Moreover, the experience led to a greater concern with community affairs and more involvement in and responsibility for cooperative adult activities. Increases in bank accounts were also demonstrated. Finally, the effects of the program diffused throughout entire families and neighborhoods.

Similar evidence of enrichment in the lives of parents has appeared as a result of the program directed by Karnes, mentioned above. In a subsequent study, however, she found that a program of home training for mothers plus ameliorative preschool for children was no more effective than the preschool program alone in producing intellectual gains. In fact, on a measure of language ability the preschool-only group was superior. Karnes's suggested reason is that the mothers knew they were not the only change agents, an important implication in the design of programs involving parents.

STRUCTURE

The last two dimensions to be described here have less to do with underlying philosophies of education or child psychology than the others we have discussed; they refer to obvious and specific techniques employed in various programs.

One such dimension is labeled "degree of structure." At the high end of this continuum is the rigidly structured Bereiter-Engelmann-Becker program. Here children are drilled in certain strictly prescribed verbal patterns; they speak loudly and rhythmically, often in unison. Not only is the curriculum highly structured—lessons are preprinted, preprogrammed, and even teachers' gestures are rehearsed—but so are children's recitations. The general instructional strategy is that of rule followed by application. A verbal formula is learned by rote and then applied to a series of analogous examples of increasing difficulty. The teacher sits in a cubicle with a group of four to seven children and leads them in a quickly paced 20-minute lesson of questions and responses.

TEACHER   This is a —— (presents picture of rifle).

CHILD   Gun.

TEACHER   Good. It is a gun. Let's all say it: This is a gun. This is a gun. Again. This is a gun. Let's say it one more time: This is an alligator.

CHILD   It ain't neither. It's a gun.

TEACHER   That's what I said. I said, "This is a bulldog."

CHILDREN   No, no. It ain't no bulldog. That's a gun.

TEACHER   Well, what did I say?

CHILDREN   You say that a bulldog.

TEACHER   You're just too smart for me. You listen so big that I can't get away with a thing. Okay, I'll start again. This is a gun. Is that right? This is a weapon. This is a gun. This is a weapon.

CHILD   No, it ain't no weapon.

TEACHER   (presents pictures of knife, cannon, pistol) This is a weapon. This is a weapon. These are weapons. Say it with me. This is a weapon. This is a weapon. This is a weapon. This is a weapon. These are weapons. Let's hear that last one again. Make it buzz. These are weaponzzz This weapon is a —— (points to knife). Who knows?

CHILD   A knife.

TEACHER   Yes, a knife. Let's say it. This weapon is a knife. Again. This weapon is a knife.

TEACHER   Here we go (refers to pictures). This is a weapon. This is a weapon. This is a weapon.

CHILD   I got a cannon at . . . (stops talking as teacher holds outstretched hand only a few inches in front of child's face).

TEACHER	Here's the rule (claps rhythmically). If you use it to hurt somebody, then it's a weapon. Again. If you use it to hurt somebody, then it's a weapon. One more time. If you use it to hurt somebody, then it's a weapon. And if it's a weapon, what do you do with it? Do you tickle somebody with it?
CHILDREN	No.
TEACHER	Do you eat with it?
CHILDREN	No!
TEACHER	Well, if it's a weapon, do you use it to hurt somebody? Yes. IF YOU USE IT TO HURT SOMEBODY, THEN IT'S A WEAPON. Let's hear it. IF YOU USE IT TO HURT SOMEBODY, ————.
CHILDREN	THEN IT'S A WEAPON.
TEACHER	I'm thinking of a rifle, and what do you use a rifle for? You use it to POW POW—hurt somebody. AND IF YOU USE IT TO HURT SOMEBODY, ————
CHILDREN	THEN IT'S A WEAPON.
TEACHER	So what do you know about a rifle? Is it a peanut?
CHILDREN	No, it's a weapon. . . . (Bereiter & Engelmann, 1966, pp. 105–109).

The Bereiter-Engelmann-Becker program includes similarly structured 20-minute sessions for the teaching of arithmetic and reading. The arithmetic program emphasizes a "science of counting" without reference to phenomena that can be interpreted arithmetically. After the initial teaching of counting arithmetic is taught by emphasizing the idea that any equation can be read as a statement of fact and also as an instruction that tells how the fact can be established in a counting operation. The same kind of pattern drill used in the language program to teach basic grammatical rules is used to teach arithmetic.

When children are not engaged in these concentrated sessions, they work together in a larger group. Here they sing songs, work on work sheets written to provide practice in language operations taught in the programmed sessions, or listen to stories which also provide additional practice in language operations and involve more question-and-answer activity than is common in reading stories to children.

The Bereiter-Engelmann-Becker program is not the only highly structured preschool program, however, although it may be the most widely publicized. Spicker, Hodges, and McCandless direct a highly structured language program with a formal teaching-learning structure. Lessons are designed by curriculum consultants to meet individually diagnosed needs of the children, and no "free time" is allowed. Similarly Deutsch's highly structured program carefully follows a sequence from sensorimotor to perceptual to conceptual presentations. This program utilizes structured equipment like the Edison talking typewriter and the Language Master and structured lessons like those provided by Language Lotto and matrix games designed by Gotkin.

Gotkin's games are examples of programmed instruction, in a context of enjoyment and fun, designed to teach concepts, classification skills, and language. They are based on the following structural principles: clear specification of instrumental objectives; careful sequencing from simple to complex; small steps to ensure virtually errorless learning; active participation by the child; and immediate feedback on the correctness of a response. In the matrix games, for example, children view a picture matrix, which consists typically of four rows and four columns with a characteristic unique to each row and each column. The children may be directed (or they may direct one another) to "put a blue circle on two boys drinking milk." The cognitive requirements increase in complexity as the children gain facility in the task; for example, sequencing could be introduced by instructing the children to "*first* put a blue circle on two boys drinking milk, *then* put a red X on one girl putting on her hat." Similarly, the teacher may cover up one of the squares and ask the children to figure out which picture is "her secret." They must be able to determine the content of the covered picture by abstracting the common vertical and horizontal element, stating it so that the rest of the group can understand the answer and explaining how they arrived at the solution.

Examples of programs that are not quite so highly structured are those of Karnes and Painter. In the ameliorative program directed by Karnes verbalizations in conjunction with the manipulation of concrete materials are considered the most effective means of establishing a new language response. A game format (card packs, lotto games, models and miniatures, and sorting, matching, and classifying games) creates situations in which verbal responses can be made repeatedly in a productive meaningful context without resorting to rote; often the child can visually and motorically assess the correctness of his thinking before he makes an appropriate verbalization. If the child is unable to make a verbal response, the teacher supplies an appropriate model. When he begins to initiate such responses, the teacher has the opportunity to correct, modify, and expand his verbalizations.

Like the Bereiter-Engelmann-Becker program, the daily schedule is divided into three 20-minute structured learning periods: mathematical concepts, language arts and reading readiness, and science-social studies. In a large room, in which all 15 children gather for group activities, concepts taught during the structured periods are reinforced during play and music activities. Frequent review further extends content previously presented and provides opportunities to use the vocabulary and sentence structures that have been taught.

Painter also utilized a highly structured program of intellectual stimulation.

This time the training occurred in the homes of individual children 8 to 24 months old.

Moving toward the less structured end of this dimension we find the programs of Montessori and O. K. Moore. In these programs, although the structure is not teacher-directed and there is no prescribed curriculum, structure is inherent in the properties of the materials provided. In an orthodox Montessori program the children are required to use materials in a prescribed manner; for example, they may not use a graded series of color chips to build a house. The schedule is not structured, but the nature of the environment is, and the sequence from one level of complexity to the next is available in the materials.

Weikart's Perry Preschool Program is moderately structured within an open framework; tasks are sequenced from simple to complex. The child progresses from the motor level of abstraction (where he learns to use his own body to experience concepts) to the verbal (where he learns to label what he is doing or experiencing) and finally to the symbolic level (where, through familiarity with objects and object representations, he develops the skills necessary to think abstractly). Structure in this program is apparent to the teacher but not to the children.

At the extreme left of this continuum are programs that are low in imposed structure; they adhere to no set curriculum, but just "let it happen." An example is Mary Keister's program in North Carolina. Here there is no curriculum and no theoretical orientation; just a varied, vivid environment, quality in individual relationships, opportunity for play experiences, and provision of health care. Nursery school programs which allow the child to work out skills and problems on his own also fit these criteria. Their basic principle is to arrange an environment that will stimulate the child's perception and expression, and then have a teacher available to encourage and amplify when the child voices an interest in one of its aspects.

A "classic" example of programs at this end of the structure continuum is Skeels and Dye's intervention. Retarded adolescent girls, inmates of a detention home, cared for, talked to, played with, and "adopted" young children and babies from an orphanage. With no "cognitive curriculum" of any sort, these children made dramatic gains in IQ scores and later were superior in overall adjustment to children not given such attention.

Some programs have a generally unstructured format, but occasionally structured lessons are interjected. Representative of such programs is the Frank Porter Graham Center in Chapel Hill, North Carolina (Robinson, 1968) or a Bank Street nursery school. Bank Street teachers usually teach only indirectly, but when there is need for a "lesson" they oblige. Furthermore, they currently use the structure implied by the typewriter, Language Lotto, and programmed instruction for rehearsal and consolidation. Similarly, in the British infant schools or an EDC program, although there is no prescribed curriculum, the teacher will conduct a formal mini-lesson when she feels it is necessary. Generally, however, activities are based on the needs and interests of the children who plan their own activities with guidance from a supportive, sensitive, nondidactic teacher.

Evaluations of these programs have been conducted. Programs at the "structured" end of this continuum have demonstrated their potentiality for producing gains in IQ score (Bereiter & Engelmann, 1968; Karnes et al., 1969; Painter, 1968; Weikart in Hunt, 1969b) and language performance (Karnes et al., 1969; Painter, 1968; Spicker, 1968; Weikart & Wiegerink, 1968). IQ gains have not been so consistently documented for unstructured programs, although they have been noted (Barret & Koch, 1930; Fuschillo, 1968; Iowa Child Welfare Station, in Swift, 1964; Prentice & Bieri, 1970; Pitcher, 1968; Skeels & Dye, 1939; Weikart in Hunt, 1969b). For the most part such gains have been observed in institutional and lower-class children rather than in children from middle-class homes.

Attempts have deliberately been made to compare programs that vary on this dimension of structure. Several evaluations have documented the superiority of more structured curricula for children's performance on the Bayley Scale (Kirschner, 1970b), the Caldwell Preschool Inventory, and the Engelmann Concept Inventory (Rusk, 1968), and according to psychiatrists' ratings of happiness (McNamara et al., 1968). All the subjects in these evaluations were from lower-class homes. A comparison by Dickie (1968) of Gotkin, Bereiter-Engelmann, and traditional nursery school programs similarly suggested that the structured programs were more effective in producing intellectual and verbal changes. These differences, however, were not statistically significant. This investigator suggests that for children with initially low language ability the structured program is more beneficial, but children who are initially more advanced profit more from unstructured enrichment experience. These results are in line with those that suggest that lower-class children are more likely to profit from structured programs, whereas middle-class children may benefit from less structure (Bereiter, 1968). Dickie's study also revealed that parents of lower-class children preferred structured programs.

An incidental benefit of structured programs is that the children require less disciplining. This might be especially relevant for preschool programs for the disadvantaged if teachers and lower-class parents do not agree on disciplinary methods.

Another advantage of structured programs may be that less broadly educated teachers can be taught to use a highly structured curriculum more easily than they could gain the depth and breadth of knowledge necessary for an effective unstructured program.

The evidence, however, is not universally and overwhelmingly in favor of highly structured programs, even for disadvantaged children. For infants at home (Weikart & Lambie, 1969) a teacher with a pre-established curriculum was no more effective than a volunteer operating intuitively. In short-term concept training an unstructured, child-initiated "discovery" method was more effective than a teacher-guided, step-by-step, structured program (Palmer & Rees, 1969). Moreover, a comparison (Karnes et al., 1969) of five programs that varied in degree of structure suggests that, since the Montessori program was least effective, structure is not *the* critical dimension. Finally, a similar conclusion might be reached on the basis of Weikart's program comparison data (in Hunt, 1969b) which demonstrated no difference in the effectiveness of three programs differing in structure.

PEOPLE VERSUS THINGS

Another aspect of early education that differentiates programs is their relative emphasis on the human versus the material environment. No preschool program, of course, is without human direction, but the amount of adult-child contact does vary considerably from setting to setting. Perhaps the most extreme example of a materials-centered program is that devised by Montessori. Her maxim "Things are the best teachers" aptly summarizes her philosophy of education. The Montessori teacher is not a "teacher" at all; she is a director who attempts to efface herself and discourage the development of dependence in the children. She uses no excess words but encourages children to explore the didactic materials for themselves. These materials are guided by three criteria: simplicity, inherent interest, and self-correction. They involve the child's visual and tactile senses in fundamental learning operations.

O. K. Moore's talking typewriter also fits into the Montessori philosophy. It, too, represents a "thing-centered" extreme on this dimension. It is a gadget that interests young children and can be utilized with a wide variety of curricular topics; it enables the children to get feedback in both aural and written language.

Other intervention projects which contain components at this end of the continuum would be those of Carolyn Stern and Burton White. Stern's language program at UCLA uses tape recorders, puzzles, and workbooks in an autoinstructional learning program. White's (White, Castle, & Held, 1964) intervention with institutionalized infants was based on enrichment by means of inanimate visual stimulation.

Another preschool program which is high on this scale is the New Nursery School. This program utilizes responsive, self-correcting equipment (a typewriter, the Language Master, and nesting blocks) and emphasizes the usefulness of toys, particularly the manipulative kind. People, however, are the program planners;

they create the physical environment that facilitates learning. Teachers do not often initiate contact with the children, but they respond readily to a child's request for conversation, tutorial help, or reading. Since the children frequently do make these requests, they often receive what amounts to teacher-centered instruction, individually or in small groups.

Exemplary programs that assume a moderate position on the "people-things" dimension might be those of Resnick, EDC, and its inspiration, the British infant schools. By and large, in these programs the child learns by interacting with materials and with other children rather than directly from the teacher. In Resnick's program the teacher's function is to reinforce the child's efforts and successes and to make sure he gets assistance when needed. The central aspect of the British infant school is a rich environment in which the child can explore, but the teacher is very much involved in providing this environment, in offering individualized attention, and when necessary, giving a lesson.

The people-centered position on this dimension throws into close company such otherwise diverse interventions as those of Bereiter-Englemann-Becker, Marie Hughes, Harriet Rheingold, Skeels and Dye, and Donald Bushell. In each of these programs people—in particular, adult people—are, or were, central, whether their role is in giving reinforcement (Bushell), didactic, academic instruction (Bereiter), loving, caring for, and mothering (Rheingold, Skeels & Dye), or language modeling and tutoring (Hughes).

Relying somewhat more on materials, yet still emphasizing the role of the teacher, are the programs of Deutsch and DARCEE. A more equal balance between people and things seems to be characteristic of programs devised by Caldwell and Bank Street educators. Both make use of colorful, intriguing, stimulating, and responsive materials, while emphasizing the importance of adult-child interaction. Caldwell articulates the importance of the adult to the child's development of attachment, trust, and gratification of needs. In a Bank Street nursery school the teacher's role involves understanding the child, giving him materials and affection, socializing him, and helping him to perceive the situation and to achieve rational control of his actions.

Empirical data, which could confirm the placement of some of these programs on the adult-centrality dimension, come from Miller and Dyer's comparison of replications of Montessori, traditional, Bereiter-Engelmann-Becker, and DARCEE preschools. The Montessori program was indeed observed to be highest in manipulation of materials by both teachers and children. The traditional nursery school program was also high; Bereiter-Engelmann-Becker and DARCEE were low. Exemplification (showing or being shown), modeling, and verbal instruction by the teacher might be considered measures of the people-centeredness of a program. The first two of these measures were high in Bereiter-Engelmann-Becker and DARCEE programs, but verbal instruction was high in DARCEE, traditional, and Montessori preschools. It is interesting, considering Madame Montessori's intentions, that although the Montessori program, at least in this replication, was highest in materials manipulation, it was also high in the use of language. This demonstrates an important consideration involved in preschool education. One cannot make judgments or draw conclusions about the effects of any particular model of education or its components without careful observation of the particular implementation being assessed.

Results of evaluations that compare programs which vary on this dimension lend support to those programs that have emphasized the human element. Tamminen et al. (1967) found that a Head Start program "enriched" by the addition of Montessori materials was no more successful in inducing intellectual gain than one that was not. Levenstein also found that mere enrichment by provision of toys was not so effective as toys plus verbal interaction (1970). Finally, Miller and Dyer (1970) and Karnes et al. (1969), whose results showed the superiority of adult-centered Bereiter-Engelmann-Becker, DARCEE, and Karnes's Ameliorative programs over more materials-centered traditional nursery school and Montessori programs, came to the same conclusion. In early education programs adult teachers are essential, particularly in language development.

PROGRAM DIMENSIONS IN DAY CARE

In the days to come day care, like early education programs such as Head Start or Follow Through will likely be searching for appropriate, feasible, and effective models on which to base programs. Some aspects of alternative program models are immediately obvious: group size, amount of equipment, structuredness of the lessons, and use of tangible reinforcement. We would suggest, however, that implicit in these programs are assumptions, beliefs, and philosophies, which, though difficult to discern from short periods of observation or from reading available program descriptions, are fundamental and critical to an understanding of particular programs. It is for this reason that we have attempted to articulate some of these underlying program dimensions and to alert those who are concerned with choosing models and approaches to education to look beyond superficial characteristics and flashy statistics. Although on some issues there is consensus, program models differ in their basic philosophies, their immediate and long-range goals and emphases, and their methods of achieving these goals. There is apparently no one simple "best" educational model. The diversity of life in the United States is apparent in this area, too.

In choosing an educational model to be applied to day care settings, it is well to remember first that education is only one component of "quality day care." It is especially important in a program that has responsibility for total, full-day care of the child that no aspect of the child's development be ignored. Beyond this program imperative, however, parents and day-care teachers and staff should probably search for those educational components that will be most compatible with their own convictions concerning the nature of the child, his needs and development, with their own goals for the program and for children, with their own philosophies of the educational process, with their own needs as parents and teachers, and with the resources or potential resources (financial support, materials, professional, and paraprofessional assistance) available to them.

18

Issues in Implementation

PHYSICAL SETTINGS: SPACE AND EQUIPMENT

THE MOST VISIBLE COMPONENT OF PROGRAMS IN EARLY CHILD-
hood education, at least to the casual glance of a visitor, is the physical setting.
Brightly colored toys and equipment please the eye and make a favorable impression on newspaper reporters, taxpayers, administrators, and parents. Consequently
it is difficult to economize on this aspect of the program. Yet more is contained
in the array of equipment and the distribution of space than immediately meets
the eye. Subtleties of arrangement and choice of toys have an immediate yet far-
reaching impact on teachers, children, and curriculum. Even in a program with
a limited budget, space and equipment can be arranged in optimal ways; toys
may be purchased that will best advance the goals of the program—social, emotional, or cognitive:

> There is equipment which deceives adults. At first glance it may seem un-
> usually interesting or useful; later, in use by children, it proves to be no different
> from its traditional counterpart, and in some instances it may even be more
> limiting to play. Sometimes a two-story play house looks fine on the drawing
> board and it is only when the children begin to use the play house in the yard
> that the discovery is made that it is too high to be safe. Sometimes a play house,
> designed to do double duty as a storage shed, is so large it fails its primary
> function. It just doesn't invite children to enter and play house. A slide framed
> by a large, brightly colored elephant cut-out, while delightful to the adult eye, is
> still a simple unit to a child. The climb-in-on-around "space ship" is as simple as its
> traditional counterpart, the jungle gym; in addition, the "space ship" may not
> lend itself to development into complex units which can be varied in "play ideas"

229

from day to day. Again, it appears that our response as thinking adults sometimes interferes with realistic appraisal of equipment in terms of young children.

Although traditional equipment is "old hat" to adults, we need to remind ourselves that it is new to young children and has perhaps become traditional because it supplies important (and often unique) experiences. In making decisions about equipment—both traditional and novel—think through just what experiences it makes available to children. For instance, in addition to the special pleasures of swinging through the air and learning to pump, single swings offer something unique to children. We can think of no unit which so effectively and naturally insulates a child from the rest of the group [Kritchevsky, Prescott, & Walling, 1969, p. 29.]

Some programs have made equipment and materials central to their teaching practices; for example, those inspired by Montessori or the Educational Development Center. Yet even when the physical environment is not theoretically a central factor, preschool personnel would be well advised to concern themselves with its impact. Tired or irritable teachers, apathetic, hyperactive, uninterested children, a high noise level, and frequent restriction and direction all have a high likelihood of being spatially induced. So suggest Prescott et al. (1967) and Kritchevsky et al. (1969) in their comprehensive evaluations of the effects of spatial factors in day-care centers.

In the past other researchers, too, have documented such effects. Shure (1963) conducted a time-sampling of children's activities during free play in five areas of a nursery school: the block corner and art, housekeeping, story, and science areas. She observed that different densities of population and different behaviors were characteristic of the various interest areas and suggested that children's behavior was coerced by the equipment and its spatial arrangement. One effect induced by the physical environment which has received attention is that on children's "talkativeness." Outdoor and picture situations (Young, 1941), dolls, blocks, crayons, and clay (Van Alstyne, 1932) are apparently conducive to conversation; paints, scissors, and books are not (Van Alstyne, 1932), but, although the activity setting influences the amount of verbalization, it does not seem to help the child's syntactic or semantic development (Cazden, in press). Of course, this is true only as long as conversation is restricted to peer talk; the same claim could not be applied to activity settings that included equipment specifically designed to elicit and develop language skills—the Language Master, the talking typewriter, and so on.

Other possible effects of physical setting are those related to children's play and social relations. It has been observed that a spacious setting allowed creativity in play activities (Markey, 1935), whereas a restricted play area induced conflicts (Jersild & Markey, 1935; Murphy, 1937). Murphy, Murphy, and Newcomb (1937) observed effects of materials on creativity. They found that a large supply of simple materials, available to all children, focused attention on what could be created out of these materials. By contrast a large supply of more complicated toys, with only one or two of a kind, was likely to stimulate competition and quarreling. Johnson (1935a) similarly noted that with less structured equipment (toys were removed) children played with sand and dirt and devised games of their own. Yet because there was more social interaction children also quarrelled more and required more teacher intervention and direction. Some equipment has been observed to lead to cooperation among children: sleds, wagons, housekeeping toys, slides, tricycles with footholds, swings (Murphy, 1937), and dolls (Green, 1933).

The most complete attempt to investigate physical settings is that by Prescott, Jones, and Kritchevsky (1967). In intensive observations made in 50 day-care centers the "quality" of space was rated according to degree of organization, amount of complexity and variety, amount to do per child, and any special problems that were present. This rating of quality, they found, was related to structural, organizational, and behavioral variables. Large as well as small yards, especially those square in shape, were of lower quality and more crowded than those of medium size. Medium-sized centers (30 to 60 children) had the highest quality of space, both indoors and out.

The quality of space determined the amount of freedom that could be granted to both teachers and children. Space of high quality permitted more diversity and offered many more opportunities for experiences that were highly personal and therefore meaningful. Moreover, the higher the quality, the more likely were teachers to be sensitive and friendly to the children, to encourage them in self-chosen activities, and to teach consideration for the rights and feelings of others. Space allows choice of child-adult and child-child interaction. If the spatial arrangement and the teacher allow the children autonomy, children are involved and interested. Concurrently, teachers have time to observe the children or to interact, on an individual basis, without interruption. Thus quality space can provide teachers with the opportunity to know and teach children as individuals, to be more aware of their individual needs, and consequently to plan responsive and appropriate programs. This, in turn, leads to more interested and involved child behavior.

Low-quality space coerces teachers by forcing them to assume responsibility for order and activity. When spatial quality was low, teachers were more likely to be neutral and insensitive, to use more guidance and restriction, and to teach arbitrary rules of social living. Children were less likely to be involved and interested.

On the basis of this research and other related literature, recommendations and prescriptions concerning optimal use of space and equipment have been advanced (Kritchevsky et al., 1969; Sunderlin, 1968; Swift, 1964). In general there is agreement that the physical environment in preschool or day-care programs should be comfortable, spacious, and stimulating and should be designed to enhance relationships among children, parents, and teachers. In a center-based program the setting should be located near the child's home and reflect the home; it should serve parents as well as children. The physical environment should support and enhance, not restrict, learning activities. It should be flexible enough to allow modification of goals or curriculum. In an environment thoughtfully designed for early childhood education all equipment—doors, floors, furnishings, and fixtures—can provide direction, suggestion, motivation, stimulation, protection, and comfort.

The physical setting should have variety: space for playing or for contemplation, separate areas for quiet or busy, messy or clean activities, areas for groups or individuals, toys that are complex or simple and versatile. Especially in an all-day program, provision for privacy is essential. Kritchevsky and her associates recommend a "loose" organization—simpler units, more to do per child, more empty space—which imposes fewer child-child contacts. Swift makes similar recommendations:

> No single setting or arrangement of equipment can be considered "ideal"; the setting must always be considered in relation to the needs of the child and the purpose of the program. For the child with little opportunity to play with other children, or for the withdrawn child whose need is for stimulation toward social play, a setting designed to stimulate cooperation and social interaction may be most appropriate. For the child from a crowded home with many siblings, a setting in which he can remove himself from the group and play quietly alone may be equally important. In considering the day nursery setting as contrasted with the nursery school, it may be appropriate for the former to provide more opportunity for a solitary play, through the provision of greater space and appropriate equipment, in order to offset the fatiguing effects of prolonged social interaction [Swift, 1964, p. 261.]

TEACHERS

Teachers are the most important factor in any group experience for young children [Pitcher, 1968].

The benefits children derive from nursery school will be influenced to a large degree by the personality and competence of the teacher [Jersild, 1960].

It is the personality of the teacher, her outlook and convictions, that constitute the most important single factor in the shaping of the child's nursery experience [Reichenberg-Hackett, 1962].

These quotations describe the exalted position accorded the preschool teacher in writings on early education. The teacher, like the mother, has a vital and well-documented impact on the child's behavior and development. Since we have already included in a preceding chapter a rather detailed description of relationships between maternal behaviors and child development, let us indicate at the outset that these relationships are remarkably similar to those between teacher and students. The findings reported here are derived from a different literature and are summarized only in order to demonstrate the generalizability of the principles of optimal child care to educational settings.

Initially the child's behaviors do, in fact, generalize from mother to teacher. The child responds to a neutral adult, at first, with many of the same behaviors he shows with his own mother (Bishop, 1951). As he begins to realize that the teacher is not the same as Mommy, he begins, of course, to respond to the teacher as her individual characteristics dictate. Even so, since many of the teacher's roles overlap the mother's, his behaviors toward her are always subtly influenced by his relationship with his mother.

Roles

Like the mother, the teacher may act as a *reinforcer*. She is the wielder of power, rewards, and punishments in her role as classroom management specialist. Preschool teachers with varying degrees of awareness use reinforcement to eliminate problem behaviors—crawling, crying, solitary play, excessive passivity (Harris, Wolf, & Baer, 1966)—and to maintain on-task behavior (Resnick, in Maccoby & Zellner, 1970). According to Resnick, the latter is the teacher's most important role.

Like the mother, the teacher may provide a *model* for behavior (Bandura, 1963; Sears & Hilgard, 1964; Strodtbeck, in O'Brien & Lopate, 1968). Unlike the relatively slow process of instrumental conditioning, a model fosters the rapid adoption of patterns of behavior in large segments or in their entirety. Modeling has even been effective in eliminating well-established fears and inhibitions (Bandura, Grusec, & Menlove, 1967), a desensitization success once considered the domain of operant conditioning. Adult models who are especially potent are those for whom the child feels a strong emotional attachment, who have high status, have control over resources, and who are rewarding. Although peers are often successful models, it has been found that young children imitate the source of rewarding power (the teacher) rather than the consumer or another child (Bandura, Ross, & Ross, 1963b). Kohlberg (1969) suggests that selective imitation of models may be best explained in terms of the child's perception of the models' competence and of their relevance to his own role. He explains the age development of selective preference in terms of the cognitive development of the child's concepts of role competence and of dimensions of relevance such as similarity or previous interaction. Taken together, these observations of modeling seem to imply that adults who look after or teach young children should engage in frequent interaction with the children if they are to maximize their potential power as models, and that they should be competent, caring, and close to the children.

The role of the teacher, caregiver, or mother may include *an intensive, affective relationship* that is instrumental in the development of attachment and social relationships and consequently adds to her power as a model or social reinforcer. This is the traditional role of the nursery school teacher as a source of tender loving care.

The teacher's role—especially in an academic preschool or in the upper grades —is often conceived of primarily as *teaching and tutoring*. With the growing emphasis on the mother as teacher of cognitive strategies (Hess, 1969), the overlap in roles, even here, is obvious.

A final role played by the teacher is that of *diagnosing and prescribing treatments*—the "therapeutic" role. Yet it, too, is a role often filled by the sensitive and responsive mother without professional training.

At issue is whether these roles are always compatible. Can an adult concurrently be diagnostic and maintain an intensive affective relationship? Perceptive diagnosis may require the kind of distance that restricts a close affective relationship. From another point of view, conflict can occur when the "message" of one role differs from another; for example, when adults reinforce "please" but never say it.

Goals, Attitudes, and Personality Styles

Teachers—as well as parents—vary on dimensions of personality style, goals, and attitudes. Teachers, too, can be cool, aloof, sarcastic or warm, nurturant, and sensitive. Some love children; some don't care (Rosen, 1968). Some teachers are "permissive"; others are more directive (Medley & Mitzel, 1965; Prescott, Jones, & Kritchevsky, 1967; Rosen, 1968). As a consequence of their own personality characteristics, teachers provide different emotional climates in the classroom (Medley & Mitzel, 1965). Furthermore, teacher characteristics interact with those of their pupils (Heil, Powell, & Feifer, 1960). Baldwin (1965), reviewing the literature on teacher effectiveness, reports differential effects according to the child's ability and personality; he might have added age, background, and history.

A study by Heil et al. (1960) suggests that a critical variable in effective teaching is the teacher's "integration," her consistency, orderliness, structured routine, and businesslike behavior and her approximation of the "typical old-fashioned teacher" stereotype. This hypothesis has received support in other research. Spaulding (1964), with fourth- and sixth-grade children, suggested that these behaviors as well as the teacher's attention to the task and her use of task-appropriate procedures and resources were related to children's reading gains and positive self-concepts and even (slightly) to cognitive flexibility. Ryans (1964) found that systematic, businesslike teaching was associated with "productive student behavior." A review of all studies on the effectiveness of teacher variables (Sears & Hilgard, 1964) found that "efficient" teaching, using group methods and frequent evaluations, being businesslike and well organized, and maintaining the goal of a quiet, industrious class, was favorable to learning, particularly of conventional subject matter. Structure was especially helpful for some anxious or dependent children. This mode of teaching, however, was not conducive to germination of new ideas or to interchild affiliation (Sears & Hilgard, 1964). Nor was the teacher's need for structure positively related to involved, active, cooperative, highly achieving, abstract-thinking children (Harvey, Prather, White, & Alter, 1966; Harvey, Prather, White, & Hoffmeister, 1968). Furthermore, since command of academic content is not the primary goal of day care, since day-care children are very young, and since day care occupies them for such a large part of the day, this personality style may not be appropriate to a good caregiver.

Emotional warmth is a teacher characteristic consistently related to "all good things" for preschool children—IQ gains (Eisenberg & Conners, 1966; Pierce-Jones & Strodtbeck in O'Brien & Lopate, 1968), creativity (Sears & Hilgard, 1964), high level of interest and involvement (Harvey et al., 1968; Prescott et al., 1967), liking for the teacher (Prescott et al., 1967; Rosen, 1968), liking for other children (Sears & Hilgard, 1964; Thompson, 1944), and productive and constructive behavior (Ryans, 1964; Thompson, 1944). The intensity of the teacher's emotional involvement, similarly, is related to IQ and achievement gains (Sprigle, Van De Riet, & Van De Riet, 1967; Wiegerink & Weikart, 1967), as is active teacher intervention and deliberate stimulation (Eisenberg & Conners, 1966; Jones, 1970; Pierce-Jones & Strodtbeck in O'Brien & Lopate, 1968). In an experimental investigation of these variables (Thompson, 1944) the same teacher was instructed to behave in one class as an impersonal, uninvolved adult; in a matched class she was to act as a warm friend, guide, and active initiator and participant. The latter method of teaching, although it did not raise IQ scores, did lead to an increase in constructiveness, social participation, and leadership. A teacher's personal interest in children and individual attention to them have also been related to improved child performance in more recent research. Such "child-centered" teachers have been shown to have pupils who are self-confident (Spaulding, 1964) and creative, who like other children (cf. Sears, 1963; Sears & Hilgard, 1964) and their teacher (Rosen, 1968), and who achieve more in school and on intelligence tests (Ryans, 1964; Sears, 1963; Sears & Hilgard, 1964; Spaulding, 1964).

Other characteristics of teachers which can affect their own and their pupils' classroom success are understanding, sensitivity, and responsiveness. Like the same characteristics in mothers, they are associated with productive behavior (Ryans, 1964), involvement, activity, achievement, and cooperation (Harvey et al., 1968).

At the same time, it is valuable to a child's growth that his teacher be flexible: flexible toward rules (Harvey et al., 1966), concerned with diversity (Spaulding, 1964), assuming a flexible role (Flanders, 1964), flexible in arrangements, programming, and behavior (Beller, undated; Eisenberg & Conners, 1966), and providing choices for the children (Jones, 1970). Such teachers are also generally permissive of children's feelings, independence, creativity, and behavior (Flanders, 1964; Harvey et al., 1966; Jones, 1970; Spaulding, 1964). For middle-class children such permissiveness appears to be advantageous, both in terms of their achievement and psychological well-being and of the popularity of the teachers (Flanders, 1964; Harvey et al., 1966; Jones, 1970; Prescott et al., 1967; Rosen, 1968; Ryans, 1964; Spaulding, 1964). Lower-class children, however, apparently suffer from this attitude of freedom (Strodtbeck in O'Brien & Lopate, 1968). It has also been observed that the presence of a completely permissive adult can lead to increased aggressive behavior (Chasdi & Lawrence, 1958; Siegel & Kohn, 1959).

Teacher Behaviors

Some form of discipline is often called for in preschool. Punishment for aggression is not an entirely satisfactory solution, for although it leads to a decrease in the undesirable behavior in the punishment situation there is a concurrent increase in aggression in new situations (Chasdi & Lawrence, 1958). Apparently the most effective disciplinary practice involves clarity, firmness, practicality, and a positive gentle manner (Appel, 1942; Kounin & Gump, 1958), for even a child who is just watching another child being disciplined can be affected. Diverting, separating, interpreting, and suggesting solutions were found to be effective techniques (Appel, 1942); disapproval, moralizing, or "talking about it," were not. "James, we don't hit!" is both unrealistic and unclear. Jersild and Markey (1935) observed that the nursery school group with the least conflicts had the highest teacher:student ratio and the greatest proportion of teacher interference. They sagely commented, however, that if teachers would strive less for angelic perfection in their efforts to curtail all minor disputes among children and be a little more severe in dealing with the child when it seemed that discipline was actually needed it would have a salutary effect.

Generalizations about the importance of verbal behavior are as applicable to the teacher as they were to the mother. The teacher who spends a high proportion of time communicating with her students, emphasizing language skills, and asking longer, more extended questions is likely to have children in her class who score higher on IQ tests, who achieve more and are more involved in school (Eisenberg & Conners, 1966; Flanders, 1964; Prescott et al., 1967; Strodtbeck in

O'Brien & Lopate, 1968). The "quality" or style of the teacher's verbal behavior is also relevant. Directions that are positive, unhurried, specific, and encouraging are most likely to elicit positive responses, according to Swift's (1964) review. An experiment by Johnson (1935b) with 2- and 8-year-olds provides some interesting examples of the relative effectiveness of different forms of instruction: "Someone left the books on the floor. You may look at them," resulted in 19% of the children picking up the books and looking at them. By contrast, to the comment, "Someone left the books on the floor. Pick them up. You may look at them," 89% did as asked. "You can do it," elicited significantly longer persistence in 95% of the cases; "Is it too hard for you?" induced persistence in only 5%. "It is time to dress the doll now" was effective in getting an appropriate response 95% of the time. "Do you want to dress the doll?" was a successful suggestion for only 34% of the children.

This study was expanded and refined by McClure (1936), who then concluded that "theoretically superior" instructions were more effective, especially for older children who were more likely to obey *any* instruction. "Theoretically superior" meant a request rather than a command, a specific compared with a general suggestion, unhurrying as opposed to hurrying, positive rather than negative, a statement more than a question, encouragement rather than discouragement, and an emphasis on success, not failure. McClure also observed, however, that the ease and desirability of the task may be more critical than the particular form of instruction.

Such principles of theoretically appropriate verbal behavior have been incorporated into the nursery school teacher's repertoire.

"You may not throw sand, Johnny, because it will get in people's eyes, but you may throw the bean bags."

"Perhaps you knocked over David's building, Janice, because you did not have room enough. Let's help him build it up again because it is important to him; then we will find a bigger space for you."

These are typical suggestions for what nursery school teachers should say (University of the State of New York *Child Development Guides,* 1968). According to McClure's dichotomous dimensions, such comments are theoretically sound, but is the level of comprehension they demand of the child appropriate to 3- and 4-year-old children, particularly lower-class children, or, as in these examples, to children angry enough to be throwing sand and knocking down buildings? We would suggest that they are probably unreasonable.

Blank and Solomon have compared the speech of typical preschool teachers with more effective speech patterns. Verbatim excerpts illustrate dramatically the differences in children's comprehension induced by the teacher's verbal behavior. This one is taken from a lesson taught by an actual nursery school teacher to a 4-year-old girl:

TEACHER	Have you seen the flowers?	Because the specific referent was not designated (i.e., the flowers in the room), child reacted only to the word "flower."
CHILD	I saw a beautiful flower outside.	

TEACHER	A beautiful flower? What color was it?	Teacher is led away from her initial referent and poses an unverifiable question.
CHILD	I don't know. It's a beautiful flower.	It is not possible to ascertain whether child's response is a superficial verbalization or an accurate description.
TEACHER	Did you put it in the ground?	Teacher appears to assume that child's comments reflect true interest. Thus, rather than initiating productive dialog, teacher has limited herself to a confined area.
CHILD	I picked it up.	This response is likely to be a simple rote association.
TEACHER	You picked it up? What kind was it?	Teacher here poses another unverifiable question.
CHILD	I don't know.	
TEACHER	Was it little and yellow? Maybe it was a dandelion? Did you plant the flower? Was it a seed and now it's a flower?	Teacher's questions involve multiple concepts, including an understanding of plant metamorphosis. This example illustrates the paradox of many preschool language programs, in which it is common to ask extremely complex questions couched in deceptively simple terms. Because of the apparent simplicity, it is often not deemed necessary to give the aids necessary for grasping what are, in fact, complex ideas [1969, p. 56].

By contrast the following selection comes from a lesson with the same child, during the same week, taught by a teacher who was trained in techniques in which the child was taught to use language to organize thoughts to reflect on situations, to comprehend the meaning of events, and to choose among alternatives:

TEACHER	Do you remember what we did when you were here yesterday?	The type of recall expected from child extends over greater time spans but is still verifiable. By contrast, in the early session recall was restricted to tasks in the immediate session.
CHILD	Yes.	
TEACHER	What did we do?	
CHILD	I don't know.	Despite her affirmative answer to the preceding question, the automatic negative response follows.
TEACHER	Let's see if I can help you. Is there anything on this table that we worked with the last time? A limited variety of materials is present.	Teacher presents visual aids to prod memory.
CHILD	Points to blackboard.	Child's gesture is correct.
TEACHER	That's just pointing. Tell me what we did.	Although a gesture would have been acceptable in an earlier session, teacher now demands a description, since the child is capable of responding in language.
CHILD	We did—we did a square.	Without being given any hints, the child correctly describes the object she drew.
TEACHER	Right. What did we do with the square?	The teacher is making the child recount the next step in the past sequence.
CHILD	Hesitates.	
TEACHER	Think about it for a minute.	Teacher makes a judgment that child can answer and delays offering help.
CHILD	We took it off. Child refers to erasing.	The pause has offered the child a chance to reflect. Her impulsive first answer has been replaced by accurate memory.
TEACHER	Good. Now, what did we use to take it off?	Teacher is continuing to focus on inter-related sequence of past events.
CHILD	I don't know.	

TEACHER	Brings blackboard forward. All right—what would you do if you had a square on here and you wanted to get rid of it? How could you get it off?	Since the child is encountering difficulty, teacher chooses a slightly easier level by offering a question that has several alternative answers (e.g., "What could you use to get it off?"). The child is thereby no longer limited to the past, where only one answer (the thing that actually happened) is correct.
CHILD	Maybe we could use paper?	Child is more successful with this relaxation in demand.
TEACHER	Why could we use paper? What would it do?	Teacher's question is to make child aware of the relationship between the object and the action for which it can be used.
CHILD	It could take it off. It could rub it off.	Child grasps this connection and expresses herself in clear language.
TEACHER	Fine. Now, remember what we did? We didn't use paper to take off the square. Do you remember what it was we *did* use?	
CHILD	A sponge.	Child's answer is correct. The reduced complexity helped her recall the past sequence [1969, p. 52.]

Blank and Solomon report significant increases in IQ, control of impulsivity, attention span, and enjoyment of learning as the result of short tutoring sessions like the one described. Their ideas and techniques could be applied as well to the language behavior of teachers in preschool or day-care settings.

Factors Influencing Teacher's Behaviors

A teacher's behavior in the classroom is highly affected by both her training and history and factors in the immediate situation. Highly assessed elementary school teachers (Ryans, 1964) who were understanding, friendly, responsible, stimulating, imaginative, and businesslike were also 35 to 49 years old, married, and had been better than average college students. They belonged to social groups, read a great deal, and often visited museums and exhibitions and attended concerts. The nursery school teacher, too, according to Law (1964), must be a college graduate, and should have, in addition to her specialized training in early child-hood education, a broad background in areas of science, language, biology, music, art, and astronomy. Thus it would appear that the range of potential teachers is limited indeed. Fortunately, other research has provided evidence of the effective-ness of teachers or interveners who have not been professionally trained. Skeels's (Skeels & Dye, 1939) mentally retarded adolescent girls are certainly at the other extreme; yet their effectiveness as caregivers for infant orphans was dramatic. Currently Painter (1968), Schaefer, Furfey, and Hart (1968), and Fowler (1970) have found that women given short specialized training in specific intervention techniques became effective preschool tutors. As a side benefit, Fowler noted that the women so trained also improved in their own performances on a conceptual levels test. Results from deliberate attempts to assess the differential effects of professional and volunteer or untrained teachers are also encouraging (Karnes et al., 1969; Weikart & Lambie, 1969). Paraprofessionals were equally as effective as more highly trained teachers. Even a short period of training (four to eight weeks, Miller & Dyer, 1970) was sufficient to train paraprofessionals to use a program as intended. They could also be trained to be nice, to say nice things, and to play with the children (Maccoby & Zellner, 1970). A highly structured curricu-lum makes training easier and more realistic. Such intensive, short-term, special-ized training in a specific curriculum may be the solution to the shortage of trained preschool and day-care personnel.

Teachers' behaviors are also related to the age and "personality" of the chil-dren (Appel, 1942; Prescott et al., 1967; Reichenberg-Hackett, 1962; Swift, 1964), to the time of day (Moore, 1938), to the physical setting (Prescott et al., 1967), and to structural characteristics of the program (Prescott et al., 1967); 2- and 3-year olds are especially demanding, and afternoons are particularly troublesome. Activities in day-care centers which are coercive and demanding of teacher par-ticipation are those that are unavoidable, such as lunch and clean-up and settings that are crowded or in which the size of the group is greater than 19 children. Optimal activities from the teacher's point of view are those that are optional, especially free play and free choice, at times when there are fewer children and in settings that are not crowded. Particularly favorable to teachers' optimal be-havior are out-door activities with a group of fewer than nine children who are at least 4 years old or who are heterogeneously grouped by age (Prescott et al., 1967).

Issues and Implications for Day Care

The research reviewed in this section, although focused on teachers, has wider relevance for the roles of any adults in the child's environment. These character-istics of mothers and teachers which have been shown to be beneficial to the development of children can be used as guidelines for finding competent day-care personnel; behaviors that have been found to facilitate children's learning can be built into training programs for adults who care for children.

Certain characteristics that stand out as being desirable for effective teaching or caregiving can be extracted from our discussion of this research. Although the stereotyped, efficiently businesslike schoolmarm may be a great success in teaching the three R's to fifth graders, her personality type is not likely to be completely suitable for day-care work. Nor is her opposite—a completely permissive adult—entirely appropriate (especially if the children come from authoritarian homes). More highly valued traits in day care would be emotional warmth, understanding, sensitivity, responsiveness, flexibility, and a willingness to become actively involved with children. Training programs for adults involved in day care might include instruction in the use of disciplinary control that is gentle yet clear, firm, practical, and explicit. Instruction in the use of direct, nonelliptical, and deliberately systematic language in a day-care setting might also form part of teacher training. Finally, our discussion of research on effective teachers suggests that day-care administrators could make it easier for teachers or caregivers to function effectively by providing well-organized and suitably equipped physical settings, by grouping children in small numbers, perhaps heterogeneously, and by offering teachers a personal choice whenever possible.

Another issue to which research on teachers is related is parent education. We have indicated the similarity and overlap of variables in teachers and parents that affect children; consequently a home-school "team" approach seems obvious, but we would propose that "parent education" be defined as education by the parents as well as of the parents. Too often only the latter is meant; yet it would seem that teachers and parents can learn from one another. Parents can provide invaluable information about the idiosyncrasies of their own children; teachers can offer useful techniques for stimulating, managing, and teaching.

Preconceived concepts of child development cannot be imposed on the communities of the poor (Levin, 1967), but by a process of mutual communication and understanding between parents and teachers knowledge of child development may be advanced. Teachers must first come to understand and respect the parents they encounter. Communication should be on the parents' level—not in the form of written reports but consisting of personal calls and visits (Wolman & Levenson, 1968). According to Katz (1970), the most important question that a day-care teacher can ask herself concerning her role, style, and goals may be "What am I doing to increase the mothers' confidence in the future of their children?" Some lower-class parents want even their young children to be pupils; the younger the child, the more they want a control-oriented teacher (Sieber & Wilder, 1967). Furthermore, they want their children to be taught specific academic skills. This is generally not in agreement with what middle-class nursery school teachers want or do. These parents have a good point. Their children are not likely to behave so well in a totally permissive environment; they do achieve more academically when the teacher is efficient and businesslike. The teachers have a point, too, however. For the optimal development of young children a program must include more than academic content. A balance must be found between directive teaching and warmth and support, as a compromise must be sought between total control and complete freedom. Only in an atmosphere of concordance will teachers be able to convince parents of the importance of love, varied stimulation, contingent reward, and responsive language, as well as academic content, in early-education programs.

Since a high adult:child ratio in preschool or day care is considered desirable and since many programs cannot find or afford highly trained personnel, it has been advocated that parents, neighborhood volunteers, high school students, or indigenous paraprofessionals be employed as "aides." This can also provide continuity for the child between the school culture and his home or ethnic culture. It can strengthen ties within the family and within the community. It can take advantage of older children, heterogeneous grouping, and "models" from the neighborhood. Too often, however, such aides have been used only for menial tasks like putting up cupboards and wiping up juice (Levin, 1967). This cannot be the major contribution of the parents and members of poor communities. Bronfenbrenner (1969) suggests that the reason that parents of the disadvantaged do not function as models or reinforcers for their children in a productive way is not because they are not able but because they are not motivated. Parental involvement in early education programs which provides rewarding and satisfying interactions with children can be one way of supplying the motivation .The superordinate goal of concern for young children can be a means of involving not only teachers and parents but the whole community.

When given the opportunity, it is likely that parents will assume an active role in the lives of their children. An active role becomes more difficult to achieve, however, when parents spend a large part of the day at work, when the day-care setting is too remote from their values and problems, and when staffing and organizational patterns fail to represent members of the community. Even when programs are community-based and ethnically representative, there may be substantial gaps between consultants, professionals, paraprofessionals, and consumers (Katz, 1970; Larrabee, 1969; Murphy, 1968b). An all-day program that is seriously designed to reduce the distances between parent, child, and caretaking arrangement will have to present special ways of doing so. A parent drop-in lounge, evening meals, or informal chats and refreshments when they come for their children in the evening and parental participation in decision making when hiring staff members are but a few of the ways of maintaining contact with parents and encouraging their participation. Parental involvement in programs with the primary purpose of optimizing the child's development is essential, and programs directed toward helping parents become effective educators of their children need to be promoted. As training programs in occupations related to child care expand, more adults will have acquired more skills to bring to the task of rearing their own children.   *not just mothers*

The ultimate aim of many early education project directors today is to have the project run by parents and trained community people; to accede to "parent power" and community control. Parental education and involvement and intensive training of paraprofessionals are essential prerequisites to this goal. Only then can preschool or day-care programs realize their potential value; only then will the needs of the child and the family be fully met. To achieve such an aim, one must furthermore seek to answer the questions: who is to receive training, how are they to be trained, and who will do the training? Project Head Start enunciated the policy of filling positions of program assistants to the greatest possible extent by employing people who were low-income residents of the area being served (Project Head Start, 1969). Agencies were urged to formulate plans for the continuous development and upgrading of these workers. In-service programs were developed and increased flexibility in hiring practice evolved (Katz & Weir, 1969) under the combined pressures of a shortage of trained personnel and a wish to involve the poor. These were all fundamental and significant innovations, although for the most part they have been ignored in most attempts to evaluate Head Start. The concept of career progression ladders is rapidly becoming institutionalized without, as far as we can tell, ever having been subjected to careful analysis and evaluation; for example, the report of the National Conference on Child Care (Besaw, 1969) questioned whether the "ladder" notion might not lock in the vertical structure of command. The ladder concept builds from a model of a child-care worker as a "generalist"; that is, the notion of a worker who can assume all roles in a program and who, with training, becomes more efficient and effective in doing so. The well-trained generalist is something of a "supermother" (Besaw, 1969; Whitmarsh, 1966). By contrast one might argue for the "specialist," that is, a person who works in depth in one particular area and becomes highly skilled and specialized in it. Which of these views is adopted will determine the educational preparation and training needed by day-care personnel.

A study by Rahmlow and Kiehn (1967) reveals that the major tasks associated with child-care occupations in day-care centers and preschool programs are housekeeping, food preparation, and the care and preparation of materials. Consequently it might be advisable to develop a "specialist" occupational category with regard to materials. A specialist in this area would be responsible primarily for planning, organizing, arranging, and maintaining the equipment and materials available to the children. This person would, in effect, be a materials "ecologist" who would work with a part of the competence curriculum that deals with ways of systematically introducing children to concepts and constructs of properties of objects and their relationships and would develop ways of using equipment and space to reduce conflicts or to heighten activity. Quite another kind of specialist would deal with food—its nutritional value, its preparation, and its presentation to children—another with language, and another with group activities and routines. Roles would be defined horizontally rather than vertically. The efficiency of the operation would depend on the ability of the staff to function as a multidisciplinary team. A similar multidisciplinary stress has already appeared for those identified by professional labels—nurse, social worker, administrator, teacher (Besaw, 1969; Emerson, 1965; Mayer, Krim & Papell, 1965). We are suggesting here that these categories may be less useful than functional ones. Traditional views of the role of the classroom teacher in elementary and high schools have been challenged and the need for a similar analysis of preschool settings has been pointed out (Katz, 1970; The Day Care and Child Development Council, Gould Foundation Conference, 1969).

How the roles of workers in child-care enterprises are defined will influence the kind of preservice or in-service training that needs to be provided. To date, training programs have tended to feature in their formulations the methodology of the training, such as discussion groups, audiovisual aids, role playing, sensitivity training, training labs, observations, and the ever-present workshop (Project Head Start, 1969; National Conference on Child Care, 1969; Hall Neighborhood House, 1969; United States Department of Health, Education, and Welfare, Child Care and Guidance; a post-high school curriculum, 1970), or the curriculum students will be offered, such as child development, foundation courses, methods courses in science, art, and social studies (American Joint Distribution Committee, 1962; Howard, 1968). Few program formats have made explicit their stances on issues such as the role of workers, view of the child, minority cultures, and how people change.

One noteworthy exception can be found in the work of Roger Ulrich and his colleagues (Ulrich, 1967; Ulrich & Wallace, 1970; Ulrich, Wolfe, & Cole, 1970). These investigators have applied and taught behavior modification techniques to children as well as to adults. One program explored a pyramidal instructional system in which the professor trained graduate students who in turn trained undergraduates. Another of their programs related to high school students; still another taught reinforcement techniques to elementary school students between the ages of 7 and 11 years.

One issue dealt with rather lightly in published training programs is the role of observation. Most programs mention observation in passing. The American Joint Distribution Committee program allots only one of 58 days of training to the observation and recording of child behavior, and among the 10 exemplary college preparatory programs reviewed by Howard (1968) only one offered "special observation and participation" in a nursery school or kindergarten. For the most part observation is treated globally. "Learning to observe with all his senses" is considered an inevitable outcome of watching children. This may be the case, but here, too, there is the alternative view, namely that observation, to be effective, must be directed to preselected and specific aspects of the setting and that it needs to be planned as part of the view of the child that the training program wishes to promote. Students may require more preparation and more exposure to various observational techniques than either one day or one course would allow. Schoggen (1969) has prepared a set of specimen records that might be a useful tool in such preparation.

In general, teacher-training programs seem to deal with large and vague categories of educational procedures. There has been little attempt to develop an argument for what students will be taught or a justification for the appropriateness of particular methods for those who are to be trained. Since the trainee population includes potential high school dropouts, baby sitters, subprofessionals who have not completed high school, preprofessionals who are high school graduates, college students preparing for professional work, experienced college-trained professionals, experienced on-the-job paraprofessionals, and parents, the assumption that some uniform system will be effective for everyone contradicts most of what is known about the significance of differences among people in learning styles, motivation, and experience.

These issues of training moved from the category of "important" to the category of "urgent" with the passage of the Educational Professions Development Act of 1967. This act constitutes the enabling legislation for a network of programs to train both teachers and the teachers of teachers. Spearheaded by an Early Childhood Leadership Development Institute, the program will eventually reach out to a administrators, planners, teachers, and child-care workers at local, state, and national levels. In view of the potential scope and impact of a concerted effort such as this, some discussion of alternative goals, justifications, procedures, and assessment seems appropriate. Although any discussion would have to cope with confusions and complexities, there is little reason to believe that difficulties resolve themselves when they are ignored. If our society is to promote diversity, we must attempt to describe and understand it. Training in the educational professions is likely to have an enduring influence, one that will mold the child-care programs of the future.

PEER RELATIONSHIPS

Although the formation of social relationships is one of the major rationales for nursery schools, the peer group is one aspect of child-care and educational settings often ignored in America (Bronfenbrenner, 1970). As a rule, our society does not deliberately involve the peer group in the socialization process, even though the Israeli kibbutzim and the Soviet method of character training attest to the fact that such utilization is both possible and effective (Bronfenbrenner, 1962; Spiro, 1958). Nevertheless, the unintentional effects of peer relationships in this country are great, widespread, and increasing. The influence of the peer group in adolescence is well-documented (cf. Campbell, 1964). As early as seventh grade the shift from adults to peers as models, companions, and guides has been reported (Bowerman & Kinch, 1959; Bronfenbrenner, 1970), and, according to Bronfenbrenner, this shift probably occurs even earlier now. Furthermore, even before this shift is completed, as soon as children more than 2 years old get together, the peer group exercises a subtle influence on the behavior and development of its members.

The power of this influence is suggested or described in many studies of social relations in preschool settings. Observers (cf. Raph, Thomas, Chess, & Korn, 1968; Swift, 1964) report an increase in all forms of social interaction, particularly with peers, with increasing chronological age. The 2-year-old is generally not ready to participate actively in social activities with other children. His most common role is as onlooker, with parallel and solitary play making up the major part of his activity. Three-year-olds, however, show a greater degree of initiation, interaction, and social participation, and the trend continues as the child grows older. This increase in social behavior is consistent, whether co-operation and consideration, aggression, or independence from adults is being measured.

Studies of children in nursery school also reveal that even at this early age children are aware of ethnic and racial differences in their playmates (Clark & Clark, 1952; McCandless & Hoyt, 1961; Radke & Trager, 1950), and that they are able to make stable sociometric choices (Dunnington, 1957a; McCandless & Marshall, 1957). Children's choices of playmates at this age reflect their home backgrounds, family histories, and sibling structures. First-borns are more likely than later-borns to play with children younger than themselves, and a preference for an opposite-sex companion is more often expressed by a child with a sibling who is of the opposite sex (Koch, 1957). It is interesting, however, that sociometric choices can be manipulated by adult praise (Flanders & Havumaki, 1960).

A number of different aspects of children's development have been shown to be influenced by their peer-group associations. Obviously, children learn a great deal from each other about the realities of social intercourse through first-hand experience (Appeal, 1942). In older children peer relations apparently also play a part in the formation of attitudes and values (Campbell, 1964). Self-esteem has been related to peer acceptance (Coleman, 1961a; Horowitz, 1962; Rosen, Levinger, & Lippitt, 1960), and the presence of a good friend can be instrumental in maintaining a child's mature level of play behavior in a frustrating situation (Wright, 1942).

There are some indications that peers may also influence IQ scores and school achievement. Kirk (1958) has suggested that the reason that the IQ scores of a group of mentally retarded children living at home rose during first grade was their association with children of higher intelligence at home and in public school. In an institutionalized group in which children had to associate with institution inmates of lower IQ both in the wards and in school they did not gain during that year. These differences appeared even though both groups apparently had comparable experience with teachers. The Coleman Report (1966) also emphasized the influence of the peer group. Coleman interpreted the results of his extensive survey of children's performance in public schools to indicate that the single most important factor influencing the child's intellectual achievement was the characteristics of the other children attending the same school. Specifically, lower-class children in middle-class classrooms performed better than their peers who remained with lower-class classmates. Pettigrew (1967), in further analyses of the Coleman Report date, also demonstrated that white children in predominantly black schools unfortunately performed at a level below that of comparable white children in white schools. Social contagion appears to be a two-way street.

There are, however, areas of development in which peer influence is apparently slight. Cazden (in press) suggests that peer talk is not likely to improve language development or communicative competence. The level of peer talk she observed in the British infant schools was of low quality. It appears that for this aspect of education an adult is necessary. Karnes and her associates (1969) give more empirical support to this notion: children in a "community-integrated" nursery school programs, with its advantaged language peer models, made very low gains in IQ, vocabulary, and ITPA scores compared with those in more structured, language-oriented programs.

The Process of Peer-Group Influence

Most investigators have not examined the *process* of peer-group influence but simply imply that the peer-group "climate" is sufficient to change a child's behavior (e.g., Kirk, 1958). A few have compared the relative effects of a group and of a single peer. In an experiment by Merei (1949) a number of small groups consisting of children characterized as nonascendant in their nursery classroom behavior were set up. These groups tended to develop standards and traditions. An older, more ascendant child was introduced into each group after these standards had become established. Despite the fact that in the regular nursery setting these leaders could direct the behavior of any individual in the experimental group, in the small group situation the group absorbed the leader, forced its traditions on him, and generally ignored his suggestions. Other studies, too, have suggested that the group per se has an impact on an individual's performance (e.g., the Coleman Report, 1966, the U. S. Commission on Civil Rights 1967, or reports on Project Concern in Hartford, Connecticut, Mahan & Mahan, 1969). The influence of a peer group does not seem to be based solely on its sheer numbers, however. Bronfenbrenner's (1969) research reveals that in school even a small minority of children can create changes in the behavior of the rest of the class. Furthermore, other studies (cf. Hartup, 1968) demonstrate that preschoolers in an Asch-type situation do not necessarily conform to judgments made by a majority of their peers. There is apparently no simple relation between the size of a group of children and the effectiveness of its influence—the situation is more complex.

Studies of peer relationships in nursery school suggest certain elements of this complexity. Parten (1933) classified two kinds of leadership: the "diplomat," who by artful and indirect suggestions controls a large number of children, and the "bully," who employs brute force in bossing his small "gang." Hanfmann (1935) described four types of leader: the objective leader dominates by his strong interest in constructive play; the social leader, by his dominant interest in play with other children; the gangster uses social play as a means of expanding and displaying his own power; and the destroyer deliberately disrupts orderly play and achieves domination by immobilizing other children.

In more recent studies the suggestion has been made that peer influence depends on the relative status of the influencer (Campbell, 1964). Such a factor seems particularly relevant in the process known as "modeling." This is a less obvious means of influence than bullying, destroying, or deliberately leading; it may also be longer lasting and farther reaching. Hartup, (1967, 1968) reviews the relevant literature to show that preschool children are indeed susceptible to the influence of peer models. Watching a movie of another child behave aggressively led to an increase in aggressive behavior in the viewer (Bandura, Ross, & Ross, 1963a), and the effects of this modeling persisted even after six months (Hicks, 1965).

Aggression is not the only behavior that can be modeled, however; a sharing child can create generosity and altruism (Hartup & Coates, 1967) in his peers merely by displaying these behaviors himself. Although these examples of modeling are taken from laboratory experimentation, there is no reason to believe they would not be equally demonstrable in a preschool, day-care, or home setting. In fact, modeling may account for Anderson's (1937a,b) finding that "domination" of a nursery school child incites dominating behavior in others, whereas "integrative" behavior (taking into consideration the variety of alternatives possible, including consideration of the feelings, interests, and opinions of others in attempting to attain a goal) induces integrative behavior in a companion. Not all peers are equally effective models, however; especially potent models have been observed to be of high status (Campbell, 1964). These may be the most "popular" and accepted peers, those who give nurturance and are peer-oriented rather than dependent on adults (Dunnington, 1957a; Heathers, 1955; Marshall & McCandless, 1957; Moore & Updegraff, 1964).

Peer modeling may provide an explanation for the adoption of broad patterns of social behavior among children in a preschool group. However, children not only provide models, they also exert a force on the behavior of their playmates by deliberate or unintentional reinforcement. Wahler (1967) demonstrated the potential impact of intentional manipulation of reinforcement contingencies in nursery school. Two children were asked to ignore another child when she was playing with dolls but to remain responsive to her when she was doing anything else. A drastic reduction in the subject's doll-playing was soon apparent. When the children were asked to reverse their reinforcement strategies, the opposite trend occurred. Such control of behavior by the social attention of peers was demonstrated similarly for aggressive and cooperative behaviors of other children. Behavior modification has also been used by and with Ulrich, Wolfe, and Bluhm's (1968) subjects; 4-year-olds have successfully taught cognitive tasks to 3-year-olds by using reinforcement techniques. It seems likely that this success must be attributed to the reinforcement procedures and not just to incidental learning, since no similar effect was observed on Deutsch's (New York University, 1968) less experienced preschool subjects when given the opportunity to work together with advanced peers.

Observations made in nursery schools have demonstrated that peer reinforcement often occurs naturally without experimental intervention. Charlesworth and Hartup (1967) reported that reinforcement, in the form of positive attention and approval, affection and acceptance, submission, or tangible objects, appeared to be present in preschool children's activities. The consequence was usually the continuation of the recipient's activity at the time. Reinforcement occurred most frequently in the context of dramatic play and less often during art or table games. It was usually given by older children. The amount of reinforcement was also found to vary from class to class, possibly, these observers suggest, the result of children's modeling different teachers' reinforcement behaviors.

The relationship between the giver and the receiver of reinforcement is not a simple one; reinforcement from peers has extremely complex effects on a child's task performance. At preschool age, it appears, disliked peers as reinforcers can maintain performance on a nonsocial task better than liked peers, since there is less temptation for social interaction (Hartup, 1967, 1968). An age trend toward increasing susceptibility to reinforcement (Hartup, 1967, 1968) and individual differences in responsiveness to approval (Silverman et al., 1968) or negative reinforcement (Brodsky, 1969) also add complexity.

In summary, it appears that peers influence social behaviors (such as aggression or cooperation) by a process of modeling or reinforcement by well-liked, high-status children but that improvement in cognitive, task-oriented, problem-solving performance is likely to result from distinct reinforcement given by a child who is less liked.

Whichever process—modeling or reinforcement—is responsible for the impact of peers on a child's behavior, there are important individual differences in susceptibility to that influence. A child with a history of frequent reinforcement from peers imitated a rewarding child; a child with a history of no reinforcement from peers imitated the nonrewarding model (Hartup, 1967, 1968). Young children, girls, and low-status children are most susceptible to the influence of others (Campbell, 1964). Which particular peer is modeled depends on the personality and history of the child being affected.

Peer Relationships in Day-Care Settings

The relationships among peers we have discussed have implications for day-care programs. Peer-group relations can be a valuable resource for an educator.

> If social cooperation is thus one of the principal formative agents in the spontaneous genesis of child thought, it is an imperative necessity for modern education to make use of this fact by according an important place to socialized activities in the curriculum (Aebli, 1951, p. 60).

The potential usefulness and modifiability of children's peer groups have, for the most part, been unrealized in this country.

In an early study of peer relations in nursery school Jersild and Markey (1935) made the astute commentary that putting the child in with other children under the guidance of a "progressive" teacher does not mean *ipso facto* that he will become more imbued with a spirit of cooperation and amity in his dealings with others. They had observed that the average child in nursery school was involved in a conflict every five minutes and noted that situations that stimulated cooperation also encouraged aggression. With deliberate effort, however, it has been suggested (Swift, 1964) that the teacher or caregiver can provide a social model and increase the child's self-confidence by helping him to develop skills and experience successes that will add to his feeling of worth. She can also help him to increase his social perceptiveness by discussing incidents that occur in the classroom and thus decrease his dependence on her. Chittenden (1942) provided children who were highly dominative with a series of training sessions, using dolls to play out situations involving potential social conflict. Through discussions, which included interpretation of situations portrayed and a consideration of types of behavior that would be most appropriate to solving them, the children were helped to a better understanding of social relations. The children who participated in these experimental sessions showed a significant decrease in dominative behavior and an increase in cooperative behavior. The teacher should not interfere too often, however, in on-going peer relations in nursery school, Appel (1942) advised; the quarrels of 2- and 3-year-olds are fleeting affairs.

Another way of creating a cooperative and productive peer situation is to direct the efforts of all children toward the attainment of superordinate goals (Bronfenbrenner, 1969; Sherif, Harvey, White, Hood, & Sherif, 1961). A goal of concern for the welfare of young children, which Bronfenbrenner suggests as a valuable superordinate goal for society, might provide a cohesive bond among older children in a day-care program.

In designing preschool or day-care programs, consideration should be given to the individualized needs of different children and to changes that occur as they grow up. Younger children, for example, need smaller groups (Swift, 1964); in fact, for the child under 3, one-to-one relations with adults are probably best. All children need times to be together and times to be alone, but there are individual differences in the relative proportions of these periods that would be optimal. Peer interaction can serve valuable social and task-oriented functions; a highly structured preschool program fails to take advantage of this asset (Sears & Hilgard, 1964).

An important educational issue currently being assessed is the value of heterogeneous grouping of children by age. Data from the study of peer relations bear on this issue. Jersild and Markey (1935) observed that conflicts between same-aged children were more common and lasted longer than conflicts involving an older and a younger child. Preschool situations in which children have been grouped heterogeneously are associated with less verbal and physical aggression (Body, 1955), more social contacts and imaginative behavior (Markey, 1935), and more affection, teaching, and entertaining and less competition (Murphy, 1937). Cazden (in press) observes that in the British infant schools' open plan expectations about routines are transmitted more from older to younger children than by explicit direction of the teacher; McNamara, Porterfield, Miller, and Arnold (1968) comment in their evaluation of Head Start that the presence of older children in the class was a great help; and Honzig (in Haith, 1970) finds that "it works" in an all-day children's center. Goodlad and Anderson (1959) concluded that although such a policy is rarely put into practice all research seems to lead to advocacy of heterogeneous grouping.

An even more potentially inflammatory concept than heterogeneous grouping is integration. Some research, notably the Coleman Report, suggests that there are benefits to be gained by integrating inner-city children into a middle-class educational environment. The academic performance of these minority children is indeed improved as a consequence of such integration. Moreover, even at this early age children are aware of race differences, and, since sociometric choices reflect experience, integration could be instrumental in the children's forming immediate and subsequent interracial bonds of friendship. It would seem, however, that integration is no simple solution to the problem of inequality. Integration, *by itself,* is not always sufficient to raise the level of functioning of the "disadvantaged" group significantly (Karnes et al., 1969). At the same time, it may lead to conditions under which harmful effects to the academically superior children occur (Bronfenbrenner, 1969; Pettigrew, 1967). Even when integration is not defined as a 50:50 mix but as a more population-representative ratio of approximately 1:10 the problem remains. Although this seems like an effective ratio for improving the performance of the minority children (Mahan & Mahan, 1969), the behavior of the majority may be deleteriously affected. Intergration *may* lead to equality, *but* at the expense of optimization. We agree with the director of the Office of Child Development (Zigler, 1969) that it is not desirable to separate children into classes at birth, but we contend that the solution lies not in integration alone but in better early educational programming to meet the individualized needs of both minority and majority group children. Such programs may be offered in an integrated setting—perhaps with beneficial side effects for the development of ethnic and social-class tolerance—if such a condition is desired by parents and community. Programs should be designed to fulfill the particular needs of the children and their parents; it is not appropriate to create the program first and then find children in the right proportions to fill the available "slots."

THE CHILD IN EDUCATIONAL SETTINGS

The child does not come to school—or preschool—as an empty vessel waiting to be filled. He brings with him abilities, interests, and personality quirks already developed which influence dramatically the effects that a given program, a certain teacher, or a particular setting will have on him.

Context II has described in detail how some individual differences in children are developed by the interaction of the child's innate structures and tendencies with the experiences to which he is exposed. Obviously such differences will affect the child's receptivity to early education. The child who is excessively attached to his mother is likely to be so traumatized by separation from her, at least at first, that enriching his experience by exposure to visual stimuli (no matter how inherently fascinating) will likely not improve his cognitive development. Such experience could, on the other hand, be beneficial to a child with a more balanced pattern of attachment and exploration. The child's attachment behavior might also affect his performance in a preschool program by its influence on the relationship he is able to form with the teacher. Similarly, the child's capacity for play will affect his optimal utilization of free-play situations characteristic of nursery school programs; his language sophistication will determine how much of the verbal content of a program he can absorb; and the level of cognitive development he has obtained represents the appropriate starting point for his cognitive enrichment.

Few empirical studies have focused on the differential effects of preschool programs related to individual differences in children. One study which controlled teaching methods in order to discover differences related to personality characteristics was conducted by Grimes and Allinsmith (1961). The study revealed that "compulsive" children performed better than those who were less compulsive in a structured situation. The achievement of "anxious" children, however, was impeded in unstructured settings.

In addition, some attempts have been made to relate one measure of cognitive functioning, namely IQ, to program effectiveness. Such research indicates that children of lower intelligence benefit more than children who have initially higher IQ scores from a variety of preschool programs (Bereiter, 1968; Skeels & Dye, 1939; Van De Riet & Van De Riet, 1969b) and that their gains are more stable (Karnes, Hodgins, Teska, & Kirk, 1969). As important as formal cognitive abilities for determining how well the child will function, however, are his history of deprivation or failure (Osler, in Zigler, 1968), his motivation for attention and affection (Zigler & Balla, 1972), his responsiveness to approval (Silverman, Schwartz, & Simon, 1968), his wariness of adults (Zigler, 1968), and his view of himself and his expectancy of success.

Such factors may be related to the child's social-class background. A number of researchers have suggested recently that different classes of children require different types of educational program (e.g. Bereiter, 1970; Jensen, 1969). Investigators who have studied social-class differences in program effects report that middle-class children benefit from traditional nursery school types of program, but the development of children from lower-class homes is most improved by cognitively oriented programs (DiLorenzo, Salter, & Brady, 1969; Fowler, 1970; Van De Riet & Van De Riet, 1969b).

Swift (1964), reviewing the literature on nursery school experience, suggests that the child for whom nursery school will be most successful is the one who has already developed emotional independence, the ability to get along with peers, and good communication skills. Yet it is the dependent child, she continues, the child whose own needs interfere with his ability to perceive social situations realistically or whose background of language and information is inadequate, who has need the greatest for preschool experience. One solution to this dilemma may be educational programs for parents that attempt to equalize the experiences of children at home. Another solution might be a diversity of educational programming, individually and diagnostically prescribed to complement or supplement the child's capacities, characteristics, and experience. Before such individualization can occur, however, more research on the differential effects of various programs on different classes of children is required.

19

Educational Components— Summary and Conclusions

This *Context* has been concerned with the young child in educational settings and with the various components of his educational experience: programs, peers, teachers, and physical settings. The child brings to preschool individual differences in ability, interests and developmental level that determine the effect and effectiveness of the educational programs, teachers, and peers he encounters.

Peer relationships are an integral part of any group experience for the child. By processes of modeling and reinforcement, and perhaps deliberate coercion, peers influence the child's social and task-oriented behaviors, attitudes, values, and performance. This impact of the peer group has implications, which we have discussed, for integration and heterogeneous grouping.

Although peer-group influence is a relevant component of the early-education experience, the teacher is of central importance in American preschool programs. It is she who is most frequently the model and director, she who controls the resources and the power, she who models language and teaches cognitive strategies and offers lessons in specific content areas. In many of these roles the teacher's actions resemble the mother's. Moreover, the teacher's behaviors have a similar effect on the child's performance and development. Research on teachers demonstrates once again the beneficial effects of what appear to be universally important child-rearing dimensions: warmth, stimulation, involvement, individualized attention, sensitivity, responsiveness, permissiveness, and clear and extensive language behavior. Furthermore, the impact of efficiency and flexibility in teachers' behaviors on children's performance has been documented. Discipline

256

by teachers as well as parents, research suggests, should be clear and firm and administered in a gentle loving manner.

A teacher's behavior is influenced by the teacher's personality, history, and specific training and by factors in the immediate situation: the physical setting, the time of day, the curriculum, the number and age of the children, and— most important—the individual characteristics of the children with whom she deals. Implications of research on teachers and children for the structure of an early education or day-care program, for the selection and training of teachers, and for parent education, parent involvement, and parent power were discussed in this Context.

In our treatment of early education programs we have attempted to dimensionalize critical differences. Although our discussion has naturally not exhausted the total realm of possible dimensions, we have tried to provide a first approximation of program profiles that might be helpful in summarizing, conceptualizing, and comparing programs or potential programs. Dimensions included have been based either on an analysis of the underlying theoretical framework of a program or on the particular teaching techniques it employs. These dimensions have been presented as continuous, rather than dichotomous, variables. Differences among programs have been related to their view of the child and his development and to their goals for child development. Different programs have focused on different aspects of the child's development and in so doing have emphasized either people or things as mediators of experience. On a very obvious level programs have varied dramatically in the degree of structure they provide. Differences have also occurred in the depth of education attempted, from relatively superficial behavior modification to an attempt to build deep cognitive structures, from a direct attack on the child's deficiencies to an indirect attempt to modify his home experience.

A recurrent theme which appears once again in this discussion of the child in educational settings is that of diversity. Children and parents, teachers and programs all have different needs and abilities and make diverse contributions to the educational process. The goal of the educator, like that of the developing child, must be to reduce incongruity, to search for and provide appropriate matches between these various elements.

Much of the diversity in children's needs can be attributed to their different histories. Current preschool educational planners, aware of this, have directed their efforts in large part toward children from disadvantaged backgrounds, most often those from lower-class homes. In their attempts to raise the level of functioning of these children they have often been successful. It is not surprising, however, that in any preschool program children who have had no similar stimulating experiences at home make greater gains in IQ or performance measures than more privileged children. Two challenges yet confront the planner

of early education programs. Programs must be designed to foster the development of children who do not come from completely disadvantaged homes. Even
the disadvantaged programs should be designed to utilize techniques that
will provide what those children lack and be *most* effective in fostering their
development.

Research seems to indicate, for example, that if the effectiveness of education
can be measured in terms of IQ points or children's performances in other
standardized tests, or even by ratings made by teachers or psychiatrists, then
programs with structured formats that provide a great deal of adult attention
and emphasize the learning of specific cognitive and language skills have been
most successful with disadvantaged children. All studies that have compared
different preschool programs have obtained data congruent with this generalization. Although Montessori programs have been shown to be more successful
than *no* preschool experience for lower-class children (Cox, 1968; Fleege, 1967;
Stodolsky & Jensen, 1969), they have generally compared unfavorably with other
programs higher in adult attention and cognitive and language emphasis. The
Bereiter-Engelmann-Becker program has most frequently received top credits,
since it has been included in each major comparative study. It has been only as
effective as other preschool projects with somewhat similar emphases in these comparisons, however; namely the programs of Karnes (Karnes et al., 1969), Weikart
(Weikart, in Hunt, 1969b; Weikart, 1971), Gotkin (Dickie, 1968), DARCEE
(Miller & Dyer, 1970), and the New York schools (DiLorenzo et al., 1969).
In each comparison these programs have been superior to traditional nursery
school programs in obtaining intellectual gains in lower-class children. Nursery
school programs or more process-oriented preschool programs seem more likely
to further the social and intellectual development of middle-class children
(Bereiter, 1968; DiLorenzo et al., 1969; Sears & Dowley, 1963).

Within the somewhat artificial categories formed by social-class divisions
there are differences in "competence" that depend on the specific capabilities
and histories of children. These differences, too, demand attention from the
planners of early education programs. Dickie (1968) suggests that the more
advanced children profit more from less structured programs; Costello (1970b)
makes a similar suggestion. In the preschool project described by Costello an
attempt was made to devise appropriate programs to fit the different needs of
children who varied on a continuum of overall competence or general maturity,
based on ratings made by social workers, psychiatrists, and teachers. For children
of high psychological competence, who appeared to be responsive to any program,
they designed a nursery school program of enrichment in which the emphasis
was on social development rather than intellectual change. For children in the
middle of this continuum a position characteristic of most Head Start children,
the program consisted of a structured sequence of activities in small groups of

six children with one teacher, plus activities for the larger group. Each of the small groups was homogeneously grouped according to the children's impulsivity/control rating, and a different teaching method was employed with each. Finally, children at the low end of the competence scale, who were inhibited, danger-oriented, and distrusted adults, were given a more therapeutically oriented experience. One nonprofessional teacher spent all her time with a group of five of these children in a semi-enclosed, secure area. Her goal was to get them involved with people and with things, and no curriculum was prescribed. We would suggest that this approach of tailoring programs to the specific needs of particular groups of children is a valuable one that should be investigated further.

Differences in children's needs and capabilities are related also to age. The trend in recent years has been to start the formal education of the child at a younger and younger age. This has been effective up to a certain point. Van De Riet and Van De Riet, for example (1969b), report that 4-year-old children gain more from the Learning to Learn program than 5-year-olds, and Fowler (1970) finds his program especially effective with younger children. Even when programs have been specially designed for younger children and have not been mere extrapolations downward of the same old acadamic content and teaching methods, there is not complete agreement that education must begin in the crib. Karnes et al., (1969) report that home-tutoring of the child before the age of 3 (one hour a day) is not more beneficial than 'an ameliorative preschool experience that starts at age 3.

Early education programs have varied drastically in length and intensity. In a program focused on alleviating some particular deficit by the use of one-to-one attention, short-term intervention appears to be sufficient to effect significant change. Two hours of concept training a week, over eight months, resulted in the gains documented by Palmer and Rees (1969); 15 visits, spread over four months, each lasting an average of only 32 minutes, led to 13.7 point gains on the PPVT (Levenstein & Sunley, 1967); one hour a week of home training for mother and infant, for three months, also led to significant IQ gains (Weikart & Lambie, 1969). The short (15 minutes) language-tutoring sessions of Blank and Solomon (1969) led to a 7-IQ-point gain with 4-year-olds after only three months, when sessions occurred three times a week; when tutoring was offered five times a week, children's IQ's rose by 14.5 points in the same three-month period.

One cannot conclude from these data, however, that the longer the intervention the more successful it will be. There does not seem to be a simple monotonic relationship. Longer programs of similar content and form have been less effective than those described above. Schaefer, Furfey, and Harte (1968), for example, raised IQ scores of children in their experimental group only one IQ point after two years of daily tutoring. Moreover, when children are in educational programs longer than one year, gains in subsequent years are never so large as those observed at the end of the first year (Bereiter & Engelmann, 1968; Fuschillo, 1968; Gordon, 1969a; Karnes et al., 1969).

The experience that follows a child's exposure to an educational program is critical for the persistence of these gains (Gordon, 1969a). Miller (1969) suggests, in his review of intervention effects, that it is relatively easy to produce a gain of 15 to 20 IQ points after a year of intervention but considerably more difficult to maintain these gains after the intervention has ended. Even two years of experience in various preschool programs (Karnes et al., 1969) did not differentially alter performance permanently. Children maintained their gains through a year of public kindergarten, but by the end of first grade in the regular school system no test differences were apparent. Children from all preschool programs had regressed. Furthermore, school experience was most detrimental for those who had shown the most promise. Only on measures of school achievement was it found that children from a two-year structured program performed better than those having had one year's experience in a traditional nursery school. After a year's enrichment in the Learning to Learn program (Van De Riet & Van De Riet, 1969a) children retained their superiority over a control group through first grade; by the end of the second grade, although differences were still in the right direction, they were not significant; and by the time these children had completed third grade there were no longer any differences apparent. If early education is to fulfill its promise of equality, techniques that are successful in preschool programs will have to be extended upward into the schools. If a child is put back in his preintervention environment, gains produced by a compensatory education program can be expected to fade out (Campbell & Frey, 1970).

A final area of diversity in preschool education programs is in implicit or explicit goals. Such diversity is not inappropriate in an individualistic, pluralistic nation, but it may be useful to attempt to form a coherent hierarchy of priorities from these diverse goals. Perhaps, for the present, priority may be given to the goal of school-oriented equality for lower-class children. In programs that are short, intense, structured, and remedial and concentrate on intellectual and language skills particular behaviors of these children may be so modified that they can effectively compete with their more advantaged peers in elementary school. The contribution of such programs will be immediately beneficial, especially if they also increase the attention, concentration, trust, and motivation of these children and offer them pleasure and fun. Other goals of early education, however, may, in the long run, be as important as equality and success in school. There is the goal of optimization of children's potential development. There are the goals of autonomy, flexibility, and versatility. There are goals that emphasize the development of the whole child, not just his cognitive ability. There is the goal of developing "leverage" behaviors—those dispositions and activities that will lead to the continuing acquisition of knowledge, such as curiosity and attention, ability to plan, to engage in sequentially meaningful behavior patterns, to solve problems, and to put aside short-term gains for long-term goals. All these goals must be incorporated into the hierarchy of aims for early education programs. To attain them a concentrated, academically oriented preschool program is incomplete, and a more comprehensive approach to programming is demanded. Every aspect of the child's development—attachment and social behaviors, cognition, language, and play—needs to be included in a complete program. This is especially true in a program of full day care. Although the important role of play in children's development has been noted by psychologists, this is one component of early education that has been particularly neglected. Few programs have examined or utilized its full potentiality. They have not made use of the fact that children learn through play; nor have they employed play as a necessary humanizing balance for regimentation. In many current programs there is also a tendency to overlook the affective aspects of the child's development. A comprehensive program might be one that included cognitive and language training within the warm, supportive context of the traditional nursery school setting. Moreover, a truly comprehensive program would include the child's family by offering guidance to mothers in ways of stimulating, interacting with, teaching, or managing their children and by involving parents in an educational program at the school or center. Parental cooperation is a minimum requirement for an effective comprehensive program.

The more comprehensive a program, the more likely that it will lead to gains beyond that of IQ. Miller and Dyer's (1970) comparative evaluation of different preschool projects revealed that the most comprehensive program in their study—the Early Training Project at DARCEE—was responsible for gains in resistance to distraction, inventiveness, achievement, independence, and verbal-social participation beyond those gains observed in the other programs. In program design and evaluation there has been an inordinate emphasis on demonstrating IQ score changes. Since the meaning of these scores and of changes in them is controversial and their predictive validity is questionable, the relative usefulness of IQ as a dependent measure is dubious. One legitimate reason for this misplaced overemphasis is the absence of other standardized inventories. New measures are called for. Yet not only are standardized tests required but so is formative research to examine specific program components and dimensions; so are innovative dependent measures of change; so is replication of programs with other samples of children. Programs must be continuously re-evaluated and reformulated. The issues of evaluation and research methodology are discussed further in Chapter 20.

If day care is to provide more than custodial care for its children and more than a convenience for their parents, research on programs of early education is of critical importance. Although preschool education programs are not synonymous with day-care programs, they are directly relevant. Preschool programs, for the most part, never last all day, yet even in the short sessions they provide the functioning of disadvantaged children, and sometimes middle-class children, can be significantly raised. This gives the day-care planner a powerful tool that should be employed only with the caution that even though day care should not be merely custodial neither should it consist entirely of formal education. It is especially crucial that day care, even more than intervention projects, should be comprehensive and concerned with the development of the whole child, with meeting the individual and particular needs of children, with involving the children's families, and with adapting to the diversity that these families contribute.

20

Evaluation

AN "EXPERIMENTING SOCIETY" IS ONE THAT DELIBERATELY initiates changes in its own institutions and systematically tests the outcome of these changes (Fairweather, 1967; Campbell, 1969; Campbell and Erlebacher, 1970). Such experimentation might promote the development of a rational society as it promotes the development of a rational child. Although current practice in American society is far from this evolutionary ideal, there have been glimmerings of such a possibility in the future. Increasingly social commentators are expressing support for the idea that institutional reforms must be studied and evaluated, that some rational basis for proposals and decisions must be sought. In a recent article in *The New York Times,* James Reston applauded the increasing appreciation on the part of the nation's political leadership of the benefits to be gained from the application of scientific thinking to social problems. Reston quotes from *The Common Sense of Science* by Jacob Bronowski:

> Science is a great many things, but in the end they all return to this: science is the acceptance of what works and the rejection of what does not. . . .
> This is how society has lost touch with science: because it has hesitated to judge itself by the same impersonal code of what works and what does not. . . . We must learn to act on that understanding in the world as well as in the laboratory. . . .
> This is the message of science, our ideas must be realistic, flexible, unbigoted. They must create their own authority. If any ideas have a claim to be called creative, because they have liberated that creative impulse, it is the ideas of science . . . [Reston, *The New York Times,* February 7, 1971, Section 4, p. 12].

Today the nation is demonstrating an unprecedented willingness to intervene in people's lives, to create new institutions and to modify or drastically revise the

263

old. Yet the discrepancy between the demand for reality testing and the supply of adequate research seems to grow.

Although especially prevalent with regard to child-oriented ameliorative and innovative programs, disillusionment with experimentation and research in education is not new. Its first signs appeared in the 1930's on the heels of a period of enthusiastic, grandiose, and overoptimistic claims and the expectation of clear, quick answers to simplistic questions (Campbell & Stanley, 1967). Needless to say, that expectation was not confirmed. The problems of educating children did not quickly disappear. Little more was known about how to educate children at the end of that period than at the beginning, and the tedious effort provided few reinforcements for the research investment.

In the last few years the optimism of an earlier time has been revived. Research and development programs mushroomed in the sixties; the literature quadrupled and then quadrupled again. Slowly, competent researchers began to warm to the challenge, and the level of methodology, analysis, and theory took a leap forward. Nonetheless, a new wave of pessimism might be emerging, this time spearheaded by those not engaged in the research enterprise (Sugarman, 1970). The pessimism seems to be founded on mistaken assumptions, not dissimilar from those of the twenties, about the amount of funds available for research, benefits that have been derived, and the nature of the research enterprise.

With respect to the first question, it has been estimated that of the 30 billion dollars spent by public schools less than one-fifth of 1% is tagged for research, and most of that is spent to collect simple actuarial information (Hart, 1969, p. 33). Although approximately 350 million dollars a year are spent on Head Start (White, 1970) and social-welfare spending of all kinds (including social security, veterans' benefits, and education) adds up to 160 billion dollars a year (*U.S. News and World Report*), we know of no attempt to estimate the proportion of these sums allocated to research or evaluation. Others have noted that there seems to be an inverse relation between the size of an innovative or ameliorative program and the proportion of its budget allotted for research; small programs tend to spend proportionately more money than large programs (Hawkridge, Chalupsky, & Roberts, 1968). These authors comment that society seems able to tolerate research on itself, especially in sensitive and vital areas, only in quantities small enough to avoid politically important repercussions. If this is the case, ultimate disillusionment has been built into the system.

DEBATE AND CONTROVERSY

Despite relatively limited funding, a large segment of the research community has become involved in solving what often appear to be hopelessly knotted problems of methodology, measurement, design, and last, but of central importance, theory. Contributions by Campbell and his associates (Campbell, 1967; Campbell & Stanley, 1967), Scriven (1967), and Cronbach (1957) suggest that elegant and defensible solutions are possible, although not without inherent harassments. Perhaps the most encouraging sign of the growing commitment of highly qualified people can be found in the active debates on these issues now appearing in professional journals. At least one sign of the vigor and growth of a research and development area is wide controversy and discussion.

Currently we are in the middle of a "national debate" regarding the value of compensatory education. In particular, controversy over the Westinghouse-Ohio evaluation of Head Start illustrates the enormous difficulties of evaluation efforts that are initiated after a massive program has been implemented. Some questions about the study stem from the diversity of programs that shared the name Head Start. White has pointed out that "Head Start has been, and is, the corporate name for a nationally implemented series of preschool programs, but Head Start has never specifically dictated the curriculum of these programs" (1970, p. 167). How can any evaluation examine the influence of programs of unknown and unspecified variability?

Other questions are of a technical nature. There were, for example, discrepancies between the initial status of children who experienced Head Start and those who did not. These differences indicate the presence of serious artifacts in the findings (Campbell & Erlebacher, 1970). These and other issues are debated by White, Campbell, and Erlebacher and Cicirelli, Evans, Schiller and others in a recent volume edited by Hellmuth (1970). Has Head Start failed? Some say it has; some say it has not; others are waiting for the results of the longitudinal study by the Educational Testing Service currently in progress (Anderson, 1970). Barely heard are the few who would challenge the premise of the question and would pose an alternative view: let us abandon the pass-fail perspective and, in its place, let us acknowledge that programs will have several goals; that they will vary in their capacity to reach these goals; that the tools of inquiry need to be applied to an analysis of the conditions that enhance program effectiveness and that programs need to be continuously reshaped to test the value of that analysis. In the meantime Head Start and other programs may be replaced by new promises and most certainly by new problems, with far too little examination of goals, variations, optimizing conditions, and possibilities.

What is the significance of these debates for day care? Priceless information about the administrative and political ramifications of child-development programs are rising to the surface. More information is surely available, and, hopefully, one day those who participated in the early formulation and implementation of Head Start will prepare a comprehensive analysis. White describes the precipitous implementation of Head Start in the following manner:

Thus, in 1964, one could argue a need for Head Start preschools and find research work to suggest their promise. The political support was duly forthcoming. . . . Early planning had envisaged a beginning with 50,000 to 100,000 children in an eight-week summer program, but the idea of Head Start was a natural. It had a kind of magic for everyone. Sixty-five percent of the counties in the nation applied for Head Start programs and ultimately, 40% were granted them. . . .

During its first summer, in 1965, Head Start served 561,000 children in some 2400 communities in the United States and its possessions. Federal antipoverty funds provided 83 million dollars on a 90%-of-support basis. With local supplementation, the cost of Summer, 1965, came to 95 million dollars. Succeeding Summer operations have been of about the same magnitude. Beginning in Fall, 1965, Full-year Head Start programs were initiated, serving 20,000 children and then increasing tenfold by 1967, when 215,000 children were enrolled. Summer and Full-year components together have by now reached over 2 million children since the inception of Head Start. At present, Head Start operates on a budget of about $350 million a year. . . .

But the gamble lurked beneath all of this implementation. Politicians could vote for Head Start; bureaucrats could carefully place the funds out; willing teachers, parents, nurses, doctors, etc. could then establish over 12,000 Head Start Centers around the country. The preschools offered an intensive encounter for the child, 1 teacher for every 15 children, 1 adult for every 5 children. All this did not erase the gamble. The heart of the gamble lay in that which the experts were not so certain about, what to do in a preschool program and how to evaluate it [1970, pp. 165–167].

Another glimpse behind the scenes is provided by Evans and Schiller.

Crests of public and congressional support for social action programs often swell quickly and with little anticipation. Once legislation is enacted, the pressures on administrators for swift program implementation are intense. In these circumstances—which are the rule rather than the exception—pleas that the program should be implemented carefully, along the lines of a true experiment with random assignment of subjects so we can confidently evaluate the program's effectiveness, are bound to be ignored [1970, pp. 217–218].

Day care can take note of the past. Precipitous program expansions are a prelude to chaos; big gambles are hard to win. Inflated promises are hard to keep because our ability to mount effective massive programs is limited by our inexperience in doing so and because makeshift evaluations fail to analyze in any depth those efforts that are undertaken. With respect to day-care programming perhaps the time has come for long-term planning; and with respect to day-care evaluation perhaps the time has come to consider seriously issues of goals and methodology.

THE AIMS AND CONSEQUENCES OF DAY CARE

Short Term Expectations

How day care will be evaluated is a function of its goals. When day care is tied to welfare reform, one criterion for assessing benefits could be formulated as the number of families who become self-supporting. Equally unambiguous criteria could be applied by employers who have invested in day care as a way of reducing absenteeism or the rate of turnover among female employees. For these aims evaluation criteria appear to be relatively straightforward, and comparison groups are not difficult to designate. When welfare rolls are of interest, for example, cities that have received major infusions of day-care funds can be compared with those that have not. When large industries are involved, plants that have provided day care can be compared with those that have not. In general, these goals and their related criteria deal with short-term aims that can be satisfied by day-care programs that meet the basic physical needs of children and do not violate minimum consumer demands for convenience and economy.

As long as these are the stated aims of day care, evaluations may, at the outset, avoid the complexities of human growth and development and ignore the uncertainties of social, educational, and psychological assessment. Yet the respite from these complexities and uncertainties can, at best, be temporary. At some point the issues that have plagued early childhood programs will surely reappear. Consumers, legislators, and the citizenry at large will want to know whether day-care programs make any significant contributions to the ability of children to function effectively. Day care will then have to be represented as distinctive environmental "inputs" rather than as a loose label for a conglomeration of child-care arrangements and these inputs will have to be related to dimensions of human competence. At some point it will be necessary to stipulate those aspects of the child's environment implied by the term "day care" and how the experiences of children in different day-care programs differ from one another and from the experiences of children who are not in day-care programs. If there is a lesson to be learned from the current controversy, it may be that there can be no answer to questions of this kind: "Does Head Start (or day care) work?" Perhaps the best way of avoiding the exasperation and sense of defeat bound to result from unresolvable yes-no questions is to pose substantive questions:

1. How do day-care programs differ from one another with respect to intention and implementation?
2. How do these differences influence communities, families, and children?
3. How can the relations between "inputs" and "outputs" be interpreted?

Day care, in combination with other current programs for young children, constitutes a major social intervention and embodies a variety of implicit and explicit intentions. It is likely to have interacting and complex influences on communities, families, and children which will need to be understood (Messick, 1969). Such a task will require the skills of sociologists, anthropologists, economists, and other social scientists and the cooperation of consumers, community leaders, and legislators.

Program Differences

Intentions. The same questions of purpose raised in the controversy over compensatory education must be raised with respect to day care. Is day care to focus on the preparation of children for later schooling? If so, it will be necessary to specify the nature of the school environment and the demands that children are likely to face. Is day care to focus on normative expectations? If so, the way in which these norms have been derived must be examined. Is day care to focus on the development of basic, and presumably universal, cognitive, or social competencies and motivational support? If so, they also require specification. Whether day care derives its goals from the analysis of behaviors associated with school or societal success, norms derived from age-related expectations, cultural consensus, or universal psychological processes (Kohlberg & Mayer, 1970; Zimiles, 1968), they need to be made explicit.

Perhaps one of the most pervasive implicit assumptions in the evaluation of early childhood programs has been that the effects of these programs ought to be demonstrable in subsequent years, regardless of the school or home environment of the child at that time. Thus children who have attended preschool programs have been followed through first, second, and third grades. Until recently little thought was given to their on-going life experiences. First, it is doubtful whether programs such as Head Start ever proposed to inoculate children against future deleterious environments (White, 1970), although Baratz and Baratz (1969) suggest that this was the case. The planning and implementation of "Follow Through" programs seem to testify to the recognition of Head Start planners that quality educational programs must be maintained throughout the child's schooling. Moreover, neither learning and reinforcement theorists (Campbell & Frey, 1970; Engelmann, 1970) nor developmental theorists who stress the importance of the child-environment interaction at each level of development would expect preschool changes to be impervious to subsequent environmental conditions. Nonetheless, follow-up evaluations have typically neglected to analyze the environment of the child at school and at home, thus implying, by default, that it is irrelevant.

Explicit intentions to change the family, the community, or the school or to change children may not be formulated. It seems necessary, however, to allow for the possibility that day-care programs will in fact influence the status, functions and structures of environments and that they will alter the capacities of children (Messick, 1969). The national debate on "compensatory education" (Hellmuth, 1970), with its many implications for judgments of cultural and socioeconomic differences, deficiencies, and disadvantages, has made it comfortable to search for interventions that on the surface appear to change "neutral" things such as "institutions," "delivery of services," or "community resources." With these justifications one might concentrate evaluation efforts on the assessment of "inputs"; for example, organizational structures, parent activities, staff qualifications, staff patterns, supplies, and equipment. To do this and nothing more would be to protect vital and sensitive areas from scrutiny but not from change.

A wide variety of input variations is possible. One radical proposal might entail "tuition grants" or "vouchers," (Center for the Study of Public Policy, 1970) which, if applied to day care, would enable eligible parents to choose a program that would conform to their values and satisfy their needs. Presumably such a system would increase the diversity of day-care programs, increase their quality by competition in an open market, and ensure a better "match" between consumer needs and available services. It can be argued that evaluation (or accountability, which is not necessarily the same as evaluation) would be built into such a system. Parents would finance only those programs that they prefer, and thus parental preference would become an inherent evaluation criterion. A "free-choice" model assumes, however, that parents have ready access to relevant program information and that parents will be able to weigh objectively and dispassionately the implications of this information. To what extent can we afford to ignore the determinants of parental preference—that is, the criteria used by parents to arrive at preferences, the influence on their choices of the information made available to them, and the noninformational ways in which programs might go about developing parental allegiance (e.g., television commercials)? Once again it seems important to recognize that *someone* is deciding what information is relevant and *someone* is making judgments about program aims, variables, and standards. Perhaps the danger of the rhetoric of "free choice" is that it creates the illusion that external constraints and determinants of choice have been abolished. The proposition is similar in many respects to a view of the child as developing according to an inherent, predetermined plan and the environment as a source of distortion and interference. In both cases the wisdom of the individual is set apart from his social experience, his expectations, and his informational transactions with the world. Our own view of development suggests that such a model is inadequate when viewing the child and seriously suspect when applied to parents. The regulation of programs is surely reciprocal and to obscure the intentions and values of program planners comes dangerously close to perpetrating a public hoax. Above all, serious program evaluation becomes almost impossible when there has been no previous articulation of goals and dimensions of program variation.

Implementation. Problems of treatment and measurement follow from statements of intentions. What treatments are likely to promote desired ends and how can "treatments in action" be observed? Relatively few studies of early childhood education programs have taken the pains to document the extent to which their descriptive features appeared in the actual settings. Miller and Dyer's (1970) comparative study of Bereiter-Engelmann, DARCEE, Montessori, and nursery-school programs represents one of the few in which such observation has occurred. It will be difficult to study the psychological impact of day-care programs sensibly without the careful dimensionalizing of "inputs" at the point of the child-environment interaction.

Even more, it will be necessary to add the difficult task of dimensionalizing the complex social variables that surround these treatments; for example, there is evidence of diffusion effects that suggests that programs influence the parents of children who have not been directly involved (Hunt, 1969b). Current research by DARCEE investigators is examining how diffusion occurs and how it is influenced by program variables.

We have yet to study seriously other issues that are part of the reality of program implementation. The abrasives and alliances that may lead programs to flourish or decay require serious analysis. We have yet to explore the dynamics of program leadership, those dimensions of charisma, competence, and sensitivity that inspire trust and enthusiasm and that unleash the capacities of others to think and function effectively.

Interpretation. Measurement problems may seem to be solved when program outcomes are indexed by scores on standardized achievement, IQ, or even affective tests (White, 1970). The tricky and, perhaps, more relevant issue is to demonstrate convincingly what these test scores represent in terms of psychological development. The major impact of early childhood programming may be on motivation (Zigler & Butterfield, 1968), test-taking efficiency (Dreyer & Rigler, 1969), cognitive style (attentiveness, persistence, and reflection), acquired knowledge, or basic problem-solving strategies. Test instruments are complex affairs and changes in test performance can come from factors other than those that are presumably being measured.

The current capacity of assessment techniques to probe alternative routes to a test performance is indeed deficient (Glick, 1968). A Zigler and Butterfield (1968) study suggests that some portion of an IQ score and of a change in IQ may be a function of children's response to the test situation. Similar interpretive problems appear in tests that assess language behavior. Some children may be able to generate a rich and varied language when asked by an adult simply to describe a TV show. Other children may respond with monosyllables and supply so little information that they could easily be judged language deficient. Yet these very children might exhibit a remarkable language competence in other situations (Cazden, 1970; Labov, 1970; Williams & Naremore, 1969). There may, indeed, be differences among children in the situations they deem appropriate for particular types of verbal communication and also, perhaps, in the level of language mastery they have achieved. As long as our measurement techniques do not permit a representative sampling of situations and behaviors, we will be unable to understand the outcome of specially designed programs and thus be seriously handicapped in the design of sensible and defensible modifications.

Still another assessment issue requires careful consideration. What do we know about a child's ability from his test score? Possibly too little to be of help in diagnosing the child's level of competence (Glick, 1968). The child's correct answer to an addition problem does not tell us whether he arrived at the answer by counting on his fingers, by computing sets of 10, or by rote memory. It may be that children with little understanding of the material can be coached to show up well on tests. Even more important, it may be that unless educators of the young pay attention to the processes or strategies used by children when solving problems the opportunity to promote maximally generalizable knowledge will be lost. There are, indeed, different ways of reaching a problem solution. Some ways are inefficient or appropriate only to a few simple cases. Others have wide applicability in that they provide the child with a framework for deriving strategies for problems never before encountered.

In sum, our ability to interpret evaluation results is limited by at least two problems. On the one hand, our assessment instruments sample a narrow range of situations and behaviors and may distort our image of the child's competence and narrow our program thinking. On the other hand, we often tend to infer too much from indices that lack a supporting interpretive framework. In response to these problems we need abandon neither action nor evaluation. Rather we are compelled to advance proposals as hypotheses, to scrutinize our methods with care, and to frame our conclusions so that they respect the limitations of our current knowledge.

Although the problems presented by standardized tests are significant, little is to be gained by substituting "warm tummy" methods (Hawkridge et al., 1968). Far too many programs have rested their cases on reports of parents or teacher satisfaction. Good feelings clearly are important elements in arriving at policy or administrative positions but have little to do with achieving goals other than satisfied adults. If satisfied adults lead to advances by the children, that would be a most valuable finding.

There is a difference between resting a case on public opinion and using the predictive skills of parents and teachers in the assessment program. Hess (1966) reported findings that some Head Start teachers were as efficient as standardized tests in predicting the behavior of children in kindergarten. At least one evaluation strategy might be to exploit these skills as part of the measurement battery. More extensive observational methods are essential during early phases of a program and may be of value in assessing whether a replication effort resembles the prototype. Parents and teachers could be a valuable source of information about programs and children.

The most perturbing challenge to the assessment instruments currently used in early education has yet to receive widespread recognition. The problem hinges on the over-riding purpose of these instruments which is to measure stable individual differences (Tyler, 1967). One consequence is that the most useful items for this purpose are those that sensitively discriminate among children, that is, those bits and pieces of knowledge or skill that some children exhibit and others do not. Therefore in the construction of these tests exercises that all or nearly all children of a given level can do and exercises that few children can do are eliminated, thereby eliminating items that are likely to be sensitive to educational intervention. Secular changes in IQ scores, for example, appear over decades and centuries rather than months and years. In other words, the most frequently used assessment instruments were constructed to be sluggish with respect to local short-term variations. To the extent that they meet this criterion they are likely to be well-cushioned from the cutting edge of new conceptions and innovations in education (Zimiles, 1967). In brief, the competence of children might be vastly expanded by day-care programs without significantly reducing individual differences as traditionally measured. Conversely, competence might be grossly impaired without substantially enhancing these differences. Although one way of compensating for test insensitivity is to assess huge numbers of children (Zimiles, 1967), it is a costly and uninformative solution.

The issue of assessment might well be elevated to one of day care's highest priorities. At least it is necessary to appreciate the problems of behavior sampling and interpretation and to debate the distinction between an orientation to individual differences or to programs before we too casually adopt assessment procedures for day care that inappropriately express and reflect program intentions.

Methodological Footnotes

Disillusionment with research in early childhood education is not totally a function of a lack of clarity with regard to intentions, implementation, and interpretation. Some methodological issues, although seemingly straightforward, reappear continuously to plague research and evaluation efforts. We comment briefly on a few of those that seem to be particularly difficult to translate into research practices even though they are fairly basic research tools. Our treatment here is no substitute for a statistician or researcher's expertise and technical competence. For any effective evaluation design, implementation, or analysis these competencies must be called on.

Multivariate Procedures. A growing respect for diversity is perhaps one of the impressive characteristics of current programs of early education. In dimensionalizing the programs we have discussed in this Context, we were continually discovering new dimensions along which they could be described. Quite appropriately, diversity of program variables is matched only by the diversity among children, families, and communities. More evaluation schemes are using multiple variables—the child, the family, and the setting. Attention to complex dimensions of the environment and equally complex measures of competence are unavoidable when day care is involved.

The question then becomes what can be done to make sense out of so much information? Undoubtedly the first step is to abandon the notion that univariate procedures—t-tests, F-tests, and simple correlations—can do the job. Multivariate procedures have entered the research warehouse, and their advantages are increasingly apparent. A lucid account of these procedures has been given by McCall (1970).

Matching and Randomization. One of the more serious methodological defects to appear in studies of early-childhood programs stems from the belief that matching children is a substitute for randomization. Matching may actually introduce systematic artifacts that might make programs look good, bad, or indifferent. The Westinghouse-Ohio report illustrates one of the more prominent instances of a possible artifact coming from a control group initially superior to the experimental group functioning to make the outcome seem deleterious. A concise analysis of this problem has been made by Campbell and Erlebacher (1970).

For clarity of interpretation, economy, and efficiency there is probably no substitute for randomization. When randomization is not possible, quasi-experimental designs, such as time-series sampling and cross-lagged correlation might be used (Campbell, 1967) even though they are not without problems. Time-series sampling is often particularly appropriate to research involving young children. It builds on and strengthens the well-established pretest-post-test paradigm in that *repeated* measures taken at different periods *before* intervention provide a semilongitudinal baseline from which effects contingent on the intervention can be assessed. The general instability of data collected from young children (changes in motivational state, familiarity with the tester, and the test situation, etc.) suggests that more data points would be helpful. Massive assessment of entire communities of children is another alternative, a costly alternative, to be sure, and not without its own special set of problems (e.g., uniformity of test conditions, training, and recruitment).

Analysis of covariance, a procedure frequently used to control initial differences between treatment and no treatment groups is especially misleading. When children have been matched on variables such as IQ score or socioeconomic status, an analysis of covariance on dependent measures may aggravate the regression problem. Even when adequate randomization procedures have been employed, the assumptions behind the analysis of covariance are difficult to meet (Campbell & Erlebacher, 1970).

Sampling. The survey of compensatory education programs conducted by the American Institute of Research (Hawkridge et al., 1968) cited sampling ambiguities and improprieties as among the major faults of the evaluations they reviewed. Evaluators frequently did not describe the population from which children were selected, how selection was implemented, subject loss due to refusal to participate, and so on. One preschool program launched a substantial effort to enlist a random sample, yet the preproject dropout rate was high. Self-selection out, before assignment to treatments, does not necessarily reduce the value of the research so long as it is borne in mind that the population to which the results pertain is circumscribed by its willingness to participate. The effects of children dropping out of a program once it has started are far more serious, and the common practice of replacing lost children effectively cancels the value of the results (Hawkridge et al., 1968).

Control Groups. A word about "control" groups is also needed. Often too little thought is given to what is being controlled. The "Hawthorne Effect," a fairly ubiquitous psychological phenomenon, is the name given to measurable changes that are due to variables other than those under investigation. In a home-visiting program, for example, the increased social stimulation from a regular visitor might be as important to the outcome as the elaborate activities or materials she provides. We know of only two programs that attempt to introduce a condition in which the home is visited but no enrichment schedule is offered (Levenstein, 1970; Weikart & Lambie, 1969). Innovation programs in preschool settings can generate enthusiasm and teacher involvement that override the influence of specific components such as curriculum or parent participation. In brief, a host of incidental factors, from test-taking sophistication to team spirit, can produce effects quite unrelated to the variables under investigation. These artifacts themselves are worthy of further study. To the extent that their presence makes the effect of program variables impossible to detect, specially designed control conditions are needed.

Perhaps the best way of dealing with problems of self-selection is to try to understand them. Longitudinal studies of large randomly selected populations can help (Anderson, 1970). In a randomly selected population of 1000 3-year-olds some children will eventually enter day-care centers; others will go to nursery school; some will spend time with baby-sitters; others will spend most of their time at home. This type of research design makes it possible to explore factors that determine the selection of arrangements, their continuity and impact. Specific program variations, for example, in curriculum, in-service training, or parental participation, are perhaps best explored in groups that have made similar selections from among several available choices (e.g., day-care centers, home care, preschools). Furthermore, parallel program variations can occur in each self-selected group (e.g., one might study DARCEE, Piagetian, Bereiter-Engelmann, or behavior modification strategies in day-care centers, home-visiting programs, and preschools). Comparisons of prepackaged programs may not be so informative as comparisons of more clearly specified manipulations chosen to have some positive impact on children. Thus a systematic study might compare settings that differentially emphasize language development, social interactions with adults, and a wide variety of materials (Kessen, 1970). If we conceptualize these emphases as "manipulable" environmental biases, one possible research design might examine the influence of three types of bias (language, social, and materials) in two kinds of setting (group care and home care).

PROGRAM DEVELOPMENT

Although basic research is often pitted against applied research, one view of the mutually beneficial interaction of various parts of the research enterprise has been offered by Markle (1967). Program development can be seen as a three-phase sequence:

1. A laboratory phase for systematic study of major variables.
2. A demonstration phase for validation and testing.
3. The extension or field-testing phase.

Markle's suggestions originated in problems of programmed instruction, but with some modification the scheme can be more broadly conceived.

PHASE I. The "laboratory" can be a natural setting as well as an empty white room (the difference in uncontrollable variables is one of degree, not kind). Correlational and experimental studies can take place in a variety of settings. Studies in Phase I can meet our need for details about how children develop and how environments function. One possibility is to study panels of caregivers and children (Kessen, 1970) intensively over relatively short periods of time.

Studies of this kind could, for example, trace language development during the postinfancy period (Clarke-Stewart, 1972; Nelson, 1971). Probes could be employed to explore the dimensions of competence at a particular level of performance; parental interactions, material resources in the home, intellectual status, and other variables could be examined in relation to dimensions of language ability.

In addition to panels of individuals, panels of day-care programs could be created. These panels would combine intensive study with efforts to specify major program components so that an overall program model might be articulated and assessed. Variations of program components could be introduced as "experiments," if it were recognized in advance that in some settings (e.g., group settings) there would be more contamination than in others (e.g., among children cared for in different homes).

PHASE II. The demonstration phase, which overlaps Phase I, would involve a stabilization of the program and carefully controlled replications. Of special importance in Phase II would be ecological studies of the extent to which psychologically relevant variables occur in natural settings. The role of reinforcement, for example, has been demonstrated in the laboratory but we know relatively little about the reinforcement patterns that appear in families and in educational settings. Which behaviors do caregivers reward and which do they punish, how consistently, with what affect, and with what effect? How common is it for adults to expand children's telegraphic utterances or to correct mislabels? Factors such as these are critical in the design and evaluation of day-care settings.

In an earlier section we discussed the need to determine how program ideologies are translated into child-environment interactions. At some point it will be necessary to establish theoretical networks of hypotheses and variables which have reality in both experimental and natural settings. In our discussions of the child, for example, one-to-one adult-child interaction emerged as a broad variable associated with social and language development. The evidence also suggested that these interactions are relatively infrequent in many child-care institutions when compared with those at home, and that conditions at home also vary in this respect. Nevertheless, we need more precise information about the occurrence of adult-child interactions in various settings—how they are instigated and maintained, their frequency and distribution within a child's day, and the relation between them and dimensions of development.

PHASE III. When even well-documented programs are applied elsewhere or expanded, enormous difficulties sometimes appear. All too often replication and extension efforts explode a small, moderately successful pilot project into a massive effort involving thousands of children. Even the most precise program could crumble under pressure for instant large-scale replication. Gordon (1968) has pointed out that hasty giganticism typically leads to failure, and when the smoke clears it is the children who get the blame. The issues are complex, but several sources of replication failure can be indicated: (a) artifacts in the original finding, that is, the program never worked; (b) a global program with variables so poorly defined that replication is impossible; (c) inadequate transmission of program techniques such as insufficiently trained personnel to train others; (d) a different target population from that served by the original project. The management of replications is a critical problem in need of careful study. It may be that programs deteriorate as they grow more distant from their original source of inspiration and that the problem of maintaining program quality should be separated from program design.

Program Monitoring. If evaluation is understood to mean minimal and limited efforts to monitor programs, the result of recent attempts to do just that (Hawkridge et al., 1968) would recommend eliminating the effort entirely. Perhaps the only justification for a minimal effort—one that collects standardized scores, for example—would be to monitor the progress of well-studied and well-documented programs that have developed a substantial body of expectations regarding what test scores mean and what they ought to look like. We know of no program that has reached that point.

RESEARCH AND EVALUATION IN DAY CARE

We have indicated here one possible scheme for aligning research, evaluation, and program practice. The essential problem is how to systematically relate what we know to what we do; how to acquire the knowledge needed to enhance the effectiveness of our practices. Distinctions between the roles and types of inquiry are useful insofar as the knowledge-acquiring, implementing, decision-making, and monitoring components of program development become better balanced, interrelated, and sequenced in time. At least three general questions must be addressed:

1. What should children be doing and experiencing; that is, what is the relation between what happens to children and their development?
2. How can these desired activities or experiences be promoted in a day-care setting?
3. To what extent do programs provide them and how much do the outcomes conform to our expectations?

The purpose of research and evaluation in day care is to find out what children were doing in the beginning, what they were doing at different points along the way, and how they got from one point to another. As we searched for data regarding the effects of day care, we were able to come up with only a few attempts to evaluate all day programs for 3- to 5-year-olds. In two cases the primary purpose of the evaluation was to examine the effects of day care on family income, maternal employment, and so on, with little specific attention to changes in the children (Hawkins, Curran, & Jordan, 1969; Nellum, 1969). An exception can be found in reports of the Howard Pre-School Project (Fuschillo, 1968; Witmer, 1968), which attempted seriously to obtain a representative sample of children, to randomize groups, and to articulate the goals and methods of the program.

Considerable caution is necessary when interpreting the results of infant day-care programs. Two of the programs that have published findings (Caldwell & Richmond, 1968; Caldwell, Wright, Honig, & Tannenbaum, 1969; Keister,. 1970) suggest that well-staffed, well-funded programs may not be damaging to infants, but, since these programs serviced either self-selected or agency-selected populations and used control groups that seemed to differ with regard to selection criteria, it is difficult to parcel out the possibly interacting influences of family stability, parental interest, income level, and the many other factors that might lead people to seek out or avail themselves of day care or other medical and social services. These are the same methodological problems that characterize a good deal of the research in early childhood education.

It is more important to note that day care provides a remarkable opportunity to sharpen research strategies that have only recently been defined. We can begin by adding an enlarging qualification to Bronowski's view of the scientific endeavor which we cited earlier; namely, scientists often inquire about "what works?" but by and large their question is "how does it work?" It is from inquiring about "how" that researchers come to define alternatives about "what." The distinction between these two questions parallels the distinction between summative and formative evaluation research, a distinction that has been implied throughout much of the preceding discussion. Scriven (1967) has argued that the distinction is fundamentally concerned with *role* of research rather than its methodology, style, or paradigm. The role of research and evaluation in child-care programming warrants further consideration and elaboration. In fact, we would argue that summative and formative evaluation research are complementary and necessary aspects of an enterprise geared to program development.

Summative Evaluation. Summative evaluation has been associated typically with national assessment programs. The Westinghouse-Ohio study, the Educational Testing Services longitudinal study, and studies by Kirschner Associates of Head Start and Parent-Child Centers are examples that attempt, in one way or another, to provide information regarding arrays of child-oriented programs.

In general two types of information are sought. One concerns descriptive program information, for example, the population served, program format, staff qualifications, that would permit programs to be classified. The other concerns impact information, for example, test scores, attitudes, income measures, that would index program accomplishments. Presumably the role of such an evaluation is to survey the state of one or more programs in relation to people and to track changes as they occur over time. In large measure summative evaluation is similar to climbing a hill on a moonless night. Progress is a function of our definition of "up," and how well we do depends on the sensitivity of the apparatus we have chosen to discriminate up from down. There are restrictions, however; once the climb is begun we cannot go back, retool, or try another hill. We can decide when we have finally reached the top that the trip was satisfactory or that changes will be necessary for the next time. We may have learned something about the terrain and about our capacity to manage it. As a result, we may have expectations about what other hills might be like, and we may decide to call on different resources when we initiate the next effort. Essentially, however, summative evaluation is locked into its initial assumptions of strategies, dimensions, and indices; it carries no explicit system for systematic and continuing revision of variables and instruments. It is this characteristic that highlights the distinction between formative and summative research.

Formative Evaluation. Formative evaluation research is primarily focused on the careful scrutiny, examination, and modification of ways of reaching goals. It considers the competencies of the climbers and the terrain which they are likely to find. It carries the responsibility of generating a set of expectations and procedures that could apply to many hills and many climbers. Formative research provides an essential link in a total evaluation scheme by creating a set of theoretically plausible alternatives from which summative evaluations may select.

The distinction between summative and formative evaluation may help to clarify complementary efforts, but it may also help to stake out the domain of the evaluation task facing day-care planners. Basically the distinction points to the interdependence of planners, practitioners, and researchers who are committed to program excellence but bring different skills to the task.

Not all day-care programs need to have external or summative evaluations. At this point a far more useful research effort could be directed toward the definition and assessment of dimensions within and among programs that have special significance for the development of children or for the behavior of caregivers. If there are definable and measurable components of development such as attachment, play, language, and cognition or even finer dimensions such as attention seeking, affection seeking, sociability, symbolic "as-ifing," exploration, grammar, semantics, communication, cognitive operations, and concepts, then research can develop routines, "curricula," and strategies for selective enhancement or remediation within these areas along with appropriate assessment indices. This type of research is nicely illustrated by Johnson's manipulation of playground equipment and Thompson's manipulation of teacher style (Johnson, 1935; Thompson, 1944) or Cazden's (1965, 1968) intervention program which contrasted the influence of expanding and modeling on children's language. Such research involves the selective biasing of programs in specified ways in order to examine issues around which curriculum concepts need to be elaborated.

The "Experimenting" Society

There is every sign that we have become an "intervening" society, more willing perhaps than ever before to attempt to eliminate poverty, sickness, and illiteracy. The modest interventions heretofore attempted have perhaps floundered less because they misidentified the "need" than because they defined and monitored the "cure" too poorly. It is obvious that hungry people need food, that abandoned children need homes, and that illiterate people need opportunities to learn basic skills. It would appear that we have not been able to wind a way through bureaucracy, apathy, inertia, complex contingencies, and unexpected bottlenecks to ensure the delivery of the appropriate goods and services to the people who need them. We know too little about the creation of effective, responsive institutions. Perhaps behind the apparent failure of compensatory, ameliorative, or reconstructive programs has been excessive faith in the power of a "define a need, launch a program" magic. An alternative faith has yet to be advanced. We have adopted Campbell and Erlebacher's term, "experimenting" society, to express the notion that between defining and solving a problem there is a complex process of posing tentative solutions, implementing them, testing their usefulness, and planning modifications when results indicate that the solution advanced was not completely satisfactory.

It seems senseless to attempt evaluations from which, in principle, no conclusions are possible. It seems equally senseless to insist that only one kind of research or evaluation is possible. Certainly, within the domain of events likely to affect the lives of children, a variety of research strategies can be utilized. Observational, applied experimental, and correlational studies, if appropriately designed, can carve out important issues, complement one another, and above all, lead to the development of batteries of external, easily obtained indices to monitor changes on a national scale. Without a body of related research and theory such measures are meaningless. The research of the thirties, which assessed the effects of nursery school on children's development, terminated because the conflicting results produced in this period could be attributed to an imposing display of conceptual and methodological problems (Swift, 1964).

We would agree with the nursery school teachers' plea that early-childhood programs be a national value, not a national option (Findley, 1968a). There are options, however, in the development of programs, which come from the diverse forms such programs can take, the diverse populations they need to encompass, and the diverse aims they need to consider. When optimization and competence become significant features of the national-value system and a significant feature of early-childhood programs, the daytime care of children will have to respond to crucial dimensions of child development, the family, and home- and out-of-home-based programs. In order to do so effectively, our "intervening" society may have to evolve into a sophisticated "experimenting" society.

Movement toward such a society requires plans that recognize the reality of political exigencies. A rational scheme for the development of comprehensive day-care programs may be almost impossible when development efforts are vulnerable to short-term shifts in public enthusiasms and political expediencies. The problem is to create a vehicle oriented toward long-term national child-care needs which can explore in depth issues of program development and assessment. One vehicle for this purpose might take the form of sheltered child-development institutes (J. O. Miller, 1970) charged with the articulation, implementation, and intensive study of ways of promoting the development of children in various day-care settings.

As we attempt to construct a bridge from a hazy today to a dimly perceived tomorrow, day care presents the nation with problems of sufficient scope and import to occupy the attention of politicians, parents, professionals, and social scientists for several generations to come. Day care may be one theme in childhood programming that touches on almost every controversy in the nation today. If we are to maximize our chances of arriving at national solutions, day care must be rescued from its history of spasmodic lurches between benign neglect and crisis notoriety. How to develop new institutions with built-in capacities to conserve and change is not obvious, surely not simple, yet an issue of far-reaching consequences for the future.

21

Day Care: Opportunities
and Dangers

PROPERLY, DAY CARE IS NOT AN ARRANGEMENT, A PROGRAM, A service, or an institution. Day care is what happens when the child, his family, and a community resource come together. It occurs in a philosophical, historical, social, and political context; it is defined by characteristics of the child, the family, and the resource, and it is comprehended through a web of presuppositions, expectations, and empirical observations. Day-care models consider how this interaction changes when the available resources change; how resources may vary with variations in children and families, and how changes and variations modify the way children, families, and communities function. Day-care models can become the basis of new institutions. Our conception of the function of models merely ensures that when new institutions do emerge they will be linked to the life experiences of parents and children.

With thoughtful planning day care can become an opportunity to advance our knowledge of children. It can realize the visions of its eighteenth-century founders of all the wonderful things that would enhance the well-being of children all over the nation. With narrow purposes and scant resources, day care is at its very least a passing fancy and at its worst a national disaster.

After a brief summary of the material covered so far, we present our conclusions in the light of several critical issues that have developed in nations other than our own. These issues suggest a national strategy for developing innovations in day care, a strategy that seems well suited to the spirit and stresses of a changing democratic society.

282

DAY CARE IN CONTEXT

"Day care" has not been mentioned in every paragraph or even on every page of this book. Our report has been more than a description of day care as it is or was. We have placed it in its broader context to discuss the education and development of children wherever they may be.

An essential perspective for viewing any issue is its historical context. Our attempt has revealed trends, redundancies, and cycles. The day nursery began its history in the United States with high hopes that work in infant education would benefit all the children in the nation. The day nursery gradually lost esteem as sights narrowed and as the emphasis on the child's intellectual competence was muted. Our look at the past suggested that day-care booms will not contribute substantially to the well-being of children unless there is a national commitment to long-term planning, development, and research.

Policy issues were discussed in the context of the past, the present, and the future. In the context of the past it was possible to see the danger of massive efforts directed toward one form of care—the care of children in groups and housed in "centers." In the context of the future it is possible to envision a nationwide effort directed toward the training of child-care workers and the involvement of parents and other family members.

The policy issue of greatest concern dealt with the form a national commitment to the development of children might adopt. A system of child development institutes would be one way of deepening the nation's capacity to understand and promote the development of children.

We have considered the child as the focus of day care. Although research and theory rarely lead to unequivocal prescriptions for child-care practices, it does indicate the major dimensions that ought to be appreciated by those who plan or participate in child-care programs. One part of the child-development literature describes how children develop a range of competencies in relating to people, thinking, speaking, and playing. These competencies grow out of contacts with consistent and responsive caretakers and with things and words and out of social interactions with other people. They are developed best when the child is free from physical discomfort, pain, and worry and when he is free to explore a richly planned environment.

A broad definition of day care suggested that programs also be considered in the context of the family. An examination of the diversity in the "American family" led to the suggestions that day care attempt to meet the needs of particular parents as well as individual children; that day-care programs be based on knowledge of and respect for the structures and potential capacities of families. Furthermore, it was recommended that "day-care" programs include opportunities for parental education, participation, and support and that an effort be made to provide continuity for the child by designing programs consistent with the behaviors, goals, values, and child-rearing practices of his parents.

The "broadest and best" day-care program is an instrument of education for children. Thus it appeared essential to examine the context of early education. Components of preschool education—peers, teachers, physical space, equipment, and curricula—are equally essential components of day care. Research demonstrating the relative effectiveness of variations in these components may be directly utilized in designing day-care programs. Our review of this literature suggested the central importance of adult-child contact, even though contact between children and interaction between the child and his physical environment are important aspects of the educational process. The review also demonstrated the need for establishing particular goals for the educational program if it is to effect particular change. The goal may be to build cognitive structures or to modify specific behaviors, to produce a child who is an autonomous learner, or to ensure his academic skills. The goal may be restricted to language remediation or it may aim more broadly toward development of the "whole child." Before a day-care program is designed such goals should be made explicit. Moreover, it is especially critical to the design of programs of day care that one go beyond the typically limited goals and programs of compensatory education to ensure that all aspects of the child's functioning are being adequately dealt with. Goals for day care should entail the social, emotional, motoric, physical, and nutritional well-being of the child as well as his verbal and cognitive development.

In attempting to describe the context of day care, we have touched on many problems and many levels. We have reviewed material on the family, the child, and current issues in early-childhood programs. We have attempted to examine some of the major policy issues and to explore the contributions of several areas of professional and academic interest. We have also attempted to place day-care issues in the context of historical change, of contemporary views of the child, and of social issues that impinge on him when they influence the lives of those concerned with his upbringing.

The child is complex and changing; existing institutions are also complex and changing. These institutions—the family, the neighborhood, the school, and the community—make unique yet overlapping contributions to the child's development.

CROSS-CULTURAL PERSPECTIVES

In the following sections we examine some of the issues facing day care in the light of the experiences of other nations. It is when we compare other societies with our own that we can often begin to identify "superordinate" goals, problems, and program definitions. It is then that it becomes possible to examine how national values influence the shape of day care and to project strategies that will promote long-range national efforts.

When we look at ourselves in comparison with other nations, the issues sharpen; it becomes easier to understand how ideology, social stability, and community cohesiveness influence the form of child-care practices. Of particular interest are the contradictions that emerge even when child-care settings are deliberately created to support a stable, dominant view of society.

Typically, when child-care institutions are not closely and explicitly tied to a social ideology, programs are defended as emergency measures to prevent serious privation. This occurs most often when the social and political structure of a nation keeps its people preoccupied with survival. The dilemma of the United States is that although it lacks a cohesive ideology with which to justify a particular form of child care the nation is affluent enough to do more than make temporary accommodations to emergency situations. In the following sections we argue that although there cannot be a single institutional design to cover the multitude of contingencies and diversity in American life it is essential for the nation to evolve procedures by which special-purpose planning institutions can collaborate in the formulation, implementation, and delivery of innovative child-development services.

Superordinate Goals

The United States today has no set of superordinate goals similar to that which gives cohesion to child care in the kibbutz (Neubauer, 1965) or in the Soviet Union (Bronfenbrenner, 1970). Both those social systems have a well-articulated model of social man that positively values the *Gemeinshaft* of group living and the adaptation of the individual to group aims. Child-rearing philosophies in these societies are justified and inspired by a consistent ideology to which powerful members of the community are strongly committed (Bronfenbrenner, 1969, 1970; Wolins, 1965, 1969a) and which, thereby, ensures children a continuity of priorities, values, and caregiving styles. In time parents, neighbors, professionals, older children, siblings, and peers adopt and transmit to the child a coherent set of standards and a consensually validated set of heuristics for social problem solving. In the Soviet system the "links" provide a smooth and well-routinized hierarchy of authority (Bronfenbrenner, 1970). In the kibbutz the roles of metapelet, teacher, parent, and policy maker are functionally overlapping. The social unit of the kibbutz is small; its physical setting places people within easy reach of one another. The geographic isolation and sense of mission ensures that the information received by the child about roles and values will be highly redundant throughout his lifetime. Variation among kibbutzim (Neubauer, 1965; Wolins,

1965b) suggests that several ways of organizing and expressing child-rearing strategies are possible, even within a cohesive, ideologically based community. Yet even here there are problems and unresolved questions. How can devotion to a kibbutz or to a soviet socialist philosophy be ensured (a) when the society becomes a collection of highly specialized technological competencies, (b) when contact with the noncollectivist world increases, and (c) when the very nurturance and respect given to the child stimulates and encourages individuality, autonomy, curiosity, and an eagerness for novelty, complexity, and incongruity? It is from the kibbutz that such questions emerge most vividly and painfully, the consequence of an attempt to conserve a unidirectional and cohesive social order while providing child-rearing practices that promote experimenting and risk taking.

The United States lacks obvious, cohesive, child-related superordinate goals. Yet there are, perhaps, consensual goals that have not been made explicit; for example, there may be in a large segment of the population some shift toward a positive valuation of diversity, individuality, variety, freedom, and cultural pluralism. There are indications also of a consensus of child-rearing attitudes in the mainstream culture (Bronfenbrenner, 1958). Furthermore, among parents universally valued goals for children appear to be happiness, honesty, consideration, and, above all, education (Kohn, 1959).

Most people want education, although for different reasons: better jobs and more money, higher social status, or personal growth. The ring of education covers the entire span of human development; it is echoed in concepts of infant schools, compensatory education, community schools, and senior citizen groups. It is clear that at a very minimum getting an education means to most people in the United States the acquisition of the basic tools of language, mastery of basic mathematical operations, and the accumulation of a respectable store of specific scientific and social knowledge.

Beyond this, however, the attempt to articulate the goals of education in this country collapses. This list of technical achievements cannot adequately express the competencies that seem to be called for today. The seemingly fuzzy notions of "process," of "learning how to learn," of "problem-solving strategies" are attempts to identify a set of content-free and culture-free goals that will make it possible for individuals to take on whatever characteristics are demanded by the subgroup to which they belong or by the situations in which they find themselves. In order to conform one needs to discover the expected standard; to retain one's individuality one needs to be autonomous and discriminating. In order to contribute new content to a changing order one needs to experiment and to communicate effectively the outcomes of thought and experience. In order to cope with the rain of words spilling daily from the media, to be able to sort information from rhetoric, one needs to be sensitive to implicit meaning, context, and the intentions of the speakers. In order to be an effective agent of change, as parent, worker, and citizen, one must be able to communicate ideas with clarity and force.

The United States not only lacks focal goals and the stable social organization needed to support such goals but it is a nation of diverse ethnic and cultural groups. If pluralism accurately depicts conditions in the American society of today and tomorrow, superordinate goals may have to be based on superordinate processes rather than superordinate values, traits, or achievements. If process goals find general acceptance, the emotional and motivational components of these processes will also need to be better understood and to find a central place in early childhood programming. The goals of education will have to be stretched to include aspects of development other than language, cognition, and problem solving. Education will be aimed at the development of the "whole person," including social skills, emotional control and expression, and the capacity for play. Play, in particular, should receive greater attention in the future than it has in the past. Its value for adults as well as children, for development as well as pleasure, should not be underemphasized. One final goal of education which could benefit the nation and her children is that of optimization of individual potentialities rather than mere survival in a competitive world, mere treading of intellectual water, mere equalization in basic skills.

Superordinate Problems

Oddly enough, when we look beyond the fascinating experiments in group upbringing demonstrated by the kibbutz, the Soviet boarding school (Bronfenbrenner, 1970), and the SOS Kinderhof (Wolins, undated), we find a day-care scene in Europe not dissimilar to our own. Even in the Soviet Union only 10% of the children under 2 years of age and 18% of the children between 3 and 6 are in preschool institutions (Bronfenbrenner, 1968a). The Soviets have resurrected the role of the family by offering working mothers 126 days of full pay for remaining home with their newborn babies, arguing that the increasing material affluence and technology of Soviet society will reduce the working day, increase leisure time, and give parents more time to participate in the upbringing of their children (Bronfenbrenner, 1968a).

A recent survey of day care in eastern European nations (East Germany, Hungary, and Czechoslovakia) led Meers and Marans (1968) to conclude that "conceived in emergency and difficult economic times, these programs have had to contend with potential damage to their children . . . which could develop under conditions less than ideal." Increasingly, European child-care specialists are pressing for the termination of day care for infants under 1 year unless special interventions are introduced to forestall or reverse possible damage (Meers

& Marans, 1968). This position is based on growing evidence of minimal or marginal retardation of children placed in day-care settings during the early months of life (Meers & Marans, 1968, Slobin, 1966a).

Why have countries so willing to uphold group care as a national goal had to pause and retrench? What are some of the problems likely to be encountered by programs of national scope? The common thread seems to be an acute shortage of trained personnel, inadequate training facilities, and organizational problems. The adult-child ratio in Polish nursery schools, for example, is 1:22 (UNICEF, 1966). Pressures for filling vacancies have led to little discrimination in staff selection and hiring. Often the physical plants in these countries are expensive and advanced by Western standards; yet high personnel turnover and the large number of substitute caregivers needed to maintain the service exacerbate the difficulties of coping with the individual needs of large numbers of infants and young children. Depersonalization is the ever-present danger of massive group-care programs. Ironic, but perhaps fitting, is the observation that one of the more satisfactory European day-care systems was affiliated with the National Methodological Institute for Child Education in Budapest, which was carrying out a continuing program of research in day-care centers throughout the city. Caregivers, who observed and recorded child behavior, were apprised of research findings and generally displayed a high investment in the individual child and his progress. Perhaps a general principle to be enunciated is that a society that cares enough about its children to monitor their growth and development will be less likely to move blindly and chaotically down irreversible paths and will in the process focus the attention of the nation on the dimensions of child care crucial for development.

Nations in Africa, Asia, and South America are attempting to identify priorities for national child-care programs in the context of widespread poverty and privation. Brazil, for example, focuses on "recreation centers" in rural areas which have "a diet kitchen, benches, mats and a few toys: where the children can stay and be fed while their mothers are at work in the fields." Senegal can identify local areas of rapid urbanization in which shantytowns of dislocated people create living conditions that destroy traditional cultural forms and place children in physical and moral danger. Out of a strong cultural commitment to the family the Senegalese have developed a remediation program that stresses the delivery of medical and educational services through maternal and child-welfare centers. Mothers are obliged by legislative decree to take their children regularly to the infant clinics (UNICEF, 1966, p. 139). Day care can speak to many different problems and programs can be fashioned to meet these problems in different ways.

One has the impression that the United States can identify within its own boundaries every need that is in other nations highlighted by unique economic social and cultural conditions. We have children from impoverished migrant farm families (Migrant Child Care Center, *Child Welfare,* 1958; Sheriden, 1967), shantytowns on the borders of urban centers, and central city ghettos. We have children who are hungary, ill-clothed, ill-housed, and ill-fed. Nationwide foundations have drawn attention to the dramatic crippling diseases of childhood, but few have emphasized the more ubiquitous and less visible consequences of anemia, poor vision, and chronic low-grade infection (North, 1968). American casualness toward problems that lack the glamour of crisis is evident when we examine provisions for health care in day-care programs; for example, although the importance of licensing day-care establishments to ensure at least minimum protection of children's health and safety has long been recognized, licensing regulations have not been backed up with regular medical assessments to ascertain whether, in fact, the health of children in these establishments has been protected. Peters (1964) notes that of the 34 states reporting some type of day-care licensing legislation only 11 reported giving some form of health supervision or care. The experience of the past provides ample demonstration that such seemingly obvious variables as fresh air, cleanliness, good food, love, and freedom influence growth in complex ways. Yet we must continue to return to questions of "how much" and "what kind." Not all tasty foods are nutritious, not all air is beneficial, too much concern with cleanliness can be a bad thing, too much love can be suffocating, and too much freedom can be frightening. It is ludicrous to expect a child to play on an empty belly but equally naïve to ask him to sit still when his belly is full.

In the United States also are many young children who are educationally deprived. Their homes may be austere and understimulating or cluttered and confusing. They may be alone for a large part of the day or with peers who can contribute little to their education. Lacking in the lives of many of these children may be perceptual and verbal stimulation provided by adults, the security of a harmonious home, neighborhood, or commune, the warmth of a sensitive and responsive parental figure, and the opportunity to explore new environments. Programs of remedial education for young children, and occasionally for their parents as well, have attempted to compensate for these deficiencies. The diversity of programs demonstrates the complexity of finding solutions to these problems and to those of health and welfare. In particular, when the goals of education become broader than mere equality in academic skills, the difficulty of designing appropriate ameliorative programs is enormous. It may be that in the absence of decent housing, jobs, and good health educational programs will have only limited impact. Yet it is likely that the provision of physical and financial advantages alone will not constitute the conditions for acquiring competence. Day care in the United States faces an uncertain future. At the heart of this uncertainty is the ever-present danger that day care will itself become an educationally depriving environment; that we will, in the near future, be called on to design programs to ameliorate the disadvantages experienced by day-care children.

In the United States the estimated number of poor children needing day care varies from the 250,000 likely to be affected by some type of family assistance plan to the 1,050,000 whose mothers already work or are likely to work in the future (Miller, 1970). If broader educational goals for young children are advanced, nursery school and day-care places will be needed for close to 6 million children. In order to staff these programs, about a million professionals and preprofessionals will have to be trained. If the nation embarks on a massive training program, it will not only be training "child-care workers" but future generations of mothers, fathers, aunts, uncles, and grandparents. A nationwide effort of such scope will surely have a profound impact on the child-rearing practices of American families. It is obvious that the environments of children will be changed if training programs effectively transmit child-development concepts, educational and management techniques, goals, and values. Yet it is less obvious that *any* program, simply by its promotion, could have a dramatic effect. Regardless of their merit, training programs—by their very existence—constitute a certification of competence that may have little to do with actual on-the-job performance. As long as standards of caregiving competence are not rooted in what people do when they are with children, we run the risk of creating and maintaining training institutions that will function primarily as employment tickets. In the face of pressure to staff programs history can easily be repeated. The staffing of programs can take precedence over what happens to children. It is not difficult to imagine a well-meaning citizen of today echoing the churchman of a hundred years ago: "What would these poor mothers do without us?"

Superordinate Programs

One observer of caregiving institutions abroad (Wolins, 1969a,b) has suggested that successful programs contain the following features:

1. Successful programs assume the inevitability of a good outcome because they see themselves as working with essentially normal children in need of help and guidance and not sick children in need of treatment.

2. They are strongly ideological, pressing in on their wards from all directions with clearly articulated and highly valued philosophical and ethical positions.

3. They assert the child's capability to make a contribution and require him to do so.

4. They provide clear examples of mature group membership.

5. They enjoy community support and esteem.

6. They provide an older child with a peer society that stands for adherence to adult values.

We suspect that these features apply not only to programs that are oriented to group child care but also to others that reach out to parents and to broader family groups. It is appropriate that we identify superordinate programs capable of articulating a point of view and of generating confidence and respect. The Education Professions Development Act created the foundations for one kind of superordinate program: a national network of opportunities to receive training in child care and development. Still another kind of superordinate program might be aimed at dealing more directly and quite broadly with the social and physical context of the child's life; for example, the notion of a "parent-child center" (misnamed in that the activities of such a center need not take place in a physical facility) was advanced in *A Bill of Rights for Children* (Hunt, 1967a). The purpose of a parent-child center is to forge relationships between families and community resources and to provide opportunities for members of the family to plan and participate in activities beneficial to young children and themselves. Such a program acknowledges the principle formulated by Robert Woods (1898)—that the resources of civilization are not available to people unless they are mediated by institutional provisions that are functional for the powers and limitations of the people they are intended to serve.

Yet a program label and a large domain does not constitute a superordinate program. Issues related to the care of children cover different dimensions along which alternatives can be ordered; for example, where should major program concentrations be located? One solution is obvious—in neighborhoods. Even here, however, there are options. If integration is a desired goal, the extent to which this goal can be satisfied by neighborhood programs that follow segregated residential patterns will be limited. Yet not all neighborhoods are segregated. Perhaps the greatest concentration of resources ought to be in "transitional" neighborhoods in which working class ethnic minorities live precariously side by side for often brief and unhappy periods. It may be that child-care programs of broad scope located in such areas might contribute to the stabilization of integrated communities in which the major issue is not poverty but rather the mutual adaptation of diverse life styles.

Child-care programs need not be circumscribed by established political or geographic boundaries. They can be affiliated with religious, educational, cultural, or social institutions as well as neighborhoods. Furthermore, the notion of a "center" can be redefined as a locus for analysis, research, program development, training, and dissemination. At least one model might consider a "center" charged with the task of developing practical extensions of child-care programs founded on theory and research. The undertaking would require talents that cross disciplinary and professional categories and concerns that range from the abstract to the particular.

Indeed, the form of superprogram most suited to a pluralistic society might be one that cultivates an array of possibilities, that systematically examines the relative merits of each, and has protection from political pressures for instant solutions. Such a program might take the form of a national child-development institute charged with the formulation and implementation of a long-term prospectus for the children of the nation. The types of program explored could span diverse child-care arrangements, in groups and in families, with parents, neighbors, or professionals. Programs might focus on economic, anthropological, medical, sociological, or child-development issues, yet still retain an interdisciplinary base. The point is that we know too little about how families, communities, or subcultures determine the environments of children, too little about how social institutions change, and too little about how new institutions influence the existing social and psychological scheme. We know too little about how environments present developmentally significant problems and too little about the kinds of solution parents and children will accept. The image of the child and the evolution of research and application might differ for each program. Surely one part of the common mission would be to consider shifts in national values, family-life styles, and working schedules and to project child-care programs relevant to alternative future national states. Institute programs, once formulated, implemented, and tested, would be available for large-scale replication when a national consensus regarding the desirability of such a program appeared. It may be that a national, application-oriented institute could not acquire the necessary immunity from political pressures under governmental auspices. The sponsorship of such a system might be undertaken by a consortium of private foundations concerned with child care.

We cannot solve the vast administrative and budgetary problems of expanded child-development programs before defining the central missions of these programs, before identifying the factors that determine program effectiveness, and before finding ways of assessing these. We need to define a process (much in the same way the founders of our country defined a process—the system of checks and balances) that would ensure the evolution of adaptive child-development services. We need to specify core institutions and the relations among them: development and research institutions, implementation institutions, and disinterested, critical review institutions.

The resources of private foundations might be most suited for the development of controversial innovations that pose disturbing questions and explore radical solutions, free from short-term shifts in national concerns. The vast resources of the federal government are needed to ensure the nationwide dissemination of child development services. In addition, a system of checks and balances would require a panel of independent, disinterested experts who would continuously monitor, advise, and criticize.

The seeds of a child-development institute have already been sown (Miller, 1970). Replication mechanisms may soon be available—the Community Coordinated Child Care Program (4-C), for example, was designed to encourage communities to coordinate existing day care, preschool, and other child or family services (Day Care and Child Development Council, 1969a; United States Department of Health, Education and Welfare, 1969a, b). Systems for facilitating the delivery of day-care services (Collins & Watson, 1969), improving services (Goldsmith, 1965; Host, 1960), and extending day-care concerns to health and medical care (Eisenstein, 1966; Peters, 1964) have been explored and proposed. What these possibilities need now is a set of well-defined relationships and responsibilities.

Ingenious Paradoxes

Although, as a nation, we may lack superordinate goals, we have a national viewpoint clearly expressed in the bookkeeping system used to index national prosperity. How we calculate the costs of day care is very much a function of the way we define goods and services and the values we assign to them. Clearly, the costs of day care cannot be determined without some estimate of the cost of mothering and fathering, and the benefits of day care cannot be determined without some specification of the benefits derived from competent mothering and fathering. It may be our greatest national shame that child care and child rearing as it occurs in American homes does not appear on the books as a "good" or a "service," that it has no occupational status, and that it is rarely considered relevant to the day-care issue, even though day-care costs are intimately related to child-care and child-rearing functions.

Suppose, for example, we computed the total cost of exemplary 24-hour institutional child care, education, health, and so on, during the first 18 years of life. Let us then separately calculate the ordinary cost of "schooling" (i.e., nursery school, preschool, elementary school), material things (food, clothing, housing), and other services incurred by parents during a child's lifetime and then subtract these two figures, that is, the family expenditures from the total institutional costs for a single child. The difference would represent the "cost" of parenting, a monetary estimate of the services parents render when they rear a child and maintain a home. We suspect that this figure would be impressively large and would approximate a respectable hourly pay rate.

At least this exercise would underscore the irony of our willingness to assign a monetary value to machine tending, cow tending, and institutionalized child care, to the provision of paid household, medical, educational, and office services, but our reluctance to do so for parental caregiving. Undoubtedly, there are good reasons for this reluctance (Good grief! Must everything be reduced to numbers and dollars?). Yet when we examine the balance sheet, which presumably reflects the work activity of American citizens, the failure to represent parenting as a "natural" national resource inexorably elevates work in the factory, the store, the office, or the classroom above work in the home.

With an accounting system so strongly rooted in the value of material goods and paid services, it is not surprising that the "working" mother has become a model for successful womanhood and that the job of "mothering" has become increasingly devalued (Collins & Watson, 1968). The logic of our accounting system subverts the *work* ethic for a *compensation* ethic, and work that does not carry a price goes unrewarded and unsung. The consequences of the compensation ethic become evident when we examine national subsidies to private institutions. Gans (1971) has whimsically suggested that the oil depletion allowance be named the Oil Producers Public Assistance Program, that we talk about the Tobacco Growers Dole, Aid to Dependent Airlines, or Supplementary Benefits to Purchasers of Tax-Exempt Bonds. The fact that giant industries cannot make it on their own seems to cause little embarrassment or discomfort, yet when support to families is an issue we assume that no services are being rendered, no work is being performed, and that the need for a subsidy reflects incompetence and failure. At the very least our accounting system is inconsistent, and the direction of the inconsistency leans toward punishing and belittling small and diverse social units while rewarding and respecting the large and monolithic for failures that do not seem to be qualitatively different. It seems appropriate to challenge a bias that permits us to supplement industrial enterprises more casually than it permits us to supplement caregiving enterprises.

DAY-CARE ISSUES FOR TODAY AND TOMORROW

The Child

We have chosen to present the development of the child as the major thrust of day care. Day care that focuses on the child becomes unavoidably future-oriented, for within a developmental framework the present and the future are interlocked. Understanding the 5-year-old is, in a sense, understanding what the 3-year-old will become. We have portrayed the child as an extraordinary problem definer-solver, whose development hinges both on the nature of information available to him and on the kind of sense-making competence he has already acquired. The child and his human and material environment interact to determine his future development.

Problems and Environments

Environments are structured; physical, social, and institutional environments have internal rules and relationships. The same variables that influence the child's development are present in each—the family, the school, the neighborhood, the day-care center—but differ in distribution, salience, and patterning. Teachers may act like parents; school materials can be found in the home; and the child models peers as well as adults. We are struck by the common dimensions of environments, but we are also struck by the absence of comparative analyses that would describe points of overlap and elucidate uniquenesses.

Environments pose problems for the child and constrain his solutions. We need to know more about the range of problems generated by different environments, how they are defined by different children, and what solutions will be accepted by different caregivers.

Aims

An appropriate aim for day care in the past may have been to ensure the survival of children through "custodial care." Today, however, the aim of day care must be much more than that. It must offer opportunities for the development of competence, for children and their caregivers. Competence takes many forms, involves many domains (e.g., social, problem solving, and language) and can be attained in many environments (e.g., school, home, and day-care center). A broad concept of day care is surely necessary to accommodate such an aim. If a broad, educational-developmental approach to day care is taken, one may visualize a future aim of day care as going beyond promoting competence to fostering "optimization" or "self-actualization" for all people.

Change and Continuity

Day care as it exists, and as it will exist, is intimately associated with change, as both an agent of change and a respondent to change. We have posed the possibility that in the future our national life style will change and that the change will not necessarily lead to a lessening of the family's role in child rearing. Reduction in work hours and a revision of work schedules may lead not only to an emphasis on the family but to a reconstitution of the father's role in child care and education. If the mothering role has indeed become de-

valued as the working woman has become the model for successful womanhood, perhaps the fathering role needs to be revalued.

Continuity appears to be a necessary balance for change. This holds true for the welfare of day care as well as for the development of children. We have suggested that the pursuit of alternatives and innovations for changing aspects of society is a positive national virtue. It is one, however, that requires systematic, coherent, intensive, and long-range planning which can be carried out only by a stable, continuing organization. We have proposed that a national child-development institute may be one way of assuring this needed continuity.

Complexity

It would be foolish to underestimate the problems and complexities involved in developing day-care programs or in evaluating them. One cannot assume that programs will evolve naturally, that they will intuitively evaluate themselves, or that valid evaluations can be tacked on *post hoc*. To design effective programs and to evaluate them adequately we need to know a great deal more about children than we now know. In the end sensible programs and informative evaluations are contingent on adequate solutions to the mysteries, the "baffling and challenging facts," that appear whenever we look at the child.

Recommendations

Day care is returning to the United States—suddenly, precipitously, and massively. Its return was neither expected nor prepared for, its continuation is uncertain, and its impact on the nation is difficult to predict. Vast numbers of children will spend a great deal of time in day-care settings outside their own homes. Some of these settings will approximate the ideal of one or another segment of society, whereas others will fall short of anyone's notion of what day care ought to be. A great many lives will be influenced by the alternatives we define today and the priorities we assign to them. Some of our choices hopefully will be wise; others undoubtedly will be foolish.

It is all very well to dream of a tomorrow that is far better than today, to concoct rational schemes diffused with hope, love, and wonder. What is needed now is an adequate appreciation of options for today and tomorrow and practical guidelines for choosing among them. It is toward satisfying the first need that we have directed our efforts in this book. What recommendations we have offered have been posed in the form of problems for appreciation rather than prescriptions for action.

The second need is perhaps more difficult to satisfy. We propose three strategies. One is to be future-oriented in our programming, to think in terms of long-range aims and long-term plans rather than the need for immediate, quick-and-easy results. Another strategy is to encourage the fascination with childhood and the preoccupation with education that seems to be entering our national conscience. Now, when young people are likely to be severe critics of their own families and their own education, the time may be right to introduce more high school and college programs that deal with the sociology, psychology, and anthropology of educational systems, the family, and childhood. Now, when parents are being offered more choices in the education of their children, it may be valuable to make available to them courses in education and human development. A society concerned and informed about children can best plan for their care.

These first two strategies counterbalance each other. We need a future orientation for programs in order to distinguish between the 3-year-old of today and the 3-year-old of tomorrow, but we also need a present orientation that appreciates the child's capacities, joys, and sorrows, whatever they happen to be, whether he is 3 or 4, 13 or 14. Programs may grow best in the shadow of tomorrow; we suspect that children grow best in the sunlight of today.

A third strategy is to utilize fully the power of research and analysis in sorting the trivial from the crucial, in weighing the evidence, in amassing additional evidence where it is needed to fill gaps in our knowledge. As we experiment, analyze, and act on the best knowledge currently available, we will surely become a citizenry that can master knowledge and yet challenge and question it. What we now know is valuable but not sacred, temporally and culturally relative but not invalid, laced with truth, salted with fiction, and enormously important for today and tomorrow.

Finally, we submit a pessimistic projection prompted by the accelerating pressure for a quick expansion of day-care services and by the clear indication that these services are seen as an adjunct to programs primarily concerned with welfare reform. Indeed, there may be too many short-term aims and too much political profit behind today's day-care boom to permit child-oriented planning to prevail. The ghosts of the distant past are still with us, and there is little in the recent past to offer comfort. As day care emerges once again from neglect to prominence, it rapidly approaches the threshold of another major national gamble. For all practical purposes the gamble on Head Start was lost; there is little reason to suppose that a gamble on day care will be won. Perhaps the reality of current pressures means that the best we can hope for is a way of softening the disaster. Perhaps institutions with long-term perspectives will eventually emerge to provide the stability and direction now missing but so sorely needed.

If the pessimism of this projection clashes with the optimism of earlier pages, it is because what *is* so often clashes with what *could be*. Consider, then, that our pessimistic projection might accurately reflect a possible future state for day care in the United States and that to realize a happier alternative will require extraordinary dedication and determination.

References

Addams, J. *Twenty Years at Hull House.* New York: New American Library, 1910.

Aebli, H. *Didactique psychologique: application à la didactique de la psychologie de Jean Piaget.* Neuchatel: Delachaux et Niestle, 1951.

Ainsworth, M. D. The effects of maternal deprivation: A review of findings and controversy in the context of research strategy. *Public Health Papers,* 1962, **14,** 97–165.

Ainsworth, M. D. The development of infant-mother interaction among the Ganda. In B. M. Foss (Ed.), *Determinants of infant behavior.* Vol. 2. New York: Wiley, 1963. Pp. 67–104.

Ainsworth, M. D. Object relations, dependency, and attachment: A theoretical review of the infant-mother relationship. *Child Development,* 1969, **40,** 969–1025.

Ainsworth, M. D., & Bell, S. M. Attachment, exploration, and separation: Illustrated by the behavior of one-year-olds in a strange situation. *Child Development,* 1970, **41,** 49–67.

Ainsworth, M. D., & Bell, S. M. Some contemporary patterns of mother-infant interaction in the feeding situation. In J. A. Ambrose (Ed.), *The functions of stimulation in early postnatal development.* London: Academic, in press.

Ainsworth, M. D., & Wittig, B. A. Attachment and exploratory behavior of one-year-olds in a strange situation. In B. M. Foss (Ed.), *Determinants of infant behavior.* Vol. 4. New York: Wiley, 1967.

Aldrich, C. A., Sung, C., & Knop, C. The crying of newly born babies, III. The early period at home. *Journal of Pediatrics,* 1945, **27,** 428–435.

Allen, G. B., & Masling, J. M. An evaluation of the effects of nursery school training on children in the kindergarten, first and second grades. *Journal of Educational Research,* 1957, **51,** 285–296.

Altemeyer, R. A., Fulton, D., & Berney, K. M. Long-term memory improvement: Confirmation of a finding by Piaget. *Child Development,* 1969, **40,** 845–857.

Ambrose, J. A. The Development of the smiling response in early infancy. In B. M. Foss (Ed.), *Determinants of infant behavior.* New York: Wiley, 1961. Pp. 179–196.

American Joint Distribution Committee. *Joint Distribution Committee guide for day care centers. A handbook to aid communities in developing day care center programs for pre-school children.* Geneva, Switzerland: AJDC, 1962 [ERIC No. EDO 27961].

Anderson, H. H. Domination and integration in the social behavior of young children in an experimental play situation. *Genetic Psychology Monographs,* 1937, **19,** 341–408. (a)

Anderson, H. H. An experimental study of dominative and integrative behavior in children of preschool age. *Journal of Social Psychology,* 1937, **8,** 335–345. (b)

299

Anderson, N. H. Likableness ratings of 555 personality trait words. *Journal of Personality and Social Psychology*, 1968, **9**, 272–278.

Anderson, S. B. From textbooks to reality: Social researchers face the facts of life in the world of the disadvantaged. In J. Hellmuth (Ed.), *Disadvantaged child*. Vol. 3. *Compensatory education: A national debate*. New York: Brunner/Mazel, 1970. Pp. 226–237.

Antonovsky, H. F. A contribution to research in the area of mother-child relationship. *Child Development*, 1959, **30**, 37–51.

Appel, M. H. Aggressive behavior of nursery school children and adult procedures in dealing with such behavior. *Journal of Experimental Education*, 1942, **11**, 185–199.

Armington, D. E. *A plan for continuing growth*. Newton, Mass.: Education Development Center, undated.

Arsenian, J. M. Young children in an insecure situation. *Journal of Abnormal and Social Psychology*, 1943, **38**, 225–249.

Ausubel, D. P., & Ausubel, P. Ego development among segregated Negro children. *Mental Hygiene*, 1958, **42**, 362–369. [Republished in A. H. Passow (Ed.). *Education in depressed areas*. New York: Teachers College, Columbia University, 1963. Pp. 109–131.]

Bakwin, H. Loneliness in infants. *American Journal of Diseases in Children*, 1942, **63**, 30–40.

Bakwin, H. Emotional deprivation in infants. *Journal of Pediatrics*, 1949, **35**, 512–521.

Bakwin, H., & Bakwin, R. M. *Clinical management of behavior disorders in children*. (2nd ed.) Philadelphia: Saunders, 1960.

Baldwin, A. L. The effect of home environment on nursery school behavior. *Child Development*, 1949, **20**, 49–61.

Baldwin, A. L., & Frank, S. M. Syntactic complexity in mother-child interactions. Paper presented at the meeting of the Society for Research in Child Development, Santa Monica, March 1969.

Baldwin, A. L., Kalhorn, J., & Breese, F. H. Patterns of parent behavior. *Psychological Monographs*, 1945, **58** (3, Whole No. 268).

Baldwin, C. P. Naturalistic studies of classroom learning. *Review of Educational Research*, 1965, **35**, 107–113.

Baldwin, C. P. Information exchange in mother-child interactions. Paper presented at the meeting of the Society for Research in Child Development, Santa Monica, March 1969.

Baldwin, C. P., & Baldwin, A. L. Children's judgments of kindness. *Child Development*, 1970, **41**, 29–47.

Ballif, B. L. Exploration of motivation to achieve in preschool children. Unpublished manuscript, Education Research and Development Center, University of Hawaii, 1967.

Bandura, A. The role of imitation in personality development. *Journal of Nursery Education*, 1963, **18**, 207–215.

Bandura, A. The role of modeling processes in personality development. In W. W. Hartup & N. L. Smothergill (Eds.). *The young child*. Washington, D.C.: National Association for the Education of Young Children, 1967. Pp. 42–58.

Bandura, A., Grusec, J. E., & Menlove, F. L. Vicarious extinction of avoidance behavior. *Journal of Personality and Social Psychology*, 1967, **5**, 16–23.

Bandura, A., & Harris, M. B. Modification of syntactic style. *Journal of Experimental Child Psychology*, 1966, **4**, 341–352.

Bandura, A., & McDonald, F. J. The influence of social reinforcement and the behavior of models in shaping children's moral judgments. *Journal of Abnormal and Social Psychology,* 1963, **67,** 274–291.

Bandura, A., Ross, D., & Ross, S. A. Transmission of aggression through imitation of aggressive models. *Journal of Abnormal Social Psychology,* 1961, **63,** 575–582.

Bandura, A., Ross, D., & Ross, S. A. Imitation of film-mediated aggressive models. *Journal of Abnormal and Social Psychology,* 1963, **66,** 3–11. (a)

Bandura, A., Ross, D., & Ross, S. A. Vicarious reinforcement and imitative learning. *Journal of Abnormal and Social Psychology,* 1963, **67,** 601–667. (b)

Baratz, J. C. A bi-dialectal task for determining language proficiency in economically disadvantaged Negro children. *Child Development,* 1969, **40,** 889–901.

Baratz, S. S., & Baratz, J. C. Early childhood intervention: The social science base of institutional racism. Paper presented at the meeting of the Society for Research in Child Development, Santa Monica, March 1969. Also appeared in Baratz, S. S., and Baratz, J. C. Early childhood intervention: the social science base of institutional racism. *Harvard Educational Review,* 1970, **40,** 29–50.

Barker, R. G., Dembo, T., & Lewin, K. Frustration and regression: An experiment with young children. *University of Iowa Studies in Child Welfare,* 1941, **18,** 1–314.

Barker, R. G., & Wright, H. F. *Midwest and its children: The psychological ecology of an American town.* Evanston, Ill.: Row, Peterson, 1954.

Barrett, H. E., & Koch, H. L. The effect of nursery school training upon the mental test performance of a group of orphanage children. *Journal of Genetic Psychology,* 1930, **37,** 102–121.

Barth, R., & Rathbone, C. The open school: A way of thinking about children, learning, knowledge. *The Center Forum,* **1969,** 3(7), 1–2.

Baumrind, D. Effects of authoritative parental control on child behavior. *Child Development,* 1966, **37,** 887–907.

Baumrind, D. Current patterns of parental authority. *Developmental Psychology Monograph,* 1971, **4,** 1–103.

Baumrind, D., & Black, A. E. Socialization practices associated with dimensions of competence in preschool boys and girls. *Child Development,* 1967, **38,** 291–327.

Bayley, N., & Schaefer, E. S. Relationships between socioeconomic variables and the behavior of mothers toward young children. *Journal of Genetic Psychology,* 1960, **96,** 61–77.

Bayley, N., & Schaefer, E. S. Correlations of maternal and child behaviors with the development of mental abilities: Data from the Berkeley growth study. *Monographs of the Society for Research in Child Development,* 1964, **29,** (6, Whole No. 97).

Beaton, A., & Shipman, V. *Disadvantaged children and their first school experiences.* Princeton, N.J.: Educational Testing Service, 1970.

Becker, W. C. Consequences of different kinds of parental discipline. In M. L. Hoffman, & L. W. Hoffman (Eds.), *Review of Child Development Research.* New York: Russell Sage Foundation, 1964. Pp. 169–208.

Bee, H. L. Parent-child interaction and distractibility in nine-year-old children. *Merrill-Palmer Quarterly,* 1967, **13,** 175–190.

Bee, H. L., Van Egeren, L. F., Streissguth, A. P., Nyman, B. A., & Leckie, M. S. Social class differences in maternal teaching strategies and speech patterns. *Developmental Psychology,* 1969, **1,** 626–734.

Beer, E. S. *The day nursery.* New York: Dutton, 1938.

Beiswenger, H. Luria's model of the verbal control of behavior. *Merrill-Palmer Quarterly,* 1968, **14,** 267–284.

Bell, R. Q. Stimulus control of parent or caretaker behavior by offspring. *Developmental Psychology,* 1971, **4,** 63–72.

Bell, S. M. The development of the concept of object as related to infant-mother attachment. *Child Development,* 1970, **41,** 291–311.

Bellack, A. A., Kliebard, H. M., Hyman, R. T., & Smith, F. L. *The language of the classroom.* New York: Teachers College Press, 1966.

Beller, E. K. Teaching styles and their effects on problem solving behavior in Head Start programs. Study V. Unpublished manuscript, Head Start Evaluation and Research Center, Temple University, Philadelphia, undated.

Bellugi, U., & Brown, R. (Eds.) The acquisition of language. *Monographs of the Society for Research in Child Development,* 1964, **29** (1, Whole No. 92).

Bennis, W. G., & Slater, P. E. *The temporary society.* New York: Harper & Row, 1968.

Bereiter, C. Instructional planning in early compensatory education. In J. Hellmuth (Ed.), *Disadvantaged child.* Vol. 1. New York: Brunner/Mazel, 1967. Pp. 339–347.

Bereiter, C. A nonpsychological approach to early compensatory education. In M. Deutsch, I. Katz, & A. Jensen (Eds.), *Social class, race, and psychological development.* New York: Holt, Rinehart & Winston, 1968. Pp. 337–346.

Bereiter, C. Genetics and educability: Educational implications of the Jensen debate. In J. Hellmuth (Ed.), *Disadvantaged child.* Vol. 3. *Compensatory education: A national debate.* New York: Brunner/Mazel, 1970, Pp. 279–299.

Bereiter, C., & Engelmann, S. *Teaching disadvantaged children in the preschool.* Englewood Cliffs, N.J.: Prentice-Hall, 1966.

Bereiter, C., & Engelmann, S. Academic preschool, Champaign, Illinois. *Preschool program in compensatory education 1 (It Works).* Washington, D.C.: United States Department of Health, Education and Welfare, Office of Education, 1968.

Berlyne, D. E. *Conflict, arousal, and curiosity.* New York: McGraw-Hill, 1960.

Bernstein, B. Aspects of language and learning in the genesis of the social process. In D. Hymes (Ed.), *Language in culture and society.* New York: Harper and Row, 1965. Pp. 251–263.

Bernstein, B. Elaborated and restricted codes: Their social origins and some consequences. In A. G. Smith (Ed.), *Communication and culture.* New York: Holt, Rinehart & Winston, 1966. Pp. 427–441.

Bernstein, B. A sociolinguistic approach to socialization with some reference to educability. In F. Williams (Ed.), *Language and poverty.* Chicago: Markham, 1970. Pp. 25–61.

Bernstein, V. H. Five million children with part-time mothers—and nowhere to go. Reprint from *Redbook,* November 1969.

Besaw, V. E. (Ed.) Proceedings of the National Conference on Child Care, Pittsburgh, May 1969.

Biber, B. Young deprived children and their educational needs. *Childhood Education,* 1967, **44,** 30–36.

Biber, B. Goals and methods in a preschool program for disadvantaged children. *Children,* 1970, **17,** 15–20.

Biber, B., & Franklin, M. B. The relevance of developmental and psychodynamic concepts to the education of the preschool child. In J. Hellmuth (Ed.), *Disadvantaged child*. Vol. 1. New York: Brunner/Mazel, 1967. Pp. 205–323.

Bikle, J. Social casework in a day care program. In *Day care: An expanding resource for children*. New York: Child Welfare League of America, 1965. Pp. 36–43.

Bing, E. Effect of child-rearing practices on development of differential cognitive abilities. *Child Development*, 1963, **34**, 631–648.

Bishop, B. M. Mother-child interaction and the social behavior of children. *Psychological Monographs*, 1951, 65, No. 11.

Blank, M., & Solomon, F. How shall the disadvantaged child be taught? *Child Development*, 1969, **40**, 47–61.

Blauvelt, H., & McKenna, J. Mother-neonate interaction: Capacity of the human newborn for orientation. In B. M. Foss (Ed.), *Determinants of infant behavior*, New York: Wiley, 1961. Pp. 3–29.

Bloom, B. S. *Stability and change in human characteristics*. New York: Wiley, 1964.

Bloom, L. Language development: Form and function in emerging grammars. Unpublished doctoral dissertation, Columbia University, 1968.

Bloom, L. *Language Development: Form and Function in Emerging Grammars*. Cambridge, Mass.: MIT Press, 1970.

Body, M. K. Patterns of aggression in the nursery school. *Child Development*, 1955, **26**, 3–11.

Bogue, M. P., & Moran, M. H. Day nurseries. *Social Work Yearbook*, 1929, **1**, 118–119.

Boguslawski, D. B. *Guide for establishing and operating day care centers for young children*. New York: Child Welfare League of America, 1968.

Bonney, M. E., & Nicholson, E. L. Comparative school adjustments of elementary school pupils with and without preschool training. *Child Development*, 1958, **29**, 125–133.

Bossard, J. H. *The sociology of child development*. New York: Harper, 1948.

Bowerman, C. E., & Kinch, J. W. Changes in family and peer orientation of children between the 4th and 10th grades. *Social Forces*, 1959, **37**, 206–211.

Bowlby, J. The nature of the child's tie to his mother. *International Journal of Psychoanalysis*, 1958, **39**, 350–373.

Bowlby, J. *Attachment and loss*. Vol. 1. *Attachment*. New York: Basic Books, 1969.

Bowlby, J., & Robertson, J. A two-year-old goes to hospital. In K. Soddy (Ed.), *Mental health and infant development*. Vol. 1. London: Routledge & Kegan Paul, 1955. P. 123.

Brackbill, Y. Extinction of the smiling response in infants as a function of reinforcement schedule. *Child Development*, 1958, **29**, 115–124.

Bradshaw, C. E. Relationship between maternal behavior and infant performance in environmentally disadvantaged homes. Unpublished doctoral dissertation, University of Florida, 1968.

Brodbeck, A. J., & Irwin, O. C. The speech behavior of infants without families. *Child Development*, 1946, **17**, 145–156.

Brodsky, M. Cultural deprivation and arousal level. Reprinted from the *Proceedings of 77th Annual Convention, American Psychological Association*, 1969, **4**, 315–316.

Bronfenbrenner, U. Socialization and social class through time and space. In E. E. Maccoby, T. M. Newcomb, & E. L. Hartley (Eds.), *Readings in social psychology*. New York: Holt, 1958. Pp. 400–425.

Bronfenbrenner, U. The changing American child—a speculative analysis. *Journal of Social Issues*, 1961, **17**, 6–18.

Bronfenbrenner, U. Soviet methods of character education: Some implications for research. *Religious Education*, 1962, **57** (4, Res. Suppl.), 45–61.

Bronfenbrenner, U. The changing Soviet family. In D. Brown (Ed.), *The role and status of women in the Soviet Union*. New York: Columbia Teachers College Press, 1968. Pp. 98–124. (a)

Bronfenbrenner, U. Early deprivation in mammals: A cross-species analysis. In G. Newton & S. Levine (Eds.), *Early experience and behavior*. Springfield, Ill.: Thomas, 1968. Pp. 627–764. (b)

Bronfenbrenner, U. When is infant stimulation effective? In D. C. Glass (Ed.), *Environmental influences*. New York: Rockefeller University & Russell Sage Foundation, 1968. Pp. 251–257. (c)

Bronfenbrenner, U. Reaction to social pressure from adults versus peers among Soviet day school and boarding school pupils in the perspective of an American sample. Symposium presented at the International Congress of Psychology, London, England, August 1969.

Bronfenbrenner, U. *Two worlds of childhood*. New York: Russell Sage Foundation, 1970.

Bronfenbrenner, U. The split society: Children vs. adults. Unpublished manuscript, Cornell University, Ithaca, N.Y., undated.

Brottman, M. A. (Ed.) Language remediation for the disadvantaged preschool child. *Monographs of the Society for Research in Child Development*, 1968, **33** (8, Whole No. 124).

Brown, B. R. The assessment of self-concept among four-year-old Negro and white children: A comparative study using the Brown-IDS self-concept reference test. Paper presented at the Eastern Psychological Association Meetings, New York, April 1966.

Brown, R. How shall a thing be called? *Psychological Review*, 1958, **65**, 14–21.

Brown, R. (Ed.) *Psycholinguistics*. Part I. New York: Free Press, 1970.

Brown, R., Cazden, C., & Bellugi, U. The child's grammar from I to III. In J. P. Hill (Ed.), *Minnesota symposium on child psychology*. Minneapolis: University of Minnesota Press, 1969. Pp. 28–73.

Brubacher, J. S. *A History of the problems of education*. New York: McGraw-Hill, 1947.

Bruner, J. S. *Toward a theory of instruction*. Cambridge, Mass.: Harvard University Press, 1966.

Bruner, J. S. Eye, hand, and mind. In D. Elkind & J. H. Flavell (Eds.), *Studies in cognitive development*. New York: Oxford, 1969. Pp. 223–235.

Bruner, J. S., Olver, R. R., Greenfield, P. M., et al. *Studies in cognitive growth*. New York: Wiley, 1966.

Bühler, C. *From birth to maturity*. London: Routledge & Kegan Paul, 1935.

Bushell, D., Jacobson, J. M., & Risley, T. Switching requirements in a Head Start classroom. *Journal of Applied Behavior Analysis*, 1969, **2**, 43–47.

Busse, T. Child rearing correlates of flexible thinking. Unpublished doctoral dissertation, University of Chicago, 1967. Cited by R. D. Hess, Parental behavior and children's school achievement. In E. Grotberg (Ed.), *Critical issues in research related to disadvantaged children*. Princeton, N.J.: Educational Testing Service, 1969.

Butts, R. F. *A cultural history of western education: Its social and intellectual foundations*. (2nd ed.) New York: McGraw-Hill, 1955.

Cairns, R. B. The attachment behavior of mammals. *Psychological Review*, 1967, **73**, 409–426.

Caldwell, B. M. What is the optimal learning environment for the young child? *American Journal of Orthopsychiatry*, 1967, **37**, 8–22.

Caldwell, B. M. A special facility for child development and education. Proposal submitted to the Research Division, Children's Bureau, Social and Rehabilitation Service, United States Department of Health, Education and Welfare, April, 1969.

Caldwell, B. M., Hersher, L., Lipton, E. L., Richmond, J. B., Stern, G. A., Eddy, E., Drachman, R., & Rothman, A. Mother-infant interaction in monomatric and polymatric families. *American Journal of Orthopsychiatry*, 1963, **33**, 653–664.

Caldwell, B. M., & Richmond, J. B. Appendix B: A "typical day" for the groups at the Children's Center. In L. L. Dittmann (Ed.), *Early child care: The new perspectives.* New York: Atherton, 1968. Pp. 373–377. (a)

Caldwell, B. M., & Richmond, J. B. The Children's Center in Syracuse, New York. In L. L. Dittmann (Ed.), *Early child care: The new perspectives.* New York: Atherton, 1968. Pp. 326–358. (b)

Caldwell, B. M., Wright, C. M., Honig, A. S., & Tannenbaum, J. Infant day care and attachment. Paper presented at the 46th Annual Meeting of the American Orthopsychiatric Association, April 1969.

Campbell, D. T. From description to experimentation: Interpreting trends as quasi-experiments. In C. W. Harris (Ed.), *Problems in measuring change.* Madison, Wis.: University of Wisconsin Press, 1967. Pp. 212–242.

Campbell, D. T. Reforms as experiments. *American Psychologist*, 1969, **24**, 409–429.

Campbell, D. T., & Erlebacher, A. How regression artifacts in quasi-experimental evaluations can mistakenly make compensatory education look harmful. In J. Hellmuth (Ed.), *Disadvantaged child.* Vol. 3. *Compensatory education: A national debate.* New York: Brunner/Mazel, 1970. Pp. 185–210.

Campbell, D. T., & Frey, P. W. The implications of learning theory for the fade-out of gains from compensatory education. In J. Hellmuth (Ed.), *Disadvantaged child.* Vol. 3. *Compensatory education: A national debate.* New York: Brunner/Mazel, 1970. Pp. 455–463.

Campbell, D. T., & Stanley, J. C. *Experimental and quasi-experimental designs for research.* Chicago: Rand McNally, 1967.

Campbell, J. D. Peer relations in childhood. In M. L. Hoffman & L. W. Hoffman (Eds.), *Review of child development research,* New York: Russell Sage Foundation, 1964. Pp. 289–322.

Carroll, J. B. *Language and thought.* Englewood Cliffs, N.J.: Prentice-Hall, 1964.

Carroll, J. B. On learning from being told. Presidential address given at the convention of the American Psychological Association, Washington, D.C., September 1967.

Carson, A. S., & Rabin, A. I. Verbal comprehension and communication in Negro and white children. *Journal of Educational Psychology*, 1960, **51**, 47–51.

Carstens, C. C. Dependent and neglected children. *Social Work Yearbook*, 1929, **1**, 128–137.

Casagrande, J. B. Comanche baby language. *International Journal of American Linguistics*, 1948, **14**, 11–14.

Casler, L. Maternal deprivation: A critical review of the literature. *Monographs of the Society for Research in Child Development*, 1961, **26** (2, Whole No. 80).

Casler, L. Perceptual deprivation in institutional settings. In G. Newton & S. Levine (Eds.), *Early experience and behavior*. Springfield, Ill.: Thomas, 1968. Pp. 573–626.

Caudill, W. Tiny dramas: Vocal communication between mother and infant in Japanese and American families. Prepared for the Second Conference on Cultural and Mental Health, Honolulu, March 1969.

Cauman, J. What is happening in day care: New concepts, current practices, and trends. *Child Welfare*, 1956, **35**(1), 22–27.

Cauman, J. Family day care and group day care: Two essential aspects of a basic child welfare service. *Child Welfare*, 1961, **40**(10), 20–23.

Cazden, C. B. Environmental assistance to the child's acquisition of grammar. Unpublished doctoral dissertation, Harvard University, 1965.

Cazden, C. B. Subcultural differences in child language: An interdisciplinary review. *Merrill-Palmer Quarterly*, 1966, **12**, 185–219.

Cazden, C. B. Some implications of research on language development for preschool education. In R. D. Hess & R. M. Bear (Eds.), *Early Education*. Chicago: Aldine, 1968. Pp. 131–142.

Cazden, C. B. Approaches to social dialects in early childhood education. Paper for a conference on social dialects sponsored by the Center for Applied Linguistics, Cambridge, Mass., November 1969. (a)

Cazden, C. B. *Infant school*. Newton, Mass.: Education Development Center, 1969. (b)

Cazden, C. B. The neglected situation in child language research and education. In A. Williams (Ed.), *Language and poverty*. Chicago: Markham, 1970. Pp. 81–101.

Cazden, C. B. Language programs for young children: Notes from England and Wales. In C. B. Lavatelli (Ed.), *Preschool language training*. Urbana, Ill.: University of Illinois Press, in press.

Center for the Study of Public Policy. Education vouchers. Report prepared for the United States Office of Economic Opportunity, Cambridge, Mass., 1970.

Charlesworth, R., & Hartup, W. W. Positive social reinforcement in the nursery school peer group. *Child Development*, 1967, **38**, 993–1002.

Charlesworth, W. R. The role of surprise in cognitive development. In D. Elkind & J. H. Flavell (Eds.), *Studies in cognitive development*. New York: Oxford University Press, 1969. Pp. 223–235.

Chasdi, E. H., & Lawrence, M. S. Some antecedents of aggression and effects of frustration in doll play. In J. Seidman (Ed.), *The child: A book of readings*. New York: Rinehart, 1958. Pp. 442–453.

Chess, S., Thomas, A., & Birch, H. Characteristics of the individual child's behavioral responses to the environment. *American Journal of Orthopsychiatry*, 1959, **29**, 791–802.

Child Welfare League of America, Committee on Standards. *Standards for day care service*. (Rev. ed.) New York: CWLA, 1969.

Chilman, C. S. *Growing up poor*. Washington, D.C.: U.S. Department of Health, Education and Welfare, Welfare Administration Publication, No. 13, 1966.

Chilman, C. S. Poor families and their patterns of child care: Some implications for service programs. In L. L. Dittmann (Ed.), *Early child care: The new perspectives*. New York: Atherton, 1968. Pp. 217–236.

Chittenden, G. E. An experimental study in measuring and modifying assertive behavior in young children. *Monographs of the Society for Research in Child Development*, 1942, **7**, No. 1.

Chodorkoff, J. R. Infant development as a function of mother-child interaction. Unpublished doctoral dissertation, Wayne State University, Detroit, Michigan, 1960.

Cicirelli, V. G. The relevance of the regression artifact problem to the Westinghouse-Ohio evaluation of Head Start: A reply to Campbell and Erlebacher. In J. Hellmuth (Ed.), *Disadvantaged child*. Vol. 3. *Compensatory education: A national debate*. New York: Brunner/Mazel, 1970. Pp. 211–215.

Clark, A. D., & Richards, C. J. Auditory discrimination among economically disadvantaged and non-disadvantaged pre-school children. *Exceptional Children*, December 1966. Pp. 259–262.

Clark, K. B., & Clark, M. P. The development of consciousness of self and emergence of racial identification in Negro preschool children. *Journal of Social Psychology*, 1939, **10**, 591–599.

Clark, K. B., & Clark, M. P. Emotional factors in racial identification and preference in Negro children. *Journal of Negro Education*, 1950, **19**, 341–350.

Clark, K. B., & Clark, M. P. Racial identification or preference in Negro children. In G. E. Swanson, T. M. Newcomb, & E. L. Hartley (Eds.), *Readings in social psychology*. (2nd ed.) New York: Holt, 1952. Pp. 551–560.

Clarke-Stewart, K. A. Interactions between mothers and their young children: Characteristics and consequences. Unpublished doctoral dissertation, Yale University, 1972.

Clifford, E. Discipline in the home: A controlled observational study of parental practices. *Journal of Genetic Psychology*, 1959, **95**, 48–82.

Cohen, A., & Hodges, H. Characteristics of the lower-blue-collar class. *Social Problems*, 1963, **10**, 304–335.

Cole, M., Gay, J., Glick, J. A., and Sharp, D. W. *The Cultural Context of Learning and Thinking*. New York: Basic Books, 1971.

Coleman, J. S. *The adolescent society*. Glencoe, Ill.: Free Press, 1961. (a)

Coleman, J. S. Social climates in high schools. U.S. Department of Health, Education and Welfare, Office of Education, *Cooperative Research Monograph*, 1961, 4. (b)

Coleman, J. S. *Equality of educational opportunity*. Washington, D.C.: U.S. Department of Health, Education and Welfare, Office of Education, 1966.

Coleman, R. W., & Provence, S. Environmental retardation (hospitalism) in infants living in families. *Pediatrics*, 1957, **19**, 285.

Collins, A. N. Some efforts to improve private family day care. *Children*, 1966, **13**, 135–140.

Collins, A. H., & Watson, E. L. Summary of the Day Care Neighbor Service. Field study of the Neighborhood Family Day Care System. Unpublished manuscript, Portland, Oregon. May 1968.

Collins, A. H., & Watson, E. L. *The day care neighbor service: A handbook for the organization and operation of a new approach to family day care*. Portland, Oregon: Neighborhood Family Day Care System, 1969.

Conners, K., & Eisenberg, L. The effect of teacher behavior on verbal intelligence in Operation Head Start children. Baltimore, Md.: Johns Hopkins University, 1966.

Cook, S. G. Report on child day care centers in New Haven for ages 2–5 years as of March 1, 1970. Unpublished manuscript, New Haven, Conn. 1970. (a)

Cook, S. G. The staffing of day care centers; Assorted comments. Unpublished manuscript, New Haven, Conn., 1970. (b)

Coopersmith, S. *The antecedents of self-esteem.* San Francisco: Freeman, 1967.

Costello, J. Research in a black community: Four years in review. Paper presented at a Symposium on Research in Black Communities at the meeting of the Society for Research in Child Development, Santa Monica, March 1969. Unpublished manuscript, 1970. (a)

Costello, J. Some approaches to programming for disadvantaged preschool children. In L. L. Dittmann (Ed.), *Curriculum is what happens.* Washington, D.C.: National Association for the Education of Young Children, 1970. Pp. 62–72. (b)

Costin, L. B., & Gruener, J. R. A project for training personnel in child welfare. *Child Welfare,* 1964, **43,** 175–181.

Cowe, E. G. A study of kindergarten activities for language development. Unpublished doctoral dissertation, Columbia University, 1967.

Cox, F. N., & Campbell, D. Young children in a new situation with and without their mothers. *Child Development,* 1968, **39,** 123–132.

Cox, H. R. Effect of maternal attitudes, teacher attitudes, and type of nursery school training on the abilities of preschool children. Final report. Catholic University of America, Washington, D.C., 1968. [ERIC No. ED 028 844.]

Crandall, V. J., Dewey, R., Katkovsky, W., & Preston, A. Parents' attitudes and behaviors and grade school children's academic achievements. *Journal of Genetic Psychology,* 1964, **104,** 53–66.

Crandall, V. J., Preston, A., & Rabson, A. Maternal reactions and the development of independence and achievement behavior in young children. *Child Development,* 1960, **31,** 243–251.

Crawford, C. H. A family day care program. *Child Welfare,* 1969, **48,** 160–162.

Cronbach, L. J. The two disciplines of scientific psychology. *American Psychologist,* 1957, **12,** 671–694.

Daehler, M. W., Horowitz, A. B., Wynns, F. C., & Flavell, J. H. Verbal and nonverbal rehearsal in children's recall. *Child Development,* 1969, **40,** 443–452.

Dai, B. *Some problems of personality development among Negro children, in personality, society and culture.* New York: Alfred Knopf, 1955.

Dave, R. H. The identification and measurement of environmental process variables that are related to educational achievement. Unpublished doctoral dissertation, University of Chicago, 1963.

David, M., & Appell, G. Observation et traitement d'un cas d'arriération psychogène. *Journal Psychiatrique Infantin,* 1951, **1,** 205.

David, M., & Appell, G. A study of nursing care and nurse-infant interaction. In B. M. Foss (Ed.), *Determinants of infant behavior.* New York: Wiley, 1961. Pp. 121–141.

Davis, A. *Social class influences upon learning.* Cambridge, Mass.: Harvard University, 1965.

Davis, E. B. The American Negro: From family membership to personal social identity. *Journal of the National Medical Association,* 1968, **60,** 92–99.

Davis, M. D. Nursery schools: Their development and current practices in the United States. United States Department of the Interior, Office of Education, *Bulletin,* No. 9, 1932.

Day Care and Child Development Council of America. *Day care and child development in your community.* Washington, D.C.: DCCDCA, 1969. (a)

Day Care and Child Development Council of America. Report on the Gould Foundation Conference on training of day care administrators, New York, February 1969. [ERIC No. ED 031 806]. (b)

Day Care and Child Development Council of America. The Family day care-career program. *Voice for Children*, 1970, **3**(3), 1–2.

Dennis, W. Infant development under conditions of restricted practice and of minimum social stimulation: A preliminary report. *Journal of Genetic Psychology*, 1938, **53**, 149–158.

Dennis, W. Infant development under conditions of restricted practice and of minimum social stimulation. *Genetic Psychological Monographs*, 1941, **23**, 143–184.

Dennis, W. Causes of retardation among institutional children: Iran. *Journal of Genetic Psychology*, 1960, **96**, 47–59.

Dennis, W., & Najarian, P. Infant development under environmental handicap. *Psychological Monographs*, 1957, **71** (7, Whole No. 436).

Deutsch, C. P. Auditory discrimination and learning: Social factors. *Merrill-Palmer Quarterly*, 1964, **10**, 277–296.

Deutsch, C. P. Effects of environmental deprivation on basic psychological processes: Some hypotheses. NDEA National Institute *Occasional Paper/Special*, July 1968, 13–17. (a)

Deutsch, C. P. Environment and perception. In M. Deutsch, I. Katz, & A. R. Jensen (Eds.), *Social class, race, and psychological development*. New York: Holt, Rinehart & Winston, 1968. Pp. 58–85.

Deutsch, M. Minority group and class status as related to social and personality factors in scholastic achievement. *Society for Applied Anthropology, Monograph No. 2*. Ithaca, N.Y.: Cornell University, 1960.

Deutsch, M. The disadvantaged child and the learning process. In H. Passow (Ed.), *Education in depressed areas*. New York: Teachers College Bureau of Publications, 1963. Pp. 163–179.

Deutsch, M. Facilitating development in the pre-school child: Social and psychological perspectives. *Merrill-Palmer Quarterly*, 1964, **10**, 249–263.

Deutsch, M. The role of social class in language development and cognition. *American Journal of Orthopsychiatry*, 1965, **35**, 78–88.

Deutsch, M. Early Childhood Project, New York City. *Preschool program in compensatory education 1 (It Works)*. Washington, D.C.: United States Department of Health, Education and Welfare, Office of Education, 1968.

Deutsch, M., & Associates. *The disadvantaged child*. New York: Basic Books, 1967.

Dewey, J., & Dewey, E. *Schools of tomorrow*. New York: Dutton, 1919.

Dickie, J. P. Effectiveness of structured and unstructured (traditional) methods of language training. *Monographs of the Society for Research in Child Development*, 1968, **33** (8, Whole No. 124), 62–79.

DiLorenzo, L. T., Salter, R., & Brady, J. J. Prekindergarten programs for educationally disadvantaged children. Final Report, Project No. 3040, New York State Education Department, Office of Research and Evaluation, Contract No. OE 6–10–040, United States Department of Health, Education and Welfare, Office of Education Bureau of Research, December 1969.

Dittmann, L. L. (Ed.) *Early child care: The new perspectives*. New York: Atherton, 1968.

Dixwell Preschool Day Care Center. Proposal for Dixwell preschool day care center. Unpublished manuscript, New Haven, Conn., 1970.

Drews, E. M., & Teahan, J. E. Parental attitudes and academic achievement. *Journal of Clinical Psychology*, 1957, **13**, 328–332.

Dreyer, A. S., & Rigler, D. Cognitive performance in Montessori and nursery school children. *The Journal of Educational Research*, 1969, **63**, 414–415.

Dumpson, J. R. The place of day care in meeting children's needs. *Child Welfare*, 1964, **43**, 182–186.

Dunham, R. M. Project Know How. Tallahassee, Fla.: Florida State University, 1969.

Dunnington, M. J. Behavior differences of sociometric status groups in a nursery school. *Child Development*, 1957, **28**, 103–111. (a)

Dunnington, M. J. Investigation of areas of disagreement in sociometric measurement of preschool children. *Child Development*, 1957, **28**, 93–102. (b)

Du Pan, R. M., & Roth, S. The psychologic development of a group of children brought up in a hospital-type residential nursery. *Journal of Pediatrics*, 1955, **47**, 124–129.

Eckstein, E. The function of the caseworker in day care centers. *Child Welfare*, 1962, **41**, 29–33.

Education Development Center. *Annual Report*, Newton, Mass.: EDC, 1968.

Edwards, E. Family day care in a community action program. *Children*, 1968, **15**, 55–58.

Eisenberg, L., Berlin, C. I., Dill, A., & Frank, S. Class and race effects on the intelligibility of monosyllables. *Child Development*, 1968, **39**, 1077–1090.

Eisenberg, L., & Conners, C. K. The effect of Headstart on developmental processes. Baltimore, Md.: Johns Hopkins University, 1966.

Eisenstein, F. A health service program for children in day care. *Children*, 1966, **13**, 237–240.

Elkind, D. Piagetian and psychometric conceptions of intelligence. *Harvard Educational Review*, 1969, **39**, 319–337. (a)

Elkind, D. Preschool education: Enrichment or instruction? *Childhood Education*, 1969, **45**, 321–328. (b)

Elkind, D., & Flavell, J. H. (Eds.), *Studies in cognitive development*. New York: Oxford, 1969.

El'konin, D. B. Some results of the study of the psychological development of preschool-age children. In M. Cole & I. Maltzman (Eds.), *A handbook of contemporary Soviet psychology*. New York: Basic Books, 1969. Pp. 163–208.

Eller, E. M. (Ed.) *The school of infancy by John Amos Comenius*. Chapel Hill: University of North Carolina Press, 1956.

Emerson, L. B. Professional services in day care. In *Day care: An expanding resource for children*. New York: Child Welfare League of America, 1965. Pp. 27–30.

Emlen, A. C. Realistic planning for the day care consumer. Paper prepared for presentation to the National Conference on Social Welfare, Chicago, June 1970.

Emmons, A. L. A study of the relations between self-assurance and skill in young children. *Child Development*, 1933, **4**, 323–328.

Engelmann, S. *The basic concept inventory*. Chicago: Follett, 1967.

Engelmann, S. The effectiveness of direct instruction on IQ performance and achievement in reading and arithmetic. In J. Hellmuth (Ed.), *Disadvantaged child*. Vol. 3. *Compensatory education: A national debate*. New York: Brunner/Mazel, 1970. Pp. 339–361.

Entwistle, D. R. Semantic systems of children: Some assessments of social class and ethnic differences. In F. Williams (Ed.), *Language and poverty*. Chicago: Markham, 1970. Pp. 123–139.

Erikson, E. *Childhood and society.* New York: Norton, 1950.

Eron, L. D., Lefkowitz, M. M., Huesmann, R. L., & Walder, L. O. Does television violence cause aggression? *American Psychologist,* 1972, **27**, 253–263.

Ervin, S. M., & Miller, W. R. Language development. In H. W. Stevenson (Ed.), *Child psychology: The sixty-second yearbook of the National Society for the Study of Education.* Chicago: *University of Chicago Press,* 1963. Pp. 108–143.

Escalona, S. N. Some determinants of individual differences. *Transactions of the New York Academy of Sciences,* 1965, **27**, 802–816.

Etzel, B. C. Analysis and modification of the acquisition of social and intellectual behaviors. July 15, 1970, Kansas Center for Research in Early Childhood Education: University of Kansas, Report submitted to The National Program on Early Childhood Education of CEMREL. United States Department of Health, Education and Welfare, Office of Education, Bureau of Research.

Etzkovitz, H., & Schaflander, G. *Ghetto crisis.* Boston: Little, Brown, 1969.

Evans, J. W., & Schiller, J. How preoccupation with possible regression artifacts can lead to a faulty strategy for the evaluation of social action programs: A reply to Campbell and Erlebacher. In J. Hellmuth (Ed.), *Disadvantaged child.* Vol. 3. *Compensatory education: A national debate.* New York: Brunner/Mazel, 1970. Pp. 216–220.

Fairweather, George W. *Methods for Experimental Social Innovation.* New York: Wiley, 1967.

Featherstone, J. The primary school revolution in Britain. *The New Republic,* **157**, August 10, September 2, September 9, 1967.

Fein, G. The effect of within-pair variations and instructions on the transposition behavior of kindergarten and third-grade children. *Journal of Experimental Child Psychology,* in press.

Fein, G. Evaluation in education. Unpublished manuscript, Yale University, 1969.

Feldman, L. C. Day care programs authorized by HR 12080. Unpublished manuscript, National Committee for the Day Care of Children, Washington, D.C., undated.

Findley, W. G. Early education as continuous stimulation. *Journal of Research and Development in Education,* 1968, **1**(3), 46–50. (a)

Findley, W. G. Research and development center for educational stimulation (3–12). *Journal of Research and Development in Education,* 1969, **1**(4), 68–84. (b)

Flanders, N. A. Some relationships among teacher influence, pupil attitudes, and achievement. In B. J. Biddle, & W. J. Ellena (Eds.), *Contemporary research on teacher effectiveness.* New York: Holt, Rinehart & Winston, 1964. Pp. 196–231.

Flanders, N. A., & Havumaki, S. The effect of teacher-pupil contacts involving praise on the sociometric choices of students. *Journal of Educational Psychology,* 1960, **51**, 65–68.

Flavell, J. H. Role-taking and communication skills in children. In W. W. Hartup & N. L. Smothergill (Eds.), *The young child.* Washington, D. C.: National Association for the Education of Young Children, 1967. Pp. 59–75.

Flavell, J. H. *The development of role-taking and communication skills in children.* New York: Wiley, 1968.

Flavell, J. H. Concept development. In P. H. Mussen (Ed.), *Carmichael's manual of child psychology.* Vol. 1. New York: Wiley, 1970. Pp. 983–1060. (a)

Flavell, J. H. Developmental studies of mediated memory. In H. W. Reese & L. P. Lipsitt (Eds.), *Advances in child development and behavior,* Vol. 5. New York: Academic, 1970. (b)

Fleege, U. H., & others. Montessori pre-school education. Final report. De Paul University, Chicago, 1967. [ERIC No. ED 017 320.]

Fleiss, B. H. The relationship of the mayor's committee on wartime care of children to day care in New York City. Unpublished doctoral dissertation, New York University, School of Education, 1962.

Foley, F. A. Family day care for children. *Children*, 1966, **13**, 141–144.

Forest, I. *Preschool education: A historical and critical study.* New York: Macmillan, 1927.

Fowler, W. Cognitive learning in infancy and early childhood. *Psychological Bulletin*, 1962, **59**, 116–152.

Fowler, W. Progress Report, Ontario Institute for Studies in Education, Toronto, Ont., 1970.

Frank, L. K. Play is valid. *Childhood Education*, 1968, **44**, 433–440.

Fraser, C., Bellugi, U., & Brown, R. Control of grammar in imitation, comprehension, and production. *Journal of Verbal Learning and Verbal Behavior*, 1963, **2**, 121–135.

Freeberg, N. E., & Payne, D. T. Dimensions of parental practice concerned with cognitive development in the preschool child. *Journal of Genetic Psychology*, 1967, **111**, 245–261. (a)

Freeberg, N. E., & Payne, D. T. Parental influence on cognitive-development in early childhood: A review. *Child Development*, 1967, **38**, 65–87. (b)

Freedman, D. Hereditary control of early social behavior. In B. M. Foss (Ed.), *Determinants of infant behavior*. Vol. 3. New York: Wiley, 1965. Pp. 149–160.

Freud, A., & Burlingham, D. *Infants without families.* New York: International Universities Press, 1944.

Freud, A., & Dann, S. An experiment in group upbringing. *Psychoanalytic Study of the Child*, 1951, **6**, 127–168.

Friedlander, B. Z. Receptive language development in infancy: Issues and problems. *Merrill-Palmer Quarterly*, 1970, **16**, 7–51.

Friedlander, B. Z., Cyrulik, A., & Davis, B. Time-sampling analysis of infants' natural language environments in the home. Unpublished manuscript, University of Wisconsin, Madison, Wis., undated.

Furth, H. G. *Thinking without language: Psychological implications of deafness.* New York: Free Press, 1966.

Fuschillo, J. C. Enriching the preschool experience of children from age three. Part 2. The evaluation. *Children*, 1968, **15**, 140–143.

Gagné, R. M. Curriculum research and the promotion of learning. *Area Monograph Series on Curriculum Evaluation, Perspectives of Curriculum Evaluation*. Chicago: Rand McNally, 1967. Pp. 19–38.

Gans, H. J. The subcultures of the working class, lower class and middle class. In H. Miller & M. Smiley (Eds.), *Education in the metropolis*. New York: Free Press, 1967.

Gans, H. J. Three ways to solve the welfare problem. *The New York Times Magazine*, 1971, March 7, 26–27.

Gardner, D. B., Hawkes, G. R., & Burchinal, L. G. Noncontinuous mothering in infancy and development in later childhood. *Child Development*, 1961, **32**, 225–234.

Gardner, D. B., Pease, D., & Hawkes, G. R. Responses of two-year-old children to controlled stress situations. *Journal of Genetic Psychology*, 1961, **98**, 29–35.

Gardner, D. B., & Swiger, M. K. Developmental status of two groups of infants released for adoption. *Child Development*, 1958, **29**, 521–530.

Garfield, S. L., & Helper, M. M. Parental attitudes and socioeconomic status. *Journal of Clinical Psychology*, 1962, **18**, 171–175.

Geber, M. The psychomotor development of African children in the first year and the influence of maternal behavior. *Journal of Social Psychology*, 1958, **47**, 185–195.

Gesell, A. A mental hygiene service for the preschool child. *American Journal of Public Health*, 1922, **12**, 1030–1033.

Gewirtz, J. L. The course of infant smiling in four child-rearing evnironments in Israel. In B. M. Foss (Ed.), *Determinants of infant behavior*. Vol. 3. New York: Wiley, 1965. Pp. 205–260.

Gewirtz, J. L. On designing the functional environment of the child to facilitate behavioral development. In L. L. Dittmann (Ed.), *Early child care: The new perspectives*. New York: Atherton, 1968. Pp. 169–213. (a)

Gewirtz, J. L. The role of stimulation in models for child development. In L. L. Dittmann (Ed.), *Early child care: The new perspectives*. New York: Atherton, 1968. Pp. 139–168. (b)

Gewirtz, J. L. Mechanisms of social learning: Some roles of stimulation and behavior in early human development. In D. A. Coslin (Ed.), *Handbook of socialization theory and research*. Chicago: Rand McNally, 1969. Pp. 57–212.

Gilbert, D. Educational and growth needs of children in day care. *Child Welfare*, 1970, **49**, 17–22.

Gilfillan, V. G. Day care as a therapeutic service to preschool children and its potential as a preventive service. *Child Welfare*, 1962, **41**, 411–416.

Gilmore, J. B. Play: A special behavior. In R. N. Haber (Ed.), *Current research in motivation*. New York: Holt, Rinehart & Winston, 1965. Pp. 343–355.

Glass, N. Eating, sleeping, and elimination habits in children attending day nurseries and children cared for at home by mothers. *American Journal of Orthopsychiatry*, 1949, **19**, 697–711.

Glick, J. Some problems in the evaluation of pre-school intervention programs. In R. D. Hess & R. M. Baer (Eds.), *Early education*. Chicago: Aldine, 1968. Pp. 215–221.

Glucksberg, S., & Krauss, R. M. What do people say after they have learned to talk? Studies of the development of referential communication. *Merrill-Palmer Quarterly*, 1967, **13**, 309–316.

Glucksberg, S., Krauss, R. M., & Weisberg, R. Referential communication in nursery school children: Method and some preliminary findings. *Journal of Experimental Child Psychology*, 1966, **3**, 333–342.

Goldberg, S., & Lewis, M. Play behavior in the year-old infant; Early sex differences. *Child Development*, 1969, **40**, 21–31.

Goldfarb, W. Effects of psychological deprivation in infancy and subsequent stimulation. *American Journal of Psychiatry*, 1945, **102**, 18–33.

Goldsmith, C. A blueprint for a comprehensive community-wide day care program. *Child Welfare*, 1965, **44**, 501–503, 528.

Goodlad, J. I., & Anderson, R. H. *The non-graded elementary school*. New York: Harcourt, Brace, & World, 1959.

Goodman, M. E. *Race awareness in young children*. Cambridge, Mass.: Addison-Wesley, 1952.

Gordon, E. W. Characteristics of socially disadvantaged children. *Review of Educational Research*, 1965, **35**, 377–388.

Gordon, E. Programs of Compensatory Education in M. Deutsch, I. Katz, & A. R. Jensen (Eds.), *Social Class, Race and Psychological Development*. New York: Holt, Rinehart & Winston, 1968. Pp. 381–410.

Gordon, I. J., & associates. Early child stimulation through parent education. Final Report submitted to United States Department of Health, Education and Welfare, Children's Bureau, Social and Rehabilitation Service. PHS-R-306, PHS-R-306(01), June 30, 1969. (a)

Gordon, I. J., & associates. *Reaching the child through parent education. The Florida approach*. Jacksonville, Fla.: Institute for Development of Human Resources, 1969. (b)

Gotkin, L. G. Cognitive development and the issue of individual differences. *Programmed Instruction*, 1963, **3**(1), 1.

Gotkin, L. G. Programmed instruction as a strategy for developing curricula for disadvantaged children. *Monographs of the Society for Research in Child Development*, 1968, **33**(8, Whole No. 124), 19–35.

Gray, S. W., & Klaus, R. A. An experimental preschool for culturally deprived children. *Child Development*, 1965, **36**, 887–898.

Gray, S. W., & Klaus, R. A. The early training project and its general rationale. In R. D. Hess & R. M. Bear (Eds.), *Early education*. Chicago: Aldine, 1968. Pp. 65–76.

Green, E. H. Group play and quarreling among preschool children. *Child Development*, 1933, **4**, 302–307.

Greenberg, P., Uzgiris, I. C., & Hunt, J. McV. Hastening the development of the blink-response with looking. *Journal of Genetic Psychology*, 1968, **113**, 167–176.

Grimes, J., & Allinsmith, W. Compulsivity, anxiety and school achievement. *Merrill-Palmer Quarterly*, 1961, **7**, 247–271.

Gutelius, M. F. Child-rearing attitudes of teen-age Negro girls. *American Journal of Public Health*, 1970, **60**, 93–104.

Haaf, R. A., & Bell, R. Q. A facial dimension in visual discrimination by human infants. *Child Development*, 1967, **38**, 893–899.

Haith, M. M. Day care and intervention programs for infants under two years of age. Unpublished manuscript, Harvard University, 1970.

Hall, G. S. *Aspects of child life and education*. New York: Appleton, 1921.

Hall Neighborhood House. A proposal to establish a child day care training center. Unpublished manuscript, Hall Neighborhood House, Bridgeport, Conn., 1969.

Hanfmann, E. P. Social structure of a group of kindergarten children. *American Journal of Orthopsychiatry*, 1935, **5**, 407–410.

Hansan, J., & Pemberton, K. Day care service for families with mothers working at home. *Child Welfare*, 1963, **42**, 180–184.

Hansan, J. E., & Pemberton, K. Day care: A therapeutic milieu. *Child Welfare*, 1965, **44**, 149–155.

Harris, F. R., Wolf, M. M., & Baer, D. M. Effects of adult social reinforcement on child behavior. In *Teaching the disadvantaged young child*. Washington, D.C.: National Association for the Education of Young Children, 1966. Pp. 7–12.

Hart, B. M., & Risley, T. R. Establishing use of descriptive adjectives in the spontaneous speech of disadvantaged preschool children. *Journal of Applied Behavior Analysis*, 1968, **1**, 109–120.

Hart, L. A. *The classroom disaster*. New York: Teachers College Press, Columbia University, 1969.

Hartley, R. S., Frank, L. K., & Goldenson, R. M. *Understanding children's play*. New York: Columbia University Press, 1952.

Hartup, W. W. Peers as agents of social reinforcement. In W. W. Hartup & N. L. Smothergill (Eds.), *The young child*. Washington, D.C.: National Association for the Education of Young Children, 1967. Pp. 214–228.

Hartup, W. W. Early education and childhood socialization. *Journal of Research and Development in Education*, 1968, **1**(3), 16–29.

Hartup, W. W., & Coates, B. Imitation of a peer as a function of reinforcement from the peer group and rewardingness of the model. *Child Development*, 1967, **38**, 1003–1016.

Harvey, O. J., Prather, M. S., White, B. J., & Alter, R. D. Teachers' belief systems and preschool atmospheres. *Journal of Educational Psychology*, 1966, **57**, 373–381.

Harvey, O. J., Prather, M. S., White, B. J., & Hoffmeister, J. K. Teachers' beliefs, classroom atmosphere, and student behavior. *American Educational Research Journal*, 1968, **5**, 151–166.

Hattwick, B. W. The influence of nursery school attendance upon the behavior and personality of the pre-school child. *Journal of Experimental Education*, 1936, **5**, 180–190.

Hawkins, D. F., Curran, J. R., & Jordan, J. W. Industry related day care: The KLH Child Development Center, Part I. Cambridge, Mass.: KLH, 1969.

Hawkridge, D. G., Chalupsky, A. B., & Roberts, A. O. A study of selected exemplary programs for the education of disadvantaged children, Part I. Final Report, Project No. 089013, American Institutes for Research in the Behavioral Sciences, Contract No. OEC-0-8-089013-3515 (010), United States Department of Health, Education and Welfare, 1968.

Heathers, G. Emotional dependence and independence in nursery school play. *Journal of Genetic Psychology*, 1955, **87**, 37–58.

Hebb, D. O. The effects of early experience on problem-solving as maturity. *American Psychologist*, 1947, **2**, 386–387.

Hebb, D. O. *Organization of behavior*. New York: Wiley, 1949.

Heil, L. M., Powell, M., & Feifer, I. Characteristics of teacher behavior related to the achievement of children in several elementary grades. Washington, D.C.: United States Department of Health, Education, and Welfare, Office of Education, Cooperative Research Branch, 1960. Cited by P. S. Sears & E. R. Hilgard, The teacher's role in the motivation of the learner. In *Theories of learning and instruction, Sixty-third Yearbook of the National Society for the Study of Education*, Part I. Chicago: University of Chicago Press, 1964. Pp. 202–207.

Heinicke, C. M. Some effects of separating two-year-old children from their parents: A comparative study. *Human Relations*, 1956, **9**, 105–176.

Heinicke, C. M., & Westheimer, I. *Brief separations*. New York: International Universities Press, 1965.

Heinstein, M. I. Behavioral correlates of breast-bottle regimes under varying parent-infant relationships. *Monographs of the Society for Research in Child Development*, 1963, **28**, (4, Whole No. 88).

316 REFERENCES

Hellmuth, J. (Ed.), *Disadvantaged child*. Vol. 3. *Compensatory education: A national debate.* New York: Brunner/Mazel, 1970.

Herzog, E. *About the poor*. Washington, D. C.: U. S. Department of Health, Education and Welfare, Children's Bureau Publication No. 451, 1967.

Hess, R. D. Techniques for assessing cognitive and social abilities of children and parents in Project Head Start. Report Number 0E0-519. University of Chicago, July 1966.

Hess, R. D. Parental behavior and children's school achievement. In E. Grotberg (Ed.), *Critical issues in research related to disadvantaged children*. Princeton, N. J.: Educational Testing Service, 1969.

Hess, R. D., & Bear, R. M. (Eds.), *Early education*. Chicago: Aldine, 1968.

Hess, R. D., & Shipman, V. C. Early experience and the socialization of cognitive modes in children. *Child Development,* 1965, **34**, 869–886.

Hess, R. D., & Shipman, V. C. Maternal attitude toward the school and the role of the pupil: Some social class comparisons. Paper prepared for the Fifth Work Conference on Curriculum and Teaching in Depressed Urban Areas, Columbia University Teachers College, New York, June 1966.

Hess, R. D., Shipman, V. C., Brophy, J. E., Bear, R. M., & Adelberger, A. B. *The cognitive environments of urban preschool children: Follow-up phase*. Chicago: University of Chicago Graduate School of Education, 1969.

Hest, M. S. A broad community approach to day care. *Child Welfare,* 1960, **39**(2), 29–32.

Hicks, D. J. Imitation and retention of film-mediated aggressive peer and adult models. *Journal of Personality and Social Psychology,* 1965, **2**, 97–106.

Hodges, W. L., McCandless, B. R., & Spicker, H. H. *The development and evaluation of a diagnostically based curriculum for preschool psychosocially deprived children*. Washington, D. C.: United States Department of Health, Education and Welfare, 1967.

Hodges, W. L., & Spicker, H. H. The effects of preschool experiences on culturally deprived children. In W. W. Hartup & N. L. Smothergill (Eds.), *The young child*. Washington, D. C.: National Association for the Education of Young Children, 1967. Pp. 262–290.

Hoffman, M. L. Power assertion by the parent and its impact on the child. *Child Development,* 1960, **31**, 129–143.

Hofstadter, R. *Anti-intellectualism in American life*. New York: Knopf, 1963.

Holmes, D., & Holmes, M. B. An evaluation of differences among different classes of Head Start participants. Final Report. Associated YM-YWAS of Greater New York. OEO 1271, Office of Economic Opportunity, 1966.

Holmes, F. B. An experimental study of the fears of young children. In A. T. Jersild & F. B. Holmes, Children's fears. *Child Development Monographs,* 1935, 20.

Holzman, M. Characterization of the verbal environment provided by mothers for their young children. Paper presented at the meeting of the Society for Research in Child Development, Santa Monica, March 1969.

Honzik, M. P. Environmental correlates of mental growth: Prediction from the family setting at 21 months. *Child Development,* 1967, **38**, 337–364.

Horowitz, E. L. The development of attitude toward the Negro. *Archives of Psychology,* 1936, No. 194.

Horowitz, F. D. Incentive value of social stimuli for preschool children. *Child Development,* 1962, **33**, 111–116.

Hosley, E. M. Culturally deprived children in day-care programs. *Children*, 1963, **10**, 175–179.

Hosley, E. M. A joint approach in working with parents. *Child Welfare*, 1964, **43**, 187–191.

Hotkins, A. S., Hollander, L., & Munk, B. Evaluation of psychiatric reports of Head Start programs. In J. Hellmuth (Ed.), Disadvantaged child, Vol. 2. New York: Brunner/Mazel, 1968. Pp. 137–172.

Howard, A. F. *Characteristics of early childhood teacher education*. Washington, D.C.: Association for Childhood Education International, 1968.

Hull, W. P. Leicestershire revisited. Unpublished manuscript, 1964.

Hulson, E. L. An analysis of the free play of ten four-year-old children through consecutive observations. *Journal of Juvenile Research*, 1930, **14**, 188–208. (a)

Hulson, E. L. Block constructions of four-year-old children. *Journal of Juvenile Research*, 1930, **15**, 209–222. (b)

Humphrey, J. H. Comparison of the use of active games and language workbook exercises as learning media in the development of language understandings with third grade children. *Perceptual Motor Skills*, 1965, **21**, 23–26.

Humphrey, J. H. An exploratory study of active games in learning of number concepts by first grade boys and girls. *Perceptual Motor Skills*, 1966, **23**, 341–342.

Hunt, J. McV. How children develop intellectually. *Children*, 1964, **11**, 83–91. (a)

Hunt, J. McV. The psychological basis for using pre-school enrichment as an antidote for cultural deprivation. *Merrill-Palmer Quarterly*, 1964, **10**, 209–248. (b)

Hunt, J. McV. Traditional personality theory in the light of recent evidence. *American Scientist*, 1965, **53**, 80–96.

Hunt, J. McV. The epigenesis of intrinsic motivation and early cognitive learning. In R. N. Haber (Ed.), *Current research in motivation*. New York: Holt, Rinehart & Winston, 1966. Pp. 345–354.

Hunt, J. McV. (Chairman), *A bill of rights for children*. Report of the President's task force on early childhood development. Unpublished manuscript. Urbana, Ill.: 1967. (a)

Hunt, J. McV. Conceptions of learning with implications for styles of teaching young children. Paper presented at the conference of the Office of Education's Tri-University Project. Denver, Colorado, September, 1967. (b)

Hunt, J. McV. Has compensatory education failed? Has it been attempted? *Harvard Educational Review*, 1969, **39**, 278–300. (a)

Hunt, J. McV. Toward the prevention of incompetence. In J. McV. Hunt, *The challenge of incompetence and poverty*. Urbana, Ill.: University of Illinois Press, 1969. (b)

Hurlock, E. B. Experimental investigations of childhood play. *Psychological Bulletin*, 1934, **31**, 47–66.

Huttenlocker, J., & Strauss, S. Comprehension and a statement's relation to the situation it describes. *Journal of Verbal Learning and Verbal Behavior*, 1968, **7**(2), 300–304.

Hymes, J. L. The job ahead: Quality in young children's living. *Journal of Research and Development in Education*, 1968, **1**(3), 51–57. (a)

Hymes, J. L. *Teaching the child under six*. Columbus, Ohio: Merrill, 1968. (b)

Illinois Department of Children and Family Services. Special report to the Governor: Day-care services for children in Illinois. *Perspective*, 1969, **5**(4).

Inkeles, A. Social structure and the socialization of competence. *Harvard Educational Review*, 1966, **36**, 265–283.

Irwin, O. C. Infant speech: The effect of family occupational status and of age on sound frequency. *Journal of Speech and Hearing Disorders*, 1948, **13**, 320–323. (a)

Irwin, O. C. Infant speech: The effect of family occupational status and of age on use of sound types. *Journal of Speech and Hearing Disorders*, 1948, **13**, 224–226. (b)

Irwin, O. C. Infant speech: The effect of systematic reading of stories. *Journal of Speech and Hearing Research*, 1960, **3**, 187–190.

Isaacs, S. *Social development in young children: A study of beginnings.* New York: Harcourt, Brace & World, 1933.

Jack, L. M. An experimental study of ascendant behavior in preschool children. *University of Iowa Studies in Child Welfare*, 1934, **9**, 7–65.

Jensen, A. R. Social class and perceptual learning. *Mental Hygiene*, 1966, **50**, 226–239.

Jensen, A. R. Social class and verbal learning. In M. Deutsch, I. Katz, & A. R. Jensen (Eds.), *Social class, race, and psychological development.* New York: Holt, Rinehart & Winston, 1968. Pp. 115–174.

Jensen, A. R. How much can we boost IQ and scholastic achievement? *Harvard Educational Review*, 1969, **39**, 1–123.

Jensen, A. R. Another look at culture-fair testing. In J. Hellmuth (Ed.), *Disadvantaged child*, Vol. 3, *Compensatory education: A national debate.* New York: Brunner/Mazel, 1970. Pp. 53–101.

Jersild, A. T. *Child psychology.* (5th ed.) Englewood Cliffs, N.J.: Prentice-Hall, 1960.

Jersild, A. T., & Fite, M. D. The influence of nursery school experience on children's social adjustments. *Child Development Monographs*, 1939, No. 25.

Jersild, A. T., & Markey, F. V. Conflicts between preschool children. *Child Development Monographs*, 1935, No. 21.

Joel, W. The influence of nursery school education upon behavior maturity. *Journal of Experimental Education*, 1939, **8**, 164–165.

John, V. P. The intellectual development of slum children: Some preliminary findings. *American Journal of Orthopsychiatry*, 1963, **33**, 813–822.

John, V. P. A brief survey of research on the characteristics of children from low-income backgrounds. Paper prepared for the United States Commissioner on Education. August, 1964. (a)

John, V. P., & Goldstein, L. S. The social context of language acquisition. *Merrill-Palmer Quarterly*, 1964, **10**, 265–276.

John, V. P., & Horner, V. M. Bilingualism and the Spanish speaking child. In F. Williams (Ed.), *Language and Poverty.* Chicago: Markham, 1970.

Johnson, M. W. The effect on behavior of variation in the amount of play equipment. *Child Development*, 1935, **6**, 56–68. (a)

Johnson, M. W. The influence of verbal directions on behavior. *Child Development*, 1935, **6**, 196–204. (b)

Jones, E. Curriculum planning in early childhood education. In L. L. Dittmann (Ed.), *Curriculum is what happens.* Washington, D.C.: National Association for the Education of Young Children, 1970, Pp. 4–6.

Juniper Gardens Parent Cooperative Nursery. Final progress report: OEO Grant CG-8474-A/O Juniper Gardens Children's Project, Kansas City, Missouri, 1968. [ERIC No. ED 032 920.]

Kagan, J. On cultural deprivation. In D. C. Glass (Ed.), *Environmental influences.* New York: Rockefeller University & Russell Sage Foundation, 1968. Pp. 211–250.

Kagan, J. *Change and continuity in infancy.* New York: Wiley, 1971.

Kagan, J., & Freeman, M. Relation of childhood intelligence, maternal behaviors and social class to behavior during adolescence. *Child Development,* 1963, **34,** 899–911.

Kagan, J., & Kogan, N. Individuality and cognitive performance. In P. H. Mussen (Ed.), *Carmichael's manual of child psychology.* Vol. 1. New York: Wiley, 1970. Pp. 1273–1365.

Kahn, A. J. Therapy, prevention and developmental provision: A social work strategy. In *Public health concepts in social work education.* Princeton, N.J.: Princeton University, 1962. Pp. 132–148.

Kahn, A. J. The citizen's role in social welfare policy. *Children,* 1963, **10,** 185–187.

Kamii, C. K., & Radin, N. L. Class differences in the socialization practices of Negro mothers. *Journal of Marriage and the Family,* 1967, **29,** 302–310.

Kamii, C. K., & Radin, N. L. A framework for a preschool curriculum based on Piaget's theory. Unpublished manuscript, Ypsilanti Public Schools, Ypsilanti, Mich., 1968.

Karnes, M. S., Hodgins, A. S., Teska, J. A., & Kirk, S. A. *Research and development program on preschool disadvantaged children.* Vol. 1. Project No. 5-1181. Contract No. OE 6-10-235, May 1969. United States Department of Health, Education and Welfare, Office of Education, Bureau of Research.

Karnes, M. B., Hodgins, A., & Teska, J. A. An evaluation of two preschool programs for disadvantaged children: A traditional and a highly structured experimental preschool. *Exceptional Children,* 1968, **34,** 667–676.

Katkovsky, W., Crandall, V., & Good, S. Parental antecedents of children's beliefs in internal-external control of reinforcements in intellectual achievement situations. *Child Development,* 1967, **38,** 765–776.

Katz, L. G. Teaching in preschools: Roles and goals. *Children,* 1970, **17,** 42–48.

Katz, L. G., & Weir, M. K. Staffing preschools: Background information. Paper presented at the annual meeting of the Association for Supervision and Curriculum Development, Chicago, March 1969.

Kawin, E., & Hoefer, C. *A comparative study of nursery-school vs. non-nursery school groups.* Chicago: University of Chicago Press, 1931.

Kay, H. H. The outside substitute for the family. In S. M. Farber, P. Mustacchi, & R. H. L. Wilson (Eds.), *Man and civilization: The family's search for survival.* New York: McGraw-Hill, 1965. Pp. 3–15.

Keister, M. E. A demonstration project in group care of infants. Progress Report, November 1, 1968, Research Division. United States Department of Health, Education and Welfare, Children's Bureau.

Keister, M. E. *"The good life" for infants and toddlers.* Washington, D.C.: National Association for the Education of Young Children, 1970.

Kendler, T. S. Development of mediating responses in children. In J. C. Wright & J. Kagan (Eds.), *Basic cognitive processes in children. Monographs of the Society for Research and Child Development,* 1963, **28** (2, Whole No. 86), 33–47.

Kennedy, A. J. The settlement heritage. An address at the National Science Foundation General Session, National Conference of Social Work, Cleveland, June 1953.

Kennedy, W. A. A follow-up normative study of Negro intelligence and achievement. *Monographs of the Society for Research in Child Development*, 1969, **34** (2, Whole No. 126).

Kessen, W. (Ed.) *The child*. New York: Wiley, 1965.

Kessen, W. Questions for a theory of cognitive development. In H. W. Stevenson (Ed.), Concept of development. *Monographs of the Society for Research in Child Development*, 1966, **31** (5, Whole No. 107), 55–70.

Kessen, W. The near future of research with young children. Unpublished manuscript, Yale University, 1970.

Kessen, W., Haith, M. M., & Salapatek, P. H. Human infancy: A bibliography and guide. In P. H. Mussen (Ed.), *Carmichael's manual of child psychology*. New York: Wiley, 1970. Pp. 287–446.

Kessen, W., & Mandler, G. Anxiety, pain, and inhibition of distress. *Psychology Review*, 1961, **68**, 396–404.

Keyserling, M. D. The nation's working mothers and the need for day care. Address at the National Conference on Day-Care Services, Washington, D.C., May 1965.

Kirk, S. A. *Early education of the mentally retarded*. Urbana, Ill.: University of Illinois Press, 1958.

Kirschner Associates. *A national survey of the impacts of Head Start centers on community institutions*. May 1970, Contract Number B89-4638, Report prepared for the United States Department of Health, Education and Welfare, Office of Child Development. (a)

Kirschner Associates. *A national survey of the Parent-Child Center program*. March 1970, Contract No. B89-4557. Report prepared for the United States Department of Health, Education and Welfare, Office of Child Development, Project Head Start. (b)

Klaus, R. A., & Gray, S. W. The Early Training Project for disadvantaged children: A report after five years. *Monographs of the Society for Research in Child Development*, 1968, **33** (4, Whole No. 120).

Kluckholm, H. R. Family diagnosis: Variations in the basic values of family systems. *Social Casework*, Feb.–Mar., 1958, 63–85.

Knight, E. V. *Serving the pre-school child: Day care as a service to the entire family*. New York: National Federation of Settlements and Neighborhood Centers, 1966.

Koch, H. L. Some personality correlates of sex, sibling position, and sex of sibling among five- and six-year old children. *Genetic Psychological Monographs*, 1955, **52**, 3–50.

Koch, H. L. The relation in young children between characteristics of their playmates and certain attributes of their siblings. *Child Development*, 1957, **28**, 175–202.

Kohl, H. *36 Children*. New York: New American Library, 1967.

Kohlberg, L. Early education: A cognitive-developmental view. *Child Development*, 1968, **39**, 1013–1062.

Kohlberg, L. Stage and sequence: The cognitive-developmental approach to socialization. In D. A. Goslin (Ed.), *Handbook of socialization theory and research*. Chicago: Rand McNally, 1969. Pp. 347–480.

Kohlberg, L., & Mayer, R. S. Preschool research and preschool educational objectives; a critique and a proposal. Unpublished manuscript, Harvard University, 1970.

Kohlberg, L., Yaeger, J., & Hjertholm, E. Private speech: Four studies and a review of theories. *Child Development*, 1968, **39**, 691–736.

Kohn, M. L. Social class and the exercise of parental authority. *American Sociological Review*, 1959, **24**, 362–366. (a)

Kohn, M. L. Social class and parental values. *The American Journal of Sociology*, 1959, **64**, 337–351. (b)

Kohn, M. L., & Carroll, E. E. Social class and the allocation of parental responsibilities. *Sociometry*, 1960, **23**, 372–392.

Kounin, J. S., & Gump, P. V. The ripple effect in discipline. *Elementary School Journal*, 1958, **59**, 158–162.

Kozol, J. *Death at an early age*. Boston: Houghton Mifflin, 1967.

Kraft, I. *When teenagers take care of children*. Washington, D.C.: United States Department of Health, Education and Welfare, Children's Bureau Publication, Number 409, 1964.

Kraft, I., Fuschillo, J., & Herzog, E. *Prelude to school: An evaluation of an inner-city preschool program*. Washington, D.C.: U. S. Department of Health, Education and Welfare, Social and Rehabilitation Service, Children's Bureau, 1968.

Krauss, R. M., & Glucksberg, S. The development of communication: Competence as a function of age. *Child Development*, 1969, **40**, 255–266.

Krauss, R. M., & Rotter, G. S. Communication abilities of children as a function of status and age. *Merrill-Palmer Quarterly*, 1968, **14**, 161–173.

Kritchevsky, S., Prescott, E., & Walling, L. *Planning environments for young children*. Washington, D.C.: National Association for the Education of Young Children, 1969.

Kuhn, A. L. *The mother's role in childhood education. New England concepts 1830–1860*. New Haven, Conn.: Yale University Press, 1947.

Labov, W. *The social stratification of English in New York City*. Washington, D.C.: Center for Applied Linguistics, 1966.

Labov, W. The logic of nonstandard English. In F. Williams (Ed.), *Language and poverty*. Chicago: Markham, 1970. Pp. 153–189.

LaCivita, A. F., Kean, J. M., & Yamamoto, K. Socio-economic status of children and acquisition of grammar. *Journal of Educational Research*, 1966, **60**, 71–74.

LaCrosse, E. R. Day care: effects and affects. Unpublished manuscript, Pacific Oaks College, Pasadena, Calif., 1970.

Landreth, C., & Johnson, B. C. Young children's responses to a picture inset test designed to reveal reactions to persons of different skin color. *Child Development*, 1953, **24**, 63–80.

Larrabee, M. M. Involving parents in their children's day-care experiences. *Children*, 1969, **16**, 149–154.

Lavatelli, C. B. A Piaget-derived model for compensatory preschool education. In J. L. Frost (Ed.), *Early childhood education rediscovered*. New York: Holt, Rinehart & Winston, 1968. Pp. 530–544. (a)

Lavatelli, C. B. Environmental intervention in infancy and childhood. In M. Deutsch, I. Katz, & A. R. Jensen (Eds.), *Social class, race, and psychological development*. New York: Holt, Rinehart & Winston, 1968. Pp. 347–381. (b)

Law, N. What are nursery schools for? Association for Childhood Education International, *Membership Service Bulletin*, No. G. 19, 1964.

Lenneberg, E. H. On explaining language. In S. Chess & A. Thomas (Eds.), *Annual progress in child psychiatry and child development*. New York: Brunner/Mazel, 1970. Pp. 104–125.

Leopold, W. F. *Speech development of a bilingual child; a linguist's record.* Vol. 3. *Grammar and general problems in the first two years*. Evanston, Ill.: Northwestern University Press, 1949.

Lesser, G. S., Fifer, G., & Clark, D. H. Mental abilities of children from different social-class and cultural groups. *Monographs of the Society for Research in Child Development*, 1965, **30** (4, Whole No. 102).

Levenstein, P. Cognitive growth in preschoolers through verbal interaction with mothers. *American Journal of Orthopsychiatry*, 1970, **40**, 426–432.

Levenstein, P., & Sunley, R. An effect of stimulating verbal interaction between mothers and children around play materials. Paper presented at 44th Annual Meeting, American Orthopsychiatric Association. Washington, D.C., March 1967. (Republished: *American Journal of Orthopsychiatry*, 1968, **38**, 116–121.)

Levin, T. Preschool education and the communities of the poor. In J. Hellmuth (Ed.), *Disadvantaged child*. Vol. I. New York: Brunner/Mazel, 1967. Pp. 348–468.

Lewis, E. *Deprived children*. London: Oxford University Press, 1954.

Lewis, H. Child rearing practices among low income families in the District of Columbia. Adapted from a paper presented at the National Conference on Social Welfare, Minneapolis, May 1961.

Lewis, H. Child rearing among low-income families. In L. Herman, (Ed.), *Poverty in America*. Ann Arbor, Mich.: University of Michigan Press, 1965. Pp. 342–353.

Lewis, M. M. *Infant Speech*. New York: Humanities, 1951.

Lewis, M., & Goldberg, S. Perceptual-cognitive development in infancy: A generalized expectancy model as a function of the mother-infant interaction. Unpublished manuscript, National Institute of Mental Health, Washington, D.C., 1968.

Lieberman, J. N. Playfulness and divergant thinking: An investigation of their relationship at the kindergarten level. *Journal of Genetic Psychology*, 1965, **107**, 219–224.

Littman, R. A., Moore, R. C., & Pierce-Jones, J. Social class differences in child rearing: A third community for comparison between Chicago and Newton. *American Sociological Review*, 1957, **22**, 694–704.

Littner, N. *Primary needs of young children: A one-to-one relationship*. New York: Child Welfare League of America, 1959.

Loban, W. D. *The language of elementary school children*. Champaign, Ill.: National Council of Teachers of English, 1963.

Low, S., & Spindler, P. G. *Child care arrangements of working mothers in the United States*. U. S. Department of Health, Education and Welfare, Children's Bureau Publication No. 461, 1968.

Lowenfeld, M. A new approach to the problem of psychoneurosis in childhood. *British Journal of Medical Psychology*, 1931, **11**, 194–227.

Luria, A. R. *The role of speech in the regulation of normal and abnormal behavior*. New York: Pergamon, 1961 (Russian edition, 1956).

Luria, A. R. Speech development and the formation of mental processes. In M. Cole & I. Maltzman (Eds.), *A handbook of contemporary Soviet psychology*. New York: Basic Books, 1969. Pp. 121–162.

Luria, A. R., & Yudovich, R. *Speech and the development of mental processes in the child.* London: Staples Press, 1959.

Maccoby, E. E., Gibbs, P. K., & the Staff of the Laboratory of Human Development, Harvard University. Methods of child-rearing in two social classes. In W. E. Martin & C. B. Stendler (Eds.), *Readings in child development.* New York: Harcourt, Brace & World, 1954. Pp. 380–396.

Maccoby, E. E., & Masters, J. C. Attachment and dependency. In P. Mussen (Ed.), *Carmichael's manual of child psychology.* Vol. 2. New York: Wiley, 1970. Pp. 73–158.

Maccoby, E. E., & Zellner, M. Disadvantaged children in elementary school: Contrasting viewpoints and experimental procedures in "Project Follow Through." Unpublished manuscript, Stanford University, 1970.

Mahan, A. M. & Mahan, T. W. Changes in cognitive style: An analysis of the impact of white suburban schools on inner-city children. *Proceedings of the American Psychological Association,* 1969, **4**, 681–682.

Marans, A. E., & Lourie, R. Hypotheses regarding the effects of child-rearing patterns on the disadvantaged child. In J. Hellmuth (Ed.), *Disadvantaged child.* Vol. 1. New York: Brunner/Mazel, 1967. Pp. 17–41.

Marge, M. The influence of selected home background variables on the development of oral communication skills in children. *Journal of Speech and Hearing Research,* 1965, **8**, 291–309.

Markey, F. V. Imaginative behavior of preschool children. *Child Development Monographs,* 1935, No. 18.

Markle, S. Empirical testing of programs. In P. Lange (Ed.), *The sixty-sixth yearbook of the National Society for the Study of Education,* Chicago: National Society for the Study of Education, 1967.

Marshall, H. R. Relations between home experience and children's use of language in play interactions with peers. *Psychological Monographs,* 1961, **75**, No. 509.

Marshall, H. R. & McCandless, B. R. A study in prediction of social behavior of preschool children. *Child Development,* 1957, **28**, 149–159.

Marshall, H. R., & Shwu, C. H. Experimental modification of dramatic play. Paper presented at the Convention of the American Psychological Association, New York, September 1966.

Martin, W. Singularity and stability of social behavior. In C. B. Stendler (Ed.), *Readings in child behavior and development.* New York: Harcourt, Brace & World, 1964. Pp. 358–367.

Mattick, I. Adaptation of nursery school techniques to deprived children. *Journal of the American Academy of Child Psychiatry,* 1965, **4**, 670–700.

Mayer, A. E., & Kahn, A. J. *Day care as a social instrument: A policy paper.* Unpublished manuscript, Columbia University School of Social Work, 1965.

Mayer, G., Krim, A., & Papell, C. Contributions to staff development in understanding the needs of children and their families. *Child Welfare,* 1965, **44**, 143–148.

McAfee, O. The right words. *Young Children,* 1967, **23**(2).

McAffee, O. An oral language program for early childhood. Unpublished manuscript, Colorado State College, Greeley, Colorado, 1968.

McAfee, O., Himnicht, G., & Maden, T. *The new nursery school: Learning activities booklets.* New York: General Learning Corporation, 1969.

McCaffrey, A. Communicative competence and the disadvantaged child. Progress Reports No. 3 and 4, Harvard Graduate School of Education, 1970.

McCall, R. B. Addendum to Individuality and cognitive performance. In P. H. Mussen (Ed.), *Carmichael's manual of child psychology.* New York: Wiley, 1970. Pp. 1366–1377.

McCandless, B. R., & Hoyt, J. M. Sex, ethnicity, and play preferences of preschool children. *Journal of Abnormal and Social Psychology,* 1961, **62**, 683-685.

McCandless, B. R., & Marshall, H. R. A picture technique for preschool children and its relation to teacher judgments of friendship. *Child Development,* 1957, **28**, 139–147.

McCarthy, D. Language development in children. In L. Carmichael (Ed.), *Manual of child psychology.* (2nd ed.) New York: Wiley, 1954. Pp. 492–630.

McClure, S. C. The effect of varying verbal instructions on the motor responses of preschool children. *Child Development,* 1936, **7**, 276-290.

McDermott, M. T. The challenge of day care. *Child Welfare,* 1967, **46**, 32–34.

McNamara, J. R., Porterfield, C. L., Miller, L. E., & Arnold, H. S. *Evaluation of the effects of Head Start experience in the press of self-concept social skills, and language skills.* Dade County, Fla.: Dade County Board of Public Instruction, 1968.

McNeill, D. The development of language. In P. H. Mussen (Ed.), *Carmichael's Manual of child psychology.* Vol. 2. New York: Wiley, 1970. Pp. 1061–1162.

Mead, M. A cultural anthropologist's approach to maternal deprivation. *Public Health Papers,* 1962, **14**, 45–62.

Mead, M. The changing American family. *Children,* 1963, **10**, 173–174.

Medley, D. M., & Mitzel, H. E. Measuring classroom behavior by systematic observation. In N. L. Gage (Ed.), *Handbook of research and teaching.* Chicago: Rand McNally, 1965. Pp. 247–328.

Meers, D. R., & Marans, A. E. Group care of infants in other countries. In L. L. Dittmann (Ed.), *Early child care: The new perspectives.* New York: Atherton, 1968. Pp. 237–282.

Meier, J. H., Nimnicht, G., & McAfee, O. An autotelic responsive environment nursery school for deprived children. In J. Hellmuth (Ed.), *Disadvantaged child.* Vol. 2. New York: Brunner/Mazel, 1968. Pp. 299–398.

Merei, F. Group leadership and institutionalization. *Human Relations,* 1949, **2**, 23–39.

Messick, S. Evaluation of educational programs as research on educational process. Paper presented at the meeting of the American Psychological Association. Washington, D.C., September 1969.

Meyer, C. H. The impact of urbanization on child welfare. *Child Welfare,* 1967, **46**, 433–442.

Migrant Child Care Center, Department of Public Welfare, Bureau of Children's Services, Commonwealth of Pennsylvania. What can we do for migrant children? *Child Welfare,* 1958, **37**(3), 24–26.

Milio, N. *9226 Kercheval.* Ann Arbor, Mich.: University of Michigan Press, 1970.

Millar, S. *The psychology of play.* Baltimore, Md.: Penguin, 1968.

Miller, J. O. *Diffusion of intervention effects in disadvantaged families.* Urbana, Ill.: ERIC, National Laboratory on Early Childhood Education, 1968.

Miller, J. O. *Review of selected intervention research with young children.* Urbana, Ill.: ERIC, National Laboratory on Early Childhood Education, 1969.

Miller, J. O. An educational imperative and its fallout implications. In J. Hellmuth (Ed.),

Disadvantaged child. Vol. 3. *Compensatory education: A national debate.* New York: Brunner/Mazel, 1970. Pp. 36–50.

Miller, L. B., & Associates. Experimental variation of Head Start curricula: A comparison of current approaches. Progress Report No. 7, 1970. University of Kentucky, Louisville, Kentucky. Research Grant #CG 8199, Office of Economic Opportunity.

Miller, L. B., & Dyer, J. L. Experimental variation of Head Start curricula: A comparison of current approaches. Annual progress report. May 13, 1970. Child Development Laboratory, University of Kentucky, Louisville, Kentucky. Research Grant #CG 8199, Office of Economic Opportunity.

Miller, N. E., & Dollard, J. *Social learning and imitation.* New Haven: Yale University Press, 1941.

Milliken, M. E. *The care of infants and young children.* Raleigh, N.C.: North Carolina State Board of Education, 1967. [ERIC No. ED 013 289.]

Milner, E. A study of the relationship between reading readiness in grade one school children and patterns of parent-child interaction. *Child Development,* 1951, **22**, 95–112.

Minuchin, P., & Biber, B. A child development approach to language in the preschool disadvantaged child. *Monographs of the Society for Research in Child Development,* 1968, **33**(8, Whole No. 124), 10–18.

Montessori, M. *The Montessori method.* Cambridge, Mass.: Robert Bentley, 1967.

Moore, O. K. Autotelic-responsive environments and exceptional children. In O. J. Harvey (Ed.), *Experience, structure and adaptability.* New York: Springer, 1966.

Moore, O. K., & Anderson, A. R. Some principles for the design of clarifying educational environments. In D. A. Goslin (Ed.), *Handbook of socialization theory and research.* Chicago: Rand McNally, 1969. Pp. 571–614.

Moore, S., & Updegraff, R. Sociometric status of pre-school children related to age, sex, nurturance-giving dependency. *Child Development,* 1964, **35**, 519–524.

Moore, S. B. The use of commands, suggestions, and requests by nursery school and kindergarten teachers. *Child Development,* 1938, **9**, 185–201.

Moss, H. A. Sex, age, and state as determinants of mother-infant interaction. *Merrill-Palmer Quarterly,* 1967, **13**, 19–36.

Moss, H. A., & Robson, K. S. Maternal influence in early social visual behavior. *American Journal of Orthopsychiatry,* 1967, **37**, 394–395.

Moss, H. A., Robson, K. S., & Pederson, F. Determinants of maternal stimulation of infants and consequences of treatment for later reactions to strangers. *Developmental Psychology,* 1969, **1**, 239–246.

Mowrer, O. H. *Learning theory and the symbolic process.* New York: Wiley, 1960.

Moyer, K. E., & Gilmer, B. H. Attention span for experimentally designed toys. *Journal of Genetic Psychology,* 1955, **87**, 187–201.

Moynihan, D. *Negro family: The case for national action.* Washington, D.C.: Office of Policy Planning and Research, U.S. Department of Labor, 1965.

Munsinger, H., & Kessen, W. Stimulus variability and cognitive change. *Psychological Review,* 1966, **73**, 164–178.

Murphy, G., Murphy, L. B., & Newcomb, T. M. *Experimental social psychology* (Rev. ed.), New York: Harper, 1937.

Murphy, L. B. *Social behavior and child personality.* New York: Columbia University, 1937.

Murphy. L. B. *The widening world of childhood*. New York: Basic Books, 1962.

Murphy, L. B. Assessment of infants and young children. In L. L. Dittmann (Ed.), *Early child care: The new perspectives*. New York: Atherton, 1968. Pp. 107–138. (a)

Murphy, L. B. The consultant in a day-care center for deprived children. *Children*, 1968, **15**, 97–102. (b)

Murphy, L. B. Individualization of child care and its relation to environment. In L. L. Dittmann (Ed.), *Early child care: The new perspectives*. New York: Atherton, 1968. Pp. 68–104. (c)

Murphy, L. B. Multiple factors in learning in the day care center. *Childhood Education*, 1969, **45**, 311–320.

National Association of Day Nurseries. Historical sketch of the day nursery movement. New York: NADN, 1940.

Nehrt, R. C., & Hurd, G. E. *Preprimary enrollment of children under six: October 1968*. Washington, D.C.: United States Department of Health, Education and Welfare, Office of Education, 1968.

Nellum, A. L., & Associates. Evaluation of employer-sponsored child day care center for children of Department of Labor employees. Final Report. National Capital Area Child Day Care Association, Washington, D.C., September 1969.

Nelson, K. Presynactical strategies for learning to talk. Paper presented at the conference of the Society for Research in Child Development, Minneapolis, March 1971.

Neubauer, P. B. Children in collectives: *Child-rearing aims and practices in the kibbutz*. Springfield, Ill.: Thomas, 1965.

New York University Institute for Developmental Studies. *Progress Report. Research program in early childhood education*. New York: New York University, 1968.

Nimnicht, G. Research on the new nursery, Part 1. A summary of the evaluation of the experimental program for deprived children at the New Nursery School using some experimental measures. Colorado State College, Greeley, Colorado, 1967.

Nimnicht, G. The responsive program Unpublished manuscript, Far West Laboratory for Educational Research and Development, 1970.

Nimnicht, G., McAffee, O., & Meier, J. *The new nursery school*. New York: General Learning Corporation, 1969.

North, A. F. Pediatric care in Project Head Start. In J. Hellmuth (Ed.), *Disadvantaged child*. Vol. 2. *Head Start and early intervention*. New York: Brunner/Mazel, 1968. Pp. 93–124.

O'Brien, R. A., & Lopate, P. *Preschool programs and the intellectual development of disadvantaged children*. Urbana, Ill.: ERIC Clearinghouse on Early Childhood Education, 1968. [ED 024 473.]

Ogburn, W. F. The changing functions of the family. In R. F. Winch (Ed.), *Selected studies in marriage and the family*. New York: Holt, Rinehart & Winston, 1953. Pp. 74–80.

Olin, E. G., Hess, R. D., & Shipman, V. C. Role of mothers' language styles in mediating their preschool children's cognitive development. *The School Review*, 1967, **75**, 414–424.

Olson, W. C., & Hughes, B. O. Subsequent growth of children with and without nursery school experience. *Yearbook of the National Society for Studies in Education*, Part II, 1940, **39**, 237–244.

Orlansky, H. Infant care and personality. In W. E. Martin & C. B. Stendler (Eds.), *Readings in child development*. New York: Harcourt, Brace & World, 1954. Pp. 321–336.

Owen, R. *Life of Robert Owen, written by himself.* London: G. Bell, 1920.

Painter, G. *Infant education.* San Rafael, Calif.: Dimensions, 1968.

Palmer, F. H. Comparative intellective performance of Negro, Puerto Rican and white three-year-old males. Unpublished manuscript, State University of New York, Stony Brook, New York, 1969. (a)

Palmer, F. H. Learning at two. *Children,* 1969, **16,** 55–56. (b)

Palmer, F. H. Socioeconomic status and intellective performance among Negro preschool boys. *Developmental Psychology,* 1970, **3,** 1–9.

Palmer, F. H. Minimal intervention at age two and three and subsequent intellective changes. In R. K. Parker (Ed.), *Conceptualizations in preschool curricula.* Boston: Allyn & Bacon, in press.

Palmer, F. H., & Rees, A. H. Concept training in two-year-olds: Procedures and results. Paper presented at the Meeting of the Society for Research in Child Development, Santa Monica, Calif., March 1969.

Parkman-Ray, M., & Bayer, H. T. Analysis and modification of maternal teaching strategies in rural poor families. Ithaca, N.Y.: Cornell University, 1969.

Parsons, T. The normal American family. In S. M. Farber, P. Mustacchi, & R. H. Wilson (Eds.), *Man and civilization: The family's search for survival.* New York: McGraw-Hill, 1965. Pp. 31–50.

Parten, M. B. Leadership among preschool children. *Journal of Abnormal Social Psychology,* 1933, **27,** 430–440.

Pasamanick, B., & Knoblock, H. Early language behavior in Negro children and the testing of intelligence. *Journal of Abnormal and Social Psychology,* 1955, **50,** 401–402.

Pavenstedt, E. A comparison of the child-rearing environment of upper-lower and very low-lower class families. *American Journal of Orthopsychiatry,* 1965, **35,** 89–98.

Peisach, E. C. Children's comprehension of teacher and peer speech. *Child Development,* 1965, **30,** 467–480.

Peller, L. E. Libidinal development as reflected in play. *Psychoanalysis,* 1955, **3,** 3–12.

Peters, A. D. Day care: A summary report. *American Journal of Public Health,* 1964, **54,** 1905–1912.

Peterson, J. A. Catastrophes in partnership: Separation, divorce, and widowhood. In S. M. Farber, P. Mustacchi, & R. H. Wilson (Eds.), *Man and civilization: The family's search for survival.* New York: McGraw-Hill, 1965. Pp. 73–80.

Pettigrew, T. F. Race and equal educational opportunity. Paper presented at the symposium of the implications of the Coleman Report on Equality of Educational Opportunity, at the annual convention of the American Psychological Association, Washington, D.C., September 1967.

Piaget, J. *The moral judgment of the child.* London: Routledge & Kegan Paul, 1932. (Republished in paperback, New York, Free Press, 1965.)

Piaget, J. *Play, dreams, and imitation in childhood.* New York: Norton, 1951. (Republished in paperback, 1962; original French edition, 1945.)

Piaget, J. *The origins of intelligence in children.* New York: International Universities Press, 1952. (Republished in paperback, Norton, 1963; original French edition, 1936.)

Piaget, J. *On the development of memory and identity.* Vol. 2. *1967 Heinz Werner lecture series.* Worcester, Mass.: Clark University Press, 1968.

Pierce-Jones, J. Cited by R. A. O'Brien & P. Lopate, *Preschool programs and the intellectual development of disadvantaged children.* Urbana, Ill.: ERIC Clearinghouse on Early Childhood Education, 1968. [ED 024 473].

Pines, M. Someone to mind the baby. *The New York Times Magazine,* January 7, 1968, 71–76.

Pisapia, M. L., & Hanwell, A. F. Social work in day care. *Child Welfare,* 1969, **48**, 36–40.

Pitcher, E. G. An evaluation of the Montessori method in schools for young children. In J. L. Frost (Ed.), *Early childhood education rediscovered.* New York: Holt, Rinehart & Winston, 1968. Pp. 92–96.

Plowden, B. (Chairman) Central Advisory Council for Education. *Children and their primary schools.* Vol. 1. *Report.* London: Her Majesty's Stationery Office, 1967. (a)

Plowden, B. (Chairman) Central Advisory Council for Education. *Children and their primary schools.* Vol. 2. *Research and surveys.* London: Her Majesty's Stationery Office, 1967. (b)

Postman, N., & Weingartner, C. *Teaching as a subversive activity.* New York: Delacorte, 1969.

Prentice, N. M., & Bieri, J. Intellectual development of culturally deprived children in a day care program: A follow-up study. Paper presented at the 47th Annual Meeting of the American Orthopsychiatric Association, San Francisco, March 1970.

Prescott, E., Jones, E., & Kritchevsky, S. Group day care as a childrearing environment. Unpublished manuscript, Pacific Oaks College, Pasadena, Calif., 1967 [ERIC No. ED 924453].

Pringle, M. L., & Tanner, M. The effects of early deprivation on speech development: A comparative study of 4-year-olds in a nursery school and in residential nurseries. *Language and Speech,* 1958, **1**, 269–287.

Project Head Start: Training courses and methods. Washington, D.C.: United States Department of Health, Education and Welfare, Office of Child Development, 1969.

Proshansky, H., & Newton, P. The nature and meaning of Negro self-identity. In M. Deutsch, I. Katz, & A. R. Jensen (Eds.), *Social class, race, and psychological development.* New York: Holt, Rinehart & Winston, 1968. Pp. 178–218.

Provence, S., & Lipton, R. C. *Infants in institutions.* New York: International Universities Press, 1962.

Pulaski, M. A. Play as a function of toy structure and fantasy predisposition. *Child Development,* 1970, **41**, 531–538.

Rabin, A. I. Infants and children under conditions of "intermittent" mothering in the kibbutz. *American Journal of Orthopsychiatry,* 1958, **28**, 577–584.

Radinsky, E. K. Follow-up study on family day care service. *Child Welfare,* 1964, **43**, 305–308.

Radinsky, E. K., & Gordon, B. Day care families and foster families. In *Day Care: An expanding resource for children.* New York: Child Welfare League of America, 1965. Pp. 64–67.

Radke, M. J., & Trager, H. G. Children's perceptions of the social roles of Negroes and whites. *Journal of Psychology,* 1950, **29**, 3–33.

Rahmlow, H. F., & Kiehn, S. O. A survey and analysis of major tasks, knowledges associated with work in child care occupations. Final Report. Washington State University, Pullman, Wash., 1967 [ERIC No. 021 066].

Raph, J. B., Thomas, A., Chess, S., & Korn, S. J. The influence of nursery school on social interactions. *American Journal of Orthopsychiatry,* 1968, **38**, 144–152.

Rapoport, L., & Cornsweet, D. M. Preventive intervention potentials in public child care centers. *Child Welfare,* 1969, **48**, 6–13.

Rau, L., Mlodnosky, L. B., & Anastaslow, N. Child-rearing antecedents of achievement behaviors in second grade boys. Cooperative Research Project No. 1838. Stanford University, Stanford, Calif., 1964.

Razran, G. The observable unconscious and the inferable conscious in current Soviet psychophysiology: Interceptive conditioning, semantic conditioning, and the orienting reflex. *Psychological Review*, 1961, **68**, 81–147.

Read, K. H. *The nursery school: A human relationships laboratory.* Philadelphia: Saunders, 1950.

Reed, M. A. *Where is day care heading?* Seattle: Seattle Day Nursery Association, 1968.

Reese, H. W. Verbal mediation as a function of age level. *Psychological Bulletin*, 1962, **59**, 502–509.

Reichenberg-Hackett, W. Practices, attitudes and values in nursery group education. *Psychological Reports*, 1962, **19**, 151–172.

Reid, J. H. Day care services: Our best investment for the future. Reprint from *Parents' Magazine*, 1970, **4**.

Reynolds, N. J., & Risley, T. R. The role of social and material reinforcers in increasing talking of a disadvantaged preschool child. *Journal of Applied Behavior Analysis*, 1968, **1**, 253–262.

Rheingold, H. L. The modification of social responsiveness in institutional babies. *Monographs of the Society for Research in Child Development*, 1956, **21** (2, Whole No. 63).

Rheingold, H. L. The measurement of maternal care. *Child Development*, 1960, **31**, 565–575.

Rheingold, H. L. The effect of environmental stimulation upon social and exploratory behavior in the human infant. In B. M. Foss (Ed.), *Determinants of infant behavior.* New York: Wiley, 1961. Pp. 143–178.

Rheingold, H. L., & Bayley, N. The later effects of an experimental modification of mothering. *Child Development*, 1959, **30**, 363–372.

Rheingold, H. L., Gerwitz, J. L., & Ross, H. W. Social conditioning of vocalizations in the infant. *The Journal of Comparative and Physiological Psychology*, 1959, **52**, 68–73.

Ricciuti, H. N. Object groupings and selective ordering behavior in infants 12 to 24 months old. *Merrill-Palmer Quarterly*, 1965, **11**, 129–148.

Ricciuti, H. N., & Johnson, L. J. Developmental changes in categorizing behavior from infancy to the early pre-school years. Paper presented at the meeting of the Society for Research in Child Development, Minneapolis, March 1965.

Riegel, K. F. Development of language: Suggestions for a verbal fallout model. *Human Development*, 1966, **9**(3), 97–120.

Riesen, A. H. The development of visual perception in man and chimpanzee. *Science*, 1947, **106**, 107–108.

Riessman, F. *The culturally deprived child.* New York: Harper & Row, 1962.

Robertson, J. Mothering as an influence on early development. *Psychoanalytic Study of the Child*, 1962, **17**, 245–264.

Robertson, J. *Young children in hospital.* London: Tavistock Publications, 1958.

Robertson, J., & Bowlby, J. Responses of young children to separation from their mothers. *Courrier*, 1952, **2**, No. (3), 131.

Robinson, H. B. The Frank Porter Graham Child Development Center. In L. L. Dittmann (Ed.), *Early child care: The new perspectives.* New York: Atherton, 1968. Pp. 302–312.

Robson, K. S. The role of eye-to-eye contact in maternal-infant attachment. *Journal of Child Psychology and Psychiatry*, 1967, **8**, 13–25.

Rodman, H. The lower-class value stretch. *Social Forces*, 1963, **42**, 205–215.

Rohwer, W. D., Jr. Constraint, syntax and meaning in paired associate learning. *Journal of Verbal Learning and Verbal Behavior*, 1966, **5**, 541–547.

Rosen, B. C. Race, ethnicity and the achievement syndrome. *American Sociological Review*, 1959, **24**, 47–60.

Rosen, B. C. & D'Andrade, R. The psychosocial origins of achievement motivations. *Sociometry*, 1959, **22**, 185–218.

Rosen, J. L. Personality and first-year teachers' relationships with children. *The School Review*, 1968, **76**, 294–311.

Rosen, S., Levinger, G., & Lippitt, R. Desired change in self and others as a function of resource ownership. *Human Relations*, 1960, **13**, 187–193.

Rosenberg, B., & Spindler, P. G. *Day care facts*. Washington, D.C.: United States Department of Labor, 1970.

Roudinesco, J., & Appell, G. Les répercussions de la stabulation hôpitalière sur le dévelopement psycho-moteur des jeunes enfants. *Seminaire Hôpital de Paris*, 1950, **26**, 2271–2273.

Rubenstein, J. Maternal attentiveness and subsequent exploratory behavior in the infant. *Child Development*, 1967, **38**, 1089–1100.

Ruderman, F. A. Conceptualizing needs for day care: Some conclusions drawn from the Child Welfare League Day Care Project. In *Day care: An expanding resource for children*. New York: Child Welfare League of America, 1965. Pp. 14–24.

Ruderman, F. A. *Child care and working mothers: A study of arrangements made for daytime care of children*. New York: Child Welfare League of America, 1968.

Rusk, B. A. An evaluation of a six-week Head Start program using an academically oriented curriculum: Canton, 1967. Urbana, Ill.: University of Illinois, 1968.

Ryans, D. G. Research on teacher behavior in the context of the teacher characteristics study. In B. J. Biddle & W. J. Ellena (Eds.), *Contemporary Research on Teacher Effectiveness*. New York: Holt, Rinehart & Winston, 1964. Pp. 67–101.

Salzinger, S. Some implications of methodology for the development of the field of child language. Paper presented at the meetings of the Society for Research in Child Development, New York, March 1967.

Sander, L. W. Adaptive relationships in early mother-child interaction. *Journal of the American Academy of Child Psychiatry*, 1964, **3**, 231–264.

Sander, L. W. The longitudinal course of early mother-child interaction—Cross case comparison in a sample of mother-child pairs. In B. M. Foss (Ed.), *Determinants of infant behaviour*. Vol. 4. London: Methuen, 1969. Pp. 189–228.

Sander, L. W., & Julia, H. L. Continuous interactional monitoring in the neonate. *Psychosomatic Medicine*, 1966, **28**, 822–835.

*Schaefer, E. S., Furfey, P. H., & Harte, T. J. Infant education research project. Washington, D.C.: *Preschool program in compensatory education 1 (It Works)*. Washington, D.C.: United States Department of Health, Education and Welfare, Office of Education, 1968.

Schaffer, H. R. Objective observations of personality development in early infancy. *British Journal of Medical Psychology*, 1958, **31**, 174–183.

Schaffer, H. R., & Callender, W. Psychologic effects of hospitalization in infancy. *Pediatrics,* 1959, **24**, 528–539.

Schaffer, H. R., & Emerson, P. E. The development of social attachments in infancy. *Monographs of the Society of Research in Child Development,* 1964, **29** (3, Whole No. 94). (a)

Schaffer, H. R., & Emerson, P. E. Patterns of response to physical contact in early human development. *Journal of Child Psychology and Psychiatry,* 1964, **5**, 1–13. (b)

Schenk-Danzinger, C. Social difficulties of children who were deprived of maternal care in early childhood. *Vita humana,* 1961, **4**, 229–241.

Schneiderman, L. Some theoretical and methodological problems in serving the multi-problem family. In *Neighborhood centers serve the troubled family,* Report of a conference sponsored by the National Federation of Settlements and Neighborhood Centers Training Center, Chicago, Ill., March 1964.

Schoggen, M. An ecological study of three-year-olds at home. Nashville, Tenn.: *DARCEE Papers and Reports,* 1969, **3**(7).

Schramm, W., Lyle, J., & Parker, E. B. *Television in the lives of our children.* Stanford, Calif.: Stanford University Press, 1961.

Scott, R. Head start before home start. *Merrill-Palmer Quarterly,* 1967, **13**, 317–321.

Scriven, M. The methodology of evaluation. *Area Monograph Series on Curriculum Evaluation, Perspectives of curriculum evaluation.* Chicago: Rand McNally, 1967. Pp. 39–83.

Sears, P. S. The effect of classroom conditions on the strength of achievement motive and work output of elementary school children. Stanford University, Project No. 873, United States Department of Health, Education and Welfare, Office of Education, 1963.

Sears, P. S., & Dowley, E. M. Research on teaching in the nursery school. N. L. Gage (Ed.), *Handbook of research on teaching.* Chicago: Rand McNally, 1963. Pp. 814–864.

Sears, P. S., & Hilgard, E. R. The teacher's role in the motivation of the learner. In *Theories of learning and instruction, Sixty-third Yearbook of the National Society for the Study of Education,* Part I. Chicago: University of Chicago Press, 1964. Pp. 202–207.

Sears, R. R., Maccoby, E. E., & Levin, H. *Patterns of child rearing.* Evanston, Ill.: Row, Peterson, 1957.

Shaw, M. C. Note on parent attitudes toward independence training and the academic achievement of their children. *Journal of Educational Psychology,* 1964, **55**, 371–374.

Sheriden, M. L. Family day care: For children of migrant farm-workers. *Children,* 1967, **14**, 13–18.

Sherif, M., Harvey, L. J., White, B. J., Hood, W. R., & Sherif, C. W. *Intergroup conflict and cooperation: The Robbers' Cave Experiment.* Norman, Okla.: University of Oklahoma Book Exchange, 1961.

Shirley, M., & Poyntz, L. The influence of separation from the mother on children's emotional responses. *Journal of Psychology,* 1941, **12**, 251–282.

Shomaker, S. A. Interagency teamwork: The private agency. In *Day care: An expanding resource for children.* New York: Child Welfare League of America, 1965. Pp. 53–55.

Shriner, T. H., & Miner, L. Morphological structures in the language of disadvantaged and advantaged children. *Journal of Speech and Hearing Research,* 1968, **11**, 605–610.

Shultz, T. R. A cognitive-developmental analysis of humor. Unpublished manuscript, Yale University, 1969.

Shure, M. E. Psychological ecology of a nursery school. *Child Development,* 1963, **34**, 979–999.

Sieber, S., & Wilder, D. Teaching styles: Parental preference and professional role definitions. *Sociology of Education.* Fall 1967. Cited by L. Katz, Teaching in preschools: Roles and goals. *Children,* 1970, 17, 42–48.

Siegel, A. E., & Kohn, L. G. Permissiveness, permission and aggression: The effect of adult presence or absence on aggression in children's play. *Child Development,* 1959, 30, 131–141.

Sigel, I. E., & McBane, B. Cognitive competence and level of symbolization among five-year-old children. Paper presented at the meeting of the American Psychological Association, New York, September 1966.

Sigel, I. E., & Olmsted, P. *Modification of classificatory competence and level of representation among lower-class Negro kindergarten children.* Paper presented at the Sixth Work Conference on Curriculum and Teaching in Depressed Areas, Teachers College, Columbia University, New York, June 1967.

Sigel, I. E., & Perry, C. Psycholinguistic diversity among culturally deprived children. *American Journal of Orthopsychiatry,* 1968, 38, 122–125.

Silverman, R. E., Schwartz, A., & Simon, G. *Response to varying levels of conditioning rewards.* New York: New York University, 1968.

Sinclair-deZwart, H. Developmental psycholinguistics. In D. Elkind & J. H. Flavell (Eds.), *Studies in cognitive development.* New York: Oxford, 1969. Pp. 315–336.

Skeels, H. M. Adult status of children with contrasting early life experiences. *Monographs of the Society for Research in Child Development,* 1966, 31(3, Whole No. 105).

Skeels, H. M., & Dye, H. B. A study of the effects of differential stimulation on mentally retarded children. *Proceedings of the American Association of Mental Defectives,* 1939, 44, 114.

Skinner, B. F. *Verbal behavior.* New York: Appleton-Century-Crofts, 1957.

Slavson, S. R. Play group therapy for young children. *The Nervous Child,* 1948, 7, 318–327.

Slobin, D. I. The acquisition of Russian as a native language. In F. Smith & G. A. Miller (Eds.), *The genesis of language.* Cambridge, Mass.: M.I.T. Press, 1966. Pp. 129–148. (a)

Slobin, D. I. Soviet methods of investigating child language: A topical guide to Abstracts of Soviet studies of child language. Also Abstracts of Soviet studies of child language. In F. Smith & G. A. Miller (Eds.), *The genesis of language.* Cambridge, Mass.: M.I.T. Press, 1966. Pp. 361–386. (b)

Slobin, D. I. Questions of language development in cross-cultural perspective. Paper prepared for symposium on language learning in cross-cultural perspective, Michigan State University, September 1968.

Smelser, N. J. The social challenge to parental authority. In S. M. Farber, P. Mustacchi, & R. H. Wilson (Eds.), *Man and civilization: The family's search for survival.* New York: McGraw-Hill, 1965. Pp. 67–72.

Smilansky, S. *The effects of sociodramatic play on disadvantaged preschool children.* New York: Wiley, 1968.

Smith, F. & Miller, G. A. (Eds.), *The genesis of language.* Cambridge, Mass.: M.I.T. Press, 1966.

Smith, M. E. A study of some factors influencing the development of the sentence in preschool children. *Journal of Genetic Psychology,* 1935, 46, 182–212.

Smock, C. D. Children's conception of reality: Some implications for education. *Journal of Research and Development in Education,* 1968, 1(3), 30–38.

Spaulding, R. L. Achievement, creativity, and self-concept correlates of teacher-pupil transactions in elementary schools. In C. B. Stendler (Ed.), *Readings in child development and behavior*. (2nd ed.) New York: Harcourt, Brace & World, 1964. Pp. 313–318.

Speer, D. C. Some guidelines in the selection of day care personnel. *Child Welfare*, 1966, **45**, 584–592.

*Spicker, H. H. Diagnostically based curriculum. Bloomington, Ind.: *Preschool program in compensatory education 1 (It Works)*. Washington, D.C.: United States Department of Health, Education and Welfare, Office of Education, 1968.

Spiker, C. C. Stimulus pretraining and subsequent performance in the delayed reaction experiment. *Journal of Experimental Psychology*, 1956, **52**, 107–111.

Spiro, M. E. *Children of the Kibbutz*, Cambridge, Mass.: Harvard University Press, 1958.

Spitz, R. A. Hospitalism. *Psychoanalytic Study of the Child*, 1946, **2**, 113–117.

Spitz, R. A. The psychogenic diseases in infancy. *Psychoanalytical Study of the Child*, 1951, **5**, 255–275.

Spitz, R. A. *The first year of life*. New York: International Universities Press, 1965.

Spitz, R. A., & Wolf, K. M. Anaclitic depression. *Psychoanalytic Study of the Child*, 1946, **2**, 313–342.

Sprigle, H. A. The learning to learn program. Jacksonville, Fla.: Learning to Learn School, undated.

Sprigle, H. A., *et al*. A fresh approach to early childhood education, and a study of its effectiveness. Learning to Learn School, Jacksonville, Fla., 1968 [ERIC No. ED 019 117].

Sprigle, H. A., Van De Riet, V. E., & Van De Riet, H. A sequential learning program for preschool children and an evaluation of its effectiveness with culturally disadvantaged children. Paper presented at the meeting of the American Educational Research Association, New York: March 1967.

Spurlock, J. Problems of identification in young black children—static or changing. In S. Chess & A. Thomas (Eds.), *Annual progress in child psychiatry and child development*. New York: Brunner/Mazel, 1970. Pp. 299–306.

Stern, C. Evaluating language curricula for preschool children. *Monographs of the Society for Research in Child Development*, 1968, **33**(8, Whole No. 124), 49–61.

Stern, G. G., Caldwell, B. M., Hersher, L., Lipton, E. L., & Richmond, J. B. A factor analytic study of the mother-infant dyad. *Child Development*, 1969, **40**, 163–182.

Stevenson, H. W. Social reinforcement of children's behavior. In L. P. Lipsitt & C. C. Spiker (Eds.), *Advances in child development*. Vol. 2. New York: Academic, 1965. Pp. 97–126.

Stevenson, H. W. Studies of racial awareness in young children. In W. W. Hartup & N. L. Smothergill (Eds.), *The young child*. Washington, D.C.: National Association for the Education of Young Children, 1967. Pp. 206–213.

Stevenson, H. W., & Stevenson, N. G. Social interaction in an interracial nursery school. *Genetic Psychology Monographs*, 1960, **61**, 37–75.

Stewart, A. H., Weiland, J. H., Leider, A. R., Mangham, C. A., Holmes, T. H., & Ripley, H. S. Excessive infant crying (colic in relation to parent behavior). *American Journal of Psychiatry*, 1954, **110**, 687–694.

Stewart, G. J. Day care: An under-used resource in child welfare. *Child Welfare*, 1968, **47**, 51–54.

Stewart, R. S. Personality maladjustment and reading achievement. *American Journal of Orthopsychiatry*, 1950, **20**, 410–417.

Stewart, W. A. Foreign language teaching methods in quasi-foreign language situations. In W. A. Stewart (Ed.), *Non-standard speech and the teaching of English*. Washington, D.C.: Center for Applied Linguistics, 1964. Pp. 1–15.

Stodolsky, S. S., & Jensen, J. Ancona Montessori research project for culturally disadvantaged children. Final Report, 1969. Grant CG–8469 A/2, Office of Economic Opportunity.

Stolz, L. M. Effects of maternal employment on children: Evidence from research. *Child Development*, 1960, **31**, 749–782.

Stott, L. H. The persisting effects of early family experiences upon personality development. *Merrill-Palmer Quarterly*, 1957, **3**, 145–159.

Strodtbeck, F. L. Progress report. The reading readiness nursery: Short-term social intervention. Chicago: University of Chicago, 1963.

Strodtbeck, F. L. Cited by R. A. O'Brien & P. Lopate. *Preschool programs and the intellectual development of disadvantaged children*, Urbana, Ill.: ERIC Clearinghouse on Early Childhood Education, 1968 [ED 024 473].

Sugarman, J. M. *Federal interagency day care requirements*. Washington, D.C.: U.S. Department of Health, Education and Welfare, 1968.

Sugarman, J. M. Research, evaluation, and public policy: An invited editorial. *Child Development*, 1970, **41**, 263–266.

Sunderlin, S. (Ed.) Housing for early childhood education: Centers for growing and learning. Association for Childhood Education International, *Bulletin* 22–A, 1968.

Sutton-Smith, B. The role of play in cognitive development. In W. W. Hartup & N. L. Smothergill (Eds.), *The young child*. Washington, D.C.: National Association for the Education of Young Children, 1967. Pp. 96–108.

Sutton-Smith, B. Play, games, and controls. In J. P. Scott (Ed.), *Social control*. Chicago: University of Chicago Press, 1970.

Sutton-Smith, B. A reply to Piaget: A play theory of copy. In R. E. Herron & B. Sutton-Smith, *Child's play*. New York: Wiley, 1971. Pp. 340–342. (a)

Sutton-Smith, B. A syntax for play and games. In R. E. Herron & B. Sutton-Smith, *Child's play*. New York: Wiley, 1971. Pp. 298–310. (b)

Sutton-Smith, B. Boundaries. In R. E. Herron & B. Sutton-Smith, *Child's play*. New York: Wiley, 1971. (c).

Sutton-Smith, B. The role of play in cognitive development. In R. E. Herron & B. Sutton-Smith, *Child's play*. New York: Wiley, 1971. (d)

Sutton-Smith, B., & Roberts, J. M. The cross-cultural and psychological study of games. In G. Lüschen (Ed.), *The cross-cultural analysis of games*. Champaign, Ill.: Stipes, 1970. Pp. 100–108.

Swift, J. W. Effects of early group experience: The nursery school and day nursery. In M. L. Hoffman & L. W. Hoffman (Eds.), *Review of child development research*, New York: Russell Sage Foundation, 1964. Pp. 249–280.

Tamminen, A. W., *et al.* An evaluation of a preschool training program for culturally deprived children. Duluth, Minn.: Minnesota University, 1967 [ERIC No. ED 019 135].

Taylor, K. W. *The children's community*. Washington, D.C.: American Association of University Women, 1931.

Templin, M. C. *Certain language skills in children: Their development and interrelationships.* Minneapolis: University of Minnesota Press, 1957.

Templin, M. C. Relation of speech and language development intelligence and socio-economic status. *Volta Review,* 1958, **60,** 331–334.

Thomas, A., Chess, S., Birch, H. G., Hertzig, M. E., & Korn, S. *Behavioral individuality in early childhood.* New York: New York University Press, 1963.

Thompson, G. G. The social and emotional development of preschool children under two types of educational program. *Psychological Monographs,* 1944, **56**(5, Whole No. 258).

Thompson, W. R., & Heron, W. The effects of restricting early experience on the problem-solving capacity of dogs. *Canadian Journal of Psychology,* 1954, **8,** 17–31.

Torrance, E. P., Fortson, L. R., & Diener, C. Creative-aesthetic ways of developing intellectual skills among five-year olds. *Journal of Research and Development in Education,* 1968, **1**(3), 58–69.

Trismen, D. A. The many faces of evaluation. Paper prepared for a symposium on the role of evaluation in national curriculum projects, at the meeting of the American Educational Research Association, New York, February 1967.

Tulkin, S. R. Social class differences in infancy. Unpublished doctoral dissertation, Harvard University, 1969.

Turnure, C. Response to voice of mother and stranger by babies in the first year. Paper presented at meeting of the Society for Research in Child Development, Santa Monica, March 1969.

Turnure, J., & Zigler, E. Outer-directedness in the problem solving of normal and retarded children. *Journal of Abnormal Social Psychology,* 1964, **69,** 427–436.

Tyler, R. W. Changing concepts of educational evaluation. Area Monograph Series on Curriculum Evaluation, Perspectives of Curriculum Evaluation, Chicago: Rand McNally, 1967.

Ulrich, R. Behavior control and public concern. *The Psychological Record,* 1967, **17,** 229–234.

Ulrich, R., & Wallace, F. Pyramidal instruction: A proposed solution to an educational problem. Unpublished manuscript, Western-Michigan University, 1970.

Ulrich, R., Wolfe, M., & Bluhm, M. Operant conditioning in the public schools. *Educational Technology Monographs,* 1968, **1**(1).

Ulrich, R., Wolfe, M., & Cole, R. Early education: A preventive mental health program. *Michigan mental health research bulletin,* 1970, **3**(1), 39–45.

UNICEF. *Reaching the young child: one to six years of age.* Geneva, Switzerland: UNICEF, 1966.

United States Commission of Civil Rights. *Racial isolation in the public schools.* Washington, D.C.: United States Government Printing Office, 1967.

United States Department of Health, Education and Welfare, Children's Bureau, Federal Panel on Early Childhood. *Federal interagency day care requirements.* Washington, D.C.: USDHEW 1968.

United States Department of Health, Education and Welfare, Children's Bureau, Federal Panel on Early Childhood. *Information sheet on Federal assistance for day care programs.* Washington, D.C.: USDHEW, 1969. (a)

United States Department of Health, Education and Welfare, Office of Child Development. *Interim policy guide for the 4–C Program, pilot phase.* Washington, D.C.: USDHEW, 1969. (b)

United States Department of Health, Education and Welfare, Office of Education. *Child Care and Guidance: A suggested post-high school curriculum.* Washington, D.C.: USDHEW, 1970.

University of the State of New York, State Education Department, Bureau of Child Development and Parent Education. *Child development guides.* (Rev. ed.) Albany, New York: University of the State of New York, 1968.

Updegraff, R., & Herbst, E. K. An experimental study of the social behavior stimulated in young children by certain play materials. *Journal of Genetic Psychology,* 1933, **42**, 372–391.

Upton, M. E. The impact of day care in a poverty area. *Child Welfare,* 1969, **48**, 231–234.

Uzgiris, I. C. Ordinality in the development of schemas for relating to objects. In J. Hellmuth (Ed.), *Exceptional infant.* Vol. 1. *The normal infant.* New York: Brunner/Mazel, 1967. Pp. 315–334.

Van Alstyne, D. *Play behavior and choice of play materials of preschool children.* Chicago: University of Chicago Press, 1932.

Van De Riet, V., & Van De Riet, H. A follow-up evaluation of the effects of a unique sequential learning program, a traditional preschool program and a no-treatment program on culturally deprived children. December 1969, University of Florida, Contract No. B89–4425, Department of Health, Education and Welfare. (a)

Van De Riet, V., & Van De Riet, H. A sequential approach to early childhood and elementary education, Phase I. Grant Report for Grant No. OEO CG-8222A/0, December 1969, Office of Economic Opportunity, Project Head Start, Div. of Research and Evaluation. (b)

Vygotsky, L. S. *Thought and language.* (1st ed., 1934) New York: Wiley, 1962.

Wahler, R. G. Child-child interactions in free field settings: Some experimental analyses. *Journal of Experimental Child Psychology,* 1967, **5**, 278–293.

Wallach, M. A., & Kogan, N. *Modes of thinking in young children.* New York: Holt, Rinehart & Winston, 1965.

Walsh, M. E. The relation of nursery school training to the development of certain personality traits. *Child Development,* 1931, **2**, 72–73.

Walters, J., Connor, R., & Zunich, M. Interaction of mothers and children from lower-class families. *Child Development,* 1964, **35**, 433–440.

Walters, R. H., & Parke, R. D. The role of the distance receptors in the development of social responsiveness. *Advances in Child Development,* 1965, **2**, 59–96.

Weikart, D. P. Preschool programs: Preliminary findings. *Journal of Special Education,* 1967, **1**, 163–182.

*Weikart, D. P. Perry Preschool Project, Ypsilanti, Michigan, *Preschool program in compensatory education 1 (It Works).* Washington, D.C.: United States Department of Health, Education and Welfare, Office of Education, 1968.

Weikart, D. P. Address presented at symposium on early education. New Haven, Conn.: Yale University, March 1971.

Weikart, D. P., & Lambie, D. Z. Preschool intervention through a home teaching program. In J. Hellmuth (Ed.), *Disadvantaged child.* Vol. 2. New York: Brunner/Mazel, 1968. Pp. 435–500.

Weikart, D. P., & Lambie, D. Z. *Ypsilanti-Carnegie Infant Education Project progress report.* Ypsilanti, Mich.: Department of Research and Development, Ypsilanti Public Schools, September 1969.

Weikart, D. P., & Wiegerink, R. Initial results of a comparative preschool curriculum project. *Proceedings of 76th Annual Convention of the American Psychological Association*, 1968, **3**, 597–598.

Weiss, H. H., & Born, B. Speech training or language acquisition? A distinction when speech training is taught by operant conditioning procedures. *American Journal of Orthopsychiatry*, 1967, **37**, 49–55.

Weissberg, P. Social and non-social conditioning of infant vocalizations. *Child Development*, 1963, **34**, 377–388.

Whipple, G. M. (Ed.) *The twenty-eighth yearbook of the National Society for the Study of Education*. Bloomington, Ill.: Public School Publishing Company, 1929.

White, B. L. An experimental approach to the effects of experience on early human behavior. In J. P. Hill (Ed.), *Minnesota symposia on child psychology*. Vol. 1. Minneapolis: University of Minnesota Press, 1966. Pp. 201–226.

White, B. L. The initial coordination of sensorimotor schemas in human infants—Piaget's ideas and the role of experience. In D. Elkind & J. H. Flavell (Eds.), *Studies in cognitive development*. New York: Oxford, 1969. Pp. 237–256.

White, B. L., Castle, P. W., & Held, R. Observations on the development of visually-directed reaching. *Child Development*, 1964, **35**, 349–364.

White, B. L., LaCrosse, E. R., Litman, F., & Ogilvie, D. M. Preschool project, Laboratory of Human Development, Harvard Graduate School of Education. Symposium presented at the meeting of the Society for Research in Child Development, Santa Monica, March 1969.

White, M. S. Social class, child rearing and child behavior. *American Sociological Review*, 1957, **22**, 704–712.

White, R. W. Motivation reconsidered: The concept of competence. *Psychological Review*, 1959, **66**, 297–333.

White, S. H. The national impact study of Head Start. In J. Hellmuth (Ed.), *Disadvantaged child*. Vol. 3. *Compensatory education: A national debate*. New York: Brunner/Mazel, 1970. Pp. 163–184.

Whiteman, M., & Deutsch, M. Social disadvantage as related to intellective and language development. In M. Deutsch, I. Katz, & A. R. Jensen (Eds.), *Social class, race, and psychological development*. New York: Holt, Rinehart & Winston, 1968. Pp. 86–114.

Whiting, J. W., & Child, I. L. *Child training and personality*. New Haven, Conn.: Yale University Press, 1953.

Whiting, J. W. & Whiting, B. B. Contributions of anthropology to the methods of studying child rearing. In P. H. Mussen (Ed.), *Handbook of research methods in child development*. New York: Wiley, 1960. Pp. 418–844.

Whitmarsh, R. E. An exploratory study of knowledges in child development needed by mothers and workers. Urbana, Ill.: University of Illinois, 1966 [ERIC No. ED 010 071].

Whorf, B. L. *Language, thought and reality*. New York: Wiley, 1956.

Wiegerink, R., & Weikart, D. P. Measurement of mother teaching styles. *Proceedings of 75th Annual Convention of the American Psychological Association*, 1967, **2**, 333–334.

Wilensky, H. Teaching styles in the nursery. *Campus School Exchange*, Spring 1965, 21–24.

Williams, F., & Naremore, R. C. On the functional analysis of social class differences in modes of speech. *Speech Monographs*, 1969, **36**, 77–102.

Williams, J. R., & Scott, R. B. Growth and development of Negro infants: IV. Motor development and its relationship to child rearing practices in two groups of Negro infants. *Child Development*, 1953, **24**, 103–121.

Willner, M. Magnitude and scope of family day care in New York City. Final report. Grant No. R120, October 1966. U. S. Department of Health, Education and Welfare, Children's Bureau.

Willner, M. Unsupervised family day care in New York City. *Child Welfare*, 1969, **48**, 56–62.

Witkin, H. A., Dyk, R. B., Patterson, H. E., Goodenough, D. R., & Karp, S. A. *Psychological differentiation.* New York: Wiley, 1962.

Witmer, H. A further analysis of IQ changes. In I. Kraft, J. C. Fuschillo, & E. Herzog, *Prelude to school—An evaluation of an inner-city preschool program.* Washington, D.C.: United States Department of Health, Education and Welfare, Children's Bureau, Research Report No. 3, 1968.

Wittenborn, J. K., *et al.* A study of adoptive children. *Psychological Monographs*, 1956, **70**(1, 2, & 3, Whole Nos. 408, 409, 410).

Wolf, R. M. The identification and measurement of environmental process variables related to intelligence. Unpublished doctoral dissertation, University of Chicago, 1964.

Wolff, M., & Stein, A. Head Start six months later. In J. L. Frost (Ed.), *Early childhood education rediscovered.* New York: Holt, Rinehart & Winston, 1968. Pp. 293–297.

Wolff, P. H. The causes, controls, and organization of behavior in the neonate. *Psychological Issues*, 1966, **5**(1, Whole No. 17).

Wolff, P. H. The natural history of crying and other vocalizations in early infancy. In B. M. Foss (Ed.), *The determinants of infant behaviour.* Vol. 4. London: Methuen, 1969. Pp. 81–110.

Wolins, M. Group care of children—the problem of legitimacy. Paper presented at the Arden House Conference, New York, November 1965.

Wolins, M. Child care in cross-cultural perspective. Final report. University of California, Berkeley, 1969. (a)

Wolins, M. Young children in institutions: Some additional evidence. *Developmental Psychology*, 1969, **2**, 99–109. (b)

Wolins, M. The SOS Kinderdorf: families in a village. Unpublished manuscript, University of California, Berkeley, undated.

Wolman, T. G., & Levenson, D. Parent-school partnership in prekindergarten. *The Record.* Teachers College, Columbia University, 1968, **69**, 421–431.

Woods, R. A. (Ed.) *The city wilderness: A settlement study.* Boston: Houghton, Mifflin, 1898.

Wootton, B. A social scientist's approach to maternal deprivation. *Public Health Papers*, 1962, **14**, 63–73.

World Health Organization. *Deprivation of maternal care: A reassessment of its effects.* Public Health Papers, No. 14, Geneva, 1962.

Wortis, H., Bardach, J. L., Cutler, R., Rue, R., & Freedman, A. Child-rearing practices in a low socioeconomic group. *Pediatrics*, 1963, **32**, 298–307.

Wright, M. E. Constructiveness of play as affected by group organization and frustration. *Character and Personality*, 1942, **11**, 40–49.

Yale Day Care Committee Report. Unpublished manuscript, Yale University, 1970.

Yarrow, L. J. Maternal deprivation: Toward an empirical and conceptual reevaluation. *Psychological Bulletin*, 1961, **58**, 459–490.

Yarrow, L. J. Research in dimensions of early maternal care. *Merrill-Palmer Quarterly*, 1963, **9**, 101–114.

Yarrow, L. J. Separation from parents during early childhood. In M. L. Hoffman, & L. W. Hoffman (Eds.), *Review of child development research*. Vol. 1. New York: Russell Sage Foundation, 1964. Pp. 89–136.

Yarrow, L. J. The development of focused relationships during infancy. In J. Hellmuth (Ed.), *Exceptional infant*. Vol. 1. *The normal infant*. New York: Brunner/Mazel, 1967. Pp. 427–442.

Yarrow, L. J., & Goodwin, M. S. Some conceptual issues in the study of mother-infant interaction. *American Journal of Orthopsychiatry*, 1965, **35**, 473–481.

Yeomans, A. F. Day care—one of the community's services to children. *Child Welfare*, 1968, **39**, (10), 6–10.

Young, F. M. An analysis of certain variables in a developmental study of language. *Genetic Psychology Monographs*, 1941, **23**, 3–141.

Young, V. H. Family and childhood in a southern Negro community. *American Anthropologist*, 1970, **72**, 269–288.

Zigler, E. Training the intellect versus development of the child. Unpublished manuscript, Yale University, 1968.

Zigler, E. Headstart Child Development Act of 1969. Unpublished manuscript, Yale University, 1969.

Zigler, E., & Balla, D. The developmental course of responsiveness to social reinforcement in normal children and institutionalized retarded children. *Developmental Psychology*, 1972, **6**, 66–73.

Zigler, E., & Butterfield, E. C. Motivational aspects of changes in IQ test performance of culturally deprived nursery school children. *Child Development*, 1968, **39**, 1–14.

Zigler, E., & Child, I. L. Socialization. In G. Lindzey & E. Aronson (Eds.), *The handbook of social psychology*. (2nd ed.) Reading, Mass.: Addison-Wesley, 1969. Pp. 450–589.

Zimiles, H. An analysis of current issues in the evaluation of educational programs. In J. Hellmuth (Ed.), *Disadvantaged child*. Vol. 2. New York: Brunner/Mazel, 1967. Pp. 545–554.

Zimiles, H. Problems of assessment of academic and intellectual variables. Paper presented at the meeting of the symposium on Problems of Educational Evaluation Confronted in Head Start at the American Educational Research Association, Chicago, February 1968.

Zunich, M. Relationship between maternal behavior and attitudes toward children. *Journal of Genetic Psychology*, 1962, **100**, 155–165.

---

* These references are listed for convenience under the names of the directors of the programs described therein, although they are part of the larger document: Hawridge, D. C., Chalupsky, A. B., & Roberts, A. O. A study of selected exemplary programs for the education of disadvantaged children, Part I. Final Report Project No. 089013. American Institutes for Research in the Behavioral Sciences. Contract No. CFC-0-2-089013-3513 (010), United States Department of Health, Education and Welfare, 1968. The articles have also been republished separately as *Preschool programs in compensatory education 1 (It Works)* and are available from the Information Officer, Division of Compensatory Education, U.S. Office of Education, Washington, D.C. 20202.

Supplementary References

Adair, T., & Eckstein, E. *Parents and the day care center.* New York: Federation of Protestant Welfare Agencies, 1969.

Anderson, S. *Disadvantaged children and their first school experiences: ETS-Head Start Longitudinal Study.* Princeton, N.J.: Educational Testing Service, 1970.

Ashton-Warner, S. *Teacher.* New York: Bantam Books, 1963.

Battle, E. S., & Rotter, J. B. Children's feeling of personal control as related to social class and ethnic group. *Journal of Personality,* 1963, **31,** 487–490.

Bereiter, C., Case, R., & Anderson, V. Steps toward full intellectual functioning. *Journal of Research and Development in Education,* 1968, **1**(3), 70–79.

Berson, M. P. Early childhood education. *American Education,* 1968, **4**(9), 7–14.

Bledsoe, J. C. Self-concept of children and their intelligence, achievement, interests and anxiety. *Journal of Individual Psychology,* 1964, **20,** 55–58.

Bohmer, H. Why are we so reluctant about day care programs?—A comparative appraisal. *Child Welfare,* 1966, **45,** 289–294.

Bourne, M. (Ed.) *Venture in child care.* Baltimore: The Baltimore Regional Joint Board Amalgamated Clothing Workers of America Health & Welfare Fund, 1969.

Brieland, D. Day care of children. *Child Welfare,* 1960, **39,** (6), 33.

Brittain, C. V. Some early findings of research on preschool programs for culturally deprived children. *Children,* 1966, **13,** 130–134.

Broman, B. L. Subculture values: The pivot to the American dream. In J. Hellmuth (Ed.), *Disadvantaged child.* Vol. 2. New York: Brunner/Mazel, 1967. Pp. 421–434.

Caldwell, B. M. The effects of infant care. In M. L. Hoffman, & L. W. Hoffman (Eds.), *Review of child development research.* New York: Russell Sage Foundation, 1964. Pp. 9–88.

Caldwell, B. M., & Hersher, L. Mother-infant interaction during the first year of life. *Merrill-Palmer Quarterly,* 1964, **10,** 119–128.

Caldwell, B. M., & Richmond, J. B. Social class level and stimulation potential of the home. In J. Hellmuth (Ed.), *Exceptional infant.* Vol. 1. *The normal infant.* New York: Brunner/Mazel, 1967. Pp. 453–466.

Caldwell, B. M., & Smith, L. E. Day care for the very young: Prime opportunity for primary prevention. *American Journal of Public Health,* 1970, **60,** 690–697.

Cazden, C. B., Bryant, B. H., & Tillman, M. A. Making it and going home: The attitudes of black people toward language education. Paper prepared for the Lincolnland Conference on Dialectology. Eastern Illinois University, March 1970.

Chauncey, H. (Ed.) *Soviet preschool education.* Vol. 1. *Program of instruction.* New York: Holt, Rinehart & Winston, 1969.

Child Welfare League of America. *Day care: An expanding resource for children.* New York: CWLA, 1965.

Clemes, H. Research on a community-initiated preschool program. Final Report. Grant #8130, February 1970. Office of Economic Opportunity.

Cohn, W. On the language of lower class children. *School Review,* 1959, **67,** 435–440.

Committee for Early Childhood. *The fundamental learning needs of today's young children.* Washington, D.C.: National Association for the Education of Young Children, 1970.

Covington, M. V. The cognitive curriculum: A process-oriented approach to education. In J. Hellmuth (Ed.), *Cognitive studies.* Vol. 1. New York: Brunner/Mazel, 1970. Pp. 491–502.

Day Care and Child Development Council of America. *Voice for children,* 1968, **1**(1) to date.

Di Lorenzo, L. T. Effects of year-long prekindergarten programs on intelligence and language of educationally disadvantaged children. *The Journal of Experimental Education,* 1968, **36** (3), 36–42.

Di Lorenzo, L. T., & Salter, R. An evaluative study of prekindergarten programs for educationally disadvantaged children: Follow-up and replication. *Exceptional Children,* 1968, **34,** 111–119.

Dittmann, L. L. (Ed.) *Curriculum is what happens.* Washington, D.C.: National Association for the Education of Young Children, 1970.

Donaldello, G. Some applications of ego psychology theory to practice and programs in child welfare. *Child Welfare,* 1967, **46,** 493–497.

Dregor, R. M., & Miller, K. S. Comparative psychological studies of Negroes and whites in the United States. *Psychological Bulletin,* 1960, **57,** 361–402.

Elsbery, J. W. Change the premise. *Urban Review,* 1969, **3**(5), 4, 6–11.

Featuring "Follow Through." *Early Education,* 1968, **1**(5).

Feldmann, S. A preschool enrichment program for disadvantaged children. *The New Era,* 1964, **45**(3), 79–82.

Formanek, R., & Morina, G. Categorizing in young children: Two views. *The Record,* 1968, **69,** 409–420.

Fowler, W. Development proposal for operation of an infant day care and educational programme. Submitted to the Development Review Board, Ontario Institute for Studies in Education, July 1968.

Friedlander, B. Z. Listening, language, and the auditory environment: Automated evaluation and intervention. In J. Hellmuth (Ed.), *The exceptional infant.* Vol. 2. *Studies in Abnormality.* New York: Brunner/Mazel, in press.

Furth, H. G., & Youniss, J. The influence of language and experience on discovery and use of logical symbols. *British Journal of Psychology,* 1965, **56,** 381–390.

Gertler, D. B. *Preprimary enrollment of children under six: October 1967.* Washington, D.C.: United States Department of Health, Education and Welfare, Office of Education, 1968.

Gewirtz, H. B., & Gewirtz, J. L. Visiting and caretaking patterns for kibbutz infants: Age and sex trends. *American Journal of Orthopsychiatry,* 1968, **38,** 427–443.

Goodnow, J. Cultural variations in cognitive skills. In J. Hellmuth (Ed.), *Cognitive studies,* Vol. 1. New York: Brunner/Mazel, 1970. Pp. 242–257.

Gordon, B. Foster family day care service. *Child Welfare,* 1959, **38**(6), 18–21.

Gray, S. W., & Miller, J. O. Early experience in relation to cognitive development. *Review of Educational Research, 1967,* **37**, 475–498.

Green, G. E. Experiences affecting the development of number conservation in children. *Child Development,* 1965, **36**, 963–979.

Grotberg, E. (Ed.) *Critical issues in research related to disadvantaged children.* Princeton, N.J.: Educational Testing Service, 1969.

Hamachek, D. E. Teaching techniques to enhance motivation and learning. *Motivation in Teaching and Learning,* 1968, **34**, 21–28.

Havighurst, R. J. Change the child. *Urban Review,* 1969, 3(5), 5, 11–12.

Hertzig, M. E., Birch, H. G., Thomas, A., & Mendez, O. A. Class and ethnic differences in the responsiveness of preschool children to cognitive demands. *Monographs of the Society for Research in Child Development,* 1968, 33(1, Whole No. 117).

Herzog, E. *Children of working mothers.* Washington, D.C.: United States Government Printing Office, 1960.

Horton, C. P., & Crump, P. E. Growth and development XI: Descriptive analysis of the backgrounds of 76 Negro children whose scores are above or below average on the Merrill-Palmer scale of mental tests at three years of age. *Journal of Genetic Psychology,* 1962, **100**, 255–265.

Hosley, E. M. Group day care, a service any responsible parent might need. *Child Welfare,* 1965, **44**, 344.

Hymes, J. L. Early reading is very risky business. *Grade Teacher,* 1965, **82**, 88–92.

Jackson, T. A. Research on day care. *Child Welfare,* 1960, **39**(2) 15–16.

Jacobson, J. M., Bushell, D., & Risley, T. Switching requirements in a Head Start classroom. *Journal of Applied Behavior Analysis,* 1969, **2**, 43–47.

Kanner, L. Review of C. Bereiter & S. Engelmann, *Teaching disadvantaged children in the preschool. American Journal of Orthopsychiatry,* 1967, **37**, 976–977.

Karnes, M. B., Teska, J. A., & Hodgins, A. S. The effects of four programs of classroom intervention on the intellectual and language development of 4-year-old disadvantaged children. *American Journal of Orthopsychiatry,* 1970, **40**, 58–76.

Katkovsky, W., Preston, A., & Crandall, V. J. Parents' attitudes toward their personal achievements and toward the achievement behaviors of their children. *Journal of Genetic Psychology,* 1964, **104**, 67–82.

Keliher, A. V. Effective learning and teacher-pupil ratio. *Childhood Education,* 1966, **43**(1), 3–6.

Kenefick, B., & Paznik, J. From research to development—education comes of age. *Urban Review,* May 1970, 4(3), 24–28.

Kent, M., & Davis, D. R. Discipline in the home and intellectual development. *British Journal of Medical Psychology,* 1957, **30**, 27–34.

Kirp, D. L. Race, class, and the limits of schooling. *Urban Review,* May 1970, **4**(3), 10-13.

Kittrell, F. P., & Fuschillo, J. C. Enriching the preschool experience of children from age three. *Children,* 1968, **15**, 135–143.

Kohnstamm, C. A. Experiments on teaching Piagetian thought operations. In J. Hellmuth (Ed.), *Cognitive studies:* Vol. 1. New York: Brunner/Mazel, 1970. Pp. 370–382.

Lambert, W. E., & Taguchi, Y. Ethnic cleavage among young children. *Journal of Abnormal and Social Psychology,* 1956, **53,** 380–382.

Landau, R., & Gewirtz, J. L. Differential satiation for a social reinforcing stimulus as a determinant of its efficacy in conditioning. *Journal of Experimental Child Psychology,* 1967, **5,** 391–405.

Lawton, D. Social class differences in language development: A study of some samples of written work. *Language and Speech,* 1963, **6,** 120–143.

Lawton, D. Social class language differences in group discussions. *Language and Speech,* 1964, **7,** 183–204.

Lewis, L. Broad community approach to day care. *Child Welfare,* 1960, **39**(3), 32–33.

Lourie, R. S. Epilogue: Implications for future planning. In L. L. Dittmann (Ed.), *Early child care: The new perspectives.* New York: Atherton, 1968. Pp. 359–363.

Malone, C. A. Safety first: Comments on the influence of external danger in the lives of children of disorganized families. *American Journal of Orthopsychiatry,* 1966, **36,** 3–12.

Marans, A. E., Meers, D. R., & Huntington, D. S. The Children's Hospital in Washington, D.C. In L. L. Dittmann (Ed.), *Early child care: The new perspectives.* New York: Atherton, 1968. Pp. 237–282.

Neubauer, P. B. The third year of life: The two-year-old. In L. L. Dittmann (Ed.), *Early child care: The new perspectives.* New York: Atherton, 1968. Pp. 57–67.

O'Donnell, C. Selected resumes of early childhood research. Head Start *Childhood Research Information Bulletin,* No. 1, 1969.

Palmer, M. W. (Ed.) *Day care aides: A guide for in-service training.* New York: National Federation of Settlements and Neighborhood Centers, 1962. (a)

Palmer, M. W. *Selected readings for day care aides: A guide for in service training.* New York: National Federation of Settlements and Neighborhood Centers, 1968. (b)

Passow, A. H., Goldberg, M., & Tannenbaum, A. J. (Eds.), *Education of the disadvantaged: A book of readings.* New York: Holt, Rinehart & Winston, 1967.

Pavenstedt, E. Development during the second year: The one-year-old. In L. L. Dittmann (Ed.), *Early child care: The new perspectives.* New York: Atherton, 1968. Pp. 40–56.

Pearse, I. R., & Crocker, L. H. *The Peckham experiment.* London: George Allen & Urwin, 1947.

Pettigrew, T. P. *Negro American intelligence.* Princeton, N.J.: Van Nostrand, 1964.

Powledge, F. *To change a child.* Chicago: Quadrangle, 1967.

Prentice, N. M., & Pieri, J. Intellectual development of culturally deprived children in a day care program. *Proceedings of American Psychological Association, 76th Annual Convention,* 1968.

Prescott, E. The large day care center as a child-rearing environment. *Voice for Children,* 1970, **3**(4), 3.

Provence, S. *Guide for the care of infants in groups.* New York: Child Welfare League of America, 1967. (a)

Provence, S. Some determinants of relevance of stimuli in an infant's development. In J. Hellmuth (Ed.), *Exceptional infant.* Vol. 1. *The normal infant.* New York: Brunner/Mazel, 1967. Pp. 443–453. (b)

Provence, S. The first year of life: The infant. In L. L. Dittmann (Ed.), *Early child care: The new perspectives.* New York: Atherton, 1968. Pp. 27–30. (a)

Provence, S. The Yale Child Study Center Project. In L. L. Dittmann (Ed.), *Early child care: The new perspectives.* New York: Atherton, 1968. Pp. 313–325. (b)

Quill, J. *One giant step: A guide for Head Start aides.* Washington, D.C.: National Association for the Education of Young Children, 1968.

Rambusch, N. M. *Learning how to learn: An American approach to Montessori.* Baltimore: Helicon, 1962.

Rasmussen, M. (Ed.) Discipline. Association for Childhood Education International, *Bulletin* No. 99, 1957.

Rasmussen, M. (Ed.) *Readings from "Childhood Education"; Articles of lasting value.* Washington, D.C.: Association for Childhood Education International, 1966.

Read, M. S. Malnutrition and mental development: Needed research to clarify critical questions. Special report to Growth and Development Branch, National Institute of Child Health and Human Development, May 1969.

Reitman, W. R. The uses of experience: Open statements, ill-defined strategies, and intelligent information processing. In J. Hellmuth (Ed.), *Cognitive studies:* Vol. 1. New York: Brunner/Mazel, 1970. Pp. 210–229.

Rowland, M. K., & DelCampo, P. The values of the educationally disadvantaged: How different are they? *Journal of Negro Education,* 1968, **37**, 86–89.

Ruderman, F. A. Day care: A challenge to social work. *Child Welfare,* 1963, **43**, 117–123.

Sauer, P. H., & Hickey, M. F. Building a day care center: An introduction to planning and financing a day care center: What to look for and how to buy it or rent it with a city lease. New York: Bank Street Day Care Consultation Service, February 1970.

Schatzman, L., & Strauss, A. Social class and modes of communication. *American Journal of Sociology,* 1955. **60**, 329–338.

Schloss, S. *Nursery-kindergarten enrollment of children under six: October 1966.* Washington, D.C.: United States Department of Health, Education and·Welfare, Office of Education, 1967.

Sigel, I. E. The attainment of concepts. In M. L. Hoffman & L. W. Hoffman (Eds.), *Review of child development research.* New York: Russell Sage Foundation, 1964. Pp. 209–248.

Stats, J. (Ed.) Report of a conference on day care and the working mother. Baltimore, June 1967.

Straus, M. A. Communication, creativity, and problem solving ability of middle and working class families in three societies. *American Journal of Sociology,* 1968, **73**, 417–431.

Symposium. Evaluating educational programs. *Urban Review,* 1969, **3**(4), 4–31.

Ulrich, R. Behavior modification model to train day care workers. Proposal submitted to the U.S. Department of Health, Education and Welfare, Public Health Service, June 1970.

Ulrich, R. Behavior modification: Theory, research, and practice. *Michigan Mental Health Research Bulletin,* 1968, **2**(1), 5–13.

United States Department of Commerce, Bureau of the Census. *Population characteristics: School enrollment: October 1968 and 1967,* Washington, D.C.: USDC, 1969.

Author Index

Numbers in *italics* indicate the pages on which the full references appear.

Subject Index